Regime Politics

STUDIES IN GOVERNMENT
AND PUBLIC POLICY

Regime Politics
Governing Atlanta, 1946–1988

Clarence N. Stone

 University Press of Kansas

Published by the University Press of Kansas (Lawrence, Kansas
66045), which was organized by the Kansas Board of Regents and is
operated and funded by Emporia State University, Fort Hays State
University, Kansas State University, Pittsburg State University,
the University of Kansas, and Wichita State University

Library of Congress Cataloging-in-Publication Data
Stone, Clarence N. (Clarence Nathan), 1935–
  Regime politics : governing Atlanta. 1946-1988 / Clarence N.
Stone
    p.   cm — (Studies in government and public policy)
  Bibliography: p.
  Includes index.
  ISBN 0-7006-0415-4 (alk. paper) — ISBN 0-7006-0416-2
(pbk. : alk. paper)
  1. Atlanta (Ga.) — Politics and government.   2. Business and
politics — Georgia — Atlanta.   3. Atlanta (Ga.) — Ethnic relations.
4. Afro-Americans — Georgia — Atlanta. — Politics and government.
I. Title.   II. Series.
F294.A857S76   1989   89-35634
975.8′231043 — dc20   CIP

British Library Cataloguing in Publication Data is available.

Printed in the United States of America
10 9 8 7 6 5 4 3 2 1

To Eleanore Bushnell
colleague, friend, and mentor

Contents

Preface

This book examines Atlanta politics, starting in 1946 and extending through more than forty years. During that time, blacks became an electoral majority and gained control of city hall. Although tension abounded throughout this period, racial polarization did not dominate the city's civic life. Instead, a biracial coalition formed and became an integral part of the city's governing regime.

Local events were intertwined with a larger set of changes. During the post–World War II era, Atlanta lost whatever regional isolation it may have had earlier. National complicity in the Jim Crow system ended and was replaced by support for the legal equality of the races. Many companion changes occurred: city-oriented federal programs abounded, from the urban-redevelopment legislation of the Truman presidency to Urban Development Action Grants (UDAGs) of the Carter administration; court-ordered reapportionment helped bring to a close the era of state politics called by V. O. Key the "rule of the rustics";[1] and the city's economy became increasingly integrated into an international economy—to name only some of the most significant. All of these are important, and I try to acknowledge their importance in the narrative of Atlanta's postwar experience. Yet the focus of this book is on the Atlanta regime—the actions of various elements of the Atlanta community in bringing together, challenging, and modifying the informal arrangements through which Atlanta was governed. Through these arrangements the forces of the larger world are mediated.

Painting the picture of governance in Atlanta requires a broad canvas. Depiction of government structure is not enough. City hall has to deal with a powerful business sector and sharp limitations on its own authority. Thus, public officeholders have to come to terms with private interests, especially business interests. That process is the core of what I call the urban regime.

The Atlanta story is, of course, not the story of every city. Yet, although

Atlanta is not a typical city, its experience can tell us a great deal that has general relevance. Atlanta in the postwar period offers a case of the formation and maintenance of a governing coalition capable of promoting far-reaching change, even in the face of substantial resistance. Atlanta's regime has been extraordinarily effective. How and with what consequences are the relevant questions. They lend significance to the Atlanta narrative.

As World War II came to a close, Atlanta emerged as a city embarked on policy activism. Gone was the caretaker stance, the minimum-service, minimum-government orientation that in the main had prevailed in the prewar years. The city's downtown business elite led the way in launching extensive redevelopment, initiating an elaborate expressway system well in advance of the federal interstate program and promoting a major alteration in land use around the central business district, in the process displacing perhaps one-fifth of the population.

Concurrently, the legal and political foundations of racial subordination came under attack, both locally and in the federal courts. Although the politics of the state in general were deeply antagonistic to blacks, Atlanta's minority community nevertheless began a successful step-by-step attack on Jim Crow—the system through which blacks were excluded from many jobs, sometimes given less pay for the same work (until legal battles in the 1940s, black teachers, for example, were paid less than their white counterparts), confined in business and professional life to serving other blacks, allowed no position of authority over whites, demeaned in forms of personal address, not allowed to try on clothes and shoes in "white" stores or drink from "white" drinking fountains, excluded from restaurants, hotels, and other public accommodations, sent to the back of the bus or separate rail cars in public transportation, residentially segregated (even to the point that street names changed as the racial character of the residents shifted), denied participation in the Democratic primary (the state's dominant party), and subjected to personal abuse and brutal treatment by police officers, especially for any sign of behavior that departed from complete submissiveness.

Others have described the system in detail, and I need not do so here. But it is important that readers understand that at the end of World War II, racial segregation was law throughout the South; and beyond the law, custom and convention—sometimes enforced by violence—subordinated blacks in a manner that made the doctrine of "separate but equal" a hypocrisy at best.

Parts of the Atlanta story are well known. What I have attempted in this book is to give an overall account, centered on the actions of the city's governing alliance. Atlanta is, of course, the site of Floyd Hunter's path-breaking study, *Community Power Structure*. Because much of my account treats bargaining and coalition-building, superficial readers of Hunter may see my study as a refutation of that book. More careful readers will see a strong kinship between the two studies, a point I have developed elsewhere.[2] My method of study (see Appendix C) focuses on the flow of events and is much different from Hunter's. Nevertheless, I owe a considerable debt to his analysis of the importance of the close but informal link between Atlanta's governmental and economic sectors. Puzzling over this link has shaped my thinking about urban politics and community power. Drawing on my first study of Atlanta,[3] I later reformulated the problem of community power in a manner intended to break the impasse between pluralists and elitists.[4] In that piece on systemic power, I analyzed what it means to combine legal equality at the ballot box with inequality in various other resources—how public officials are affected by the mix of formal democracy and social stratification that provides the context for their behavior. Officials are greatly constrained by the need to court popular favor and win elections, but, I concluded, they are also predisposed to cooperate with those who can provide them with useful resources and opportunities to achieve results. Thus, an electoral coalition, even when it wins, is not the same as a governing coalition.[5]

This current study of Atlanta builds on my earlier argument; yet it is also a departure from that argument. The concept of systemic power highlights how and why public officials are attracted to a partnership with business, and, by extension, it shows why other groups—Atlanta's black middle class, for example—might also seek political partnership with business. Thus, the idea of systemic power enables us to see how Atlanta's business elite, despite its electoral weakness, was able to retain a central part in the city's postwar regime. Yet, the question that systemic power directs us toward, but does not itself answer, is how, in the face of complex and sometimes divisive forces, an effective and durable capacity to govern can be created. That capacity is not to be taken for granted, as is illustrated by such experiences as the Lindsay administration in New York,[6] or the failure of many communities to manage racial conflict.[7]

While by no means typical, the Atlanta experience speaks directly to the point of what makes a community governable. It is not the formal machinery of government; American urban regimes are noted for their weak legal position.[8] Systemic advantages do not automatically cumulate into an effective regime; resources must be tapped and efforts made to bring together institutional capacities in different sectors of community life and to coordinate and sustain them. Atlanta's business elite is extraordinarily important because it excels in getting strategically positioned people to act together, thereby expanding its realm of allies and imposing opportunity costs on those who decline to go along.

There are long-standing arguments, at least as far back as Edward Banfield's "imperatives of metropolitan growth," that cities are more the product of economics and technology than of politics.[9] More recently, both structural Marxists and market-centrist Paul Peterson have argued that cities are limited by competition for mobile capital.[10] Intergovernmental relations and forms of assistance are still another dimension of the "dependent city."[11] Yet there are counterarguments about the importance of coalition building and political struggle.[12] Or, as the late Governor James Folsom said: "Nothing just happens. Everything is *arranged*."[13] Politics, then, as the art of arranging, is not to be ignored. It is at the heart of the Atlanta story.

A caution is in order, however. Political scientists tend to be a bit romantic about politics, linking it to enlightened choice as opposed to the mechanistic determinism of economics. Indeed, at its best, politics *is* about reason-giving and efforts to further the common weal.[14] But these are ideals; how do we reach them? Although politics is "the art of arranging," it is not an infinitely flexible art. We cannot simply design a pattern and expect the world to follow it. In addition to economic imperatives, there may be political imperatives as well.

Long ago, Robert Michels warned that the very fact of political organization entails rigidities that can displace formally agreed-to ends.[15] The need for political organization, for bringing together a shared capacity to act, itself builds in constraints. Max Weber's examination of bureaucracy led him to believe that more effective forms of organization will drive out less effective ones. And Mancur Olson has also argued that whoever best solves the problem of collective action is likely to enjoy a substantial power advantage, undermining any optimistic version of pluralism.[16] Thus the problem of collective action has wide implications.[17] Indeed, Michael Taylor argues that "politics is the study of ways of solving collective action problems."[18]

Although I would not carry the argument as far as Taylor does, there is no question that a capacity for common action is at the heart of politics. That being so, collective action is too important a problem to be left in the hands of public-choice analysts. At the same time, these analysts concern themselves with a body of theory that cannot be ignored. This theory can alert us to difficulties in politics that we might otherwise underrate. If indeed politics can enhance the urban condition, then we must learn how to act in concert on those matters that people might choose by reasoning together. That, the Atlanta experience cautions us, is no easy task.

Many years ago, V. O. Key observed that "the South may not be the nation's number one political problem, . . . but politics is the South's number one problem."[19] I can only paraphrase: Urban areas may not be the nation's number one political problem, but politics is urban America's number one problem. It is not easy to have a regime that is both effective and equitable, but no regime is truly effective unless it is also equitable. Tension between equity and effectiveness is largely a matter of how regimes are put together. The problem is that the path of least resistance lies in the direction of slighting equity. The Atlanta case richly illustrates the problem, and regime analysis enables us to examine it.

Acknowledgments

I have drunk from wells I did not dig, I have been warmed by fires I did not build.

Writing a book cannot be done without the help of many people, and this book is no exception. If anything, I have incurred more than the ordinary debts to others. Many have contributed to the wellspring of ideas from which I have drawn, and even the list of references falls far short of naming them all. But let me concentrate here on those who have aided me in direct ways. Several people have read all or part of the manuscript in one draft or another, and I owe a special debt to them for their comments and suggestions: Ronald Bayor, Madelyn Bonsignore, Amy Bridges, Stephen Elkin, Steven Erie, Floyd Hayes, John Hutcheson, Bryan Jones, Norton Long, Mark Stone, Mary Stone, and Robert Whelan. I exempt them from all shortcomings in the book, but must credit them with much of its merit. They have played the role of constructive critic well.

I am also indebted to a number of people for research assistance. At the University of Maryland during various stages of this project, I have been helped by Pamela Edwards, Adam Goldstein, David Imbroscio, Brooke Randolph, Amy Rosenthal, and Elaine Yannotti. At Georgia State University, I have been assisted by Edith Sage.

In doing research on Atlanta, I have also benefited from the opportunity to talk with a number of scholars who have a current or past connection with Atlanta. I assume responsibility for the interpretation of the Atlanta experience given here, but I have gained understanding of the Atlanta context and sources of information about Atlanta from the following: Glenn Abney, Numan Bartley, Ronald Bayor, Timothy Crimmins, Arnold Fleischmann, Robert Holmes, John Hutcheson, Alton Hornsby, Jr., Larry Keating, Thomas Lauth, Eleanor Main, Adolph Reed, Jr., Bradley Rice, Dana White, and Alex Willingham.

The General Research Board of the University of Maryland has been generous in providing time free of teaching responsibilities for field research. In Atlanta, I have been assisted greatly by the Department of Political Science at Georgia State University. The chair, Donald Fairchild, provided me with desk, telephone, and the generous help of the office under the able supervision of Thelma Williams. That arrangement saved me countless hours and bolstered my spirit during the arduous task of arranging interviews. The staff of Central Atlanta Progress has also been unsparing in its cooperation.

The nearly one hundred individuals who consented to interviews and provided access to information (including correspondence, minutes, reports, clippings, etc.) are due a special debt that is not lessened by the absence of their names here.

The staff of the University Press of Kansas have been a joy to work with, combining efficiency with good will. Laura Poracsky provided cartographic expertise, as she did with my earlier book on Atlanta.

Finally, writing a book calls for much more than processing information and analyzing ideas. Support comes in many forms. I especially appreciate the willingness of John Hutcheson, Carol Pierannunzi, and their daughter Christine to provide me with a home away from home during my sojourn in Atlanta and for their warm support and encouragement. To Stephen Elkin, I am indebted for a happy and very special merger of colleagueship and friendship. To my wife, Mary, go thanks beyond measure. She has read more draft pages than should be asked of anyone, and through it all has been my emotional mainstay in the ups and downs of authorship. From her I have been privileged to receive more than thirty years of unselfish giving and sound advice. I look forward to at least another thirty.

PART ONE
INTRODUCTION

1

Urban Regimes: A Research Perspective

I have come across men of letters who have written history without taking part in public affairs, and politicians who have concerned themselves with producing events without thinking about them. I have observed that the first are always inclined to find general causes, whereas the second, living in the midst of disconnected daily facts, are prone to imagine that everything is attributable to particular incidents, and that the wires they pull are the same as those that move the world. It is to be presumed that both are equally deceived.

—Alexis de Tocqueville

What makes governance in Atlanta effective is not the formal machinery of government, but rather the informal partnership between city hall and the downtown business elite. This informal partnership and the way it operates constitute the city's regime; it is the means through which major policy decisions are made.

The word "regime" connotes different things to different people, but in this book regime is specifically about the *informal arrangements* that surround and complement the formal workings of governmental authority. All governmental authority in the United States is greatly limited—limited by the Constitution, limited perhaps even more by the nation's political tradition, and limited structurally by the autonomy of privately owned business enterprise. The exercise of public authority is thus never a simple matter; it is almost always enhanced by extraformal considerations. Because local governmental authority is by law and tradition even more limited than authority at the state and national level, informal arrangements assume special importance in urban politics. But we should begin our understanding of regimes by realizing that informal arrangements are by no means peculiar to cities or, for that matter, to government.

Even narrowly bounded organizations, those with highly specific func-

3

tional responsibilities, develop informal governing coalitions.[1] As Chester Barnard argued many years ago, formal goals and formal lines of authority are insufficient by themselves to bring about coordinated action with sufficient energy to accomplish organizational purposes;[2] commitment and cooperation do not just spring up from the lines of an organization chart. Because every formal organization gives rise to an informal one, Barnard concluded, successful executives must master the skill of shaping and using informal organization for their purposes.

Attention to informal arrangements takes various forms. In the analysis of business firms, the school of thought labeled "transaction cost economics" has given systematic attention to how things actually get done in a world full of social friction — basically the same question that Chester Barnard considered. A leading proponent of this approach, Oliver Williamson,[3] finds that what he terms "private orderings" (as opposed to formal and legal agreements) are enormously important in the running of business affairs. For many transactions, mutual and tacit understanding is a more efficient way of conducting relations than are legal agreements and formal contracts. Williamson quotes a business executive as saying, "You can settle any dispute if you keep the lawyers and accountants out of it. They just do not understand the give-and-take needed in business."[4] Because informal understandings and arrangements provide needed flexibility to cope with nonroutine matters, they facilitate cooperation to a degree that formally defined relationships do not. People who know one another, who have worked together in the past, who have shared in the achievement of a task, and who perhaps have experienced the same crisis are especially likely to develop tacit understandings. If they interact on a continuing basis, they can learn to trust one another and to expect dependability from one another. It can be argued, then, that transactions flow more smoothly and business is conducted more efficiently when a core of insiders form and develop an ongoing relationship.

A regime thus involves not just any informal group that comes together to make a decision but an informal yet relatively stable group *with access to institutional resources* that enable it to have a sustained role in making governing decisions. What makes the group informal is not a lack of institutional connections, but the fact that the group, *as a group*, brings together institutional connections by an informal mode of cooperation. There is no all-encompassing structure of command that guides and synchronizes everyone's behavior. There is a purposive coordination of efforts, but it comes about informally, in ways that often depend heavily on tacit understandings.

If there is no overarching command structure, what gives a regime coherence? What makes it more than an "ecology of games"?[5] The answer is that the regime is purposive, created and maintained as a way of facilitating action. In a very important sense, *a regime is empowering*. Its supporters see it as a means for achieving coordinated efforts that might not otherwise be realized. A regime, however, is not created or redirected at will. Organizational analysis teaches us that cognition is limited, existing arrangements have staying power, and implementation is profoundly shaped by procedures in place.[6] Shrewd and determined leaders can effect purposive change, but only by being attentive to the ways in which existing forms of coordination can be altered or amplified.[7]

We can think of cities as organizations that lack a conjoining structure of command. There are institutional sectors within which the power of command may be much in evidence, but the sectors are independent of one another.[8] Because localities have only weak formal means through which coordination can be achieved, informal arrangements to promote cooperation are especially useful. *These informal modes of coordinating efforts across institutional boundaries are what I call "civic cooperation."* In a system of weak formal authority, it holds special importance. Integrated with the formal structure of authority into a suprainstitutional capacity to take action, any informal basis of cooperation is empowering. It enables community actors to achieve cooperation beyond what could be formally commanded.

Consider the case of local political machines. When ward politicians learned to coordinate informally what otherwise was mired in institutional fragmentation and personal opportunism, the urban political machine was created and proved to have enormous staying power.[9] "Loyalty" is the shorthand that machine politicians used to describe the code that bound them into a cohesive group.[10] The political machine is in many ways the exemplar of governance in which informal arrangements are vital complements to the formal organization of government. The classic urban machines brought together various elements of the community in an informal scheme of exchange and cooperation that was the real governing system of the community.

The urban machine, of course, represents only one form of regime. In considering Atlanta, I am examining the governing coalition in a nonmachine city. The term "governing coalition" is a way of making the notion of regime concrete. It makes us face the fact that informal arrangements are held together by a core group—typically a body of insiders—who come together repeatedly in making important decisions. Thus, when I refer to the governing coalition in Atlanta, I mean the core group at the center of the workings of the regime.

To talk about a core group is not to suggest that they are of one mind or that they all represent identical interests—far from it. "Coalition" is the word I use to emphasize that a regime involves bringing together various elements of the community and the different institutional capacities they control. "Governing," as used in "governing coalition," I must stress, does not mean rule in command-and-control fashion. Governance through informal arrangements is about how some forms of coordination of effort prevail over others. It is about mobilizing efforts to cope and to adapt; it is not about absolute control. Informal arrangements are a way of bolstering (and guiding) the formal capacity to act, but even this enhanced capacity remains quite limited.

Having argued that informal arrangements are important in a range of circumstances, not just in cities, let me return to the specifics of the city setting. After all, the important point is not simply that there are informal arrangements; it is the particular features of urban regimes that provide the lenses through which we see the Atlanta experience. For cities, two questions face us: (1) Who makes up the governing coalition—who has to come together to make governance possible? (2) How is the coming together accomplished? These two questions imply a third: What are the consequences of the *who* and *how*? Urban regimes are not neutral mechanisms through which policy is made; they shape policy. To be sure, they do not do so on terms solely of the governing coalition's own choosing. But regimes are the mediating agents between the ill-defined pressures of an urban environment and the making of community policy. The *who* and *how* of urban regimes matter, thus giving rise to the further question of *with what consequences*. These three questions will guide my analysis of Atlanta.

URBAN REGIMES

As indicated above, an urban regime refers to the set of arrangements by which a community is actually governed. Even though the institutions of local government bear most of the formal responsibility for governing, they lack the resources and the scope of authority to govern without the active support and cooperation of significant private interests. An urban regime may thus be defined as *the informal arrangements by which public bodies and private interests function together in order to be able to make and carry out governing decisions*. These governing decisions, I want to emphasize, are not a matter of running or controlling everything. They have to do with *managing conflict* and *making adaptive responses* to social change. The informal arrangements through which governing decisions are made differ from community to community, but everywhere they are driven by two needs: (1) institutional scope (that is, the need to encompass a wide enough scope of institutions to mobilize the resources required to make and implement governing decisions) and (2) cooperation (that is, the need to promote enough cooperation and coordination for the diverse participants to reach decisions and sustain action in support of those decisions).

The mix of participants varies by community, but that mix is itself constrained by the accommodation of two basic institutional principles of the American political economy: (1) popular control of the formal machinery of government and (2) private ownership of business enterprise.[11] Neither of these principles is pristine. Popular control is modified and compromised in various ways, but nevertheless remains as the basic principle of government. Private ownership is less than universal, as governments do own and operate various auxiliary enterprises from mass transit to convention centers. Even so, governmental conduct is constrained by the need to promote investment activity in an economic arena dominated by private ownership. This political-economy insight is the foundation for a theory of urban regimes.[12]

In defining an urban regime as the informal arrangements through which public bodies and private interests function together to make and carry out governing decisions, bear in mind that I did not specify that the private interests are business interests. Indeed, in practice, private interests are not confined to business figures. Labor-union officials, party functionaries, officers in nonprofit organizations or foundations, and church leaders may also be involved.[13]

Why, then, pay particular attention to business interests? One reason is the now well-understood need to encourage business investment in order to have an economically thriving community. A second reason is the sometimes overlooked factor that businesses control politically important resources and are rarely absent totally from the scene. They may work through intermediaries, or some businesses may even be passive because others represent their interests as property holders, but a business presence is always part of the urban political scene. Although the nature of business involvement extends from the direct and extensive to the indirect and limited, the economic role of businesses *and the resources they control* are too important for these enterprises to be left out completely.

With revived interest in political economy, the regime's need for an adequate institutional scope (including typically some degree of business involvement) has received significant attention. However, less has been said about the regime's need for cooperation — and the various ways to meet it.[14] Perhaps some take for granted that, when cooperation is called for, it will be forthcoming. But careful reflection reminds us that cooperation does not occur simply because it is useful.

Robert Wiebe analyzed machine politics in a way that illustrates an important point: "The ward politician . . . required wider connections in order to manage many of his clients' problems. . . . Therefore clusters of these men allied to increase their bargaining power in city affairs. But if logic led to an integrated city-wide organization, the instinct of self-preservation did not. The more elaborate the structure, the more independence the ward bosses and area chieftains lost."[15] Cooperation can thus never be taken as a given; it must be achieved and at significant costs. Some of the costs are visible resources expended in promoting cooperation — favors and benefits distributed to curry reciprocity, the effort required to establish and maintain channels of communication, and responsibilities borne to knit activities together are a few examples. But, as Wiebe's observation reminds us, there are less visible costs. Achieving cooperation entails commitment to a set of relationships, and these relationships limit independence of action. If relationships are to be ongoing, they cannot be neglected; they may even call for sacrifices to prevent alienating allies. Forming wider connections is thus not a cost-free step, and it is not a step that community actors are always eager to take.

Because centrifugal tendencies are always strong, achieving cooperation is a major accomplishment and requires constant effort. Cooperation can be brought about in various ways. It can be induced if there is an actor powerful enough to coerce others into it, but that is a rare occurrence, because power is not usually so concentrated. More often, cooperation is achieved by some degree of reciprocity.

The literature on collective action focuses on the problem of cooperation in the absence of a system of command. For example, the "prisoner's dilemma" game instructs us that noncooperation may be invited by a number of situations.[16] In the same vein, Mancur Olson's classic analysis highlights the free-rider problem and the importance of selective incentives in inducing cooperation.[17] Alternatively, repeated interactions permit people to see the shortcomings of mutual noncooperation and to learn norms of cooperation.[18] Moreover, although Robert Axelrod's experiments with TIT FOR TAT computer programs indicate that cooperation can be instrumentally rational under some conditions, the process is not purely mechanical.[19] Students of culture point to the importance of common identity and language in facilitating interaction and promoting trust.[20] Size of group is also a consideration, affecting the ease of communication and bargaining among members; Michael Taylor, for example, emphasizes the increased difficulty of conditional cooperation in larger groups.[21]

What we can surmise about the urban community is thus twofold: (1) cooperation across institutional lines is valuable but far from automatic; and (2) cooperation is more likely to grow under some circumstances than others. This conclusion has wide implications for the study of urban politics. For example, much of the literature on community power has centered on the question of control, its possibilities and limitations: to what extent is domination by a command center possible and how is the cost of social control worked out. The long-standing elitist-pluralist debate centers on such questions. However, my line of argument here points to another way of viewing urban communities; it points to the need to think about cooperation, its possibilities and limitations—not just any cooperation, but cooperation of the kind that can bring together people based in different sectors of a community's institutional life and that enables a coalition of actors to make and support a set of governing decisions.

If the conventional model of urban politics is one of social control (with both elitist and pluralist variants), then the one proposed here might be called "the social-production model." It is based on the question of how, in a world of limited and dispersed authority, actors work together across institutional lines to produce a capacity to govern and to bring about publicly significant results.

To be sure, the development of a system of cooperation for governing is something that arises, not from an unformed mass, but rather within a structured set of relationships. Following Stephen Elkin, I described above the basic configuration in political-economy terms: popular control of governmental authority and private ownership of business activity. However, both of these elements are subject to variation. Populations vary in characteristics and in type of political organization; hence, popular control comes in many forms. The economic sector itself varies by the types of businesses that compose it and by the way in which it is organized formally and informally. Hence there is no one formula for bringing institutional sectors into an arrangement for cooperation, and the whole process is imbued with uncertainty. Cooperation is always somewhat tenuous, and it is made more so as conditions change and new actors enter the scene.

The study of urban regimes is thus a study of who cooperates and how their cooperation is achieved across institutional sectors of community life. Further, it is an examination of how that cooperation is maintained when confronted with an ongoing process of social change, a continuing influx of new actors, and potential break-downs through conflict or indifference.

Regimes are dynamic, not static, and regime dynamics concern the ways in which forces for change and forces for continuity play against one another. For example, Atlanta's governing coalition has displayed remarkable continuity in the post–World War II period, and it has done so despite deep-seated forces of social change. Understanding Atlanta's urban regime involves understanding how cooperation can be maintained and continuity can prevail in the face of so many possibilities for conflict.

STRUCTURE, ACTION, AND STRUCTURING

Because of the interplay of change and continuity, urban regimes are perhaps best studied over time. Let us, then, take a closer look at historical analysis. Scholars make sense out of the particulars of political and social life by thinking mainly in terms of abstract structures such as democracy and capitalism. Although these are useful as shorthand, the danger in abstractions is that they never capture the full complexity and contingency of the world. Furthermore, "structure" suggests something solid and unchanging, yet political and social life is riddled with contradictions and uncertainties that give rise to an ongoing process of change and adjustment. Much of the change that occurs is at the margins of basic and enduring relationships, making it easy to think in terms of order and stability. Incrementalists remind us that the present is the best predictor of the near future. But students of history, especially those accustomed to looking at longer periods of time, offer a different perspective. They see a world undergoing change, in which various actors struggle over what the terms of that change will be. It is a world shaped and reshaped by human efforts, a world that never quite forms a unified whole.

In historical light, social structures are less solid and less fixed than social scientists have sometimes assumed. Charles Tilly has argued that there is no single social structure. Instead, he urges us to think in terms of multiple structures, which "consist of shifting, constructed social relations among limited numbers of actors."[22] Philip Abrams also sees structures as relationships, relationships that are socially fabricated and subject to purposive modification.[23]

Structures are real but not fixed. Action does not simply occur within the bounds set by structures but is sometimes aimed at the structures themselves, so that a process of reshaping is taking place at all times. Abrams thus argues that events have a two-sided character, involving both structure and action in such a way that action shapes structures and structures shape actions. Abrams calls for the study of a process he labels as "structur*ing*," by which he means that events occur in a structured context and that events help reshape structure.[24]

Abrams therefore offers a perspective on the interplay of change and continuity. This continuity is not so much a matter of resisting change as coping with it. Because the potential for change is ever present, regime continuity is a remarkable outcome. Any event contains regime-altering potential — perhaps not in sudden realignment, but in opening up a new path along which subsequent events can cumulatively bring about fundamental change.[25] The absence of regime alteration is thus an outcome to be explained, and it must be explained in terms of a capacity to adapt and reinforce existing structures. Events are the arena in which the struggle between change and continuity is played out, but they are neither self-defining nor free-formed phenomena. They become events in our minds because they have some bearing on structures that help shape future occurrences. It is the interplay of event and structure that is especially worthy of study. To identify events, one therefore needs to have some conception of structure. In this way, the researcher can focus attention, relieved of the impossible task of studying everything.

There is no escaping the necessity of the scholar's imposing some form of analysis on research. The past becomes known through the concepts we apply. Abrams sees this as the heart of historical sociology: "The reality of the past is just not 'there' waiting to be observed by the resurrectionist historian. It is to be known if at all through strenuous theoretical alienation."[26] He also reminds us that many aspects of an event cannot be observed in a direct sense; too much is implicit at any given moment.[27] That is why the process, or the flow of events over time, is so important to examine. That is also why events are not necessarily most significant for their immediate impact; they may be more significant for their bearing on subsequent events, thus giving rise to modifications in structure.

PROLOGUE TO THE ATLANTA NARRATIVE

Structuring in Atlanta is a story in which race is central. If regimes are about who cooperates, how, and with what consequences, one of the remarkable features of Atlanta's urban regime is its biracial character. How has cooperation been achieved across racial lines, particularly since race is often a chasm rather than a bridge? Atlanta has been governed by a biracial coalition for so long that it is tempting to believe that nothing else was possible. Yet other cities followed a different pattern. At a time when Atlanta prided itself on being "the city too busy to hate," Little Rock, Birmingham, and New Orleans pursued die-hard segregation and were caught up in racial violence and turmoil. The experience of these cities reminds us that Atlanta's regime is not simply an informal arrangement through which popular elections and private ownership are reconciled, but is deeply intertwined with race relations, with some actors on the Atlanta scene able to overcome the divisive character of race sufficiently to achieve cooperation.

Atlanta's earlier history is itself a mixed experience, offering no clear indication that biracial cooperation would emerge and prevail in the years after World War II. In 1906, the city was the site of a violent race riot apparently precipitated by inflammatory antiblack newspaper rhetoric.[28] The incident hastened the city's move toward the economic exclusion and residential segregation of blacks, their disenfranchisement, and enforcement of social subordination; and the years after 1906 saw the Jim Crow system fastened into place. Still, the riot was followed by modest efforts to promote biracial understanding, culminating in the formation in 1919 of the Commission on Interracial Cooperation.

Atlanta, however, also became the headquarters city for a revived Ku Klux Klan. During the 1920s, the Klan enjoyed wide support and was a significant influence in city elections. At this time, it gained a strong foothold in city government and a lasting one in the police department.[29] In 1930, faced with rising unemployment, some white Atlantans also founded the Order of Black Shirts for the express purpose of driving blacks out of even menial jobs and replacing them with whites. Black Shirt protests had an impact, and opportunities for blacks once again were constricted. At the end of World War II, with Atlanta's black population expanding beyond a number that could be contained in the city's traditionally defined black neighborhoods, another klanlike organization, the Columbians, sought to use terror tactics to prevent black expansion into previously all-white areas. All of this occurred against a background of state and regional politics devoted to the subordination of blacks to whites — a setting that did not change much until the 1960s.

Nevertheless, other patterns surfaced briefly from time to time. In 1932, Angelo Herndon, a black Communist organizer, led a mass demonstration of white and black unemployed protesting a cutoff of work relief. Herndon was arrested, and the biracial following he led proved short-lived. Still, the event had occurred, and Atlanta's city council did in fact accede to the demand for continued relief.[30] In the immediate postwar period, a progressive biracial coalition formed around the successful candidacy of Helen Douglas Mankin for a congressional seat representing Georgia's fifth district. That, too, was short-lived, as ultra-conservative Talmadge forces maneuvered to reinstitute Georgia's county-unit system for the fifth district and defeat Mankin with a minority of the popular vote.[31]

It is tempting to see the flow of history as flux, and one could easily dwell on the mutable character of political alignments. The Atlanta experience suggests that coalitions often give expression to instability. Centrifugal forces are strong, and in some ways disorder is a natural state. What conflict does not tear asunder, indifference is fully capable of wearing away.

The political incorporation of blacks into Atlanta's urban regime in tight coalition with the city's white business elite is thus not a story of how popular control and private capital came inevitably to live together in peace and harmony. It is an account of struggle and conflict — bringing together a biracial governing coalition at the outset, and then allowing each of the coalition partners to secure for itself an advantageous position within the coalition. In the first instance, struggle involved efforts to see that the coalition between white business interests and the black middle class prevailed over other possible alignments. In the second instance, there was struggle over the terms of coalition between the partners; thus political conflict is not confined to "ins" versus "outs." Those on the inside engage in significant struggle with one another over the terms on which cooperation will be maintained, which is one reason governing arrangements should never be taken for granted.

Atlanta's urban regime therefore appears to be the creature of purposive struggle, and both its establishment and its maintenance call for a political explanation. The shape of the regime was far from inevitable, but rather came about through the actions of human agents making political choices. Without extraeconomic efforts by the city's business leadership, Atlanta would have been governed in a much different manner, and Atlanta's urban regime and the policies furthered by that regime might well have diverged from the path taken. History, perhaps, is as much about alternatives not pursued as about those that were.

2

Prewar Background

Had it not been for the automobile, which was the prevailing means of urban transportation during the period when Atlanta entered its initial period of economic growth, the Georgia capital of [today] would be structured entirely differently.

—Howard Preston

Southern politics have . . . always been the politics of race.

—Alton Hornsby, Jr.

While transportation has had and continues to have a profound influence upon Atlanta's physical structure and social ecology, so too has the system of caste. Caste . . . left an indelible mark on the pattern of the city in its creation of two separate "sides" of the city, two "communities."

—Dana F. White and Timothy J. Crimmins

Any time span chosen for historical analysis is somewhat arbitrary. However, the four-plus decades of this study do have a rationale. In 1946, when a federal court ended Georgia's white primary, black voting was minuscule; today blacks enjoy electoral dominance. The mounting impact of black voting on city politics and the evolving response to that impact, especially by Atlanta's downtown business elite, are the focus of this study.

The enfranchisement of Atlanta's black population occurred in a context of national political change and against a setting of prior Atlanta history. This chapter treats the latter, at the same time acknowledging the influence of national trends. However, the perspective is that of local actors and their response to the larger flow of events.

Four features of prewar Atlanta are important background for the postwar years: (1) An agenda of development concerns took shape in the 1920s and

1930s. (2) The white business elite unified, and it organized for action separate from the Chamber of Commerce. (3) Ward-based politics that depended on the distribution of city jobs and favors lost ground to good-government practices and centralized political leadership. (4) Even though constrained within a system of racial subordination, middle-class blacks showed a capacity to act independently in both political and business affairs.

A CHANGING CITY

Atlanta is a young city. Incorporated in 1847, Atlanta's early rise was tied to its being a rail center.[1] Though it became the capital of Georgia in 1868, under the state's reconstruction government, Atlanta remained a small town by most standards; it was not until 1920 that its population reached two hundred thousand. By 1940, the city had grown past the three hundred thousand mark, but cautious public spending meant that services and facilities lagged. Funding for education, in particular, was an ongoing struggle.[2] Moreover, the city, designed as a rail hub, was not handling the automobile era well.[3] Suburban sprawl had begun; traffic congestion was enormous, and the downtown was divided by railroad tracks, which added to the city's traffic problems.

The city's politics was ill-suited to a bold response to the challenge of urban growth.[4] Ward politicians engaged in a struggle for patronage,[5] and personal rivalries — for a time anchored in competition between the city's major newspapers, the *Constitution* and the *Journal* — were important. Blacks were largely excluded from electoral politics, and the white working class was mostly confined to choosing between factions led by the city's civic and business elite.[6] Although there was some tension between those who adhered doggedly to a minimum-taxation position and those who were willing to use public authority and resources to promote growth and development, "friends and neighbors" loyalties were primary. Class politics was scarcely evident in city elections. Atlanta was not scandal-ridden on the scale of older and larger cities in the North, but confidence in government was weakened by corruption, particularly in the police department.

As the 1920s gave way to the 1930s and then to the 1940s, a trend became evident. While sheer growth enhanced the transition into a modern city, Atlanta was doing more than becoming bigger. The automobile had altered the range of urban life; population and business moved away from downtown to a degree that affected the city's agenda of civic action. Immediate problems were the traffic congestion and demands for more services. For the future, there was the question of the changing role of downtown in a metropolitan area increasingly spread out. The automobile brought powerful technological, economic, and social change that city policymakers would be challenged to cope with.

Small businesses and ward-based interests increasingly lost out to larger businesses and interests that operated on a citywide scale. For example, jitneys were prohibited in 1925, leaving what is now the Georgia Power Company with a monopoly of bus and streetcar transportation.[7] Despite some initial opposition by merchants, the 1920s also saw the construction of a viaduct system, elevating street traffic over rail lines. Disruption caused by construction and a change in the street level — combined, of course, with the centrifugal pull of the automobile — greatly decreased the number of small, retail businesses in the central business district.

The character of downtown was changing. One merchant, upon closing the cigar store he had operated in downtown for thirty-two years, offered this view:

> Now instead of having one community center, Atlanta has many — Tenth Street, Pershing Point, Buckhead, Little Five Points and a number of others. Five Points [the center of downtown] has become more like a Wall Street business section.
>
> In the old days, people used to go "to town" in the evening. Now they take their cars and ride away from town, and at night Five Points is almost deserted.[8]

The Chamber of Commerce was active in a range of issues, particularly planning.[9] In 1920, eight of twenty-four members of the city's first planning commission were appointed by the president of the Chamber of Commerce, and another seven commissioners, appointed by others, were also members of the chamber.[10] In the 1930s, the chamber also began to press for governmental reform to counter the inefficiency and corruption that tarnished the city's image and hampered the provision of services.

Some business leaders foresaw the impact of the automobile on the future of the city. The viaduct system built in the 1920s eased traffic congestion, but the problem persisted. Many small merchants resisted parking restrictions on city streets, even though their own businesses were damaged by the problem of congestion. In the long run, outward growth meant a changing purpose for the central business district, as it became increasingly clear that downtown Atlanta was not assured of remaining as the economic hub of a spreading metropolis.

As the scale of activity increased and the pace of change quickened, a division within the business community became evident. Large businesses, big money, and major property holders can afford to plan, take risks, absorb short-term losses, and aim for long-range payoffs; small businesses cannot. In a period of transformation, the two types of businesses react differently.

One illustration is slum clearance. Taking advantage of an opening provided by the New Deal, Charles Palmer, the owner and manager of downtown office buildings, put together a coalition of business leaders to create the nation's first slum-clearance project in the 1930s. Palmer saw public housing as a means by which slums could be replaced and nearby property values protected. However, backers of slum clearance had to overcome the opposition of residential real-estate interests, who saw the use of eminent domain for redevelopment as a threat to their income from substandard housing.

The pioneering slum clearance and public-housing projects were followed in 1941 by the creation of the Central Atlanta Improvement Association, an organization of major property holders in the downtown area. Its creation signaled that "big money" in Atlanta had interests that were not always acknowledged and supported by small businesses. By creating a separate organization with a small membership, the major property holders were better able to act together on their shared interests.[11] They could bypass the Chamber of Commerce with its more diverse membership, especially in the early stages of planning, and dominate programs of action. The chamber was unlikely to offer a challenge, and, indeed, had a strong inclination to follow the business elite's lead.[12]

In 1941, Atlanta was still small enough that private social contacts were as effective as formal associations as ways of planning. Private clubs — in particular, the Piedmont Driving Club, the Capital City Club, and the Commerce Club — provided gathering places where informal plans of action could be worked out. Floyd Hunter described that pattern in his initial study of Atlanta,[13] but the practice dates back much earlier.

What made the Central Atlanta Improvement Association (later called the Central Atlanta Association and, still later, the Central Atlanta Progress — CAP) important was that it provided a structure for more than ad hoc cooperation. With CAP, the major players could launch long-range planning and engage in sustained action in support of a comprehensive program of redevelopment.[14] To plan and act collectively on behalf of large property interests thus seemed to call for something more than informal association. Perhaps delays that business leaders encountered in promoting the viaduct system in the 1920s, combined with ongoing resistance to parking and traffic regulation, was the initial inspiration for creating a more formal organization for future planning and development. Perhaps the crucial event was the opposition of small realtors to the use of eminent domain in slum clearance; unless they could be isolated from business interests generally, land assembly for redevelopment could be enormously difficult. However, if the major downtown businesses could set an action agenda first, then opposition by realtors could be countered as obstructionism.

With the advent of the automobile, urban development ceased to be an "everybody wins" game for city commercial interests. Suburban sprawl changed the character of the central business district, and decisions about a new role for downtown meant losses to some, gains to others. Against this background, major downtown business interests came out of the Great Depression organized to act on behalf of their collective interests as soon as wartime restrictions on building and development came to an end.

POLITICAL REFORM

Throughout the pre–World War II period, business interests promoted, with limited success, good-government reform. Highlighted by police corruption, the city's ward-based politics came under attack. In a 1929 graft investigation, fifteen individuals, six of them members of the city's legislative body, were convicted.[15] Further weakened by the Great Depression and the consequent squeeze on local finances, Atlanta's traditional system of ward politics was dealt a further setback with the 1936 election of William B. Hartsfield as mayor. Running as a reform candidate, Hartsfield garnered the financial and personal support of major business leaders,[16] including Robert Woodruff, the Coca Cola magnate found by Floyd Hunter to be "the biggest man" in town.[17]

In a city on the verge of bankruptcy, patronage politicians had no way of sustaining themselves, and they could expect little support from higher levels of government. The state was oriented toward rural courthouses, not Atlanta's city hall. And with Governor Eugene Talmadge openly hostile to the New Deal, the Roosevelt administration was more inclined to look upon friendly reform-minded business leaders as allies in Atlanta than it was to try to cultivate party support.[18]

Assuming office in January 1937, Hartsfield was mayor of a city in such financial crisis that it was paying its employees in scrip.[19] Hartsfield turned to business leaders like Woodruff and to the banks to guarantee the scrip and refinance the city so it could once again function as a going concern. In the words of Hartsfield's biographer, "The word was out in financial circles that Robert Woodruff had full confidence in the honesty, character, and financial ability of Bill Hartsfield, and thus reassured, the banks willingly helped the new mayor refinance the more pressing obligations."[20] For his part, Hartsfield set up a new budget system, eliminated 165 positions, and put into office a new police chief.[21] Without mass patronage and a precinct network, Hartsfield was dependent on his good-government image and the civic network centered around the city's major businesses. That image, of course, depended greatly on sympathetic coverage in the news media (the two newspapers also owned three radio stations).[22] But since the major newspapers had ceased their rivalry and were each an integral part of the business alliance, favorable press was assured so long as Hartsfield consulted with Woodruff and other business leaders.[23]

Education politics in Atlanta also underwent a change.[24] Long caught up in the city's bifactional politics, Atlanta's school system struggled for funding. In the 1920s and 1930s, the teacher's union and their labor allies formed a coalition with an organization of middle-class parents on Atlanta's affluent northside. As bifactionalism declined, this coalition successfully backed Ira Jarrell, till then president of the teacher's union, as superintendent of Atlanta schools in 1943. Once in office, Jarrell distanced herself from the labor movement and relied mainly on business support.[25] For its part, the teachers' union — an all-white organization — proved unable to deal with black restiveness, including a successful suit by black teachers for equal pay.[26]

RACE RELATIONS

The efforts by whites to keep blacks subordinate continued unabated in the period between the two world wars. And in Atlanta as elsewhere, the goal of white supremacy was not confined to less-educated whites, as an all-white teachers' union illustrates. Though the Ku Klux Klan had a particular appeal to the white working class and marginal middle class, educated and well-off whites were frequently at the center of encouraging and exploiting racial antagonism.[27] For example, Hoke Smith, a prominent member of Atlanta's civic and business elite, stirred racial fear and promoted the disenfranchisement of blacks during his otherwise progressive political career in state politics.[28]

Yet the pre–World War II period did lay a preliminary foundation for the later view that racial progress was best promoted by seeking the support of Atlanta's better educated and more prosperous whites. In 1919, white ministers and church groups, along with a local banker, formed the Commission on Interracial Cooperation, providing a means whereby communication and negotiation could be conducted across racial lines in Atlanta and a few other cities.[29] The organization offered no challenge to segregation but sought to eliminate the worst abuses of the Jim Crow system. It proceeded from the belief that "once the 'best people' of both races learned to cooperate for mutual benefit the way would be opened for all Southern people to accept a more just treatment of blacks."[30] However, during this period, there were few white moderates of any class with whom blacks could ally. Any concessions blacks gained came mostly through their own efforts. Indeed, what is noteworthy is just how adept black leaders were in positioning themselves to make the most of the restricted opportunities available.

Although the white primary, the poll tax, and the general atmosphere of racial hostility kept black voter participation at a very low level, there was nevertheless a small but real black electorate. Blacks were not barred from bond referendums, and they used that narrow opening to bargain for improved educational and other facilities. A successful bond referendum required a two-thirds vote of those *registered* to vote. Merely by increasing registration before a referendum, blacks could exert pressure and did in fact defeat bond referendums in the 1920s and 1930s to make that point.[31] It was by such electoral pressure and by negotiating through the Commission on Interracial Cooperation that blacks gained a commitment from the Board of Education to build Atlanta's first black high school in 1921.[32]

The interwar period is also notable for the various steps to organize the black community politically and to lay the groundwork for more extensive voter participation. Starting in 1932, at the suggestion of Mrs. John Hope (wife of the president of Atlanta University) and A. T. Walden (an attorney and president of the Atlanta chapter of the National Association for the Advancement of Colored People—NAACP), citizenship schools were conducted each year for six weeks in the black community. Under the direction of the Atlanta University faculty, these schools provided general citizenship education, information about registration and voting procedures, and inspirational talk about the importance of the ballot. During this same period, John Wesley Dobbs (a black Republican untouched by the exclusion of the white Democratic party primary) formed the Atlanta Civic and Political League, which sponsored mass meetings to raise political consciousness and promote voter registration.

Although black voter registration remained low during this period, these endeavors were important as independent efforts by blacks to become an electoral force. They afforded blacks opportunities to become knowledgeable about procedures and to develop organizational skills in voter mobilization. Significantly, many of the same individuals played important roles in forming and operating the All-Citizens Registration Committee, the organization created to promote black voter registration when Georgia's white primary was declared unconstitutional in 1946.

The white primary was only one area of restrictions that blacks sought to maneuver around. Residential exclusions were especially limiting. After the race riot of 1906, blacks who were already concentrated in older areas of the city—east, south, and west of the business district—became even more confined. The section to the east, particularly Auburn Avenue, became a hub of black commercial and civic activity.[33] The westside included the area that became the home of the Atlanta University complex, as over time the black colleges in the city came to concentrate in one place.[34]

Terror tactics discouraged dispersion of the black population, and ghettoization was furthered by city ordinance as early as 1913.[35] When the initial ordinance was declared invalid under the state constitution, the city devised new plans, in 1917 and again in 1922.[36] These laws were also declared invalid, but they marked the beginning of a firm understanding that northside Atlanta was "off limits" to black property owners.[37] With city actions reinforced by threats of violence and restrictive covenants, all that blacks could expect was a chance to expand into areas that whites no longer found desirable or that were undeveloped, which Atlanta as a young city did indeed possess.

In this context, a pioneer black entrepreneur, Heman E. Perry, made the bold move of buying up some three hundred acres of land on Atlanta's westside. Since his small but interlocking business empire brought together real estate, finance, and construction, he could build houses and offer financing without the participation of white mortgage lenders.[38] Though Perry eventually overextended himself and lost his whole enterprise, the westside residential opening had been made, and Atlanta's black community was no longer locked into older, close-in neighborhoods.[39] While northside remained "off limits," a pattern of success had been demonstrated: black-controlled real estate, finance, and construction gave Atlanta blacks maneuverability in coping with efforts to prevent them from expanding into new residential areas.

Thus, long before their postwar enfranchisement, blacks in Atlanta had developed a substantial middle class with an array of organizational and financial skills. The schools making up the Atlanta University complex contributed greatly to both their political and business efforts. In various ways, the black community came into the postwar era as a group with significant resources and a proven capacity to take advantage of the slender opportunities available in a system of racial domination.

The Jim Crow system in places like Atlanta contained seeds of its own destruction. Segregation built a sense of community among blacks[40] and gave their business and civic leaders a base of support independent of whites. Moreover, segregation was a pattern that could be perpetuated only with considerable effort, since racial friction was not a self-managing problem. As a growing population, blacks needed land, while white neighborhoods resisted their expansion, in some cases by force and violence.

The white business elite was itself dissatisfied with the status quo. To them, a changing central city meant that downtown would need a new relationship to the larger urban community—one that they believed could not be allowed to develop out of a filtering process through which older neighborhoods around the business district simply became more crowded and continued to deteriorate.

The automotive city and racial friction were conditions that grew out of forces well beyond any single group's mastery of the process of social change. As Atlanta entered the post–World War II era, the questions were how to cope with these conditions, and on whose terms and with what set of concerns would policy be made.

CONCLUSION

For most people, these various actions emanated from no broad understanding of what was happening, but were largely responses to immediate pressures and opportunities. However, by creating the Central Atlanta Improvement Association, Atlanta's business elite was providing itself with an organizational means to look more broadly, both in area and time, than other elements of the community were likely to do. It is significant that the formation of this association occurred after downtown Atlanta became less populated by small merchants and after homeowners began to disperse. As the big property holders recognized the concerns that differentiated their interests from those of more modest property holders, they positioned themselves to act independently. Furthermore, they controlled enough resources to make themselves attractive allies on Atlanta's civic scene.

At the same time, when the politics of personal rivalry, friends-and-neighbors loyalty, and ward-based organization lost ground, the importance of small business in city politics also declined. So too did the policy of minimum services and minimum taxation. For the downtown elite determined to achieve economic transformation, public authority was too useful in reshaping the city to be employed meagerly. In retrospect, it is understandable that Atlanta's business elite would create their own organization for planning and development, that they promoted reform of the city's traditional politics, that they were willing to use public authority and funds to redesign the flow of traffic and to clear slums, and that proponents of increased expenditures on education and other services saw them as vital allies.

As we turn to Atlanta's politics in the post–World War II period, we need to remember that both the white business elite and elements of the black middle class had already made substantial efforts to shape arrangements that would attend to their concerns. The postwar period is a time in which those efforts were joined.

For those who debate whether history should be a narrative of events *or* an analysis of structures, the Atlanta experience offers no such choice. Far from being one or the other, Atlanta's postwar history reveals continuing attempts to shape and reshape the structures (that is, efforts at structur*ing*) within which future events would unfold. Narrative and structur*ing* blend into one.[41]

PART TWO
POSTWAR EVENTS, 1946–1988

3

The Era of
Negotiated Settlements

*Nearly always in Atlanta it's the manipulative adjustment of interests rather
than the head-on clash.*

—Harold Fleming

Urban regimes are not fixed entities. They form and re-form as groups with
differing aims seek to shape arrangements in ways that promote their sometimes competing goals. In the process, groups adjust to one another, and individual groups themselves undergo change.

Atlanta enables us to see that struggle over regime arrangements is ongoing and evolutionary. From the pre–World War II period came three emerging trends that set the stage for the city's post–World War II regime. First,
without a large industrial sector, Atlanta's business elite saw early the need
to move toward a service economy.[1] The challenge of redevelopment strongly
invited a collective effort to plan and promote a transformed central business
district, and the formation of the Central Atlanta Improvement Association
(later shortened to Central Atlanta Association) provided the means whereby
the major property holders could act in concert. Principal members of the
business elite included Coca Cola, the banks, the utilities, the two major
newspapers (eventually brought under joint ownership), department and
other large downtown stores, and the biggest development and real estate
firms. All had a huge stake in the future of Atlanta's downtown. They were
also businesses with a tradition of civic involvement, businesses that gave
homage to the norm of a corporate responsibility to take an active part in
community affairs.[2]

As we saw in the background chapter, Atlanta's major economic enterprises
have not always enjoyed unity. In the early 1900s, newspaper rivalry guided
or at least reinforced bifactional conflict in the city's ward-based politics of

patronage and personal rivalry. So it is of more than passing importance that newspaper competition eventually declined, and in the postwar period, the two remaining major dailies came under the same ownership. The post–World War II period was thus marked by a shared concern about the future of downtown *and* a unified capacity to act on that concern.

The task of downtown redevelopment also increased business dissatisfaction with ward-based political arrangements. Their pre–World War II alliance with Mayor Hartsfield and the early ventures into slum clearance and public housing foreshadowed an activist postwar agenda that called for a unified city government. In short, redevelopment required not just an accommodation between business and city hall, but a close working relationship— one not hampered by the protection of ward-defined turf. Hence, a second significant trend was the decline of ward-based contention and the emergence of citywide concerns as focal points of Atlanta politics.

Groups differ not only in aims but in their capacity to further aims. In the post–World War II period, as the big downtown businesses pushed their ambitious goal of redevelopment, they inevitably encountered opposition, especially from small and vulnerable property holders. In this struggle, the downtown elite possessed many useful resources but lacked the essential component of numbers. This situation provided the setting for the third significant trend: Atlanta's restive black middle class, increasingly able to assemble a significant body of resources including a sizable bloc of voters, determined to make a bid for political influence and move against the strictures of the Jim Crow system.

As someone in the middle of these emerging trends, Mayor Hartsfield had a strong inducement to be politically innovative, and he had the foresight to recognize that an expanded coalition reaching across racial lines could be put together. However, the formation of this new governing coalition was only a first step; it had to be solidified by a series of biracial settlements, negotiated backstage in the face of significant popular opposition. Thus the mid 1940s saw the emergence of a system of biracial agreements that lasted until the student-led protests in the early 1960s. Both the beginning and the end of this era illustrate that structur*ing*, rather than fixed structure, is the appropriate way to consider urban regimes.

HARTSFIELD AS A POLITICAL LEADER

When Atlanta emerged from the World War II years, William B. Hartsfield was completing his second term as mayor.[3] Although the ward system with its friends-and-neighbors attachments had not disappeared, it had largely yielded to a more centralized form of politics. Hartsfield's political attachment to the city's business leadership was the prime mover of this transition, but ac-

companying alterations in the formal structure of government also contributed to Atlanta's evolution away from ward politics.

Faced with a large city debt coming into office, Hartsfield worked with
bankers to draw up a new budget law that tightly restricted the spending tendencies of patronage-minded aldermen. A more complete package of reforms was promoted by the 1938 Reed report—a study initiated and supported by the Chamber of Commerce—but it was put into effect only in
stages. The first major step, creating a civil-service system, came quickly in
1939. Other steps had to wait until the Plan of Improvement of 1951.[4]

Paving the way for these formal changes was the mayor's approach to politics. Hartsfield distanced himself from the fading ward organizations and relied on support from the city's business elite, not only for himself but also
for his allies on the Board of Aldermen. Without a precinct organization of
the old friends-and-neighbors kind, the Hartsfield administration found ample campaign money essential.

As noted earlier, Hartsfield was also acutely sensitive to the importance
of the news media, and he mastered the art of garnering good press. In doing
so, he relied in particular on Helen Bullard of Rawson Associates, a major
advertising firm, to head his reelection campaigns and other public relations
efforts. (She later served in a similar capacity for Ivan Allen.[5])

Hartsfield constantly projected a good-government image, and he played
on a larger stage than just the local community. He coined the phrase, "the
city too busy to hate," to describe Atlanta in the 1950s, revealing himself,
at a time when others of his generation were hesitant or unwilling to face
social change, as savvy enough to see that a reputation for good race-rela-
tions made favorable national press for his city.[6] But he was no mere manipu-
lator of public images; his political base was more securely founded than
that. His habit of first consulting the business elite before moving on an important issue led Floyd Hunter to talk about the "community power structure" and to depict Hartsfield as subordinate to the city's business elite.[7]
Although others credit Hartsfield with a stronger leadership role and describe
him as an initiator of major policy efforts and a skillful mobilizer of the
business elite,[8] on major issues such as the Plan of Improvement[9] and urban
redevelopment,[10] his role appears to be quite modest.

Even though Hartsfield moved solely in tandem with the business elite, his
alliance with them would work only with an appropriate electoral base. His
appeal to Atlanta's white working class was weak,[11] since reform-style politics
held little attraction for them. And the logical supporters of "good government," Atlanta's white middle class, had migrated to the suburbs. With electoral support for the governing coalition sure to be severely strained by redevelopment, Hartsfield's recurring concern was to recapture the out-migrating
educated and affluent white middle class—the group he saw as his core constituency. However, attempts at annexation failed in 1938, 1943, and 1947.

It was in this context that the black middle class gained entry to the governing coalition. Atlanta was still very much in the throes of the Jim Crow system, and the city's black leadership was eager for change. Even so, in an era of continuing white racial domination, aligning a black constituency with the governing coalition would be no simple matter. How that came about is the gist of the remainder of the chapter.

SHAPING AND RESHAPING
AN ELECTORAL CONSTITUENCY

The 1940s was a decade of some fluidity in city and even state politics. At the state level, Ellis Arnall (1943–1947) brought a degree of reform and progressivism into the governor's office. A 1946 special election for Georgia's Fifth Congressional District gave Atlanta blacks an opportunity to tilt the outcome toward a progressive candidate, Helen Douglas Mankin, by an alliance with organized labor and others.[12] But the conservative Talmadge forces regained control of the state party machinery and put the district under the county-unit system, thus negating Mankin's strong Atlanta vote in her reelection bid. Nevertheless, the black community was encouraged by its initial success and by the capacity of a progressive candidate to garner votes inside the city — with its backing. The congressional election was thus a signal to Hartsfield and his business allies that adjustments had to be made, and they proved receptive to overtures from the black middle class.

It was a textbook case of the theory that skillful exercise of the vote affects the behavior of officeholders. Early in his career, Hartsfield had been a conventional segregationist.[13] He had fought the idea of creating a federal Fair Employment Practices Commission,[14] and in 1944, he asked the House Un-American Activities Committee to investigate the NAACP.[15] On occasion, he attacked "so-called liberals, alleged sociologists, advanced educators, agitators, left wing radicals and South haters."[16] Yet Hartsfield was no racial demagogue. After a protest march to city hall asking for fair law enforcement and the hiring of black police officers, Hartsfield met with black leaders.[17] That meeting began a pattern of resolving issues by quiet, behind-the-scenes negotiation between the mayor and black leaders.[18] Hartsfield is quoted as having said that "Your vote will buy you a ticket to any place you want to sit."[19]

In 1946, blacks launched a major drive that raised black registration from approximately three thousand voters (4 percent of the electorate) to twenty-one thousand voters (27 percent of the electorate)[20] — a phenomenal feat, particularly in a Deep South city in the 1940s. Building on earlier efforts in the black community, an All-Citizens Registration Committee formed under the auspices of the local chapter of the NAACP. Several Atlanta University professors played key parts in the organization. The Atlanta Urban League, headed by Grace Hamilton, provided block-by-block analysis and organized an 870-person volunteer force to canvass the more than one thousand blocks on which blacks lived. The committee touched all bases — car pools, a speakers' bureau, sermons in black churches, handbills and placards, Boy Scouts distributing literature, numerous community meetings and social events, a barrage of publicity through the black newspaper (the Atlanta *Daily World*), special projects by churches, labor unions, and college fraternities, and targeted registration drives by project managers of public housing and black employers such as the Atlanta Life Insurance Company. The black community was well endowed with organizational resources; they needed only to be mobilized to produce results.

The virtues of a coordinated effort had been boldly demonstrated, and in preparation for the city's nonpartisan elections in the fall of 1949, black Democrats under attorney A. T. Walden and black Republicans under John Wesley Dobbs (maternal grandfather of Maynard Jackson, who would be elected in 1973 as Atlanta's first black mayor) merged to form the Atlanta Negro Voters League. The advantages were clear: a single organization could hold off making its endorsements known until the last minute and still get the word out to the black community; and, a united front was stronger in dealing with public officials and other white leaders.

With blacks constituting more than a quarter of the electorate, it was time to move forward on the issue of black police officers. Hartsfield did so, consulting, as usual, with leading business figures, one of whom was the councilmember who introduced the resolution to employ black policemen.[21] The resolution passed in late 1947, and recruitment began in 1948 — despite the filing of a suit, the opposition of a former mayor and some state officials, and resistance within the police department.

The city's action was largely symbolic. Only eight black policemen were hired, and they were under the command of a white captain, operating out of a separate substation. And for a time they were not authorized to arrest whites. Nevertheless, in the Deep South of the 1940s, it was a significant step, and Hartsfield exploited it for its full symbolic value within the black community. According to the mayor's biographer, the employment of black police officers "was the first real breakthrough in race relations in Atlanta."[22] He also observed:

> Hartsfield . . . was to use his black officers most effectively as stage props in his campaigns. He would appear to speak before a black rally, and all of a sudden the black policemen in full uniform would appear, to the loud applause of the black audience. One of his favorite ploys, particularly when campaigning against his perennial opponent, Charlie Brown, was to wait outside a Negro mass meeting until Brown was in the middle of his speech. He would then enter with his entourage, to

loud applause, shaking hands right and left and leaving the hapless speaker frothing in rage.[23]

This breakthrough in race relations paid off for Hartsfield in the next election and thereafter. In 1949, he rebuffed a challenge by Charlie Brown and two other opponents, avoiding a runoff by just 102 votes—a victory made possible only by the huge majorities he received in black precincts.[24] Hartsfield also received a majority of the white vote on Atlanta's affluent northside, but not an overall majority among white voters.

Despite such demonstrations of the value of support from a growing black electorate, Hartsfield always saw educated and well-to-do whites as the linchpin of the governing coalition and of responsible politics in general. Hartsfield described them to blacks as "the decent folks" and the best bet for good race relations. He maintained to blacks and whites alike that a black majority was an unworkable political arrangement.[25] Prior to the large black voter registration, Hartsfield had written a letter to numerous community leaders, asking their support for the annexation of the affluent suburbs to the north of Atlanta. In this letter he said:

Our Negro population is growing by leaps and bounds. They stay right in the city limits and grow by taking more white territory inside Atlanta. Out-migration is good, white homeowning citizens. With the federal government insisting on political recognition of Negroes in local affairs, the time is not far distant when they will become a political force in Atlanta if our white citizens are just going to move out and give it to them. This is not intended to stir race prejudice because all of us want to deal fairly with them; but do you want to hand them political control of Atlanta?[26]

After blacks were mobilized electorally, Hartsfield argued to them that northside Atlanta represented a reasonable element, one capable of counterbalancing the state's antiblack politics. In a state where Eugene Talmadge, Herman Talmadge, and Marvin Griffin had served as governors, it was a telling point, and it persuaded the Atlanta Negro Voters League to support annexation of northside suburbs as part of the Plan of Improvement in 1951.

This plan expressed the strategy of maintaining a white majority city, but one dominated by the affluent middle class. Though it had the short-run effect of reducing black electoral influence, it protected the coalitional foundation of that black participation at a time when federal activity on behalf of minority voting rights was modest at best. The Plan of Improvement tripled the size of the city from 37 to 118 square miles and added an estimated 100,000 to its population, bringing the total to 428,299. It also realigned functions between city and county and created a smaller city council elected at-large.[27]

The predominantly upper-class white constituency that was now folded into the enlarged city helped Atlanta elect its first black to citywide office in the twentieth century, when Dr. Rufus Clement, president of Atlanta University, was elected to the school board in 1953. As part of the same move, A. T. Walden of the Atlanta Negro Voters League and Dr. Miles Amos, another black leader, were elected to an obscure body, the City Executive Committee.[28]

Getting the Plan of Improvement adopted was an enormous accomplishment, requiring the support of two county delegations to the state legislature and then a successful referendum. Although Hartsfield backed the plan, it was the city's business leadership that led the campaign to have it approved.[29] They secured the support of good-government organizations like the League of Women Voters, and with Hartsfield's groundwork, they also received backing from the strategically important Atlanta Negro Voters League. The newspapers predictably were strong backers as well.

Extensive behind-the-scenes bargaining was as important to the success of the Plan of Improvement as was the public campaign. With Hartsfield often serving as the mediating link, the two key elements in the governing circle "negotiated settlements," not just in pushing through the plan but in many matters. Coalition insiders favored this practice over the "divisive applications of political pressure," believing that backstage negotiations lessened the chances for racial polarization.[30]

The approach was highly incremental. Hartsfield, for example, eliminated the "white" and "colored" signs from the restrooms at the Atlanta airport by gradually reducing them in size until they could hardly be seen. Then, without public notice, they simply disappeared.[31] In other instances, Hartsfield took the position that he was only abiding by the law. In 1958, after federal courts had declared bus segregation unconstitutional in other cities, Atlanta was hit by protests challenging segregated seating, which was still required under state law. After considerable negotiation with key black ministers, a prearranged test case was staged, in which a group of blacks were arrested for "violating state segregation law" and immediately released on bond.[32] The state statute was declared unconstitutional, and Atlanta's buses were then integrated.[33]

With its policy of racial moderation and negotiated gradualism, Atlanta appeared to be an isle of reasonableness in a sea of die-hard resistance. Moreover, while there was tension between city and state officials, segregationist governors were not eager to attack an urban regime supported by Atlanta's economic elite and affluent northsiders.

Much of what Atlanta offered the black community in the Hartsfield era was largely symbolic, but for black leaders, the city's modest steps represented movement in the right direction. However, that was only part of the picture; the full vista includes the governing coalition's handling of controversial land-use issues. Expressway construction and redevelopment implied massive displacement, forcing the city to face the dual problems of housing for blacks and neighborhood transition. Here the workability of negotiated settlements would be severely tested. On the other hand, the issues were not unconnected; the 1952 enlargement of the city provided vacant land that could be used to increase housing for blacks, which was one reason that black leaders supported the Plan of Improvement. It had literally expanded the field of negotiated settlements.

LAND AND THE TASK OF GOVERNANCE

However politically useful annexation was, in itself it could do nothing to preserve the central business district as a hub of economic activity. For that to happen, business leaders concluded, it would be necessary to link downtown with the suburbs by means of expressways. Some early plans had called for an expressway west of downtown, elevated over the rail lines running through that area.[34] Such a route would minimize residential dislocation and by some estimates would be less costly than the alternatives. However, the business elite—having long been concerned about the proximity of blighted residential areas to the business district, as evidenced in their backing for slum-clearance projects in the 1930s—had different ideas about the best location for highways. Instead of acting directly, business leaders proposed the use of private consultants, and they strongly backed the consultants' "Lochner report" when it was issued in 1946.

Long before the creation of the federal interstate highway program, the Lochner report called for a $60-million issue of local bonds (by Atlanta, and Fulton and DeKalb counties) to fund both a north-south and an east-west expressway.[35] Not surprisingly, the Lochner plan involved more than simply linking downtown and the suburbs. The north-south expressway was to curve around the edge of downtown, forming a buffer between the business district and the black neighborhoods to the east. Gone was business support for close-in public housing. Instead, the business community feared that such projects would anchor blacks to these areas and hamper downtown revitalization.[36] The Lochner plan would shift that population away from the business district and place a barrier between downtown and the black population.

Although the plan spread the highway building over ten years, it was not an ideal time to embark on a program that involved displacement. The postwar housing boom had not yet taken off, and housing was still in short supply—acutely so for Atlanta's black population. Except for the partially developed westside (some of which fell beyond the preannexation city limits), Atlanta's black population was largely locked into older areas around the business district. Even some older black neighborhoods outside of the city were subject to public actions that sacrificed them to white priorities. For example, the county commission turned a black neighborhood in the north-side community of Buckhead into a public park — for whites only.[37]

In 1946, the same year that the Lochner report was released, the Atlanta Urban League convened a meeting on the need for land for black residential areas.[38] A Temporary Coordinating Committee on Housing was created, chaired by a black contractor and consisting of representatives of the business, social agency, and political sectors of the black community. The group developed two organizations to pursue a housing program: a land committee, headed by a real estate broker, to search for "outlet areas for Negro expansion";[39] and a corporate committee, to consider forming a corporation to build on sites obtained by the land committee.

It was wholly appropriate that the local Urban League should take the lead in mustering resources and planning an attack on what had long been a critical problem. Organized in 1919 in the offices of black entrepreneur Heman Perry,[40] the Atlanta branch of the Urban League was firmly tied to the city's black business class. It was in close contact with the Butler Street Young Men's Christian Association (in the business section of Auburn Avenue) as well as the leadership of Atlanta University. It was also linked to the city's white business elite.[41] And, unlike the NAACP chapter, it was funded partly by what was then called the community chest — a fact that worked as a moderating influence on the pursuit of the black agenda. Thus the Urban League made no frontal assault on the idea of racially exclusive neighborhoods, but instead pursued a policy of improved housing opportunities for blacks within the system of segregation.

The regime-supporting role of the Urban League is illustrated in an incident related by Hartsfield's biographer. Prior to the city election of 1953, John Wesley Dobbs pulled his Republican followers out of the nonpartisan Atlanta Negro Voters League. Dobbs was dissatisfied that Hartsfield was unwilling to follow the police precedent and hire black fire fighters. Hartsfield's campaign and public relations chief, Helen Bullard, went to Grace Hamilton, the executive director of the Atlanta Urban League, for advice about how to handle the situation. Hamilton provided Bullard with a list of fifty-four names — black ministers, university officials and professors, and businessmen — all of whom were leaders in the Atlanta Negro Voters League. Hartsfield was advised to invite this group to meet him at the Butler Street YMCA. In this meeting, Hamilton suggested that Hartsfield should

> begin by saying that his opponents were calling him "the Negroes' representative," but that he denied this. He should say instead that he had tried to be mayor of all the people; that he had been deeply aware of the special needs of the Negro population, but he had had to work on these needs in terms of what was possible for the whole population. He should point out that he had been able to keep city government free of

some of the anti-Negro forces so rampant in the state government, but that in this race he strongly believed his opponent was making a strong effort to turn Atlanta over to those elements in the state, thus punishing him, the mayor, for having resisted them.

It would also be wise, Mrs. Hamilton suggested, to admit that all had not been done that should have been done — and that the Negro did have legitimate gripes. The sore spots should be brought up and discussed — no Negro firemen, more Negro policemen, better schools and parks for Negroes, appointment of Negroes to planning boards, and the elimination of police brutality. Bringing all these into the open and discussing them fully would rob the disgruntled of their ammunition.[42]

Hamilton's advice to Hartsfield through Bullard is noteworthy for several themes. First and foremost, a vote against Hartsfield was a vote for the most racist element in the state. Second, Hartsfield had to work within the bounds of what was feasible and that meant not being perceived as a representative of only black interests. Third, it was necessary to acknowledge that there was room for further negotiation. All of this was to be said in a context in which Hartsfield would display respect for black leaders by going to their home turf, since the Butler Street YMCA was *the* meeting place for black civic leaders.[43]

Thus, the Urban League was a central connector in the city's governing coalition. White leaders saw it as nonthreatening, and it worked closely with the mayor in mediating black-white relations. It could do so, in part, because it was immensely valuable to leaders in both racial communities. It also played a very concrete role. The Temporary Coordinating Committee on Housing looked to the Urban League for staff support in estimating housing needs, making contacts, purchasing land, enlisting Federal Housing Administration (FHA) cooperation, and performing numerous other tasks. As land was obtained and housing projects built, black-white cooperation became extensive. For example, an analysis of nineteen black subdivisions built in the early postwar years showed that two were financed by blacks, four by whites, and thirteen by both.[44]

Building new housing developments for blacks was intertwined with the complexities of racial transition, as existing residential areas shifted from white to black. White resistance to black residential expansion was organized and intensive. Aside from various neighborhood "protection" associations, a klanlike organization, the Columbians, formed to use terror and violence to discourage blacks from moving into white areas.[45] Even where the Columbians were not operating, the process was difficult. To be sure, much transition in Atlanta occurred through the private market and the enormous profit opportunities it offered. Because there was a huge, pent-up demand for housing in the black community, blacks were willing to pay a premium for older housing at the very moment that whites were looking at vast new housing opportunities in the suburbs. Even so, the process of racial turnover in housing was fraught with violence, panic-selling, and the kind of deep emotion that made it anything but a free market. As upholder of law and order, the city was drawn in, and an unofficial group known as the Mayor's Committee was established to negotiate particularly difficult transitions.[46]

Court decisions precluded any legal designation of areas by race, but unofficial agreements did in fact guide the residential development of west- and southside Atlanta. There was also some transition on the eastside, but north Atlanta remained firmly off limits to black expansion. Greatly expanded by annexation, the westside contained most of the undeveloped land, with blacks controlling the resources to acquire and build on property, and provide mortgage financing. However, the scope of movement and especially the amount of new housing were dependent on black-white cooperation, once again negotiated backstage.

The Atlanta Housing Authority and the Metropolitan Planning Commission both participated in identifying areas for black expansion; and, in building the projects of Carver Homes (opened in 1953 on the southside) and Perry Homes (opened in 1955 on the westside), the Housing Authority was integral to the opening of residential land for blacks. By one estimate, between 1945 and 1956, 3,450 new owner-occupied homes, 3,100 new private apartments, and 1,990 new public housing units were built for blacks.[47]

Providing blacks with land both for expansion and replacement of old areas lost to expressway construction was much more than a technical process of building and financing. Not only did the Mayor's Committee negotiate disputes, but other elements of the mayor's alliance played strategic roles as well. The support of the police department was crucial, and the mayor and police chief were apparently inclined to hold back protection unless an expansion was part of an approved plan.[48] As usual, the newspapers were important, opposing violence in general and the Columbians in particular while minimizing the publicity around specific conflicts over residential areas.

Housing is not an isolated good; its use is integrally related to the availability of other facilities and services. A particularly long struggle was waged over a westside area called Mozley Park.[49] Eventually the transition, which included a park and school, was completed in 1954, but other services, in particular a bus line for the area, were also at issue. The privately owned Atlanta Transit System did not extend service to the full Mozley Park area until two years after the transition struggle was over.[50] Although the owner of the transit system was an insider in the Hartsfield-business alliance, the provision of bus service required prolonged negotiation. And Mozley Park was not unique. Deliberate efforts to retard black residential expansion took the form of not building through-streets in many parts of the newly enlarged city.[51]

Isolation of blacks in remote sections of Atlanta was thus a serious problem, not easily remedied. In this period, any benefit extended to blacks was a break with the prevailing system of racial subordination.

Will W. Alexander, director of the Commission on Interracial Cooperation (headquartered in Atlanta), once said, "The best way to change men's minds about each other is to set them to work on some concrete task."[52] Housing for blacks in Atlanta in the immediate postwar years was such a shared task, which cemented the governing coalition in its biracial form. There were abundant opportunities for backstage negotiations — the hallmark of the Hartsfield era. These negotiations involved city hall, the school system, the police department, black business interests, black social-agency staff, black political leaders, white financial interests, the news media, and eventually the private transit company. Facing vehement and, on occasion, violent opposition, the interacting parties drew support from one another. Moreover, the fact that the task they accomplished was socially, organizationally, and technically formidable gave rise to a shared sense of accomplishment.

Institutionally, this governing coalition represented major white business enterprises, local government in the hands of white officials, and key organizations in the black community. Together they demonstrated that they could make things happen; they could set policy and carry it out. But why would such a wide array of community actors undertake a task so surrounded by controversy and, on every count, so filled with potential frustrations? The answer lies in the common need shared by Atlanta's white business elite and black middle class: Both wanted change.

Restructuring land use brought the elements of the coalition together into complex and repeated interactions that did indeed build a foundation for cross-racial understanding and habits of biracial cooperation. No one had a master plan of how cooperation could be managed, and relations within the coalition were not always smooth. But negotiated settlements did emerge. Some agreements, particularly about racial control of land, were explicit; a few were written and others were tacit.

The main contours of the biracial agreements of that period are clear. The white business elite wanted to move blacks and low-income whites away from the fringe of the business district, especially on the east- and southsides. (Railroads constituted a buffer on the westside.) They also wanted no black expansion into northside Atlanta, and segregated residential life was a given. For their part, blacks wanted expansion land, including the opportunity to build new housing for both homeownership and rental units. Land-use agreement was accompanied by a political agreement. Blacks would give electoral support to Mayor Hartsfield and his allies; they in turn would support the gradual shrinking of the Jim Crow system, engage in no race-baiting rhetoric, accord blacks personal respect, and hold in check the potential for white violence against blacks.

On both sides, there was a general understanding that negotiation was preferable to grandstanding and open conflict. For the white business elite, behind-the-scenes bargaining was desirable because they lacked numbers. For blacks, the specter of mass white violence of the kind perpetrated in the 1906 riot and on a smaller scale in some of the housing transition areas was an inducement to embrace quiet negotiation.

The benefits of the arrangements were multiple, which is why they were so durable. Both groups gained important objectives that could be touted before larger publics. Blacks of all classes, formerly squeezed into a restricted area of the city — "one-third of the population on one-ninth of the land" was the shorthand description used by the Urban League — got land for expansion and housing built for a range of income levels. The business elite could point to economic growth and a revitalized downtown that promised gains across class and racial lines.

Some of the benefits were psychic — civic pride, and a strong sense of accomplishment over the joint furtherance of economic growth and racial peace. But there were also material and particular benefits, since restructuring land use unfolded significant opportunities for contracts, retainer fees, jobs, speculative profits, and the enhancement of land values.[53] Especially for black businesspeople, so long confined, large-scale restructuring of land use offered a chance to exercise their entrepreneurial aspirations fully. The chance to push back barriers (even within the bounds of continuing segregation) and make profits in the process was an irresistible inducement. However, it is noteworthy that accomplishment came at the upper level between black and white elites, not at the mass level. There, racial antipathy and a sense of being manipulated remained strong.

Seen in the light of the coalition program of restructuring land use, the Plan of Improvement takes on added meaning. It gave the city's governing coalition a larger territory in which to pursue their policy. Blacks faced diminished electoral weight but enlarged housing and entrepreneurial opportunities. In the realignment of functions, law enforcement inside and outside the city was a responsibility of the city police department. The Housing Authority could operate outside as well as inside the city limits. Further, the addition of a voting constituency responsive to the leadership of Atlanta's civic elite was not an alarming prospect to blacks; in fact, in some ways, it was reassuring. And when the enlargement of the city was followed by the election of a black member of the school board, prospects for racial progress seemed promising.

Since, in relation to the enactment of the Plan of Improvement, the crucial elections were in 1950 (and the 1951 referendum), they preceded the Supreme Court's ruling that declared segregated schools unconstitutional. Thus the racial fears of middle-class whites were not fanned by that issue. Indeed, the major concern that had to be allayed was whether additional parts of DeKalb

County would be incorporated into the city. Once DeKalb was excluded from further annexation, legislative opposition to the Plan of Improvement eased.

Despite earlier defeats for annexation, the 1950 plan had the united backing of the governing coalition. Opposition was still significant, but the governing coalition behind the active leadership of the white business elite was able to draw together the necessary elements of support.

LAND USE, PHASE TWO

In the first phase of restructuring Atlanta land use, the city built expressways and responded to the growing housing needs in the black community by providing sites for expansion or (since land was being lost to nonresidential uses) for replacement. In the second phase, the city's urban-renewal program took center stage.[54] Redevelopment officially came onto Atlanta's policy agenda with the passage of the Federal Housing Act of 1949. Urban renewal — federal financial assistance for locally planned and executed redevelopment projects — was enormously controversial, and it faced numerous legal, political, and organizational obstacles. Central to this program was the use of the power of eminent domain, through which land was acquired and resold to developers, typically at a written-down cost. The federal government covered two-thirds of the cost of planning, land acquisition, relocation, and implementation; it also regulated the entire process and approved projects one by one. Local governments could meet much of their one-third share by spending money to make improvements in the renewal areas.

Though urban renewal was legally and financially complicated, the basic approach was clear: land was taken from one set of owners and given to another to alter its use. Whole neighborhoods could be changed or even eliminated. Although cleared sites could be used for public facilities (Atlanta, for example, built a stadium and a civic center in renewal areas), the process typically involved private development.[55]

Only a coalition able to draw on a wide variety of resources could even undertake a renewal effort. To actually carry out a program required an ability to keep resources mobilized over a period of years in the face of considerable resistance. Urban renewal was a *political* process at heart, which attempted to disaggregate opposition while holding support together. In Atlanta, renewal was every bit the challenge that the Plan of Improvement was and more.

Once again, the Central Atlanta Association was the prime mover. Even before the 1949 Housing Act, it was working with the newly created Metropolitan Planning Commission (formally an independent body, supported by both the city and downtown business leaders) to rejuvenate and expand the central business district. In 1950, the city designated its first redevelopment project: the white Hemphill Avenue area, adjoining the Georgia Institute of Technology just north of the business district. Even though the Hemphill area was chosen to avoid the issue of black relocation, the proposed project was highly controversial. Small businesses and residents who would have to move were strongly opposed. Others, especially smaller realtors oriented toward residential properties, were also fearful; they especially objected to the building of additional public housing to accommodate displacees. Some saw urban renewal, with its ominous use of eminent domain, as a socialist assault on private enterprise.

The Hemphill venture predated the Plan of Improvement and the large addition of affluent northside whites to the electorate. Proponents of urban renewal feared that small business and lower-income whites might coalesce into solid opposition, and the Hemphill project was shelved. A legal test of state enabling legislation seemed certain, but what was the best site for such a case if not Hemphill Avenue? Redevelopment had also made the black community apprehensive; its *Daily World* warned that clearance in and around Auburn Avenue would be resisted "by whatever influence" blacks could "bring to bear, politically, legally or otherwise."[56] Auburn Avenue had already been affected by the north-south expressway, and black leaders had fought off a suggested world's-fair site in the vicinity.

Backers of urban renewal finally chose a black area south of the business district, away from Auburn Avenue. Despite significant opposition, the city council approved the project and the legal contest was set. The Georgia Supreme Court ruled that the use of eminent domain for redevelopment purposes was not permitted under the state constitution. However, in a remarkable display of their ability to get their way through a state government, characterized by V. O. Key as the "rule of the rustics,"[57] Atlanta business leaders, working with the Georgia Municipal Association, succeeded in having the state constitution amended and new enabling legislation passed.

With legal issues resolved, the next step called for the allocation of city funds through a general bond referendum.[58] Significantly, funds for urban renewal received the weakest support of the various elements of the bond issue. Thus, while the referendum did succeed, it also indicated that popular support was shaky.

But all sorts of specific backing, not just general citizen endorsement, were needed. One challenge was to prevent Atlanta's business community from fragmenting over site selection and reuse planning. Another was to cope with potential black opposition and the strictures of federal rules regarding relocation. Without succeeding on these two fronts, the urban-renewal process would be immobilized. Meanwhile, the mayor was unenthusiastic about the program and the thorny displacement problems it posed.[59] Although the Atlanta Housing Authority was responsible for execution of the program and much of its planning, city hall nevertheless had to take action itself.

The first step in building an urban-renewal coalition was to unify the white business elite. Two site decisions overcame the first hurdle: placating Rich's Department Store and the lower downtown faction by designating an area just south of the business district (Rawson-Washington); and bypassing competing priorities by choosing a site (Butler Street) east of the business district that satisfied the uptown faction, led by Davidson's (the Atlanta link in the Macy's chain). The second crucial decision was an informal understanding that no public housing would be built *on urban-renewal land*, in order to reassure the Atlanta Real Estate Board in particular, with its strong orientation toward private residential properties. That agreement, of course, complicated the provision of relocation housing.

Next, support had to be built within the black community, and in this venture, past experience proved important. The Urban League was a central actor and was instrumental in suggesting that expansion land for the Atlanta University system be included as a separate urban-renewal area. Hence, the original urban-renewal package included three projects that bore the clear signs of logrolling within the city's biracial coalition. When these three projects proved insufficient to meet relocation requirements, two more were added. Rockdale and Thomasville were low-density neighborhoods in outlying sections of the city—on the west- and southside, respectively. They were designated as redevelopment areas for single family dwellings under FHA's "221" program for home ownership by moderate-income families.

The shape of the urban-renewal program was clear. It would continue what had started earlier under the Lochner plan. Blacks would be moved away from the business district and relocated in outlying areas to the west and south. Land for new black housing developments would be made available. Black colleges would gain room for expansion and a diminution of substandard housing in the areas around them. Even a massive relocation of blacks, though painful to those uprooted, opened the prospect of substantial opportunities for black businesses. Contractors could benefit from the significant building in prospect; black real-estate companies could be prime beneficiaries of the property acquisition and rehousing that were inevitable in urban renewal. Predictably, the Empire Real Estate Board was much more enthusiastic about urban renewal than was its white counterpart, the Atlanta Real Estate Board.

Despite coalition-building efforts, a white group formed an organization called the Fourth Ward Zoning Committee to oppose relocation through the "221" program. Black opposition also surfaced. The Butler Street project in the Auburn Avenue area was especially controversial, since it followed extensive displacement for expressway construction. A nonfederally assisted alley-clearance program, launched by the city in 1955 to remove substandard dwellings in what had once been servant quarters, increased concern about "Negro removal."[60] The local chapter of the NAACP and several black ministers formed the Localities Committee, which succeeded in getting a federal mediation officer sent in but could not have redevelopment stopped.

Federal authorities took the narrow view that the city had to guarantee housing for those displaced by the federal urban-renewal program but not for displacees from other forms of government action. Federal mediation did enable the "221" program to survive, and the Atlanta Housing Authority did agree to conduct a further housing study in 1958. The results showed that by 1963 government action would uproot more than ten thousand *families*, many with extremely low incomes. Those figures convinced city officials that additional public housing would be necessary to sustain the renewal program.

Officials took other steps as well to dampen black opposition. For example, they made generous appraisals of the value of black churches to be acquired by eminent domain, thus enabling black congregations to buy churches vacated by white flight. Moreover, black opposition, though substantial, never became unmanageable. Black business and institutional interests received enough benefits to prevent their making common cause with lower-class blacks. Poor blacks at least obtained some new public housing, though it was late in coming, insufficient, and often in remote areas. As with the building of expressways, blacks were losing close-in land, but were gaining expansion areas. Nonaffluent whites on the southside and, as displacement mounted, on the eastside paid the main social costs of rapid racial turnover.

Though events are only sketched briefly here, it is enough to indicate that a great deal of social and political conflict had to be managed in order for Atlanta's urban-renewal program to be launched. Opposition was ineffective because it never aggregated into a sustained and unified force. Biracial support for urban renewal took shape, biracial opposition did not – even though there was substantial disapproval by blacks and whites.

Perhaps more than any other issue in Atlanta, urban renewal involved the "complexity of joint action."[61] Certainly the program could have been stymied at any number of points. The actions of ten or more official bodies had to be coordinated for urban renewal to proceed: the state government and the state voting public that approved the changes in the Georgia constitution and laws to allow urban renewal; the city's voters who approved an omnibus bond referendum, including funds earmarked for urban renewal; the Atlanta Housing Authority as the city's official redevelopment agency; the mayor's office; various city departments, such as public works and parks and recreation, which provided complementary facilities that helped the city meet its local share of the financial costs of urban renewal; the Atlanta school system, for the same reason; the Joint Planning Board (of the city and county) that recommended rezoning actions; the Board of Aldermen of the city and its various committees; and various federal officials, regional and national, in the Urban Renewal Administration, Public Housing Administration, and FHA. That lineup omits the assorted citizens' committees, some with quasi-official status, that performed studies, made recommendations, and rallied voters in the face of heavy opposition.

It was Atlanta's governing coalition, driven by the city's business elite, that made it all work. They lobbied the state for legal changes, and they played a central role in the omnibus bond issue. Federal officials perceived them as essential supporters, as indeed they were. At one point, key figures in the business elite met privately with Hartsfield and insisted that he get the program on track, while the daily newspapers attacked him for foot-dragging.[62] After the meeting, Hartsfield passed the warning around city hall that "our downtown citizens, together with the newspapers" would "go to the extent of rooting the entire government out if they feel we have been remiss in the face of federal opportunities to make progress."[63] The program moved forward.

The Housing Authority proved an especially strong facilitator. It was officially independent of the mayor, though he appointed the governing board. Significantly, most of its members were also members of the Central Atlanta Association, reflecting Hartsfield's alliance with the downtown elite.[64]

CRACKS IN THE GOVERNING COALITION – MORE LAND-USE CONTROVERSY

Despite its institutional bases of strength, the governing coalition was vulnerable to defeat on specific issues, and the selection of a site for public housing in 1960 was one of them. After many years of tension over displacement and residential transition, the Housing Authority had great difficulty finding sites to accommodate the one thousand units whose need had been identified in the survey triggered by the Localities Committee protest.

With the search under way, the authority bought an eastside parcel (once the site of Egleston Hospital) large enough for 350 units of public housing, 210 of which would be for the elderly. The area, which had recently become black, contained significant commercial and industrial activity as well. It was also near the all-white Georgia Baptist Hospital and Druid Hills Baptist Church, a large white church pastored by Louis Newton. Newton was not only influential in his church denomination, but also had substantial ties in the extended business community, having once edited the news magazine of the Atlanta Chamber of Commerce.[65] As chairman of the Georgia Baptist Hospital Commission, Newton feared that the hospital was being encircled by a spreading ghetto. The stage was thus set for a confrontation, with the governing coalition and its supporters on one side, and white neighborhood interests allied with Georgia Baptist Hospital on the other.[66]

Before public housing could be built, the site had to be rezoned. The battleground was the city's Board of Aldermen, which Hartsfield was supposed to be able to lead. In 1959, after an initial rejection of the rezoning proposal, the business elite took an active part in gathering support for a reconsideration, from good-government organizations such as the League of Women Voters and from other groups ranging from the Georgia Engineering Society to the Atlanta Association for Mental Health. In the meantime, a second and less controversial site, for 650 units of public housing, had been located on westside Atlanta. The two items came before the aldermanic board in March 1960. Rezoning of the westside site was approved by a vote of eleven to five, and reconsideration of the Egleston rezoning lost nine to eight, with board president Lee Evans casting a tie-breaking vote.

The timing of the votes is important, considering the broader milieu. Student sit-ins had just begun, signaling a new assertiveness in the black community and growing impatience with the pace of racial progress. No black had yet been elected to the city council; it remained a body largely oriented toward a past in which white dominance was unquestioned and blacks received only token gestures.

The Egleston defeat threw the governing coalition into a crisis. Hartsfield came under considerable criticism for not delivering an aldermanic majority. Seventy years old, he had been mayor for nearly twenty-five years, and some in the governing coalition believed it was time for new leadership in city hall. One person observed, "Hartsfield and his colleagues are getting old; he has absorbed few new people into his orbit."[67] Another noted that "For years the business side of the power structure has relied on Hartsfield to keep the board in line. They would back him and not pay too much attention to the aldermen because they were in with him. Now that Hartsfield's control is slipping, we are going to have to start watching the aldermen more closely."[68]

Discontent ran even deeper in the black community, and some white civic leaders were fearful that "moderate and responsible" blacks would lose leadership. One cautioned that "we must restore their leadership and keep their cooperation if Atlanta is going to have stable housing."[69] The white establishment believed that all-out black opposition to urban renewal was possible, and they feared that blacks might disregard existing racial agreements and expand into several previously white residential areas. The Egleston defeat thus endangered the commitment of blacks to the planned restructuring of land use initiated in 1946.

For their part, blacks regarded the Egleston decision as a rejection of the tacit understanding that they should be able "to develop in their own areas." After the vote, a mass rally was held in protest and to air concerns. At the meeting, A. T. Walden, head of the Atlanta Negro Voters League, made the case for sticking with the coalition. While acknowledging that blacks "do not like what happened," he urged that they "not be thrown off . . . balance" so as to "lose liaison" with "the people who have the best interests of Atlanta at heart."[70]

The biracial alliance held, but change was in the offing. The following year, Hartsfield decided not to run again for mayor. Ivan Allen, Jr., ran as the coalition candidate and defeated segregationist Lester Maddox, his principal opponent, by rallying once again northside whites and Atlanta's growing black population.[71] Even though the 1952 annexation had added whites to the city, white flight and black in-migration gave Atlanta a 1960 population that was 38 percent black. (It seems that the city's white civic leadership was not fully aware of the long-range trend toward a black majority. Interviews of the early 1960s referred to the in-migration of poor whites as a possible dominant factor in the future politics of the city.[72]) With black voting power gaining in importance, black leaders marked Lee Evans for defeat in his reelection bid for presidency of the Board of Aldermen. Evans was succeeded by Sam Massell, who, with strong black support, became Atlanta's first Jewish mayor eight years later. Thus the alliance that had defeated Egleston rezoning was a passing phenomenon. In retrospect, the Egleston vote was the "last hurrah" of traditionalist white opposition in Atlanta.

Blacks now pressed for further accommodation to their housing needs. In the 1950s, Hartsfield had been less than aggressive: of the city's quota of 5,500 housing units under FHA's "221" program, only 3,008 had been built. Racial tensions over relocation grew as urban renewal proceeded, yet Hartsfield had rejected a staff proposal to create a blue-ribbon citizens' committee to lead the search for relocation housing sites.[73]

In the effort culminating in the Egleston proposal, much debate had occurred inside the governing coalition over various ideas about alternative housing. The business elite rejected close-in sites, especially just east of the business district, claiming that residential density in that area needed to be decreased. Even before the Egleston decision, the accommodation-minded Urban League and Empire Real Estate Board expressed dissatisfaction with the "artificial" land shortage imposed on blacks.[74]

To stabilize the governing coalition, it was time to make some concession to black housing; specifically, to find another site for the 350 units lost in the Egleston defeat. With white neighborhood opposition aroused, that was no easy task; however, the Housing Authority came up with a compromise to build 140 family units as an annex to an existing project in far westside Atlanta and put 210 units for the elderly in the Butler Street project area near Auburn Avenue, also adjoining an existing public-housing project. This close-in location was a significant concession to the black leadership concerned about the future of Auburn Avenue, and the white business elite could accept housing for the elderly close to the business district. One- and two-person households did not create the kind of density it was concerned about, and the units could go into a single high-rise apartment building that would occupy little land. Business leaders moved to resolve the one complication—the earlier informal agreement that no public housing would be built on urban-renewal land—by endorsing the proposition that "this high rise facility will be considered an 'exception.'"[75] With business support, the close-in site for elderly housing was approved.

Both the original understanding and the negotiated "exception" indicate that the white business elite was the central element in the city's governing coalition. Although defeated in an aldermanic vote, they still set policy direction for the city, *mindful of their need for black allies.* White traditionalists had exerted a temporary veto but were unable to exercise the governing power of the community. Furthermore, after the passion of the Egleston issue faded, white traditionalist neighborhoods, including those on the eastside, once again absorbed the impact of black displacement and expansion.

Significantly, the Atlanta Real Estate Board did not fight the exception to the past understanding, but their acquiescence was no sign of growing acceptance of public housing. As late as mid 1959, the board president presented a resolution to the city's Urban Renewal Policy Committee opposing "socialistic public housing subsidized by taxpayers."[76] It is noteworthy, then, that realtors did not mobilize against public housing when site location became the principal issue.

Real-estate interests in Atlanta were fragmented. There was a racial division, separating the black Empire Real Estate Board from the white Atlanta Real Estate Board, and some real-estate dealers were part of neither organization. Moreover, the Atlanta Real Estate Board itself had incompatible elements. Smaller companies concerned mainly with residential properties had expressed their fear of public housing as early as the 1950 Hemphill-area battle. Larger companies, concerned mainly with commercial properties in downtown Atlanta, were part and parcel of the Central Atlanta Association and were more concerned about maintaining coalitional support and federal approval for urban renewal than about opposing public housing.

Further, real-estate interests found that their sorties into the issue were subject to hard-hitting counterattacks. Their policy stands were vulnerable to the charge of being nothing more than self-serving positions, since some brokers dealt in slum housing and others were engaged primarily in the pursuit of speculative profits. In 1958, the newspapers leveled editorial fire against realtors engaged in challenging the constitutionality of the city's newly enacted housing code (drafted to help the city qualify for federal urban-renewal funding): "Are Atlanta real estate developers opposed to urban renewal? Is the motive behind this move an attempt to block and delay a program which is vital to the city's future? Are some property owners who make money on incredibly filthy slums so greedy they would perpetuate blight which threatens to destroy all property values in the downtown area?"[77] That the newspapers were an integral part of the governing coalition was a matter of consequence, easing some paths of action and making others more difficult. Faced with the possibility of public attack as well as bad relations within the business community, realtors steered clear of both the Egleston issue and its aftermath.

There would be no dominant standpat coalition. Egleston was followed by another major battle between racial moderates and traditionalists — one fought mainly at the state level, but in which Atlanta's business elite played an important role. The battle was over school desegregation, and this time traditionalists failed to exercise a veto.

SCHOOL DESEGREGATION

As Hartsfield's mayoralty was coming to a close in 1961, few tangible changes in race relations had occurred. In the fifteen years since blacks had mobilized electorally, their concrete gains were few: the hiring of black police officers, the elimination of Jim Crow signs from the airport, the court-ordered desegregation of public transportation and of municipal golf courses, and the election of a black member of the school board. Housing segregation had actually increased from 1950 to 1960.[78] What Hartsfield offered was mainly a moderate tone in race relations: "racial moderation in campaign speeches and other public utterances."[79] Yet Atlanta was regarded as a pacesetter in the South, "an island of reason in a sea of bigotry."[80] Georgia, Ivan Allen observed, was for years "one of the most racially spiteful states in America."[81] The climate of moderation brought about in the state's capital city was thus no small accomplishment.

Under Hartsfield's leadership, Atlanta had made significant progress in the realm of the less tangible. Whites in the governing coalition had been educated to the changing times. School desegregation was thinkable; when it came, they were not surprised.[82] By contrast, the rural-oriented Georgia Association of County Commissioners was on record as opposed to "any race mixing in any Georgia schools anywhere, at any time, under any circumstances."[83]

The NAACP set the Atlanta school desegregation process in motion with a suit initiated in 1958. At that time, the state had on its books a legislative arsenal for massive resistance, the centerpiece being a requirement that schools be closed before mixing the races. Georgia's governor and governor-elect used the unequivocal rhetoric of never-say-die for the "southern way of life." Locally, prosegregation forces formed two distinct organizations — MASE, the Metropolitan Association for Segregated Education, and Lester Maddox's GUTS, Georgians Unwilling to Surrender.[84]

However, school desegregation was no replay of the Egleston site controversy. Momentum for keeping the schools open built slowly; as it did, all parts of the city government (including a unanimous Board of Aldermen), the business community, church groups, the Atlanta *Constitution*, the League of Women Voters, the Board of Education, Parent-Teacher Associations (PTAs), the Georgia Education Association, and a wide array of other civic organizations came together to oppose massive resistance.[85] The strategy was twofold: to argue that the local community should decide; and to link school desegregation in particular and moderation generally with economic growth.

The moral issue was not excluded. Even before the filing of the court case, eighty Protestant clergy of Atlanta issued a statement calling for obedience to the law and for the preservation of public schools. In 1959, 311 ministers signed a second statement.[86] On another front, Atlanta mothers concerned about schools for their children formed an organization called Help Our Public Education (HOPE). By 1960, as the federal case worked its way through the courts to an implementation decree, HOPE had thirty thousand members in several Georgia cities.[87]

Although there is some uncertainty about when and how forcefully business leaders entered the fray, there is no doubt that business lobbying was crucial in turning around massive resistance in a rural-dominated state.[88] In 1960, under Ivan Allen, the Atlanta Chamber of Commerce pounded the lessons of Little Rock and New Orleans, and the business community was on record as firmly committed to open schools.[89] That same year, Georgia's governor and legislature established a blue-ribbon citizens' commission, headed by John A. Sibley — banker, lawyer, counsel to Coca Cola, and a leading member of the Atlanta business establishment.[90] After hearings in every congressional district in the state, the Sibley Commission recommended repealing massive-resistance legislation, replacing it with local option, and preserving public education. That became the rallying ground for moderates.

When black plaintiffs won their case, the Atlanta Board of Education was ordered to submit a desegregation plan by December 1959, for the opening of school in the fall of 1960. The school board proposed a one-grade-per-year plan (starting with seniors) on a freedom-of-choice basis, and the court assented. Acceptance of school desegregation in the Deep South was still very much in doubt then, and Atlanta stood as the likely indicator of the future.

Since Georgia law at that point would have denied state funds to Atlanta's school system, the court delayed implementation until fall of 1961 to allow time for the state to reconsider its stance, setting the stage for the Sibley Commission to make its recommendations. For the session of the legislature opening in January 1961, everyone anticipated that the desegregation of the Atlanta schools would be the focus of a struggle over repeal of massive-resistance legislation. But a successful admissions suit for the University of Georgia, timed for January, accelerated events.[91] The state was thus faced with the immediate issue of closing the university. Throughout the state, church people, educators, and education groups, joined first by the Atlanta Chamber of Commerce and then by other business leaders, spoke out for the end of massive resistance. According to one chronicler, "nearly a thousand Georgia businessmen" called on the governor and state legislators to keep the schools open. Many signed a resolution stating that "disruption of our public school system would have a calamitous effect on the economic climate of Georgia."[92] Georgia officially abandoned massive resistance. As historian Numan Bartley has observed, "Open schools had become part of the economic growth consensus."[93]

Atlanta still faced the challenge of peaceful implementation. Desegregating schools, after all, was enormously more difficult than quietly desegregating municipal golf courses. When Atlanta desegregated its schools, the entire nation was watching, and the city feared that its high profile would draw "troublemakers from all over the country."[94] There was also significant local opposition, and the potential for violence was real, as experiences in other places indicated. Atlanta itself had suffered the bombing of a synagogue as recently as 1958.

The image-conscious Hartsfield wanted not only to avoid violence but to have the city look very good in the process. The governing coalition agreed. Public rhetoric stressed the benefits of racial progress for business, and it included statistics showing how damaging Little Rock's 1957 riots had been economically.[95] Drawing in PTAs, religious groups, and professional groups as well as the usual array of civic organizations, the governing coalition launched an elaborate campaign to prepare the city for peaceful school desegregation. Jane Hammer (wife of the first director of Atlanta's Metropolitan Planning Commission and an insider in the governing coalition) chaired an organization of organizations — OASIS, or Organizations Assisting Schools in September.[96] During a law-and-order week before school opened, churches and synagogues conducted special prayers for peaceful desegregation.[97] The mayor, the police chief, and the school superintendent all made public statements, reassuring parents about safety, making it clear that no disruption would be allowed, and affirming the inevitability of the change.[98]

Despite Atlanta's good reputation in race relations, not all of the signs favored a smooth transition. Student sit-ins had come to Atlanta in 1960, and Atlanta University students had engaged in direct-action protests against Jim Crow practices in downtown Atlanta extending into the early months of 1961. Emotions were at a peak, and a cooling-off period was negotiated for the opening of school. Meanwhile, Lester Maddox, Atlanta's most flamboyant segregationist, continued his shrill calls for resistance, expressing his anxieties that school desegregation might lead to "white girls being found in negro hotels."[99]

As the school-opening date neared, the Atlanta police undertook an elaborate surveillance program — watching individuals known for racial agitation, infiltrating organizations, and giving gun merchants and sellers of commercial explosives pictures of individuals thought to be potential troublemakers.[100] Police informers infiltrated the Klan, and according to one account, another extremist group "was so ridden by police watchers and strict enforcement that it moved its headquarters to Birmingham in search of freedom."[101]

After all this preparation, Atlanta's school desegregation in the fall of 1961 involved only nine black students, divided among four formerly all-white high schools. Even so, the step was momentous, not just for Atlanta, but for the nation, still unsure that school desegregation could be achieved peaceably. On opening day, police and school officials declared that school facilities were off limits to everyone except students and staff.[102] The press corps, swelled by two hundred out-of-towners, was briefed in a pressroom at city hall, given a handbook prepared by OASIS, driven from school to school, and at the end of a peaceful day ("the quiet heard around the world"), offered a bus tour of Atlanta. At a cocktail party at the downtown Biltmore Hotel, the mayor reminded the press that the racially mixed party under city auspices was itself a landmark event.[103]

The smooth school desegregation was "a giant public relations coup for Atlanta."[104] President Kennedy, the United States Attorney General, and the national news media all congratulated the city, perhaps sensing that Atlanta's successful transition marked the end of massive resistance. The schools, in fact, remained largely segregated over the next several years,[105] and new litigation was started; still, an important symbolic bridge had been crossed.

Whereas urban renewal was a policy in which the white business elite was the driving force, desegregation was an issue in which the black community was the central factor. In both situations, the coalition held together, once again displaying its capacity to formulate and carry out policy. Every element in the coalition handled its part well. The mayor's office, the school system, and the police department acted with unity of purpose. The business community and its civic allies played an active and crucial role. The Atlanta news media again was cooperative, contributing to a climate of order and peaceable acceptance.

The cooling-off period negotiated in the parallel issue of public-accommodations desegregation in downtown Atlanta was part of the coalition's overall plan for coping with racial change. Though the governing alliance was experiencing great tension at this time, its continuing strength was much in evidence. Past experience and long-established ties were vital components. And school desegregation was treated in a way that was consistent with the coalition's past commitments to amicable race relations and the promotion of economic growth.

School desegregation provided Hartsfield with his crowning achievement; in his words, it was Atlanta's "finest hour." As he was leaving office, this one-time segregationist called for acceptance of social change and of the need "to live in peace and without hatred."[106] In the wings was Ivan Allen, Jr., elected in the fall of 1961 to the first of his two terms as mayor. As president of the Chamber of Commerce, Allen had been active in promoting peaceful school desegregation. But he also had an ambitious agenda of redevelopment in mind that would test further the durability of the coalition between the black middle class and the white business elite. Meanwhile, the student sit-ins demonstrated that the black community itself was undergoing major change. Backstage negotiation and "the manipulative adjustment of interests" came under attack.[107] Fundamental political change appeared to be in the offing.

4

Protests and Coalitional Stress

In politics neither defeat nor victory is permanent.

— Richard Rich

Change is often treated as the transition between *periods* of stability. The study of electoral politics in particular focuses on periods of dominance by a given coalition, followed by its eventual breakdown and the emergence of a new alignment.[1] There is wisdom in this cyclical view. Once a workable political arrangement proves itself, it can maintain support and even draw new allies into its orbit. In Atlanta, that is what the alliance between Hartsfield and the business elite succeeded in doing. Blacks were incorporated into the governing coalition as junior partners, and the coalition was bound by the double theme of economic growth and racial moderation.

There is, however, something that the cyclical view misses. Seen close up, political arrangements are often not firmly fixed and perhaps subject to coming unraveled or at least to being reshuffled. Even something as seemingly settled as the Daley machine in Chicago involved considerable change and significant readjustment.[2] It would be easy to slip into calling this ongoing process of readjustment "pluralism," but change within a relatively stable regime is not that open and unstructured. Some groups have a superior capacity for adjusting to changing conditions in order to offset unwanted developments, but this ability should not obscure the fact that established arrangements come under pressure.

In Atlanta in the 1960s, the governing coalition was subject to enormous strain. A generational divide weakened the position of established black leaders, bringing forth new and vocal champions of black interests and increasing friction between black and white leaders. As civil-rights activism, federal policy, and, eventually, state politics altered the conditions under which black

51

leaders and the downtown business elite had achieved their initial accommodation, there was no guarantee that past arrangements would hold. Student sit-ins provided the first, but only the first, test of the durability of established coalitional lines. As the 1960s unfolded, the practice of negotiated settlements gave ground to protests, and a variety of groups openly expressed dissatisfaction with city policy.

SIT-INS VERSUS "THE ATLANTA PLAN"

In reflecting on the early 1960s, Martin Luther King, Sr. — known affectionately within the black community as Daddy King — talked about the city's coalition politics "grinding slowly to a halt":[3] "Our warnings to Hartsfield and the others that it was increasingly difficult to convince younger people to wait any longer for the rights their Constitution guaranteed them just weren't being heard. The storm kept brewing."[4]

Ivan Allen, Jr., offered a parallel assessment in his recollection of meeting with student protesters during the time he was president of the Chamber of Commerce: "We listened to them and said we would take the matter up with the other members of the Chamber, but then we made no serious moves toward eliminating segregation. . . . What we were doing was closing our eyes and hoping the problem would go away."[5] Indeed, initial resistance was so strong that Rich's Department Store, a principal target of the sit-ins, considered becoming an all-white store.[6]

When black college presidents met with white business executives to negotiate on behalf of students, the exchange became heated. One "outstanding businessman" said, "You go back and tell your students that they will never eat in a white restaurant in Atlanta."[7] When students (over opposition from older leaders) targeted Rich's Department Store for a sit-in as the bellwether for downtown Atlanta, an angry Richard Rich had them arrested under Georgia's new antitrespassing law.[8] The newspapers also rejected the legitimacy of student demands. The Atlanta *Journal* editorialized that "old customs and traditions are not changed by battering rams and dramatics but by time and attrition and with the help of good will."[9]

Friction and misunderstanding between the races was matched by generational cleavage within the black community. There was no conflict over goals, but there were sharp differences over tactics and timetable. On the one side were students, seized with the excitement and promise of mass action outside established channels. Impatient for an end to segregation and with little vested in the status quo, they were quite open to the expressive appeal of the historic moment. As participant-observer Howard Zinn said, "It is hard to overestimate the electrical effect of the first sit-in in Greensboro."[10] It not only introduced a change in technique but also increased resolve.

Still, the generational divide was not all-inclusive. The older black generation broadly supported the student goal of ending segregation. Black lawyers defended students, the Empire Real Estate Board provided bail, ministers made their churches available for mass meetings, black physicians and their spouses picketed, and the presidents in the Atlanta University system made no effort to stop students from demonstrating—though they did urge caution and insist that academic work proceed.[11] But on tactics and pace, the cleavage was deep. To some of the students, the older generation was hopelessly compromised by their financial and other ties to Atlanta's white civic elite—an elite that made deposits in black financial institutions, advertised in the black newspaper (the Atlanta *Daily World*), donated to black colleges and social agencies, and helped to make business opportunities available. A. T. Walden and the Atlanta Negro Voters League came under especially sharp criticism as Uncle Toms, who had "done little but feather their own nests."[12]

Clearly, some of Atlanta's black leaders had benefited from being "reasonable," whether materially or in status as representatives of Atlanta's black community.[13] Martin Luther King, Sr., himself had deep stakes in the established procedures, which he saw as providing "a sophisticated exchange of viewpoint."[14] He was a long-standing member of the city's Interracial Commission,[15] able, as he put it, to speak "often with the mayor, the chief of police, the head of the Atlanta Board of Education."[16] The elder King recounted how he used that network to see that his daughter was not excluded from employment with the Atlanta school system. This was no simple patronage matter, since King had played an important part in the 1940s suit to equalize teachers pay and feared that his daughter was being sanctioned for his past action. To King, the network was valuable as a means of communication between the races.[17] His view was not universally endorsed. When he attempted to persuade a mass audience that accepting a negotiated settlement with a cooling-off period was desirable, he reminded the younger generation that he had been working in Atlanta to improve race relations for thirty years. At that point, someone yelled out, "That's what's wrong."[18] And Daddy King was booed.

The matter is too complex, however, to dismiss Atlanta's older leaders as Uncle Toms, willing to accommodate the status quo for personal advantage. They had grown up in the rural, small-town South, and they knew how oppressive that South was. They had themselves taken risks during times when white violence and intimidation were present dangers. Although they favored the new protest tactics for places like Montgomery, Alabama, which was part of the older South,[19] they saw Atlanta as different. Linking racial oppression with the landed elite of the traditional South,[20] they believed that the New South business elite had a different agenda. The new group would provide a modernizing leadership, capable of pushing aside the old elite committed to racial domination.[21]

In the eyes of some of the less sophisticated older black leaders, the issue boiled down to money and power. Theirs was an if-you-can't-beat-them-join-them argument: "Don't you know you can't force Rich's to change? Rich's has millions of dollars."[22] They thought it unwise to turn powerful allies into adversaries. Both kinds of older leaders leaned toward what Martin Luther King, Sr., called "the Atlanta Plan," based on the bus desegregation effort in Atlanta during the late 1950s: "nonviolent action, arrests, and subsequent integration through court decree."[23] The key element was the court decree. Looking back years later, King made a revealing observation: "I maintain to this day that there was nothing basically wrong with this approach, except that it took too long and never got to the roots of segregation, those deeper places in the human soul where the law did not reach."[24] It was precisely those deeper places that students sought to reach—and without taking "too long."

To the older generation, the special appeal of the Atlanta Plan and its ultimate reliance on court action was that it did not threaten the bonds that held the coalition together. The senior King spoke repeatedly of the Atlanta Plan as a tactic that enabled those who made concessions to save face.[25] In that way, trust could be preserved and communication maintained, even as segregation was being challenged.

When Atlanta University students planned their first sit-in, older leaders initially persuaded them to take two actions in line with the tactical spirit of the Atlanta Plan. One was to begin by drawing up a statement of grievances, and a small committee, including the eloquent Julian Bond, drafted "An Appeal for Human Rights" that called for an end to segregation and specified areas for redress, ranging from education to movie theaters. President Rufus Clement of Atlanta University arranged to have it published in both white and black newspapers in advance of any direct action.[26] Response to the appeal from within the biracial coalition was largely favorable, but Governor Vandiver, by contrast, attacked it vehemently. With the sit-in movement already spreading rapidly, the manifesto served to alert the community that direct action was coming.

In deference to the Atlanta Plan, the students also agreed initially to concentrate on public buildings (city hall, the county courthouse, and the state capitol) and on facilities indisputably included in interstate commerce (the bus and train stations). This tactic not only offered the best opportunity for successful litigation but also spared downtown merchants. However, when this effort yielded little, Rich's Department Store (a mainstay of the biracial coalition) was targeted for a sit-in. Boycotts and mass picketing downtown followed. It was at this stage that the biracial coalition was most severely strained and generational cleavage was at its peak. The publisher of the old-line black newspaper, the *Daily World*, criticized the students for lawlessness, and younger black leaders, including some from the business sector, retaliated by starting a new newspaper in the black community, the Atlanta *Enquirer.*

Despite the deep divisions and the angry words between generations, the negotiating team that was eventually named included younger business people and student leaders, though it was weighted toward the older and established figures. When the settlement did come (in the second year of protests), it was initially opposed by students. Martin Luther King, Jr., bridged the generational divide and made a successful appeal to support the settlement—a written agreement to end the demonstrations for several months until after the public schools were desegregated. Students in jail would be released immediately, and after a cooling-off period, downtown stores would be desegregated.[27] Another important actor in the negotiated settlement was Ivan Allen, Jr., still president of the Atlanta Chamber of Commerce but soon to be mayor. As the student protests ran into a second year, Allen, a business insider, was instrumental in bringing about an agreement (though a few establishments refused to become parties to it) where Mayor Hartsfield had been unsuccessful.

Police Chief Herbert Jenkins was also critically involved. During the early stages of the student protests, at a meeting with President Benjamin Mays of Morehouse College, Jenkins said, "Go back and tell your students that when they are going to demonstrate, sit-in, or picket, let me know in advance so that I will be able to dispatch the right officers to the scene. You know we have all kinds of men on the police force, some are members of the Klan. It makes a lot of difference who the officer in charge is."[28] Jenkins also came on campus and talked to the students. His openness helped to avert what could have been a bloody confrontation between students and armed state troopers at the state capitol. Jenkins, who had no jurisdiction on the capitol grounds, persuaded protesters to bypass them and go through the downtown.

Even though the Atlanta Plan gave way to direct action against downtown businesses, the governing coalition held. Hartsfield, Jenkins, and Allen maintained a close working relationship with black leaders, and bonds of cooperation were kept intact. Within the black community, the links were less secure. Lacking substantial stakes in a system of cooperation with white business leaders, the younger generation found gradualism unappealing, and their political attachments remained unfixed.

IVAN ALLEN'S ELECTION: THE COALITION HOLDS

When Ivan Allen, Jr., heir to a business-supply firm, became mayor in 1962, his inaugural speech called for greater business participation in the affairs of the city,[29] and his mayoral platform was based on his six-point program as president of the Chamber of Commerce. Allen was a long-standing member of Atlanta's civic elite, following in his father's footsteps. In the election, he was, as he later said, the "silk-stocking" candidate.[30] Allen represented a generational change much different from the one at work in the black community; in his words,

> the older group, which included my father, had guided Atlanta from behind the scenes for nearly four decades. Sometimes altruistic but most often pragmatic — with a businessman's view that what was good for Atlanta was good for them — they had brought Atlanta from an overgrown country town to a metropolis totaling nearly a million people. Woodruff [the Coca Cola magnate] embodied the best of this group: for more than two decades he had been an unofficial advisor to Mayor Hartsfield, and I think it is correct to say that not a single fund-raising drive in Atlanta during that time had been successful without help (usually in the form of an anonymous gift) from the Woodruff interests. Woodruff was the symbol of the benevolent, civic-minded patriarch.[31]

In line with the "power structure" lore of the city, Allen said that "Woodruff was turning over the management of Coca Cola — and the direction of Atlanta, since the two were to a degree synonymous — to younger men, and his peers were doing the same."[32]

The group that Allen described was a highly cohesive one: "when I looked around to see who was with me in this new group of leaders, I found my lifelong friends. Almost all of us had been born and raised within a mile or two of each other in Atlanta. We had gone to the same churches, to the same golf courses, to the same summer camps. We had played within our group, married within our group, partied within our group, and worked within our group."[33] Floyd Hunter could not have said it better. Who was this group? As Allen described, "We were white, Anglo-Saxon, Protestant, Atlantan, business-oriented, nonpolitical, moderate, well-bred, well-educated, pragmatic, and dedicated to the betterment of Atlanta as much as a Boy Scout troop is dedicated to fresh milk and clean air."[34]

It was also a group, as the Allen administration proved, that could get things done. It pushed through a rapidly moving development agenda; it played a key role in the peaceful desegregation of Atlanta schools; and it was the group that protesters targeted to end the exclusion of blacks from public accommodations in downtown Atlanta.

In running for mayor, Ivan Allen had ample campaign funds, Hartsfield's longtime campaign director, four hundred employees of the Ivan Allen Company, newspaper support, and prestigious endorsements — such as ones from the presidents of the five major banks.[35] Yet it was no foregone conclusion that he would be elected mayor. He also had well-known opponents in the race, including die-hard segregationist Lester Maddox — owner of the Pickrick Restaurant and organizer of GUTS, who had run a strong but losing race against Hartsfield four years earlier. Challenging Allen for votes in the black community was "Muggsy" Smith, a state legislator with political ties to the black community. Smith tried to capitalize on the younger generation's discontent with the Atlanta Negro Voters League, and he did succeed in gaining about one-third of the black vote.

Allen deliberately pitted his racial moderation against Maddox's unyielding commitment to segregation.[36] That strategy led the Atlanta Negro Voters League to back Allen, claiming that "a vote against Ivan Allen is a vote for Lester Maddox."[37] In a runoff between Maddox and Allen, Maddox attacked Allen as a "silver spoon hypocrite, with inherited wealth."[38] Maddox pointed out that the Atlanta civic elite did not hire black executives in their businesses, send their own children to integrated schools, or patronize racially mixed swimming pools. Maddox received a majority of white votes, but Allen won nearly unanimous support from blacks and heavy support among affluent, northside whites. The coalition held. Allen assumed the office of mayor in January 1962. Three black candidates lost their bids for aldermanic seats, but Dr. Rufus Clement, president of Atlanta University, got a third term on the Board of Education.[39]

POINT, COUNTERPOINT—
BLACK PROTESTS AND LIBERAL WHITE STANDS

Coming from a "crowd" accustomed to guiding the affairs of the city off-stage, Allen stumbled at first as a political leader. In his first year in office, he lost an $80-million bond proposal, but he came back the following year with a much smaller proposal ($39 million) that passed.[40] His major blunder was with the black community. In late 1962, responding to white concerns about racial transition in southwest Atlanta, Allen put up a barrier on Peyton Road, a street in that area. It was a public-relations disaster on the national scene,[41] and Atlanta's black community invoked Iron Curtain symbolism to call it the Peyton Wall.

The previous year, Mayor Hartsfield had put up a similar barricade in the same section of the city,[42] without such damaging reaction. And, as Allen pointed out, Atlanta city-maps were dotted with various buffer zones that were typically areas zoned for commercial use.[43] In the tradition of many past trade-offs, Allen proposed to offer in exchange to rezone 250 acres of industrial land on which low-to-middle-income housing for blacks could be built. What Allen had not reckoned with was a rising tide of expectations in the black community that made explicit barriers no longer acceptable.

When Mayor Allen called for a meeting that included city officials, the Atlanta Negro Voters League, the Empire Real Estate Board, and white home-owners, the two black organizations declined to attend. Instead, they announced that in these matters they would now be represented by the newly formed Citizens Committee for Better City Planning.[44] In addition to long-established black organizations, the CCBCP represented such newcomers as the Southern Christian Leadership Conference (SCLC), the Student Nonviolent Coordinating Committee (SNCC), and the Committee on Appeal for Human Rights (the student organization that had directed the sit-ins). The Board of Aldermen and the mayor refused to do away with the Peyton Road barrier on their own, but when a Fulton County Superior Court judge ruled against it, the mayor had the barrier taken down immediately — as he said, to make sure that no more pictures of it would be taken.[45]

In other housing developments, the new Uptown Association succeeded in its specific goal of preventing blacks from moving north of Ponce de Leon Avenue, but black expansion continued in southwest Atlanta and on east- and southside Atlanta. In the mid 1960s, as redevelopment continued its massive displacement in the center of the city, black residential expansion spilled over the city limits to the east into DeKalb County. A move welcomed by city officials, it was reportedly brought about with the help of federal officials in the regional office of the U.S. Department of Housing and Urban Development (HUD).

The CCBCP evolved into the Atlanta Summit Leadership Conference, an organization with a broad civil-rights agenda. While students and other civil-rights activists directed protests at sundry targets — including hospitals[46] and the public schools, where desegregation was slow,[47] — the Summit Leadership Conference launched a campaign for total desegregation of Atlanta, advocating a local public accommodations ordinance, an open-occupancy housing law, and the establishment of fair employment machinery.[48] The Board of Aldermen balked at any move, but demands did not lessen.

The city came under strong pressure on jobs in particular. Marches, demonstrations, and, eventually, a boycott were employed.[49] The presence of entertainer and activist Dick Gregory, Martin Luther King, Jr., and SNCC in support of these efforts were signs that the Atlanta Plan and the established black leadership had indeed been replaced by a new, or at least more diverse, team and by a new strategy of protest and activism. Significantly, however, Martin Luther King, Jr., was only sporadically involved in city affairs. By all accounts, he was kept on a short rein by established black leaders.[50]

In 1963, when a demonstration against the recalcitrant Heart of Atlanta Motel resulted in the arrest of three hundred students, the aging A. T. Walden resigned from the Summit Leadership Conference, stating that he was "not in agreement with excess, like the recent demonstrations." He added, "Disorderly demonstrations tend to drive people away."[51] Other established leaders were not so negative. Dr. Benjamin Mays suggested that "the demonstrations may be necessary to speed the desegregation of Atlanta."[52] Clearly past practices were not holding. Walden's death in 1965 completed the passing of an era. Virtually all the other black leaders had moved to a more assertive stance, and despite significant intragroup tensions, various black organizations worked together. Eventually, the more militant members faded away from the Summit Leadership Conference, but in positions of influence was left a younger and more assertive, though not highly militant, group.[53]

Mayor Allen responded to this demonstrated assertiveness. He appointed a biracial committee to increase job opportunities for blacks,[54] and, in 1963, at the request of President Kennedy, he testified in favor of the newly introduced federal civil-rights bill.[55] He was the first and only southern mayor to do so; from the South, he was joined in support of the bill only by Charles Weltner, Atlanta-area congressman. Allen had been at the center of negotiations that occurred after student sit-ins began, and in office he was confronted with the uneven results of voluntary desegregation. The importance of convention business to Atlanta added pressure against leaving the issue unresolved. He was also mindful of the good national press that the city had received from peaceful school desegregation—and the bad press from the Peyton Road barrier. Still, he took a risk in getting so far ahead of sentiments held by white business and newspaper officials.

Why, then, did he endorse federal legislation? Allen later gave as reasons his own awakening liberal conscience and the deep-rooted notion of Atlanta as a unique southern city. From all indications, what drove him was not vote-seeking, but an attachment to the established black leaders in Atlanta; he spoke of them as individuals "who had been at my side during years of crises . . . with whom I shared mutual respect and support."[56] This loyalty to individuals included the idea that the biracial coalition was an effective and sensible way to govern the city. These same considerations led Allen two years later (in 1965) to be part of the successful effort to sponsor a biracial dinner in Atlanta honoring Martin Luther King, Jr., as a Nobel Peace Prize recipient. That dinner was again an occasion when white business leaders were initially reluctant to participate, but the risk of adverse national publicity and the efforts of coalition insiders, including the legendary Robert Woodruff, overcame their hesitation, making the event a success attended by an estimated one thousand five hundred people.[57]

With Ivan Allen, as it had been with William Hartsfield, Atlanta's governing coalition had a very strong personal dimension. Consultation, reciprocal support, and personal respect facilitated actions that might otherwise have been stymied by mistrust and friction. Three years after the Nobel dinner, when word came to Allen of King's assassination, the mayor could go to Coretta King without his comfort and assistance appearing contrived. Allen's actions were part of a long-established pattern, and he in turn was bolstered by Robert Woodruff. Woodruff and Paul Austin, both of Coca Cola, have been credited with major roles in fostering business support for racial accommodation in Atlanta at various points, including participation in the dinner honoring Dr. King. Moreover, after King's assassination occurred, Woodruff telephoned Allen, and, according to the mayor, said: "Ivan, the minute they bring King's body back tomorrow—between then and the time of the funeral—Atlanta, Georgia, is going to be the center of the universe. . . . I want you to do whatever is right and necessary, and whatever the city can't pay for will be taken care of. Just do it right."[58]

Allen's ability to reach across racial lines personally and symbolically, combined with his capacity to draw on business support, placed him at the heart of the governing coalition, with a reputation for being able to get things done.

DEVELOPMENT PROJECTS

The six-point program Allen developed as president of the Chamber of Commerce was carried over into his platform as a mayoral candidate. Although the program reflected the biracial character of Atlanta's governing coalition (peaceful school desegregation was one of the points), the overall program was heavily weighted toward redevelopment of the city.

As a strategy for making Atlanta a "national city," Allen wanted major-league sports brought to town. He also wanted a new civic center, with auditorium and exhibition hall, as part of a convention complex within walking distance of downtown hotels. These, in turn, were linked to an aggressive use of urban renewal (see Map 4.1); in the process, downtown would be given a wide buffer zone between it and lower-income neighborhoods. The capstone of revitalization was to be a mass transit system centered in the city's downtown.

Atlanta's first round of urban renewal had shown how difficult redevelopment might be. For any additional displacement of residents, relocation loomed as a major complication.[59] Business unity behind the general idea of growth and development would also come under pressure as the city moved from concept to concrete action.

Allen emulated the strategy used in launching Atlanta's first round of urban renewal, but with significant modifications. The basic plan was to aggregate support within the business elite by pursuing projects both south and east of the central business district, each of which had unique considerations attached to it. (For a close-up of the central area of Atlanta at the beginning of the Allen era, see Map 4.2.)

To the south, the first round of urban renewal had cleared land for the Rawson-Washington project—now an embarrassment, since it still lay vacant. One wing of Rawson-Washington, immediately south of the business district, had been intended to provide new, close-in housing for middle-income families, replacing dilapidated housing and the lower-income population who lived there. No developer regarded the project as feasible. Mayor Allen hit upon

Map 4.1   Urban Renewal and Public-Housing Projects, 1970

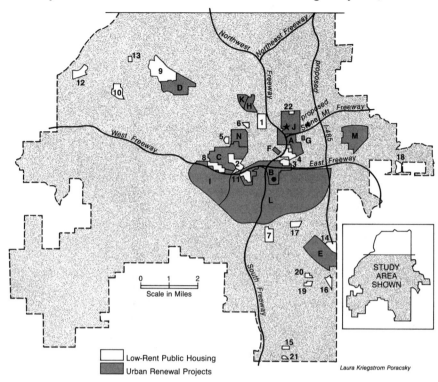

Low-Rent Public Housing

Urban Renewal Projects

Laura Kriegstrom Poracsky

Low-Rent Public Housing

EXISTING PROJECTS
1. Techwood (1936)
   Clark Howell (1940)
   Palmer House (1966)*
   North Ave.-Techwood
   (in planning)
2. University (1937)
   John Hope (1940)
3. Capitol (1941)
4. Grady (1942)
   Antoine Graves (1965)*
5. Eagan (1941)
6. Herndon (1941)
7. Carver (1953)

8. Harris (1956)
   John O. Chiles (1965)*
9. Perry (1955, 1969)
10. Bowen (1964)
    (Field Road Site)
11. McDaniel-Glenn (1968)
12. Bankhead (1969)
13. Hollywood (1969)
14. Thomasville Heights (1970)
15. Gilbert Gardens (1970)
16. Leila Valley (1970)
17. Wellswood (1970)

UNDER CONSTRUCTION
18. East Lake
19. Jonesboro Road I
20. Jonesboro Road II
21. Gilbert Gardens Annex
22. North Ave.-Linden**

Urban Renewal Projects

A. Butler Street
B. Rawson-Washington
C. University Center
D. Rockdale
E. Thomasville
F. Georgia State
G. Howard High
H. Georgia Tech
I. West End
J. Bedford-Pine
K. Georgia Tech II
L. Model Cities
M. Edgewood
N. Vine City

● Stadium Site
★ Civic Center
▲ Egleston Site

( ) Date Opened for Occupancy   * Housing for the Elderly
**Housing Predominantly for the Elderly

Map 4.2 Central Atlanta at the Beginning of the Allen Era

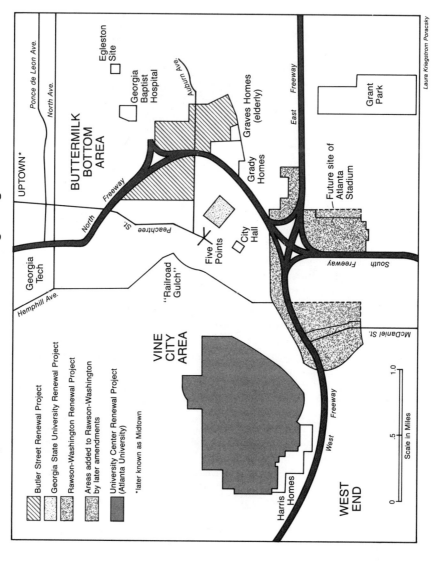

Butler Street Renewal Project

Georgia State University Renewal Project

Rawson-Washington Renewal Project

Areas added to Rawson-Washington by later amendments

University Center Renewal Project (Atlanta University)

*later known as Midtown

UPTOWN*

Ponce de Leon Ave.

North Ave.

BUTTERMILK BOTTOM AREA

Egleston Site

Georgia Baptist Hospital

Auburn Ave.

Graves Homes (elderly)

North Freeway

Georgia Tech

Hemphill Ave.

Peachtree St.

Five Points

City Hall

"Railroad Gulch"

Grady Homes

East Freeway

Grant Park

Future site of Atlanta Stadium

South Freeway

VINE CITY AREA

Harris Homes

WEST END

West Freeway

McDaniel St.

0   .5   1.0

Scale in Miles

Laura Kriegstrom Poracsky

this area as a site for a new Atlanta Stadium,[60] but the city's planning staff were wary. The necessary parking would displace still more low-income families, and the site would present major traffic problems. As a result of conflict over the site and the related issue of housing, a top city planner resigned, but Allen moved ahead.

The building of Atlanta Stadium is itself a remarkable event.[61] Later, Atlantans were to remember how the city had built a stadium for a team not yet signed, with money it did not have, on land it did not own (the land was controlled by the Atlanta Housing Authority). The key was Ivan Allen's close tie with the business elite and his ability to persuade banker Mills Lane that a stadium on the Rawson-Washington site was a good idea. According to Allen, Lane's response was: "You've got it. . . . Tell you what. If you'll recreate the old Stadium Authority and appoint the people I recommend, and make Arthur Montgomery chairman [Atlanta Coca Cola Bottling Company executive] and me treasurer, I'll pledge the full credit of C&S Bank to build it."[62] Lane put up money for architectural plans before a major-league team was signed. The resurrected Stadium Authority paid a $600,000-premium to the contractors to finish the construction within a year — which they did, but it was another year before the Braves moved to Atlanta.

The building of Atlanta Stadium on urban-renewal land, adjoining downtown, was a major development project by any standard. It was, however, only part of what was taking place. The city also launched its effort to build a civic center and auditorium (and a huge parking lot) to the east of the business district. Urban renewal and the Atlanta Housing Authority (the redevelopment agency) were once again put to use.[63] Officials chose a site in the Buttermilk Bottom area, a black residential section of run-down housing immediately east of the business district. Also located just north of Auburn Avenue, the area was of keen interest to businesses and churches in that traditional center of black community life.

The Uptown Association (whose membership included some of the business elite) was eager to have the Buttermilk Bottom site selected, in order to remove its black population and to upgrade the area physically as an adjunct to the central business district. Together, the civic center and the stadium once again combined uptown/downtown business support. And, despite the racial aspects of the civic-center site, the Urban League concurred because the housing in the area was badly dilapidated. The implicit stipulation was that replacement housing would be provided, but the details of that understanding remained vague.

The city did agree to build an additional one thousand units of public housing, and the mayor tagged the western wing of the Rawson-Washington project (land originally designated for industrial development but still vacant) for most of those units. The proposal ran contrary to the "understanding" that urban-renewal land would not be used for public housing. Since the business community regarded this informal compact as a "community decision," it could not be revoked without another such decision. The Central Atlanta Association "studied the issue," found "a heavy ground swell" for additional urban renewal and a need to deal with relocation. Its report also noted that public housing could be built on urban-renewal land at a written-down cost and that "some of the least salable areas" in the city's renewal inventory could be used.[64] After this report was issued, Mayor Allen met informally with representatives of the business community, including realtors, to announce that "the gentlemen's agreement" was no longer applicable to renewal land. He simply said that rapid completion of the civic center and stadium was the overriding objective. The newspaper firmly backed both projects and stood ready to attack as slumlords those who might oppose them.[65] Opposition from the Atlanta Real Estate Board was thus effectively squelched.

The mayor confined his consultation with the black community to the accommodation-minded Urban League; hence, the strategy in this case was not to head off resistance but to delay its outbreak until plans were already set. Despite opposition from within the planning staff over the massive displacement of blacks, city hall used an expedited procedure known as Early Land Acquisition and began clearance for the civic center within a month of federal approval. In short order, despite school board concerns, the Buttermilk Bottom area's C. W. Hill Elementary School was slated for clearance to make way for an exhibition hall adjoining the civic-center auditorium. The resulting controversy is detailed elsewhere.[66] Suffice it to say here that the city's quick action was a choice made consciously over an alternative approach, one that called for careful planning and staged redevelopment. Proponents of this latter approach—principally the Urban League and members of the city planning staff—preferred a general plan effected in carefully designed stages in order to minimize neighborhood disruption and provide relocation housing close in. They were also concerned that rapid and massive displacement would spill over into adjoining neighborhoods, worsening their condition and spreading the blight of slums.

The head of the city's Urban Renewal Department favored "quick and dirty" action. He proposed presenting the neighborhood with a *fait accompli*, arguing that "there is no need to get a large segment of the population in that area exercised and riled up over the possibility of having to move eventually. . . . This could be disastrous and could conceivably kill the entire project before it really gets started."[67]

Urban League and planning staff opposition had been discreet. Still, the closing of C. W. Hill School triggered an aggressive response. The president of the school's PTA went to Jesse Hill, one of the younger and more assertive black businessmen who had become a key figure in the Atlanta Negro Voters League and the Summit Leadership Conference. Later to become president of Atlanta Life Insurance, Jesse Hill was then a vice president. Earlier, at the time of the student sit-ins, Hill had been regarded as one of the "young turks" in the black community and had supported the upstart Atlanta *Enquirer*. Hill's first move was to fire off a strongly worded statement in which the PTA urged the school board "to spare Atlanta's history of the pending ugly scar" brought on by "the pressure of commercial power and other prestige interests," and by "poor planning or the lack of proper regard for the 800 Negro elementary school children."[68] The actual request, however, was a temperate one. It asked the Board of Education to set up a review committee that would include three citizens *named by the C. W. Hill PTA.*

This proposal was a departure from past practice and a sign of how profoundly the student movement had influenced the whole black community. Hartsfield had worked mainly through his chosen contacts. In the early 1960s protests, the negotiating team consisted mainly of blacks with whom Hartsfield and other white leaders were accustomed to dealing, plus an admixture of younger leaders. The C. W. Hill PTA's idea about the selection of a biracial committee would bestow a power equality not recognized before.

When the school board took no action, Jesse Hill touched base with other black leaders and with federal officials. He suggested that there might be a legal challenge and even hinted at "protests detrimental to the public relations of our city [which] could endanger the orderly progress of the new auditorium complex."[69] When the board chairman became angry at what he saw as threats, Hill responded that negotiations were at an end. Black leaders then escalated the conflict by asking for the complete desegregation of the public schools rather than the token plan then in operation.

At that stage, with a nudge from a member of the business elite, the board chairman took himself out of the process so that talks could resume. The mayor then appointed a special committee consisting of three members of the school board and three representatives chosen by the black community — evidence that the rules had indeed changed. But the mayor also would not allow stopping or even delaying civic-center construction. Out of the negotiations came an agreement to build a new elementary school and adjoining park in the Bedford-Pine area, just east of the renewal land now given over to the civic-center complex. (For details of the project, see Map 4.3.) The Housing Authority gave assurances that this area, also designated for urban renewal, would remain predominantly residential. The new school was to be built on an accelerated schedule; in the meantime, temporary facilities would be provided.

Responding to the broader school desegregation demand, board members on the committee also agreed to citywide acceleration. It replaced the one-grade-per-year transfer rights to allow transfers for all grades. The agreement is revealing. Once citywide black leaders were asked for help, citywide concerns became paramount. Though the neighborhood was promised a new school, the Buttermilk Bottom project area was totally cleared, displacing

Map 4.3 The Buttermilk Bottom/Bedford-Pine Renewal Project Area

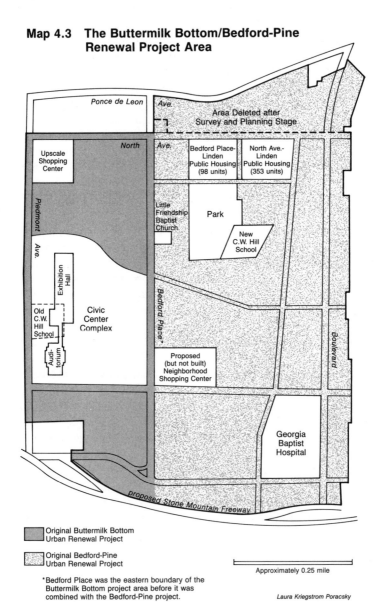

Original Buttermilk Bottom
Urban Renewal Project

Original Bedford-Pine
Urban Renewal Project

*Bedford Place was the eastern boundary of the
Buttermilk Bottom project area before it was
combined with the Bedford-Pine project.

Approximately 0.25 mile

Laura Kriegstrom Poracsky

nearly nine hundred households. Ironically, the new school and park caused still further displacement. The close-in vicinity east of the central business district was changed dramatically, in exactly the way Allen and his business allies wanted; the black population in that area was reduced, just as it had been earlier by expressway construction and renewal. Yet the coalition tie between Mayor Allen and citywide black leaders, though strained, was not broken because, once again, there were gains for citywide black leaders: a move toward negotiating parity and accelerated school desegregation. That the neighborhood lost heavily was glossed over with the guarantee of a new elementary school.

In 1965, on the heels of the C. W. Hill School controversy, Ivan Allen was reelected with extremely heavy support from the black community. Because neighborhood conservation and housing improvement were hardly visible as issues in the campaign, Allen had little indication that his second term would see widespread protests, directly challenging the policy priorities that focused so heavily on the revitalization of the central business district.

Neighborhood discontent was picking up steam even as city hall and the white business elite were using FHA's "221(d)3" housing program to defuse black opposition to renewal activity. Under this program, nonprofit groups could sponsor the building of apartments for moderate-income families, with costs lowered by a subsidized interest rate. Black churches, in particular, were encouraged to undertake sponsorship, and several did.[70] Since the program was complicated, these inexperienced church sponsors needed technical assistance and sympathetic lenders. White developers and the white financial community provided both. But even though these projects helped to maintain a pattern of biracial cooperation, discontent was mounting, in Atlanta as in other urban communities.

NEIGHBORHOOD DISCONTENT

Atlanta politics did not occur in isolation from the flow of national events. New federal programs encouraged neighborhood participation; and the civil-rights movement itself underwent significant change in 1966, spawning a Black Power ideology that totally rejected traditional white paternalism. Court-ordered reapportionment altered the climate of state politics and provided a new entry point for black representation. Each of these developments affected Atlanta, but initially at least, city hall hewed to conventional practice.

Just as Mayor Allen had supported national civil-rights legislation in 1963, he also supported Great Society legislation. In 1964, Atlanta was one of the first cities to set up an antipoverty program — Economic Opportunity Atlanta, known as EOA. In 1966, with the model-cities program, Atlanta was again one of the first to participate. In both cases, involvement had a particular Atlanta imprint.

EOA was set up as an independent agency serving poor people outside as well as inside the city.[71] Its structure encouraged the pursuit of private as well as government support. The governing board was not elected but appointed, and the white civic elite was the major force. Boisfeuillet Jones, president of the Woodruff Foundation (hence, close to Coca Cola's leadership) was chairman. The agency primarily facilitated and coordinated service delivery and dealt with individual complaints; it was no pioneer in either citizen participation or social policy experimentation.[72] Housing was a case in point. Though it remained one of the city's most troublesome problems,[73] EOA precluded anything but a case-by-case approach to housing code violations. Aggressive action on the issue came from unofficial neighborhood groups, not from the EOA structure.

Neighborhood concerns came into sharp focus in Bedford-Pine. When Bedford-Pine, which included the site of the new C. W. Hill School, was designated as an urban-renewal area, long-standing anxieties about "Negro removal" reached a peak. Among other causes for concern, the Bedford-Pine project area contained Georgia Baptist Hospital in one corner. Like many other large urban institutions, it was recognized as land-hungry. The hospital had also mustered opposition to using the Egleston site for public housing; hence, the neighborhood perceived it as eager to reduce the black population in its environs.

When a routine newspaper item mentioned displacement of 966 families, alarm bells went off.[74] Three black ministers (one of them a state legislator) of large neighborhood churches and two local white merchants organized a fight against displacement. Each of the ministers pastored a church that had been dislocated in an earlier wave of urban renewal, and Buttermilk Bottom was fresh in everyone's mind. When the five leaders decided that they wanted a more formal and broadly based organization, they did not attempt to work through citywide black leaders but chose to operate as a strictly neighborhood group, U-Rescue. They invited city and housing authority officials to mass meetings, where angry residents made it clear that they did not trust vague promises about keeping the area residential, citing broken promises in the past.

U-Rescue did not take a hard and fast line against urban renewal. Instead, it demanded a citizens' advisory committee and assurance that the area would not only remain residential but would be within the means of those living there. It also asked for express protection of one of the area's small churches, Little Friendship Baptist Church, located on the border of the project closest to the civic-center complex. City officials concluded that U-Rescue was indeed a formidable grass-roots organization, capable of wielding significant electoral power and of bringing an effective legal challenge. The Reverend J. D. Grier, the state legislator from the area, was a particularly savvy negotiator. Although U-Rescue could not convince the city to reduce the amount of displacement in the area, it did gain concessions to preserve the residential character of the neighborhood. Specifically, public housing would be built within the project area, and displacement would occur in stages so that the substitute housing could be phased in accordingly. The three churches also began negotiations to sponsor "221(d)3" housing.

Long-term results were mixed. U-Rescue did not last, partly because it lost two of its founders: Grier was moved out of the area by his church hierarchy, and one of the white merchants was killed in an automobile accident. Though the original agreement was eroded somewhat over time, Bedford-Pine nevertheless has retained a significant residential component. Public housing, "221(d)3" apartments, and some residential rehabilitation served that goal, even as Little Friendship Church was lost to the bulldozer.

U-Rescue is notable in several respects. In a black neighborhood, the organization's leadership was biracial. And its small merchants, with a background not so different from Lester Maddox's, helped prove that biracial cooperation could occur at the neighborhood as well as the citywide level. Further, U-Rescue showed that neighborhood leaders had the skill and, indeed, the political muscle to negotiate effectively with city officials, at least in the short run. They gained major concessions, even in the face of official recalcitrance that was encouraged by the Uptown Association and Georgia Baptist Hospital.

At the same time, the leaders of U-Rescue knew the limits of their clout. Perceiving Allen as extraordinarily powerful, as a mayor with unimpeachable business-elite credentials, they never attempted to put him on the spot. To them, he was "the power structure." So, when they threatened early on to "raise hell," the threat was directed at the Board of Aldermen. U-Rescue never pursued a pure strategy of confrontation. Its leadership had a significant institutional base, and its most active constituents were homeowners. Its successors as neighborhood advocates—Crisis House and later an elected project-area committee (mandated by HUD regulations)—were based more among the poverty-level, rent-paying residents and did use confrontational strategies; the concessions they gained proved to be smaller and more ephemeral.[75]

Bedford-Pine was not the only site of protests. Vine City and Lightning, adjoining neighborhoods close to the rail lines on the western fringe of the business district, also voiced discontent. The long-existing Vine City Improvement Association, as the spokesman of homeowners, was not inclined to take up the cause of poverty-level renters. However, a white Quaker interested in community organizing among the poor moved into the area and helped form a new organization, the Vine City Council,[76] which sponsored a rent strike, picketed the slum landlord's house, and challenged the incumbent black legislator (Grace Hamilton). The group also petitioned the city for street paving and staged demonstrations calling for playgrounds in the area. Through the rent strike, the organization helped dramatize the city's housing problem, but it achieved only limited results. The Vine City Council did not survive for long. In addition to opposition from established black leaders and from property holders, the organization came under attack from SNCC.

SNCC began working in Atlanta shortly after Julian Bond's election to the state legislature in 1965. At first, it worked with the Vine City Council, appropriately enough, since the council believed that the city's white establishment and moderate black allies neglected the problems faced by the black masses.[77] But in 1966 SNCC turned toward racial separatism and the expulsion of whites from the civil-rights movement.[78] Whites, they argued, should be involved in organizing the white poor. The Atlanta SNCC group saw America as a racist society; therefore, only a racial basis of organization would do. They expressed no confidence in any structure formed or joined by blacks "who are emotionally, socially, politically and economically dependent upon those individuals who are nonblack."[79]

SNCC's Atlanta project concentrated on propagandizing about race consciousness. The staff played down the role of class and indeed gave surprisingly little attention to economic issues. Between an unending search for ideological correctness and a struggle over control of resources, the Atlanta project came into conflict with the national organization, and so, like the Vine City Council, it also failed to become a lasting presence in the neighborhood.

Meanwhile, community discontent had spread, and a temporary coalition of neighborhoods petitioned city hall for redress of their grievances, especially on housing. There was even talk of a "tent-in" at city hall.[80] In 1966, there were also outbreaks of civil disorder. In Summerhill (immediately adjoining Atlanta's new stadium), a police detective wounded a black man suspected of auto theft; as rumors spread, a crowd gathered. Stokely Carmichael and other SNCC members arrived with a soundtruck.[81] Mayor Allen came to the scene, and, by prior arrangement, he was accompanied by twenty-five black ministers who tried to calm the crowd. At one point, the mayor was rocked off the top of a police car as he tried to address the street throng. When the ministers were not able to quiet the crowd, the mayor instructed the police to use tear gas. Carmichael was among those arrested, but his conviction on a charge of disorderly conduct and inciting a riot was overturned by a federal court.

A few days later, in the fringe of Bedford-Pine, another minor riot occurred. Moderate black leaders, however, gained the upper hand and helped quiet the neighborhood. The following year, a west Atlanta neighborhood, Dixie Hills, was also the scene of violence, and again moderate black leaders gained control.[82] A black state senator, Leroy Johnson, organized a youth patrol for the area after residents asked that all regular police patrols be withdrawn.

Publicly, the mayor blamed the riots on SNCC, which indeed came on the scene during each of the disorders. Moreover, the mayor took some comfort from the fact that, in two of the three incidents, it was moderate black leaders who restored order. Even so, it was clear that city priorities had neglected the poor, and neighborhood residents deeply distrusted the city. The mayor, social agencies, federal officials, and even some officers of the Chamber of Commerce agreed that there had to be better communication between neighborhoods and city hall.[83]

The newspapers joined in, and one series went so far as to question the effectiveness of urban renewal. An editorial asked, "Is Atlanta, the city too busy to hate, also the city too busy to care?" The answer offered was no, but there was an admission that past policies would not solve current problems.[84] The image of a new stadium sitting next to old slums was also too dramatic to be passed up. One headline writer could not resist: "City's Shame in Shadow of Its Pride: Atlanta's Plush Stadium Towers over Slum's Poor."[85]

As early as 1965, Allen's new biracial Commission on Crime and Juvenile Delinquency had prophetically identified Summerhill as the city's most likely spot for unrest.[86] Perhaps unfortunately for sound policy planning, it pinpointed "rootless migrants" as the key to crime and disorder. But, as later events were to show, discontent was widespread among old as well as new residents. Mayor Allen adjusted to the unfolding events. He singled out the city's ten worst slums for concentrated action to intensify service delivery and enforce housing code. Some of these ten were included in the model-cities program;[87] specifically, Summerhill and a larger area around the stadium. Other neighborhoods were brought into the urban-renewal program, this time for conservation, not for clearance. In 1966, the city also created a Community Relations Commission to hear complaints and receive recommendations from the citizens of low-income neighborhoods.[88] This was perhaps the major effort to institutionalize better communication between city hall and neighborhood.

Through various channels, the message came that housing was the principal source of grievance. And in November 1966, Allen signaled a commitment to new priorities by calling a Mayor's Conference on Housing that set a five-year goal of 17,000 new units of low- and moderate-income housing, with a crash program of 9800 units in two years. To pursue the goal, Allen appointed a Housing Resources Committee headed by architect Cecil Alexander — a socially-minded member of Atlanta's white civic establishment who was close to him.[89]

Starting in 1965 and put into official policy in 1966 and 1967 — through the model-cities program, neighborhood renewal planning, and the Housing Resources Committee — a reversal of city priorities came about, mainly out of concern over civil disorder. Neighborhood activism played a part, and reapportionment of the state legislature, coupled with district elections, broadened representation. Federal provisions for citizen participation in the antipoverty, model-cities, and neighborhood-development (urban renewal) programs also contributed to a wider array of concerns being expressed. But worry about civil disorder was the most urgent matter being expressed at city hall, a worry shared by moderate and established black leaders as well as by the white business elite.

For a time, it seemed that more than policy priorities had changed. Certainly, an enlarged set of concerns was guiding policy. New voices *were* being heard, and new instruments of representation were in the making that might produce a more diverse and inclusive governing coalition. However, these nascent changes did not endure.

Conflict hampered both the city's new agenda and the widening of the governing coalition. Many neighborhoods were wracked with internal conflict, particularly between homeowners and renters.[90] The model-cities area added the dimension of interracial tension. Neighborhood organizations, especially in sections with a high proportion of renters, kept falling apart. Even Bedford-Pine, blessed with skillful leaders and a solid base of churches, homeowners, and businesses, could not maintain a stable organization. And the high level of distrust of city officials that prevailed in poorer neighborhoods, though warranted by past experience, nonetheless made cooperation and quick action difficult. For example, when the mayor came to a mass meeting in Vine City to discuss launching a neighborhood improvement project, he came under sharp criticism and bitter accusations. He himself became angry and refused to make any further personal effort on behalf of Vine City. As delay, intraneighborhood factionalism, and distrust of public officials took their toll, programs appeared empty and indeed became so, thus reinforcing neighborhood alienation from city hall. Coalition building across neighborhood lines was virtually absent, as each area concentrated on its own internal problems and quarrels. The upshot was that neighborhood improvement did not generate a durable and cohesive constituency capable of working smoothly with city officials.

To be sure, there were other complications. Local officials were inexperienced in working with poorer neighborhoods, besides being wary of citizen participation. Red tape was abundant, and regulations changed, especially whenever a new federal administration came into office. Federal money was always uncertain and limited. As those funds shrank, neighborhoods had even less incentive to organize around improvement goals. When Atlanta's business elite declined to back a bond issue for neighborhood improvement, local funds also began to dry up. Together, these negative forces created a self-perpetuating cycle. There was no easy way to break through and establish a cooperative relationship that could yield quick and visible program results.

An expanded supply of low- and moderate-income housing also proved to be a difficult goal to achieve. Under the mayor's leadership, the city made a substantial start,[91] but subsidized housing suffered under multiple handicaps. Under federal regulations, public housing could not be built in areas already concentrated with minority residences. The noble ideal of class and racial integration behind this regulation guaranteed that site selection would be controversial. Although several rezonings occurred, opposition hampered progress. As the threat of civil disorder receded, Mayor Allen became less supportive of the program, responding in part to worries in the business community that subsidized housing would serve as a magnet for the poor and hasten the day that Atlanta would become a black majority city. When the Central Atlanta Association (reorganized in 1966 as Central Atlanta Progress — hereafter CAP), finally took an official position on housing, it called for a regional solution. New low-income housing, the business elite argued, should be built beyond the city limits of Atlanta.

THE BIRACIAL COALITION WAVERS

The city's governing coalition had not, in fact, broadened. Concessions to neighborhood interests and concerns with housing were short-term. Advocates of the poor and defenders of the neighborhoods failed to gain an institutionalized place in the city's informal structure of governance.

Yet there could be no return to earlier days. Atlanta was approaching a black majority, and the expectations of black leaders rose correspondingly. They saw Mayor Allen and the virtually all-white Board of Aldermen as highly resistant to change. Further, they perceived black aspirations as blocked not only by white political pressure, but also by the informal and highly personal network of social relations in which white officeholders (Ivan Allen, especially) were encased. Peer pressures from friends and acquaintances countered efforts by blacks to make the system more open and inclusive.[92]

Two events revealed how tenuous the long-standing biracial coalition was: a low-publicity conflict over the awarding of a bid for subsidized housing in Rockdale and a highly visible referendum defeat for Atlanta's proposed mass transit system, MARTA (Metropolitan Atlanta Rapid Transit Authority).

Spurred by the Mayor's Housing Conference, the Atlanta Housing Authority decided to designate the Rockdale area in northwest Atlanta (cleared for FHA "221" single-family homes but never developed) for "221(d)3" multifamily housing. Since the land price was fixed, bids were to be judged on design quality, an inherently subjective criterion.[93] The choice narrowed down to two developers. One was black and was endorsed as the bid recipient by the city's Citizen Advisory Committee on Urban Renewal, a group with substantial black representation. The other bidder was white and was selected by the Housing Authority.

Black leaders were angered by this action. The Summit Leadership Conference appeared before the Urban Renewal Policy Committee, accused the Housing Authority in particular of being hostile to the well-being of blacks, and conveyed a long list of grievances to the mayor. The city's only black alderman offered the view that "Atlanta must let Negroes participate and become part of urban renewal if it is to survive."[94]

On behalf of the Summit Leadership Conference, the NAACP filed a formal complaint with HUD, charging that the city virtually excluded blacks from business and job opportunities in urban renewal, challenging the Rockdale bid award specifically, and accusing the city of excluding blacks from model-cities planning. Other objections focused on public-housing location and the failure to provide support facilities and services for public-housing projects. The complaint was not upheld, but the mayor did appoint a black to head the model-cities program in its implementation phase. Two more years went by before EOA got a black director, and city employment remained a point of discontent among black leaders.[95]

In November 1968, an even deeper split in the coalition became evident. Blacks opposed the MARTA referendum, a heavy blow for Allen, since mass transit had been one of the items on his original six-point program. A 1964 vote amending the Georgia state constitution had indicated public support for the *concept* of a mass transit system. Allen had seen state enabling legislation enacted, and a MARTA Board had been appointed, representing the city of Atlanta and its suburban jurisdictions.[96] Atlanta's four representatives on the board were business executives, the lone black member being bank president L. D. Milton of Citizens Trust Company. Department store head Richard Rich was chosen MARTA chairman.

Though federal funding was to cover much of the construction cost, the 1968 referendum was on an *actual* plan, and it included property taxes to cover the local share. The plan was the joint product of the Atlanta business elite and the Atlanta Regional Metropolitan Planning Commission.[97] The Summit Leadership Conference had warned the MARTA Board a year before the vote that it would not support a system that failed to serve poor neighborhoods adequately, and it opposed the 1968 referendum.[98] After a short campaign of only three weeks, the MARTA referendum was soundly defeated: all of the suburban counties taking part turned it down, as did voters in the city. Strong black opposition marked a decided break in the electoral coalition that had prevailed for more than twenty years. Blacks even had an effect in the suburbs, where the metropolitan offshoot of the Atlanta Summit Leadership Conference added significantly to the no-vote in DeKalb County. Jesse Hill, by then a veteran of numerous civic struggles, was a particularly vociferous opponent, citing the lack of black participation in the planning process, the neglect of black employment, and shortcomings in a system designed only to serve downtown needs.[99]

The following year (1969) brought a further rupture in the coalition, this time in the mayoral election. Former coalition partners were again in opposing camps, as the Summit Leadership Conference and Mayor Allen failed to agree on whom to back as a successor.[100] An account of that election is considered in the next chapter. As Atlanta moved from the 1960s to the 1970s, the coalition arrangement that had held for nearly a quarter of a century seemed to be unraveling. Even personal ties, long in place, are not invulnerable to forces of social change and to new political alignments emerging from those changes.

CONCLUSION

The 1960s were years of protest and direct action that called into question the practice of settlements negotiated quietly behind the scenes. College students, who set the pace for that decade, were suspicious of established biracial attachments, which they attacked as self-serving and incapable of promoting basic social change. The older generation did indeed have material and psychic stakes in established arrangements, but they also regarded these biracial attachments as too useful in a complex and uncertain world to be lightly discarded. They preferred a reform strategy of mediated litigation and open communication to one of confrontation and polarization. The older generation saw white leaders, not as adversaries to be surprised or embarrassed, but as potential partners to be courted and shown consideration.

The demands for a reordering of city priorities appeared in more and varied forms, from a lengthening list of constituencies. Black voices in local affairs became more numerous. Although some of the younger and more militant leaders had only transitory roles, durable black leaders — the new black establishment — became more assertive.

During Ivan Allen's two terms as mayor, discord beset the governing coalition. On the one side, the white business elite, long accustomed to calling the shots in civic affairs, seemed tempted to disregard new elements and demands. Only sustained protests led them to end the exclusion of blacks from public accommodations in downtown Atlanta. When civil disorders generated new policy priorities, the business elite still held back; they failed to support a bond issue to fund a systematic program of neighborhood improvement. The mayor's housing proposal fared little better.

The mayor could draw his business colleagues into ending the Jim Crow system and even into attending a dinner honoring Martin Luther King, Jr. But he could not persuade them to support redistributive measures. Instead, the mayor himself seemed to be pulled back by his close personal ties within the business community. Communication between black and white leaders did not end, but as Allen's second term came to a close, the mayor and the black community appeared to be in pursuit of sharply conflicting policy goals.

Even though the 1960s saw Atlanta's black leaders become more assertive, they nevertheless remained realistic about the limits on their power locally. They were not reluctant to invoke federal authority or the pressure of national opinion, but with Ivan Allen as mayor, local political and economic power were combined in the same hands—a combination that some dissenters discovered could not be challenged unreservedly. Still, the days of this formidable union were numbered; black voters would soon outnumber white. With blacks pushing for a greater role in governing the city, Atlanta had entered a period of political uncertainty.

5

Challenge and Response

Continuity is without doubt one of the fundamental puzzles of social life.
— Ralf Dahrendorf

Continuity is the key to an exchange relationship.
— William K. Muir

As the 1960s came to a close, Atlanta's long-standing governing arrangements appeared vulnerable to challenge. Not only had the 1960s provided a more assertive black leadership, but the decade witnessed a significant shift in population balance. White population declined by 60,000, black population increased by 70,000, and proposals to annex or to consolidate the city with Fulton County foundered on suburban opposition. The 1970 census revealed Atlanta to be a city with a black majority. Although differences in age composition still left Atlanta with a narrow white electoral majority for the election of 1973, the shift to a new balance of voting power became a central fact in the city's political life.

Sheer numbers, of course, are only part of the picture. The greater concern of the national government for the rights of minorities *and* the diminishing state electoral base for antiblack politics altered the context in which city politics was waged. A growing black electorate inside the city took on added significance with a general empowering of blacks on the state and national scene. Atlanta's business elite thus lost on two fronts: It was no longer needed as a buffer between the city's black population and race-baiting demagogues in state politics, and its close allies in the white middle class no longer held a swing position in city elections.

Ivan Allen's decision not to run for reelection in 1969 brought the changed context of Atlanta politics into sharp focus, but exactly how the city's political life would be reshaped by the approaching black electoral majority was unclear. Although Atlanta saw new forces move onto the political stage, the business elite possessed important resources that were useful in readjusting its role in the civic life of the city. In this chapter, I forego chronological treatment to follow first the movement toward regime change and then the countermovement bolstering regime continuity. (For a chronological sequence of major events, see Appendix B.)

BUSINESS LOSES ELECTORAL INFLUENCE

The 1968 MARTA referendum loss foreshadowed the electoral future for the white business elite. As the 1969 mayoral election approached, black leaders were unable to reach agreement with Ivan Allen about his successor.[1] Mindful that other cities had elected black mayors and that, even in predominantly white Los Angeles, black mayoral candidate Thomas Bradley was in a strong challenging position, representatives from the Summit Leadership Conference met with Allen for discussion. Allen indicated that the downtown elite would support Rodney Cook, a white member of the Board of Aldermen. The Summit Leadership delegation regarded Cook as unacceptable, but Allen offered no encouragement for a black candidacy.

Black leaders were inclined to back State Senator Leroy Johnson. The first black elected to the Georgia legislature since Reconstruction and a protege of A. T. Walden, Johnson had been elected to the state senate in 1962, following a court-mandated reapportionment. Though the white business elite was politically comfortable with him and the Walden tradition, they did not encourage Johnson to run for mayor in 1969. Then, when Los Angeles Mayor Yorty upset Bradley in the runoff to win reelection, Johnson concluded that the timing was not right and made no move.[2]

Since blacks constituted only 41 percent of the city electorate in 1969, the black establishment decided to concentrate on city council and school board seats rather than the mayoralty. They were therefore taken aback when a young black attorney, Maynard Jackson, announced his candidacy for the position of vice-mayor. An eloquent and imposing speaker, Jackson had filed at the last minute to oppose Herman Talmadge for U.S. Senate in the 1968 Democratic primary. Jackson lost statewide, but he carried Atlanta.

When he failed to clear his candidacy for vice-mayor with senior black leaders, he earned considerable resentment for "leap-frogging," for his "irreverence of pecking order, timetables and especially the perquisites of age." One black leader commented that Jackson had not "made the stations of the Cross." Another asked, "Who'd he *check* with?"[3] Despite the prominence of his family in Atlanta's black community, Jackson, only thirty-one at the time, was not part of the inner club. In the end, however, key black business leaders — insurance executive Jesse Hill and contractor Herman Russell — held offices in the Jackson campaign, and black solidarity gave Jackson 99 percent of the black vote and a victory citywide.

However, black solidarity did not prevail in the mayoral contest. After Leroy Johnson backed away from running, Dr. Horace Tate, a black educator, entered the race. Meanwhile, Johnson and other established black leaders decided to support the candidacy of Sam Massell, vice-mayor during Allen's two terms. Although Massell was a businessman by background, he was known as a political maverick, and his political connections were strongest to liberal and labor groups. He was also Jewish and not in the dominant Protestant mold associated with Atlanta's civic elite. In reaching out for black support, Massell was calling in his chits for his earlier defeat of the incumbent vice-mayor, who had cast the tie-breaking vote on the Egleston-site issue.

The upshot was that the black vote split between Tate and Massell, and when Tate failed to make the runoff, Massell then received an overwhelming black vote and won the election. Black representation on the city council went from one to five (of sixteen), and on the Board of Education, from one to three (of nine) — all in addition to Maynard Jackson's election as vice-mayor. These gains were offset by continuing black disunity. The failure of Johnson and his allies to support Tate created enmity between the two, and Tate subsequently challenged and defeated Johnson for his senate seat. Nor was the traditional black-white coalition much in evidence. Black representation had increased greatly, but the key black victory (Jackson's) was itself an overturning of traditional leadership lines within the black community. Maynard Jackson was not beholden to established black political leaders; he had few links to the past of negotiated biracial settlements and no history of ties to the white business elite. He was well positioned to run for mayor in the next round, and that promised a further scrambling of old alliances.

Massell had run on a platform that called for the appointment of blacks to major city hall positions and for an increase in the proportion of black city employees to 50 percent by 1975. Once in office, he named a black as director of personnel, and he created an Office of Affirmative Action within the department.[4] In his first year, he appointed black members to all aldermanic committees and as chairs of the important finance and police committees.[5] That first year marked the high point of Massell's effort to add blacks to city government. Facing a highly uncertain political future, he adjusted accordingly. Since he was sure to face one or more black challengers in 1973, his subsequent actions suggested a search for white voter support. The tone and appeal of his administration changed. In his campaign, he had opposed the extraordinary influence of business in Atlanta politics;[6] in office, he worked closely with business on several issues, including a new campaign for the MARTA system.

There was, however, some friction between Massell and particular business leaders. For example, he replaced the businessman chairing MARTA with the president of the Atlanta Labor Council, stating that "it is most important to have organized labor have a voice in MARTA deliberations."[7] Even so, Massell's policy agenda was essentially the same as that of the business elite. Despite electoral support from blacks and labor, the mayor opposed wage demands of the predominantly black sanitation workers and broke their attempted strike.[8] Also, he did not resist a Housing Authority plan that gave Park Central Communities, a subsidiary of CAP, development rights for a highly prized 78-acre tract in the long-contested Buttermilk Bottom/Bedford-Pine urban-renewal area. Aside from MARTA, Massell's main development interest was on the westside of the business district, not on the eastside where Buttermilk Bottom was. The mayor actively supported the building of Atlanta's indoor coliseum, Omni, on the western periphery of the business district.[9]

Further, though Massell had campaigned against annexation or city-county consolidation, he shifted position and sought the annexation of a northside area that would have increased the city's white population by an estimated fifty thousand.[10] Even though his justification was economic, the mayor undoubtedly had his political future in mind as well. His rhetoric also underwent an in-office change. At one point, the mayor addressed a major black forum, the Hungry Club at the Butler Street YMCA. In his speech, Massell cautioned about the economic consequences of white flight and admonished black leaders to "think white" in order to make the city more attractive to whites. Massell urged his black audience to represent the views of all segments of the city and not have just a distinctively black perspective.[11]

This speech foreshadowed Massell's 1973 reelection strategy, when he argued that black control of city hall, particularly under a forceful advocate of black interests such as Maynard Jackson, would not be good for the city's economic future. In the campaign, Massell used the slogan "Atlanta's Too Young to Die."[12] He made a particular pitch that property values in the city would decline with the election of a black mayor, and Massell (a realtor before becoming mayor) got the Atlanta Real Estate Board's endorsement. One ad on Massell's behalf proclaimed, "It's Cheaper to Vote Than to Move."[13]

Massell's effort to fend off black control of city hall failed, as he lost in a runoff contest to Maynard Jackson, gaining only 41 percent of the vote. Massell did win more than three-quarters of the white vote, but no appreciable black vote. Moreover, he had only limited support among the business elite[14] and came under criticism by the newspapers for his use of racial issues.[15]

In general, the 1973 city election indicated how the traditional voting alignment had splintered. Leroy Johnson, with the endorsement of the Atlanta *Constitution* and some support from the white business elite, also entered the mayoral race, as did Maynard Jackson. It looked as if the black vote would split between two black candidates, but Johnson received only 4 percent of the vote in the primary contest. The black community was solidly behind Maynard Jackson and handed him first place for the runoff.

The white business elite proved to be much more divided. Some of them supported Charles Weltner, congressman from the Atlanta area during the Allen years, who came in a close third behind Massell. Harold Dye, a former state administrator, had some appeal on the northside, but finished a weak fourth. And some of the white business elite backed Jackson, though this appeared to be mainly a calculated move to preserve access. A banker offered this explanation: "I'd always been persuaded that Maynard was going to be elected. We did a poll, and it showed he was a winner. So I thought somebody in the business community better get behind this guy so that we'd have a line of communication."[16]

The 1973 election was a stark reversal of the political past. *Electorally*, the white business elite was reduced to junior partner in the biracial coalition. Unlike 1969, the black community was united in the mayoral contest from the outset, and their electoral success thus seemed inevitable. There was, however, no single black, citywide campaign organization.[17]

The new city council was evenly divided between nine black and nine white members, with a separately elected president — Wyche Fowler (now U.S. senator) — white but not the business elite's candidate. The newly elected school board consisted of five blacks and four whites. With a black mayor and a white city-council president, Atlanta engaged in a certain amount of self-congratulatory rhetoric about racial balance and understanding. In fact, the underlying political reality was much more complicated.

Increased black electoral power and Jackson's election in particular had shaken profoundly the past foundations of biracial cooperation in Atlanta. Although low-key, Jackson's campaign emphasized the need to make the city's political and economic life more inclusive. In response to Massell's 1973 tactics, Jackson called for an end to fear-mongering and urged unity.[18] Jackson said that he wanted "strong lines of communication between City Hall and the business community," he also intended to see "*other* power structures — also grass-roots leadership" included.[19] Jackson likened the political and economic life of Atlanta to a table provided with food: He did not want to push anyone away; he only wanted to see that previously excluded groups could join in the feast.

This language of unity and inclusion somewhat obscured the fact that Atlanta was a city where the traditional form of biracial cooperation could no longer be taken for granted. Before assuming office, Jackson described his aim: to produce "a situation whereby grass-roots leaders, white and black, will be sitting alongside of persons who are quite wealthy, quite influential, and sometimes not as attuned as they need to be to what it is really like to be living close to disaster."[20] For a city accustomed to elite-level cooperation, Jackson's aspiration represented a fundamental change.

The new mayor took office in a city in which the base of political activity had significantly diversified. Jackson looked forward to a social-reform agenda that would build on that fact. Not only had the black community become more diverse in its participation, but a neighborhood movement centered in predominantly white areas had also become an important actor in the city's politics. Just how important is indicated in the shaping of a new city charter under which the 1973 winners would function.

NEIGHBORHOOD MOBILIZATION
AND THE NEW CITY CHARTER

The immediate stimulus to Atlanta's neighborhood movement was opposition to proposed expressways, but it was slow to emerge.[21] The 1946 Lochner plan had committed the city to linking the central business district with outlying suburbs — a development strategy that had continued largely unopposed until the late 1960s. The original north-south and east-west expressways mostly disrupted black neighborhoods, especially those close to the central business district. By one estimate, 50 percent of downtown land was devoted to expressways, streets, and parking; additionally, hundreds of acres were consumed by interchanges and connectors on the periphery of the business district.[22] In the 1960s, the state highway department proposed two more major expressways: I-485, with a main artery through northeast Atlanta, and the Stone Mountain Tollway, to connect Atlanta with the suburbs to the east. This time, the neighborhoods most affected were white and many of them quite affluent.

Initial opposition came from two sources. The Morningside–Lenox Park Civic Association, inside the city, targeted I-485; and the suburban area known as Druid Hills, east of the city in the path of the proposed Stone Mountain Tollway, led that opposition. The Chamber of Commerce and CAP, the city's two main business organizations, endorsed the expressways, and state transportation officials largely ignored community opposition. But these were neighborhoods accustomed to having weight in community affairs, and they possessed resources useful in prolonged controversy. Further, after MARTA was approved in 1971, highway opponents could point to it as an alternative to expressways.[23] The newly enacted federal requirement for environmental impact statements provided grounds for a court challenge, and a suit temporarily delayed construction of I-485. Meanwhile, political organization gained strength, and yet another neighborhood group, BOND (Bass Organization for Neighborhood Development), began fighting both proposed roads, which would intersect in the heart of the Bass area.

As the controversy progressed, the lawyer bringing the case against I-485 strongly advised an effort to rally popular opposition, so that the neighborhoods could enlist the help of elected officials.[24] The neighborhoods moved from a fragmented set of organizations, concerned only with impacts on their individual areas, to form the Atlanta Coalition on the Transportation Crisis. This umbrella organization raised funds for research and legal fees *and* for a program of political action. They gained the support of newly elected Congressman Andrew Young and got federal officials to stop I-485. Governor Jimmy Carter, also newly elected, agreed to appoint a committee of citizens to reconsider the Stone Mountain Tollway; when they recommended against the tollway, he scrapped it.

Once mobilized, the neighborhoods did not simply fold their tents after their expressway victories. The changing composition of Atlanta's middle-class, "in-town" sections offered the politicized neighborhood movement a yeasty agenda. As the older white middle class moved away or died, these neighborhoods had begun to decline. But "white flight," combined with highway-related disinvestment, made their once fine, large homes affordable to a young, city-minded generation adventurous enough to be pioneers in gentrification.[25] According to one analysis, between 1970 and 1980, median income in two of the eastside gentrifying neighborhoods (Inman Park and Candler Park) doubled, and job and education levels rose correspondingly.[26] Perhaps more important than census data was the change in outlook. One neighborhood leader, whose activism in the area dated back to the 1960s, said, "You had a bunch of people in here who believed they could solve problems, and who weren't afraid to change things and tear down walls [figurative as well as literal]."[27] By all accounts, they experienced a "unifying camaraderie" and the kind of solidarity that can come from having a common enemy (even if ill-defined), especially one perceived to be in retreat.[28] Feelings of efficacy and accomplishment abounded.

When the BOND area had a community congress, the talk among gentrifiers was not all about killing rats or which brand of stripper paint was best. "There was a lot of 1960s-style activism,"[29] and the activists saw highway-builders, red-lining bankers, and an old-guard city government as barriers that could be overcome. Furthermore, as the politically conscious neighborhood movement gathered momentum, it achieved notable victories — defeating highways (and contributing support to MARTA), gaining concessions from banks on the availability of mortgage money for in-town neighborhoods, and joining with black leaders to work for a new city charter. Self-help formed part of the movement as well; BOND established a child-care center, a newspaper, and a credit union.

Within a short time, the agenda of policy concerns grew to include the development of neighborhood shopping facilities, crime prevention, and zoning. The neighborhood movement got a timely boost from two directions. First, the Atlanta Regional Commission reported that the city's demolition of some thirty-four thousand homes during the 1960s had contributed to a housing shortage, and it called for a policy that would "promote all appropriate actions to conserve existing housing resources and protect existing neighborhoods."[30] Second, neighborhood mobilization occurred in time to get a strong say-so on the citizen commission drafting a document to restructure city government (with final action to come from the state legislature). The charter commission gave community groups a way to make known their lack of confidence in city planning and zoning.[31] Promoted by black legislators (in particular Grace Hamilton), the charter contained two significant provisions that the leaders of the neighborhood movement keenly favored. One required citizen participation in the city's planning process — a direct response to neighborhood complaints. The other provided for district elections.

Neighborhood leaders reasoned that with at-large elections, money and mass media support were crucial to electoral success, but that with district elections, grass-roots organizations and "politically active volunteers" could "make a difference."[32] Under the old charter, all sixteen aldermen were elected at-large. The vice-mayor presided, and the mayor appointed all aldermanic committees. The new council had eighteen members, twelve elected by district and six at-large. In addition, the president of the city council (elected at-large) would both preside and appoint council committees. The school board was changed in a parallel way. Its size remained at nine, but instead of all members being elected at-large, six of the nine were shifted to district election.

The mustering of support to achieve a basic change in Atlanta's government led the neighborhood movement to assume a more permanent political form. When they started in 1971 as the Atlanta Coalition on the Transportation Crisis, the neighborhoods constituted an organized coalition. Sam Massell, mayor at that time, wavered on the expressway issue, as did much of the city council;[33] however, Maynard Jackson, then vice-mayor, became a staunch neighborhood supporter, at one point casting a crucial tie-breaking vote against city support for I-485.[34] In the 1973 election campaign, Jackson ran on a strong neighborhood platform.[35] Thus, his election not only provided the city with its first black mayor, but it gave the in-town neighborhoods a victory as well.

Reaching beyond transportation, the neighborhood movement constituted itself as an explicitly political and widely focused organization called the Citywide League of Neighborhoods, succeeding the Atlanta Coalition on the Transportation Crisis. It interviewed candidates, made endorsements, raised money, and channeled volunteer workers into the campaigns of proneighborhood candidates. Gathering strength quickly, the neighborhood movement soon could claim as close allies not only the mayor and the president of the city council but one-third of the city council itself.

By the time Jackson took office under the new charter in January 1974, several remarkable changes had occurred, all of which challenged the long hegemony of the downtown elite. The black community no longer meekly followed the electoral choice of Atlanta's white leaders. Maynard Jackson had not come up through the old system of negotiated settlements, and he was not the first choice of most white business leaders. Also, the neighborhood movement represented a new form of political consciousness, independent of the white business elite and even in opposition to it at times. A city council that as recently as the early 1960s had been all white and male, with fifteen of its sixteen members either attorneys or businessmen, gave way to city councils that included more than token numbers of women and blacks, as well as a diversified range of occupational backgrounds.[36] The council elected in 1973 under the new charter was evenly split between blacks and whites. Business representation declined, and neighborhood activists were a substantial bloc, reaching across racial lines.

Maynard Jackson appeared to be the linchpin for a new urban regime, bringing together independent-minded blacks and politically conscious and organized neighborhood activists, predominantly (though not exclusively) white. Although Jackson did not emerge from the traditional black leadership structure, he nevertheless had deep roots and strong popular support in Atlanta's black community, in addition to his appeal to in-town whites. He was sympathetic to city promotion of the arts, culture, and historic preservation. Besides being ideologically progressive, he was an articulate and polished ambassador for Atlanta, in cultivating outside investors. Maynard Jackson's labors as architect of a prospective new governing coalition in Atlanta are thus signally important.

JACKSON'S AGENDA AND THE BUSINESS RESPONSE

Maynard Jackson's 1973 electoral victory seemed like a revolution by ballot box. His connections to Atlanta's traditional civic establishment were even more tenuous than those of his predecessor, Sam Massell, and his constituency had a freshness and vigor to it that Massell's had lacked. By comparison with Jackson, Massell appeared to be very much a transitional figure who had put together a temporary victory out of the remnants of a disintegrating old order.

Change was afoot. Annexation had been rejected, leaving no way to prevent the city population from tilting to a black majority. The Citywide League was giving the neighborhood movement political clout. Different bases of electoral power were plainly visible, and many city officeholders were new incumbents: mayor, city-council president, and eight councilmembers under a new charter. The Board of Education was undergoing parallel changes. One of the five new members — Dr. Benjamin Mays, president of Morehouse College — was elected president of the school board. Whereas most school board members had been recruited in the past from within the white business community,[37] that was no longer the case. Also, a majority of the first, post-charter school board was female, not male, and black, not white, marking other sharp departures from the past.

More city hall changes would flow from the new charter, since it made the mayor a genuine chief executive with full powers of administrative appointment and reorganization; in short, a "strong mayor" to replace the old "weak mayor" structure which gave formal administrative control to the Board of Aldermen. However, the full situation was somewhat more complicated. Under the old charter, Atlantans talked about a weak-mayor *form* with strong mayors. That characterization was partly a tribute to the forceful city hall leadership of Hartsfield and Allen. But the so-called weak mayor had one especially potent tool—the right to appoint aldermanic committees. That important power was lost under the new charter; the president of the city council made committee appointments. The new charter also limited mayors to two consecutive terms in office. The underlying reality was that in some ways the office was left politically weaker. Nevertheless, as Atlanta's first black mayor took office in January 1974, he did so formally empowered to control the administrative operations of the city. Jackson proved quite willing to use that power.

The new city council was an agent of change as well. To carry out the charter mandate for citizen participation, the city was divided into twenty-four neighborhood planning units, known as NPUs.[38] Each unit made up a cluster of the city's more than two hundred neighborhoods and were designed to bring representatives from more than one neighborhood into contact with each other. The new ordinance setting up the NPU system required that all planning and zoning proposals be referred to the NPUs affected, for their reaction and comments before the official city government acted. An ongoing process of developing one-, five-, and fifteen-year plans encouraged the NPUs to take both a short-run and long-run view of their situations and how they fit into the overall city picture.

Mayor Jackson, using his new administrative powers, backed the ordinance by creating a Division of Neighborhood Planning and providing staff (in reality, "advocacy planners") to give each NPU the help they needed to argue their positions effectively. The division reported to Commissioner of Budget and Planning Leon Eplan, a prominent member of the planning profession who regarded the earlier period when so much of the city's population had been displaced by urban renewal and expressways as a social disaster: "A neighborhood was redeveloped and its residents moved to an adjoining neighborhood, and then *those* people moved to the next. Recipient neighborhoods sometimes doubled or tripled their population." As a result, the city "ended up with worse housing after urban renewal than before. All social organization was destroyed. The population was disorganized."[39] Eplan obviously intended a different form of planning for the city.

Eplan and the NPU system were only one indication of an innovation-minded city hall. Mayor Jackson himself represented a fount of change. He was firmly committed to a progressive policy agenda and not intimidated by opposition. Though young (only thirty-five when he assumed office), he was forceful and articulate. Jackson believed that he had a mandate for social reform, and he was explicit about rejecting a tradition of what he termed "slavish, unquestioning adherence to downtown dicta."[40] Self-assured and nondeferential, Jackson was perceived by business leaders as aloof and arrogant,[41] lacking "a spirit of give-and-take."[42] When the chairman of the Community Relations Commission maintained that the mayor gave white business leaders "very limited opportunities in decision making," Jackson responded, "I will not cater exclusively to the old-line establishment leaders of Atlanta commerce, whose wishes were often granted by past administrations."[43] Furthermore, Jackson used his office as a "bully pulpit" to deplore the near absence of blacks and women from the boardrooms and executive offices of Atlanta businesses.[44]

Jackson set out to change more than the planning process. Affirmative action enjoyed high priority. Although the post of affirmative-action officer had been created during Massell's administration, it was not actually filled until Jackson became mayor.[45] Besides actively seeking black recruits, Jackson also altered city procedures, imposing a residency requirement on all appointed personnel and modifying procedures to reduce emphasis on standardized exams.[46] The city council helped to widen opportunities for women and minorities with an ordinance specifying guidelines for participation in city contracts and appointing a contract-compliance officer to oversee these provisions.[47] Special attention was given to promoting minority business enterprises, including joint-venture arrangements when minority firms were nonexistent or too small to compete for contracts.

Although contractors and other business executives resisted this policy and made charges of "reverse racism," Jackson had enormous leverage in achieving acceptance. He had become mayor as the city embarked on the development of a new $400-million airport.[48] To the white business elite, Jackson's insistence that 20 percent of the contracts be awarded to minority firms was a startling departure from past practice. It generated complaints about using a vital project as a "social experiment."[49]

Jackson was willing to use bold language on behalf of affirmative action. He put banks on notice that they could not take for granted the traditional formula by which city deposits were divided among them. In a statement variously interpreted (as an ultimatum to the banks or merely as a dramatic way of getting their attention), Mayor Jackson suggested that he would deposit the city's money in Birmingham banks if Atlanta banks were unwilling to name women and minorities to their boards and to implement plans by which women and minorities could rise to executive-level positions. In response to opposition to minority participation in airport construction, Jackson indicated his willingness to let grass grow on the runways if minority firms were not brought into the construction process.

Reform of the police department was Jackson's severest test. The black community regarded John Inman, the white police chief, as racially insensitive and too inclined to condone police use of force in doubtful circumstances. Compounding the situation, Inman announced he would disregard the city personnel board's affirmative-action recommendation. At that point, Jackson ordered Inman dismissed, even though Inman had a contract for another six years. In defiance, Inman brought in members of the SWAT squad to keep out Jackson's designee as acting chief, then took the matter to court, where his contract was upheld. The mayor countered with reorganization, creating a new Public Safety Commission to be headed by Reginald Eaves — his chief administrative assistant, a former penal officer in Boston, and a friend from college days. Inman went to court again, but this time the mayor won. Inman was effectively removed from command of the department.

Eaves quickly became popular in the black community. He pushed affirmative action in police and fire department recruitment and promotion, and he curbed the police's tendency to resort to force.[50] However, Eaves became involved in politically embarrassing actions; the most damaging concerned incidents of cheating on a police exam. At one point, some state legislators proposed shifting control of the police department from the city to the state.[51] A joint meeting of police officers and fire fighters about grievances produced a vote of "no confidence" in the administration.[52] The business elite also complained about Eaves and sought an end to "turmoil" in the department.[53] And breaking with the agreement dating back to the Plan of Improvement, the Fulton County Commission voted to set up a separate county police department.[54] As the controversies cumulated and the exam-cheating scandal broke, Mayor Jackson concluded that he had to remove Eaves from office and did so. Eaves subsequently demonstrated his continuing popularity by being elected to the Fulton County Commission. He failed, however, in a 1981 bid to succeed Jackson as mayor.

Although the attempted firing of Inman and the later replacement of Eaves were perhaps the most publicized conflicts in Jackson's mayoralty, the mayor's first few years in office were filled with controversy. The white city-council president, Wyche Fowler, was openly critical of Eaves and attacked the mayor's budget and tax proposals.[55] In addition, the Bedford-Pine urban-renewal area became the locus of a major struggle between the business elite and the neighborhood-based PAC (Project Area Committee), elected under federal requirements. The Reverend Ted Clark, a black minister in the district and a practitioner of confrontation politics, gained control of the PAC and made major demands about subsidized housing and community facilities that ran counter to CAP plans for the area. With Jackson in a mediating role, some agreements were reached; mainly, redevelopment of the area was delayed, as CAP outwaited Clark until he eventually left the area.

Along with controversies over substantive policy issues came attacks on Jackson's efforts to extend the domain of his office. Proceeding from a new charter, Jackson's executive power was not legitimized by long-standing practice. Inevitably, the strong-mayor form invited executive-legislative conflict, especially since the new charter had also reduced mayoral leverage over the council by taking away his power to appoint council committees. The daily newspapers were especially critical of Jackson's expansion of mayoral staff not covered by civil service and of his efforts to extend his control over redevelopment, complaining that "Jackson's grasp for the levers of power is tenacious."[56] In redevelopment, a new charter and enhanced executive powers were not all that strengthened the mayor's hand; 1974 marked the year when federal categorical grants programs (such as urban renewal and model cities) were folded into the new Community Development Block Grant (CDBG) program. This shift in structure paved the way for replacing the Atlanta Housing Authority with a regular city department as the site of redevelopment activity.

Jackson also faced criticism from other quarters. He split politically with State Representative Grace Hamilton — a key figure in bringing about a new charter — who indicated that the legislature might curtail the city's powers by expanding the state's direct role in meeting problems traditionally regarded as local.[57]

Business Resistance

Confronted with a new mayor acting under a new charter with new political alliances and a new policy agenda at work, white business leaders experienced considerable anxiety. After many years as the central actor in the city's governing coalition, the downtown elite was being challenged at the very time that the city was undergoing a shift in racial balance.

Giving shape to these apprehensions, CAP conducted a survey among downtown business executives and reported the results in a letter from its board chair, Harold Brockey, to the mayor.[58] The letter cited a number of concerns — "fear of crime," "white flight," "growing racial imbalance of the labor force," "perceived racial split in leadership," and others.[59] Ironically, many of these items echoed Sam Massell's unsuccessful reelection campaign, for which he had been roundly condemned by the newspapers. However, the main worries expressed in the Brockey letter related to governing arrangements: a lack of easy access to the mayor and the breakdown of close government-business cooperation. The letter also reported that the mayor was *perceived* to be antiwhite, and it expressed fears that there might be disinvestment in downtown. Specifically, the letter noted that some business operations "have moved and more are considering moving for other than economic or management reasons."[60] Aside from the Brockey report, a business forum held concurrently served as the occasion for black leaders (including, of course, Mayor Jackson) to come under attack for their opposition to annexation or consolidation.[61]

When the national press picked up the Brockey letter incident, Atlanta found itself depicted as a community with a deep split between city government and downtown business.[62] As a result, the two camps joined in denying any serious rift. Furthermore, business leaders sought quickly to play down any hint that disinvestment would occur (presumably out of fear that they might provoke such an action), and they asserted their loyalty to the city.[63]

Just as this controversy cooled down, the Atlanta *Constitution* ran a series titled "A City in Crisis," in which publisher Jack Tarver was quoted as saying: "The unfortunate thing . . . is that we are not attracting the kind of people to run for office that you need."[64] The conflict was partly personal. Tarver was used to being an insider;[65] Ivan Allen had consulted him regularly, and now he was outside looking in. One business executive commented that "he acts like somebody took his candy."[66] Though Tarver made no secret of his disdain for Jackson's leadership, the series was not simply part of a two-person conflict. The newspaper articles (as well as the informal word) made it clear that the animus was broadly shared among business executives.

"A City in Crisis" reinforced the view already suggested by the Brockey letter — namely, that effective governance of the city required cooperation between city hall and downtown business. Within the black community, a number of established leaders were concerned about the turn of events. One black politician explained that "the major problem in Atlanta . . . is the loss of faith on the part of white folks, a loss of cooperation. If folks do completely lose faith, the downtown buildings will be empty."[67] On their side, the white business elite feared that too much publicity about conflict would be bad for the city's image and discourage investment. Hence, CAP arranged a meeting with outside investors to reassure them that Atlanta could indeed restore civic harmony.[68]

The flow of events in the early years of Jackson's mayoralty thus revealed significant crosscurrents. New foundations of electoral power consistent with the mayor's social-reform tendencies pulled city hall away from the traditional close alliance with downtown business. For their part, business leaders resented Jackson's independent path of action, and they were fearful about their loss of special access to the mayor's office. In various forums — the news media, civic-association meetings, and informal conversations — they attacked the mayor. The newspapers in particular kept up a drumfire of criticism, portraying Jackson as inexperienced, inaccessible, unskillful as a manager, excessively concerned about enhancing his power, and unwilling to consult. The message was not very subtle: Jackson sought power but was not to be trusted with it. The mayor and other black leaders resented this treatment and deplored the negativism, both publicly and privately. In short, the city's traditional biracial coalition could easily have come apart if personal resentments had prevailed.

But counter pressures were at work. Black leaders saw a need for a robust economy and for government-business cooperation on behalf of that goal, while business executives saw that they had to curtail open criticism of and conflict with the mayor, even though personal antagonisms abounded. Having once sounded the alarm about disinvestment, they soon realized that a massive exodus from downtown Atlanta would be enormously costly to themselves as the major property holders in the business district. In sum, both black and business leaders had a strong incentive to overcome differences and reestablish biracial cooperation in governing the city.

The task would not be easy. Conflicting interests worked against any durable form of cooperation. The black community itself was divided into several elements, each with a somewhat different base of support and set of concerns.[69] Black business leaders were motivated to pursue cooperation with the white business elite. Black community activists, practiced in confrontation politics, had no such incentives. Black political leaders in state and city offices had to juggle these diverse constituencies while trying to be effective within their own institutional settings. Black state legislators had to cope with a predominantly white peer group, with a much different constituency base from the one that city hall politicians had. Personal rivalries also hurt black solidarity—the conflict between Maynard Jackson and Grace Hamilton, for example. But there was also a realization, as one black clergyman put it, that "if Maynard fails, we all to an extent fail. But if he succeeds, we succeed. I think what we ought to do is support him."[70]

The Neighborhood/CAP Rift

Into these crosscurrents flowed another stream, with its own potential for conflict. With the new city charter giving neighborhoods a voice in planning and development, both CAP and the Chamber of Commerce initiated contacts with the neighborhood movement.[71] The Chamber of Commerce established a liaison program called Outreach, and CAP cofunded a "Back to the City" study, focused on in-town housing.[72] CAP also worked with the local banks to create a mortgage pool to finance homeownership and rehabilitation efforts in neighborhoods previously red-lined.[73]

However, when CAP supported a revived effort to build an expressway through northeast Atlanta, the Citywide League of Neighborhoods promptly breached its uneasy peace with the downtown business organization.[74] League president Joe Drolet wrote to CAP stating that communications were henceforth broken off. CAP officials viewed the letter as an emotional overreaction to a difference in policy, but Drolet regarded the issue as a "clash on basics." He believed that the Citywide League had to distance itself from any group that took a stand fundamentally in conflict with the goals of the neighborhoods. Drolet explained, "We only have people, and their political power and our movement depend on the good faith of the neighborhoods. The way things are viewed is important."[75]

As a mass-based organization, the Citywide League of Neighborhoods depended on its ability to rally support around deeply held objectives shared by an otherwise diffuse public. Complex alliances — particularly with organizations that sometimes pursued antagonistic interests — conveyed an unclear message. Mass mobilization hinges on a clarion call to arms, unsullied by the appearance of compromise and expedience. Fervor does not rise from complex calculations about what, on balance, is the most effective way to advance a set of interrelated aims; and fervor is essential to a voluntary association like the Citywide League of Neighborhoods.[76]

Maynard Jackson's vision of an inclusive coalition in which neighborhood representatives would sit down with members of the business elite came to naught because of the inability of the coalition partners to surmount their differences. In Drolet's judgment, CAP, as the voice of downtown business, and the Citywide League, as the voice of neighborhoods, were fundamentally different kinds of organizations whose interests diverged on important issues; therefore, alliance was impossible.

Jackson Regroups

As Jackson's mayoralty took shape, it was far from clear what coalition would prevail. There was not only conflict between neighborhoods and downtown business but also deep tension between the black and business communities. Jackson remained in alliance with the neighborhood movement throughout his mayoralty, but his support for the NPU system weakened. Responding to city-hall staff complaints that neighborhood leaders sometimes had superior information to their own on city issues, Jackson cut back the NPU planning staff to six, but he did not eliminate it.

At the polls, the Citywide League peaked in 1977, as Jackson ran successfully for a second term. Six members of the city council elected that year were closely connected with the neighborhood movement. Although some councilmembers felt threatened by neighborhood organization, at least three other members were sympathizers.[77] Jackson was unable, however, to resolve the most troubling issue for the eastside, in-town neighborhoods: what would happen to the land bought by the state for the Stone Mountain Tollway. The I-485 land acquired by the Georgia Department of Transportation was resold to its original owners or others, but the Stone Mountain Tollway property was not. No agreement could be reached, and the affected neighborhoods were left with great uncertainty.

Jackson did make headway on other fronts, especially in economic development, which was a top priority. In pursuit of that goal, he worked out a set of accommodations with the business elite: 1) a detailed compromise over the building of the airport, which included encouraging but not requiring joint ventures where no black firms could compete for contracts; 2) setting up regular Pound Cake Summit meetings at city hall with business leaders, through which they reached an agreement on a hotel-motel tax — earmarking part of it for the privately run convention bureau to promote Atlanta as a convention city; 3) creating an independent agency, the Atlanta Economic Development Corporation, to serve as a public-private entity to oversee economic development projects; and 4) making numerous trips with members of the Chamber of Commerce to promote Atlanta as an investment site. These direct contacts between city hall and business allowed cooperation to take place, despite continuing tensions.

Jackson's experience with his black working-class constituency offered a telling contrast. Under pressure to oblige business and unable to impose his own ideas about city finance on the city council, Jackson had little budgetary slack. (He also had the misfortune to come into office in the midst of a national recession.) When Jackson faced wage demands from municipal workers and eventually a strike, he broke the strike and mobilized the black clergy to support his position.[78]

How did the alliance with business, conflict-ridden as it was, gain ground while other constituencies lost ground? In the first place, the conflict was not between two groups bent on defeating one another at all costs[79] but was more about how relationships would be realigned. Both parties saw a need for business-government cooperation. Furthermore, business proved quite able to accept affirmative action and various provisions for minority contracting, including joint-venture arrangements. After all, moves by city hall to promote minority business and employment opportunities paralleled action at the federal level and hardly constituted a radical new policy direction. Moreover, as will be discussed later, extensive and substantive affirmative-action agreements had been worked out both with MARTA and with the Atlanta school system before Jackson was elected mayor. In itself, this fact suggests that the Brockey report of business perceptions of Jackson as being antiwhite was something of a smokescreen; the real issue was business access to city hall.

When Jackson insisted on the independence of his authority as mayor, he did so as a popularly elected officeholder with a reform mandate. Though criticisms centered on matters of personal style, reactions to his recruitments suggest otherwise. His willingness to enlist outsiders — for example, Jules

Sugarman from the Lindsay administration in New York City as his chief administrative officer — came under fire because they *were* outsiders. His appointment of Reginald Eaves to head Public Safety was labeled as cronyism, because there was a personal tie between the mayor and Eaves. But Jackson's appointment of George Berry — longtime confidante of the business elite — to oversee the airport project (part of the compromise over joint ventures) was received as a sound management decision. The pattern is clear.

Jackson's independent stance altered understandings about power relationships that had long been in place. The black community traditionally had beseeched favors or concessions from the community's "top" leaders. For Jackson to inform the business elite what their obligations were — whether about bank hiring or city contracts — upset that understanding. Similarly, when Jackson was not deferential to business contributors to his campaign, he was regarded as impertinent, even though "money from whites didn't begin to roll in until late in the campaign."[80] To treat business supporters as simply self-interested actors attempting to buy into an already winning campaign turned the power relationship around.[81] The business elite was not accustomed to having electoral power asserted as a basis for legitimate action, one that might even be superior to an economic foundation. Since they were never fully comfortable with Jackson's mayoralty, there was some residual sense of a "city in crisis" among civic insiders, both black and white. Yet the old coalition was reconstituted, albeit on altered terms and with no air of stability.

What drove the coalition toward restoration while other possible alignments faltered? Specifically, why could Jackson not establish a progressive regime? Certain explanations can be eliminated. Maynard Jackson was *not* a weak figure, averse to risk or unwilling to explore new bases of support. Quite the contrary, he was able, self-assured, and assertive — even aggressive in pursuing his goal of making the political and economic life of Atlanta more inclusive. An eloquent speaker, Jackson was capable of rallying support, and there was a significant popular constituency to be rallied. As mayor, he also had a firm intellectual grasp of what he was doing, both in a broad sense and in a highly detailed way. In short, he had the personal capacity to provide strong leadership and did so.

Jackson's move toward reconciliation might be explained by the need to attract and hold investment capital.[82] Yet, because of their substantial sunk investment in downtown property, the business elite never declared its independence from city hall. Instead, it repeatedly asserted the need for a business-government partnership. Downtown businesses — the banks and other financial institutions (with which Coca Cola was interlocked), department stores, utility companies, developers and commercial realtors, and the newspaper — had too much at stake to disengage from city governance and disinvest.

Foundations of Coalition Reconstitution

Why was the governing coalition reconstituted on grounds not only favorable to business but also increasingly inattentive to the electorally potent neighborhood movement and the numerically large black working class? One can grant that city governance requires an accommodation between economic and electoral power, that some form of city hall/business alliance is essential — and still acknowledge that political leaders and community groups have some leverage in bargaining with business.

From the business perspective, the challenge becomes how to minimize the leverage of other community groups exercised through popular control of local government. That is a contest in which Atlanta's business elite has long displayed considerable skill. Of course, skill amounts to little without resources. The regime concept introduced earlier is vital for understanding the resources Atlanta's business elite used to reposition itself and divert the city from a progressive agenda.

As mayor, Jackson's bold assertion of a reform agenda was based on the assumption that he had a popular mandate to lead in that direction. After all, he was a capable exerciser of the formal authority of the office, and as a popular leader, he was able to mobilize mass support. *But he lacked command of the informal system of cooperation that was so important in the civic life of Atlanta.*

The powers of the office of mayor enabled him to do some things, such as alter the leadership of the police department. But a broad agenda of action would require support from several sectors of the community and from the state government as well. To pursue economic development, Jackson would need business cooperation, and in seeking it, he operated from a distinct disadvantage. His constituency was loose-knit and had to be mobilized issue by issue. By contrast, the Atlanta business community was highly cohesive, and it controlled key resources that enabled it to facilitate a variety of projects. Moreover, the business elite operated from multiple points of strength that made it a formidable adversary. Jackson was pulled inevitably toward accommodation.

Under ongoing media criticism, Mayor Jackson needed to show that he was willing to cooperate with business, especially with economic development as a priority. Hence, he devoted time to travel with Chamber of Commerce officials and inaugurated the Pound Cake Summit meetings. Another factor that gave business leaders ample opportunity to argue their claims was the "buddy" system of the Chamber of Commerce, whereby each city councilmember was assigned to a business person, who kept in close contact with the councilmember. In short, what the NPU system and district elections provided to neighborhoods was easily matched by the informal and direct access of business leaders to city hall.

Jackson's perception that he needed business cooperation increased his responsiveness to business lobbying for an independent authority to create public-private partnerships in the area of economic development. The resulting Atlanta Economic Development Corporation was set up outside city hall (for several years, it was physically located across the hall from the Chamber of Commerce offices), with a joint public-private board of directors. Government-business cooperation was thus given an institutional foundation. The devolving of redevelopment in Bedford-Pine to the private Park Central Communities during Sam Massell's administration had already set the precedent for that pattern.

The partnership was not restricted to economic development. The business elite's capacity to raise money and deploy credit quickly served to link city hall closely to the business community. As one example, when the city was agonizing over the serial murder of black children, a boiler exploded at the day-care center in Bowen Homes, a public-housing project, killing four children and a teacher. Although the explosion was unconnected to the murders, it aggravated an already tense situation. The mayor needed a quick response, preferably one displaying biracial concern as a sign of reassurance. Jackson worked with CAP to raise money for a new day-care center,[83] and he later recalled that the construction of the facilities "happened almost overnight."[84]

The Context of Biracial Cooperation

It is important to recognize that particular incidents of cooperation possess a history. Past events shape later expectations, and established relationships are valued for the accomplishments they made possible, becoming in turn bridges over which new projects can be moved. These relationships need not be overtly political to have profound political consequences. When Maynard Jackson came into office with an agenda that put him at cross-purposes with the downtown elite, past biracial affiliations limited the support he could command within the black community. Before and during Jackson's mayoralty, white business leaders were forging links with the black middle class. Timely assistance to black businesses was a well-established pattern, and one that continued. During the early years of Jackson's mayoralty, one of the major banks, C&S, established a Community Development Corporation to make minority business loans. In addition, a consortium of banks and foundations provided a bail-out to the black-owned Citizens Trust Company.[85]

Particular instances of financial assistance formed only part of the picture. The white business elite sought to build multiple bridges between itself and the black middle class. In 1969, the Chamber of Commerce launched Leadership Atlanta, a program that brought together people of both races from business, government, the professions, and the voluntary, social welfare, and religious sectors to consider community problems and solutions.

Leadership Atlanta included both men and women and recruited largely a younger, up-and-coming group. It was tied to the business elite mainly through the Chamber of Commerce sponsorship and because upward-moving business managers were involved. The first "class" of fifty included thirty business members deemed by their firms to have the ability to become company president. For black participants, this was a rich networking opportunity, especially for those with entrepreneurial aspirations.

Also formed in 1969 was Action Forum, an organization linking the white business elite and top-level black leaders. It grew out of the realization that if MARTA were to make a comeback after its 1968 defeat, black support would be essential.[86] All of the white participants were chief executive officers of major businesses. Black participants came from more diverse backgrounds — social and voluntary-agency heads and college presidents as well as business executives. They met informally and quietly once a month, with no officers or minutes, for frank and open discussion about major community issues. Action Forum was another networking opportunity for blacks, facilitating their integration into the economic life of the white business elite. Significantly, it was also a key contact point for those blacks named to the boards of major white businesses.[87] Eventually, some black members of Action Forum landed executive positions with such major firms as Coca Cola and Delta Airlines.

Concurrently with the formation of these groups, the Chamber of Commerce continued efforts to integrate black businesspeople into its activities. (Action Forum has remained all male; Leadership Atlanta and the Chamber of Commerce include women and men.) Jesse Hill of Atlanta Life became the first black president of the Chamber of Commerce in 1968; contractor Herman Russell became the second in 1971. Both men were also members of Action Forum.

All of this activity occurred *before* Maynard Jackson was elected mayor, and significantly, Hill and Russell played important roles in Jackson's campaign. Hence, when Jackson received the Brockey letter, he could not count on united black support in a confrontation with the white business elite. In fact, there were influential voices in his camp promoting accommodation, since several black leaders with valued ties to the white business elite were reluctant to endanger them by racial discord. Also, the Chamber of Commerce had instituted a practice of sending small biracial teams to other cities in the United States and abroad, to promote investment in Atlanta. Close ties, everyone understood, would be forged during these trips, making it easier to communicate on a personal basis when community tensions rose.

The existing biracial network meant that even in the midst of conflict, the mayor was tugged toward reaching accord by the personal and material links that members of the black middle class had to the very elite that was challenging Jackson's leadership. The reemergence of the old biracial coalition out of the political fluidity of the 1970s thus seems to stem in part from the efforts of the white business elite to ensure that they would indeed continue to occupy a central place in the city's governing coalition.

The interplay between the progressive challenge and the business response reveals how deeply embedded Atlanta politics is in a network of biracial cooperation. This network operates beyond the electoral arena, and it was firmly in place when Jackson became mayor. Most visibly represented in Action Forum, the biracial network demonstrated its problem-solving capacities before Jackson assumed office. Thus, although the flow of electoral politics suggested a possible realignment, starting in 1968, the handling of major issues pointed to a reconstituted regime in which the business elite would continue to play a central part.

In the next section, a flashback to two of these issues—the successful MARTA referendum in 1971 and the "Atlanta Compromise" on school desegregation in 1973—shows that accommodation between the downtown elite and the black middle class was in progress before Maynard Jackson came to office. Jackson's policy on minority-business participation therefore built on clearly established precedents.

PORTENTS OF A NEW ACCOMMODATION

MARTA

In retrospect, the 1971 launching of MARTA, the mass transit system, proved to be a turning point in Atlanta politics. This issue made the white business elite realize that it must have the active support of the black middle class, and so it used the bridges it had constructed to work out new understandings—understandings that left the biracial coalition intact but with significant concessions to the black community and its increased electoral power. In this section, as we flashback to the period immediately preceding Maynard Jackson's election as mayor, we can see how he both built on and was constrained by the MARTA experience.

The first MARTA Board was designed to fit the good-government image of a body "above politics"; no public officeholder, for example, could serve as a board member.[88] This blue-ribbon group representing Atlanta and the four participating counties was all male and included only one black member— L. D. Milton, an elderly, conservative, and quiescent banker. Engaged in technically complicated planning and design and intertwined with complex intergovernmental relationships, MARTA made little effort to involve the public.[89] It held few public hearings, and these came after, rather than as part of, the planning process.

In the 1968 referendum campaign, MARTA officials relied on an organization composed mainly of downtown businesspeople (the Committee for Rapid

Transit Now). Helen Bullard, the veteran of several mayoral contests for William Hartsfield and Ivan Allen, managed the campaign. Although the black community made its opposition known, especially through Jesse Hill and the Atlanta Summit Leadership Conference, MARTA officials offered no accommodation. In the November vote that would have moved MARTA from planning to construction, the referendum lost in all jurisdictions, failing to gain majority support from either the black community or white suburban voters. As one report concluded, "The Board's carefully developed image — detached, aloof, and non-political — did not generate positive responses from ordinary citizens."[90] The harsh reality of defeat forced some rethinking, and the small circle of business backers and regional planners who had brought MARTA into being decided that they must broaden support and involvement. The referendum proposal had been attacked as serving only the interests of downtown business, and an internal MARTA memorandum called for the board to become more inclusive, "moving away from the image of a downtown interest to a city-wide and representative body."[91]

MARTA backers realized that they had to make a special effort to cultivate support in the black community, which one board member described as "a community unfortunately ignored in the last referendum, and a population without any representatives in MARTA."[92] The MARTA Board also discarded the "above politics" approach, believing that the absence of vocal advocacy by local officials was harmful and resulted from their lack of "ownership and involvement" in the plan.[93] In this climate, Sam Massell became mayor; he took the lead in shaping the new plan for financing MARTA and assumed a high visibility role in promoting its passage in the 1971 referendum.[94]

The MARTA Board created a Citizens Transportation Advisory Committee, but not until late 1970, only a year before the new referendum. More important were the informal consultations initiated in Action Forum and pursued within the MARTA Board. Right after the 1968 referendum defeat, Mayor Allen had taken a vital corrective step by appointing Jesse Hill to the MARTA Board. Hill had been the most vocal black critic of the first referendum proposal, and he was also a "charter" member of Action Forum. He thus enjoyed both informal contact with the city's white business elite through this organization and a formal position of authority on the MARTA Board.

In that position, Hill's special concern was to increase black employment and black business opportunities with MARTA. One of his earliest moves was a call for the creation of the position of Community Relations Director. Since the person would work specifically with Atlanta's black community, it was therefore especially appropriate for a black appointee. Agreements to extend affirmative action to MARTA employment and contracts were also worked out, consistent with federal requirements. In addition, when the 1971 referendum was approaching, Hill engineered the hiring of a black public-relations firm by the privately organized campaign committee, to work specifically in the black community.[95]

Hill and other black leaders also pressed the case that MARTA had to be more than a rapid-rail system for white suburbanites working downtown. At one point, technical consultants proposed a stripped-down version of a north-south railway and an east-west busway; given Atlanta's residential pattern, that amounted to a white railway and a black busway. The scheme was discarded as politically unacceptable.[96] The final plan included railways on both axes, plus a spur off the western line to serve the Perry Homes public-housing project. This Proctor Creek spur later took on enormous symbolic significance for the black community.

Since white suburbanites had also rejected the initial plan, MARTA strategists decided that they would have to give up reliance on the property tax to win support in that sector. Elected officials all had their preferences. Suburban officials leaned toward the use of a local add-on to the state sales tax, a regressive measure. Initially, Mayor Sam Massell and the black community preferred a local income tax, a progressive measure. The impasse was finally resolved by a compromise worked out by Massell and the counsel for MARTA: a 1-percent sales tax for the first ten years of MARTA development and a heavily subsidized busfare of 15 cents for the first seven years.[97] The proposal gave the suburbanites the form of revenue they preferred, while reduced fares offset the regressiveness of the sales tax (but only for limited time).

The revamped proposal held out the carrot of immediate improvement in public transportation: MARTA would buy the privately owned Atlanta Transit Company and expand and improve its service both in the city and in the suburbs. This revised MARTA plan was narrowly approved by voters in the two core counties of Fulton and DeKalb (which contain Atlanta), but was rejected overwhelmingly in the two smaller counties of Gwinnett and Clayton. Race, rather than issues of finance or alternative transportation, dominated the campaign. There was some scattered black opposition on the ground that MARTA was a transportation system to serve whites. Some suburban opponents characterized it as a plot to scatter blacks throughout the metropolitan area and bring about metropolitan school integration. Overall, more votes were cast against than for MARTA, but the victories in Fulton and DeKalb counties enabled MARTA to start collecting local revenue, begin construction, and purchase the bus company. The core of the metropolitan area would be served.

Seen in the context of MARTA, Maynard Jackson's social-reform agenda appears to be no radical departure from existing practice. Through MARTA, affirmative-action steps became part of local practice. Decision making opened up to include more groups, and the black community in particular assumed a more prominent place in shaping policy. Moreover, elected officials generally and Mayor Massell specifically were active in the decision process. The inauguration of MARTA also shows that, despite tensions, black leaders and the white business elite were far from alienated from one another. MARTA came about through their joint efforts.

The requirement that MARTA's local financing be approved in referendum served to heighten the importance of popular control and clearly limited the business elite's capacity to go it alone. Indeed, the launching of MARTA suggests a weakening of elite domination and the emergence of a more pluralistic form of policymaking. In that sense, the political changes surrounding the referendum approval appear to follow naturally from the general changes in Atlanta's politics that began with the student sit-ins in 1960. Yet to characterize the MARTA referendum as a flowering of pluralism paints a picture only partially accurate. Atlanta's business elite remained centrally involved in promoting MARTA, and the core of what they sought from a *public* transportation system remained intact.

Consider the essential features of MARTA. Fixed rail is an expensive system, subject to telling criticisms.[98] There are alternative ways of meeting urban transportation needs. Extensive bus service, for example, costs less and provides better city-to-suburb access for job-seeking residents of the city. (In fact, the owner of the Atlanta Transit Company actually made such a proposal as an alternative to MARTA's rail-centered system.[99])

Nor is Atlanta a "natural" site for rapid-rail transit. It is the smallest city in North America to have such a system, and its population density is relatively low for fixed rail.[100] The appeal of a rail system lies in its centripetal impact; it fit exactly the goal of the downtown elite. The same is true of its financing. The 15-cent busfare was only an interim policy, now lapsed in the face of rising costs, and the sales tax has been extended.

How did it happen that a costly transportation system centered around fixed rail, financed locally by a regressive tax, and offering limited city-to-suburb access came to be favored? Strongly backed by the city's business elite, it is unlikely that it simply emerged out of the random play of many crosscutting forces. The choices were: (1) the status quo of minimal costs and minimal public transportation, which could be perpetuated without the support of Atlanta's business elite, or (2) MARTA. Improved bus service by itself lacked support from the business elite and was not a viable alternative.

One might explain Mayor Massell's support of MARTA as an action in the economic interest of the city. With substantial federal funding, the local cost of enhancing downtown property values was reduced. Probably that was a contributing factor, but elected officials are seldom overridingly concerned with the long run. What they do care about is acquiring a reputation for action and accomplishment. For Massell, MARTA was what could be done with the resources and allies at hand.

If Atlanta's business elite is viewed as making the difference between being able to do nothing and being able to do something, then we can see how policy comes to serve their interests so well. Consider the part of downtown business in promoting MARTA. It had played a major role in lobbying the state government on the various legal provisions needed to make MARTA possible. Afterwards, although the business elite failed on its own to leap the referendum hurdle in 1968, it was vitally involved in the 1971 electoral victory. MARTA itself was prohibited from campaigning, so a privately constituted Committee for Sensible Rapid Transit was created. Its staff and other expenses were paid for by funds collected by a blue-ribbon task force drawn from the business elite. Moreover, a volunteer from a downtown business firm ran the Speakers Bureau supporting MARTA. No comparable efforts were available for nonrail alternatives for improving public transportation. Those interested in bus service found that a link with fixed rail was the easiest way to finance improvement. To integrate better bus service into the rail system, six Atlanta banks loaned MARTA $8.5 million to purchase the Atlanta Transit Company.[101] No such loan was forthcoming simply to improve bus service.

The moral of the story is that large and complicated projects stand little chance of becoming viable without business support. For Mayor Massell, MARTA offered the chance for him to make a mark politically. In public transportation, it was the only practicable game in town. For the black community, the story was much the same. Die-hard opposition to MARTA offered only the status quo, whereas support could gain minority jobs and contracts and improve public transportation in the bargain. That the trade-offs on local financing would end up thoroughly regressive was not entirely apparent at the outset. Nor was it fully evident in the beginning that the costliness of the system would increase the pressure to appeal to suburban riders. And possibly only transportation experts could foresee clearly that suburb-to-city commuting is what rail transit is integrally about.

Politically, MARTA provided a set of issues through which the biracial coalition could begin to be reconstituted — but on altered terms. The need for popular approval was pivotal in the launching of MARTA, and that meant leverage for the city's black majority, which translated mainly into individual benefits in the form of access to jobs and contracts and short-term gains through reduced fares.

MARTA was followed by the building of Omni coliseum and by another round of negotiations over minority participation.[102] When Maynard Jackson assumed the office of mayor in January 1974, MARTA and Omni had already revived a pattern of biracial accommodation centered around particular material benefits. And, as we shall see in the discussion of school desegregation, Action Forum contacts again provided a basis for biracial negotiations.

The School Settlement of 1973

After the initial court order requiring Atlanta public schools to begin desegregation in 1961, the process moved slowly.[103] In that first year, only nine black students, eleventh and twelfth graders, were involved, as four previously all-white high schools received their first black students. In 1962, the number increased to forty-four black students, as the tenth grade was included. Atlanta was using a form of "freedom of choice" in which individual students had to take the initiative in requesting transfers. At that point, federal courts had not yet struck down such plans.

In fact, Atlanta did not even have a genuine freedom-of-choice plan. School administrators established a procedure whereby black students wanting to transfer were screened through interviews with parents, "personality interviews" with applicants, and a set of scholastic and aptitude tests. Transfer students had to have test scores equal to the average score of that grade of the receiving school. Meanwhile, this painfully slow desegregation was taking place at a time when there were substantial discrepancies in the allocation of resources to schools.[104]

Under this procedure, the initial nine students came from a pool of 130 applicants; the 44 the second year, from a pool of 266 applicants. A spokesperson for the NAACP remarked publicly: "We've got a saying around here that it's easier to go to Yale than to transfer from one public school to another in Atlanta."[105] Faced with litigation, the school system eased these procedures, and in 1965, as part of the agreement over the closing of the old C. W. Hill School in Buttermilk Bottom, the Board of Education ended the grade-a-year plan and made "free choice" applicable to all grades. Even so, in the 1969–70 school year, only 20,000 Atlanta pupils out of more than 100,000 total were in desegregated schools. With "desegregated" defined as enrolling at least 10 percent of each race, only 34 schools met that standard; 117 did not.

In *Green v. New Kent County, Virginia*, the U.S. Supreme Court had ruled that ineffective "freedom of choice" plans had to be replaced. Under local NAACP pressure, integration of faculties was mandated and "freedom of choice" was replaced with majority-to-minority transfers. This plan required the Atlanta school system to provide free transportation for students making such moves. Several crosscurrents were at work. By 1970, white enrollment in the public schools was little more than half its 1963 peak. From an even division between blacks and whites in the 1964–65 school year, student enrollment had shifted to two-to-one black over white by 1969–70. White enrollment continued to drop year by year thereafter, so that there were fewer and fewer white students available to provide racially mixed schools.

In April 1971, the Supreme Court in *Swann v. Charlotte-Mecklenburg* held that massive busing was allowed as a tool for achieving desegregation and ending the effects of past discrimination. Lonnie King, a leader of the student sit-ins in 1960, had become president of the local NAACP chapter and was pressing for large-scale busing in Atlanta.[106] King, however, was also a member of Action Forum, which now turned its attention to school desegregation.[107] Business leaders in this biracial group saw busing as a scheme that would simply accelerate "white flight." Action Forum proposed to seek a negotiated settlement, and the federal district court concurred. The judge also named a biracial committee with Action Forum member Lyndon Wade (executive director of the Atlanta Urban League) as chairperson.[108] Within this committee (essentially a replication of the Action Forum coalition), the prevailing view was that Atlanta could not afford the economic consequences of racial turmoil, and biracial agreement was preferable to a decision reached by adversarial legal procedures.[109] Significantly, the agreement was negotiated in the downtown offices of two of Atlanta's major banks.[110]

The NAACP proposal for large-scale busing gave way to a negotiated settlement containing four parts:

1. A student assignment plan under which each school would have at least 30 percent black enrollment (and many schools would be preponderantly or all black);

2. Staff desegregation in which individual school staffs would be in line with the racial proportions of the overall staff (reassignment by lottery resulted in a large number of white teacher resignations);

3. An expanded majority-to-minority transfer plan for students, with magnet programs to attract whites to black schools (in actual practice, the latter simply concentrated middle-class black children in selected schools);[111]

4. Administrative desegregation, which specified the racial composition of a newly created top organizational structure and included the appointment of the city's first black superintendent to replace the soon-to-retire John Letson.

The first three points were essentially elaborations of the court decree of 1970. Administrative desegregation in exchange for foregoing busing was what black negotiators got. To provide a biracial "cabinet," thirteen upper-level administrative positions were created. Extensive busing in Atlanta was abandoned, as was litigation seeking a metropolitan solution to the problem of racial imbalance in the schools. (The Supreme Court had not at this time ruled against that remedy, though a case was pending.)

A metropolitan-wide plan was opposed by Dr. Benjamin Mays, the black president of what was still a white-majority school board, and it was rejected by the biracial committee. Earlier the business elite had favored a metropolitan solution to the problem of low-income housing, but the school-desegregation negotiations got under way just as MARTA had won narrowly, and then only in the two core counties. Metropolitan school integration had come up during the referendum campaign, and MARTA supporters had denied any connection between the two issues.[112] Business backers of MARTA, hoping to bring additional jurisdictions into the MARTA system later, wanted no controversy over metropolitan school integration. A busing controversy would also harm chances for achieving annexation or city-county consolidation.

Lonnie King had a different but not incompatible view of what was at issue: "If the metropolitan plan had come about, it would have meant there would have to be some power sharing. . . . If we went for a metropolitan school system, blacks would still have gotten the short end of the stick."[113] Given that the Atlanta school system had a tradition of strong superintendents and deferential school boards, the position of superintendent was especially important.[114] Furthermore, many blacks regarded John Letson as unsympathetic; during his tenure, the school system had moved slowly on desegregation, taking only those steps required by court action. In addition to being segregated, black schools were also overcrowded and undersupplied. Clearly there was much that black administrators could do to improve the school situation for the city's black pupils.

Local supporters of the negotiated settlement of 1973 viewed it as conferring "control by Blacks of the administrative and staff assignments" and as putting the black community in strategic "positions of authority" in order to make the school system more responsive to the city's black majority.[115] The national NAACP attacked the settlement as an abandonment of integration in exchange for high-level jobs. In looking back on this period, Thomas Atkins, former general counsel for the national NAACP, said that "it was viewed in the national civil rights community as a thoroughly unprincipled compromise in which black politicians sought to preserve their own privileges at the expense of their children."[116] The conflict between the national and local organizations was sharp, and the national organization ousted Lonnie King from the presidency of the local chapter because of his backing for the compromise settlement.

King's presettlement proposal had called for greater school integration and substantial busing, but inside the city of Atlanta. Without drawing suburban schools into a metropolitan plan, that approach offered little long-term promise. The number of white students in the city school system was small and shrinking. In the 1972–73 school year, when the compromise was reached, whites made up only 23 percent of the city school enrollment, down from 59 percent ten years earlier. This is not to suggest that school desegregation was the sole or even the main cause of white departure from the city; that seems unlikely. White, middle-class out-migration to the suburbs happened long before school integration, perhaps gaining momentum from the large-scale displacement of blacks and neighborhood disruption brought about by massive redevelopment.

After all, school desegregation proceeded at a modest pace throughout the 1960s. Atlanta followed "freedom of choice," not "forced busing." The city operated under no plan to promote racial balance. In 1969–70, for example, only 38 percent of the city's white students were in desegregated schools.

Because there was no requirement for white enrollment in previously all-black schools, whites outnumbered blacks in desegregated schools about two-to-one. Furthermore, at that point, only 34 of the city's 151 schools were integrated.[117] Yet white enrollment had already shrunk to one-third of the total school population. In short, white departure from the school system was far out of proportion to the modest degree of school desegregation achieved under the city's "freedom of choice" plan. Whatever the causes of the white migration, it had been massive, and there was little prospect that a significant number of whites would remain in the system to make racial balance through busing workable. Without a metropolitan solution, there would be too few whites. Moreover, many blacks opposed busing away from their neighborhoods.[118]

The general political significance of the 1973 compromise settlement is twofold. First, the presence of the issue meant that Maynard Jackson came into office at a time when the problem of white exodus was salient; hence, white business anxieties about race and the future of the city were at a high level. Second, it was a time when, despite past tensions and frictions, Action Forum in particular, but other organizations and contacts as well, provided an ongoing bridge between the white business elite and key black leaders. Reinforced by negotiations over MARTA and school desegregation, this ongoing network pressed Jackson in the direction of accommodation with the white business elite. He could not command black solidarity in the face of conflict with the downtown business elite; the jobs and contracts that came through the MARTA and school-desegregation negotiations demonstrated that biracial accommodation was no empty exercise. Tangible benefits could be gained.

CONCLUSION

Why did the white business elite so strongly resist Jackson's leadership as mayor? After all, MARTA had made affirmative action and minority contracts an established part of the Atlanta scene before he came into office. Moreover, Jackson was not the first black occupying a position of executive authority. Dr. Benjamin Mays had become the city's first black school board president in 1970, and Alonzo Crim its first black school superintendent in 1973 as a result of the compromise agreement.

When all of these events are considered together, it seems likely that race per se was less troubling to the white business elite than the more particular point that Jackson was electorally independent and had little background in Atlanta-style negotiation. Maynard Jackson was a largely unknown factor to them, and most of the staff he chose were not civic insiders; like him, many of them had no history of negotiation and cooperation with the white business elite. That was at the beginning of Jackson's eight years as mayor, when friction was greatest.

By the time Jackson's second term drew to a close, a pattern of interaction and cooperation with the white business elite had taken shape, even though the earlier tensions had not completely faded away. Crises (in particular, the serial murders of black children) brought the mayor and business elite into closer contact and a degree of mutual dependence. To the mayor, the business elite demonstrated that it could respond quickly and constructively to events such as the boiler explosion at Bowen Homes. Their timely assistance in showing concern and providing new day-care facilities was enormously helpful to the mayor when he sorely needed it. For their part, the business elite realized that Jackson indeed possessed strong mayoral leadership qualities. During the time when racial fears were at a peak over the child murders, Jackson was an effective and eloquent spokesman to the national media and to his Atlanta constituents. He also initiated the raising of reward money, which evoked a sympathetic national response and helped reassure people locally that significant action was being taken. As a further measure to promote calm, the mayor also created a task force of black ministers to talk with people and help ease tension.

As Jackson's second term ended, the serial child-murder case was closed, and racial peace held. Cooperation between a black-controlled city hall and a white business elite had emerged, albeit tenuously, despite the early friction. The political future of the neighborhood movement was somewhat in question. Atlanta's population was no longer evenly balanced between blacks and whites. By the time the 1981 municipal elections were held, blacks constituted two-thirds of the city population. It was in this demographic context that Andrew Young made his successful bid to become Atlanta's second black mayor.

6

The Neighborhood Movement Falters

High ideals, devotion to duty, and honor are not, in themselves, passports to victory.

—Ralph McGill

As Jackson's second term came to a close, political arrangements in the city remained somewhat unsettled. Jackson had been unable to convert his electoral base into a progressive governing coalition. The business elite had too many strategic alliances to be pushed aside. Faced with an unfriendly media and handicapped by having key black supporters tied into a business-centered network, Jackson lacked a political foundation strong enough to create an independent system of civic cooperation.

Consider his pattern of successes and failures. For budgetary reasons, the mayor had broken a strike of city employees. With limited state leverage, he was unable to stifle the ambitions of state highway officials to build an expressway through eastside neighborhoods. Jackson's mediating role in the Bedford-Pine urban-renewal area produced few visible results. Further, some of his appointees—especially Reginald Eaves as Public Safety Commissioner—became political embarrassments that were magnified by hostile press.

Besieged, especially at first, by newspaper and business voices who questioned whether or not he could govern the city,[1] Jackson made concessions to the downtown elite and was drawn into a degree of partnership with his critics. And, indeed, those issues on which Jackson cooperated closely with the business elite—whether at the state level in support of building the Georgia World Congress Center[2] or in the nongovernmental arena in replacing day-care facilities at Bowen Homes during the child-murder crisis—produced quick and visible results.

Yet, despite the fact that city hall and the downtown elite found working together productive, the 1981 mayoral campaign offered no clear indication of an accommodation between white economic and black electoral power. Once again, the business elite backed a losing candidate for the mayoralty. Nevertheless, this election set the stage for later developments.

ANDREW YOUNG BECOMES MAYOR

Three major contenders ran for mayor. Andrew Young, a minister by training, had been a principal lieutenant for Martin Luther King, Jr., in the Southern Christian Leadership Conference. He also had headed the city's Community Relations Commission and had served the Atlanta area in the U.S. House of Representatives before being appointed by President Jimmy Carter as United Nations ambassador. As a member of Congress, Young had worked closely with neighborhood leaders in stopping expressway construction.

A second black candidate was Reginald Eaves, whom Maynard Jackson had appointed and later removed from the post of Public Safety Commissioner. As the official most directly involved in altering police department practices, Eaves enjoyed substantial popularity in the black community, and six months after Jackson removed him from city office, he was elected to the Fulton County Commission from a predominantly black district.

The third major candidate, Sidney Marcus, was white and a member of the state legislature. Marcus had a long history of involvement in civic affairs and enjoyed strong backing from the business elite. He also had substantial support within the neighborhood movement and was on record as an opponent of in-town expressways.

In the first round, Young had a lead of only two percentage points over Marcus—41 percent to 39 percent—but he won the runoff comfortably with 55 percent of the vote. The outcome, however, was by no means preordained by demography. To be sure, the 1980 census revealed that Atlanta's black population had grown to two-thirds of the city's total population. However, with significant age differences along racial lines, the voting balance between blacks and whites was much closer: 56 percent black, 44 percent white. Further, Atlanta blacks had helped elect such white officials as Congressman Wyche Fowler, so a black city majority did not guarantee a win for a black candidate. However, in the runoff, voting followed racial lines closely.[3]

Even so, lines of political alliance remained somewhat muddled throughout the campaign. Most of the business elite backed Marcus, but the Atlanta *Constitution* endorsed Young. The Citywide League of Neighborhoods did not make a straightforward endorsement, instead rating candidates on the basis of their "understanding of issues important to neighborhoods." All were deemed "acceptable," but the league gave Eaves and Marcus higher marks, noting that these two talked their language more clearly than Young did. League officials stated that while the former congressman had "a track record of working with neighborhoods," they would "have to educate Mr. Young about what the neighborhood issues are."[4] Although such public pronouncements hardly build strong bridges, it should be noted that neighborhood leaders who had worked with Young on past issues signed an endorsement as individuals.[5] And Young's prepared campaign statement called for the city's neighborhoods to "be protected from encroachment by unnecessary development and destructive highway projects."[6]

Young's relationship with the business elite took a different form. Though most business leaders backed Marcus, Young spoke their language in his campaign. Economic development occupied a major place in his platform, and Young proposed making Atlanta a headquarters for business with Third World countries. Once the election was over, Young—an admirer of Action Forum—was quick to talk about "peace and harmony" between the races and move toward cooperation with the business community. Even before election day, with polls showing a Young victory, the peace-making efforts had begun. Young recalls that Coca Cola executive Roberto Goizueta "had 25 CEO's to breakfast with me in private. We put it back together." The day after the election, the lone white business executive active in Young's campaign organized a "peace-making" luncheon for Young and downtown business leaders, which Young opened with the comment, "I didn't get elected with your help," but then repeated a view he had expressed during his campaign: "I can't govern without you."[7]

The newspaper editorialized about the need for a "healing time," and City Council President Marvin Arrington hosted a meeting of "several dozen political and community leaders" to promote cooperation between city hall and the business elite.[8] As future events would confirm, the old coalition was reconstituted on a firm footing. Whereas Maynard Jackson's alliance with the business elite was slow in coming, uneasy at best, and compromised by other constituency ties, Andrew Young's alliance was quick, firm, and unambiguous.

THE PRESIDENTIAL PARKWAY CONTROVERSY

In office, Young moved to disarm the NPU system, reducing its staff support to a single person housed in the mayor's office. The Neighborhood Planning Division was no more, and NPUs could no longer look to city hall for advocacy planners. Although Young initially retained Maynard Jackson's planning director—Panke Bradley, who had been among the first councilmembers elected by the neighborhood movement before her subsequent appointment by Jackson to head the planning bureau—she was not part of Young's inner circle. After a few years, a transportation planner from the staff of the regional planning commission replaced her, completing Young's break with the neighborhood movement.

Other events also marked Young's new attachment to the business elite. For example, he brushed aside earlier concerns in the black community about the regressive character of sales taxes. Young aggressively backed a local add-on to the state tax in order to fund a variety of projects while lowering property taxes—a measure long favored by business interests.[9] He also gave high priority to other items on the policy agenda of downtown business: the redevelopment of Underground Atlanta and the building of housing *for the affluent* on the periphery of the central business district.

Young's most publicized decision involved the Carter Presidential Library, a decision filled with ironies.[10] As governor, Carter had stopped expressways planned for eastside Atlanta; as a U.S. representative from the Atlanta area, Andrew Young had worked to withdraw federal funding from these same roads. In their new roles, however, Carter and Young joined with the state Department of Transportation (DOT) director to revive a key segment of the moribund Stone Mountain expressway. The highway polarized the city, pitting Young, a former principal in the civil-rights movement, against liberal whites and the neighborhood movement.

Young's decision also aligned him unequivocally with the downtown business elite, thus helping to end the political fluidity of the 1970s. The city's most visible black political leaders—Mayor Andrew Young, Fulton County Commission Chairman Michael Lomax, City Council President Marvin Arrington, and Council Finance Committee Chair Ira Jackson—individually and collectively came into close alliance with downtown business. Once again, electoral and economic power were joined in an effective governing coalition, and the neighborhood movement was left in the position of political outsider.

The Presidential Parkway issue both cemented the alliance and demonstrated its power. In broad outline, the issue evolved as follows. The area east of the business district in the path of a proposed Stone Mountain Tollway had remained in limbo throughout the 1970s. A short interchange with a downtown connector, known as "the stub," and an outlying section had already been built when the expressway was suspended. The state DOT still owned 219 acres of cleared land in the heart of the eastside, in-town neighborhoods (see Map 6.1).

In Jackson's era, various proposals suggested using some of that land for housing and reserving a key portion for park land and perhaps an amphitheater. The area even became known as the Great Park area. A Jackson commission was heavily weighted toward the neighborhood movement, but the state DOT, which had already built two chunks of the expressway, was not inclined to consider alternative purposes. Even a later governor's commission, the Great Park Authority, though weighted toward downtown business interests, could not budge the state DOT. But a member of the authority, architect and developer John Portman, did at one point propose that the area be used for a Carter library.

Map 6.1 Selected Intown Areas

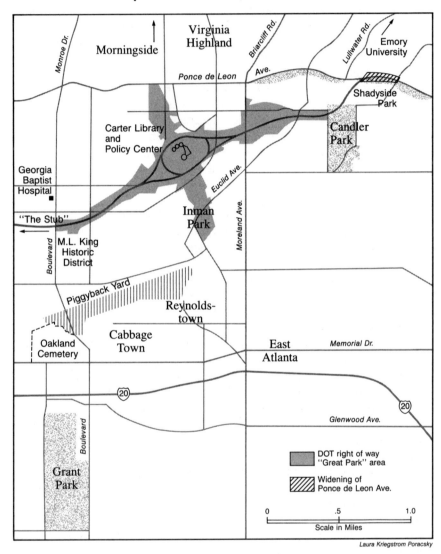

Monroe Dr.

Morningside

Virginia Highland

Briarcliff Rd.

Lullwater Rd.

Emory University

Ponce de Leon Ave.

Shadyside Park

Carter Library and Policy Center

Candler Park

Georgia Baptist Hospital ■

Euclid Ave.

"The Stub"

Inman Park

Moreland Ave.

Boulevard

M.L. King Historic District

Piggyback Yard

Reynolds-town

Oakland Cemetery

Cabbage Town

East Atlanta

Memorial Dr.

20

Boulevard

Glenwood Ave.

20

Grant Park

DOT right of way "Great Park" area

Widening of Ponce de Leon Ave.

0   .5   1.0

Scale in Miles

Laura Kriegstrom Poracsky

Following Carter's defeat in November 1980, plans for his presidential library took shape. Carter wanted it to be accessible. He was also exploring the idea of a Carter Policy Center, to be situated next to the library but affiliated institutionally with Emory University. The Great Park area looked ideal, both to Carter and to downtown business interests. In mid 1981 — just before Young's election as mayor — a Carter representative, the president of Emory, and the head of the state DOT reached an informal agreement on the Great Park site for both buildings. Shortly thereafter, Carter announced publicly that Great Park would be the library site.

Meanwhile, the governor's top aide told the Great Park Authority that unless they recommended a road as well as the library and center, "the governor would cut us off at the knees," as one authority member put it.[11] As negotiations proceeded, the understanding was that the Carter library and center could lease and control the site, but ownership would remain with the state DOT. Money raised for the Carter library could then be devoted to the building itself and its operation; land costs would be saved. The state highway department would be able to connect the library with downtown on the very route laid out for the Stone Mountain Tollway. It could even extend that road farther eastward, taking it closer to the outlying segment of the Stone Mountain expressway built years earlier.

Emory University's position vis-á-vis both the Carter center and the highway was complex. The university itself lies just outside the eastern city limits of Atlanta, but some of the neighborhoods that form the university community are inside the city. In addition, some of the university environs *outside* the city limits, though not cleared, were in the path of the once-proposed Stone Mountain Tollway. In 1972, the Emory faculty had gone on record as opposing the tollway, and the president of Emory in that period had signed a Bicentennial Conservation Covenant "to uphold the character and integrity of the Fernbank-Druid Hills area."[12] Druid Hills is a vaguely defined residential area on Atlanta's eastside that lies both inside and outside the city boundaries. Portions of its parks and landscaping designed by Frederick Law Olmstead in the 1890s are designated as historic districts. Another complication was the fact that members of Atlanta's economic elite have traditionally played important roles on Emory's Board of Trustees and in fundraising efforts for the university. At the same time, many Emory faculty lived in the affected area, and thus their personal interests as well as the institutional interest of Emory were at stake.

Shortly after taking office, Mayor Young asked an architect to draw up a plan for the Great Park area, including the presidential library and policy center as well as a four-lane special access road, using the right-of-way owned by the state. Affected neighborhoods opposed this plan, fearing that any four-lane road would be connected to the already-completed segment of the Stone Mountain expressway. To allay opposition, Young attended a community meeting, but the road opponents were adamant, and his attempts to reassure were greeted with hostility.

Young took the position that the parkway would not harm the in-town neighborhoods and that as a whole the plan would be an asset. It included parks, jogging trails, and bike paths, as well as land for housing. At that stage, the state DOT had said that the city could design the plan, including the parkway. The state agency also assured Young that there would be minority participation in the construction, although neither the specifics nor a monitoring mechanism was established. In any case, it is not apparent that anything beyond the federal guidelines for federally funded road projects was promised.

Faced with vociferous opposition from white eastside neighborhoods, Young rallied black support around the theme that road construction would provide jobs. The downtown business elite and the Atlanta *Constitution* also supported the parkway. In July 1982, a divided city council, before approving the mayor's plan eleven to eight, decided to narrow the width of the proposed parkway to prevent it from being easily converted into a major expressway. Next came a state-required review by the Atlanta Regional Commission, the planning commission for the metropolitan area. Ignoring the thirteen-to-one vote of its citizens' advisory committee against the plan, the commission approved the parkway, thirteen to seven.

While the regional body deliberated, neighborhood and civic associations were busy. Ten of them, in the predominantly white areas that would be most immediately affected, formed CAUTION—Coalition Against Unnecessary Thoroughfares in Older Neighborhoods. CAUTION mounted a legal challenge to the parkway, raising $100,000 in its first year; by its fifth year, that amount had grown to $350,000. The organization hired a highly regarded lawyer with the reputation of being unafraid to take on the state and other large institutions. CAUTION also assembled a large volunteer team of lawyers, law students, and paralegals. University faculty and other professionals from the affected neighborhoods provided a wide range of technical specialists. In short, CAUTION was formidable opposition.

When the state DOT released its detailed engineering plan for the road, the worst fears of its neighborhood opponents were fulfilled. The plan called for a four-lane road with a continuous flow of traffic, taking more park and historic land than had the earlier "conceptual plan" prepared for Mayor Young and supported in the original council resolution. State planners designed the road as a commuter highway, not simply as a tree-lined avenue to the presidential library, and acknowledged that the level of use was likely to lead to the eventual widening of Olmstead-designed Ponce de Leon Avenue.[13]

The neighborhoods not only opposed the harm to parks, historic areas, and residential quality, but also challenged the need for a commuter highway parallel to the east-west line of MARTA.[14] Road proponents and the state Environmental Impact Statement linked the highway to the overall development of the Great Park area and thus emphasized cultural and educational enhancement as well as the creation of two thousand jobs (by including all phases of the development of the plan).[15]

CAUTION had strong backing from historic preservationists in opposing a four-lane road, especially one that incorporated the celebrated Ponce de Leon Avenue, and was little inclined to compromise on the major issues—during the early years of the struggle. Backers of the state road plan were equally unbending, and the state transportation commissioner, by linking the provision of land for the Carter library and policy center to the four-lane road designed for commuter traffic, enjoyed the support of not only the governor but Atlanta's economic elite, Mayor Young, and President Carter—though Carter's lobbying was discreet.

Despite several attempts, opponents never got a city council vote to overturn its original support of the mayor's "conceptual plan." They came close in September 1984, when a council committee voted four to zero for a resolution opposing the parkway; but the council majority they were counting on dissolved under a combination of heavy lobbying, state insistence that no road meant no library site, and a controversial ruling and tie-producing vote by City Council President Marvin Arrington. Had city support for the parkway been reversed, both state and federal officials indicated that they would withdraw funding, thus effectively killing the road.[16]

Arrington's move to defeat the resolution opposing the parkway subsequently proved embarrassing. Three months later, it became known that his firm had been hired as a minority subcontractor to perform $890,000 of hauling work for the company given the bid for the Presidential Parkway. Arrington, it turned out, had also voted for a city transfer of land to the parkway project in November (after being named a subcontractor), but then had switched to an abstention after the measure passed eleven to eight. Arrington explained his vote by saying that he had intended to abstain, but "someone called me and diverted my attention, so I voted."[17]

Arrington's financial stake in parkway construction called into question the legitimacy of the September tie vote, and after strong urging, he withdrew his firm from the project.[18] The 1984 tie vote sustaining the parkway withstood challenge, even though subsequent opposition moves—efforts to delay and modify the project by federal reviews, the emergence of a new organization (Roadbusters) ready to use civil-disobedience tactics, state legislative action, and court suits—have prolonged the controversy through both terms of the Young administration.

The library is now completed, but the road is still unfinished. Nevertheless, the parkway appears inevitable, and it is likely to be constructed as the commuter road planned by the state DOT. Few legal maneuvers are left to the opponents of the road, and the in-town neighborhoods failed to dislodge road supporters in the 1985 city elections. Furthermore, when councilmember and civil-rights leader John Lewis—a staunch supporter of neighborhood causes and opponent of the parkway—left the city council to run for Congress in 1986, the neighborhood movement could recruit no strong candidate to replace him. In Congress, however, Lewis has been able to delay federal funding.

To date, highway officials have rejected all negotiations and have also refused to cooperate with the neighborhoods in the disposition of vacant land.[19] All in all, the issue suggests that the once formidable Citywide League of Neighborhoods is a spent force. Without demonstrated electoral clout, parkway opponents have had to rely heavily on litigation.

OTHER NEIGHBORHOOD DEFEATS

Neighborhood defeat on the Presidential Parkway issue might be dismissed as a unique event, resulting from an exceptional array of proparkway forces. But this defeat was followed by others that, together, signaled a basic shift in the city's politics away from responsiveness to the neighborhood movement. More than a signal, the parkway controversy may even have contributed to this shift; certainly it reinforced the newly emerged alignment of political forces. Vituperative criticism of the mayor by neighborhood groups on one side, and the mayor's unbending support for the state's plan on the other, combined to magnify the distance between these former allies. The mutual hostility had an emotional dimension similar to that surrounding a bitter divorce.

Still, all neighborhood groups —black, white, biracial, and from different parts of the city—lost ground, not just those that fought the parkway. In a series of skirmishes, the outcome was uniform: Projects with detrimental effects on neighborhoods went forward.

An In-Town Piggyback Facility

Literally across the tracks from Inman Park (one of the fully gentrified neighborhoods fighting the Presidential Parkway) lies a group of nonaffluent neighborhoods (see Map 6.1). One is Cabbagetown, a white neighborhood surrounding a textile mill (closed in 1974) that is now a historic district. To the west toward downtown, is the Oakland Cemetery, also a historic site, and east of Cabbagetown is the separate but equally neglected black neighborhood of Reynoldstown. On their north rim runs the Seaboard Coastline Railroad (now CSX). Further south is Grant Park, a neighborhood named for the large city park in its midst. Grant Park had been middle-class white, then working-class white and part of Atlanta's model-cities area, and later racially mixed and working class; in the 1980s, it was undergoing substantial gentrification. These neighborhoods are joined by East Atlanta, now predominantly poor and black but experiencing a modest degree of white gentrification. The area south of the railroad tracks is thus mixed by both race and class. It contains a significant number of educated professionals, though nothing like the affluence of the neighborhoods to the north.

North of the tracks, closer in than Inman Park, is a set of significant institutions, including the Martin Luther King, Jr., birthplace and historic district, the Martin Luther King Center, the Rhodes Nursing Home, and Georgia Baptist Hospital. Less than a mile south of the railroad lies I-20, Atlanta's major east-west interstate, which intersects Atlanta's north-south connector (I-75 and I-85) a little more than a mile farther west. Next to Cabbagetown and Reynoldstown on the railroad line is Hulsey Yard, a major switching facility.

In 1983, CSX chose this site for a piggyback facility, proposing that trucks come in from I-20 and make their exchange with rail cars at the rate of five hundred truck trips per day — an average of one truck entering every three minutes around the clock. That kind of congestion threatened levels of noise and pollution that could destabilize the residential character of the area, undermine efforts to conserve and upgrade its neighborhoods, and have a detrimental effect on nearby institutions and historic sites.

As soon as residents became aware of the proposal, they began to take steps opposing the piggyback facility. They formed NIP (No Intown Piggyback), which represented a coalition of black and white residents from several affected neighborhoods plus various institutions—the Rhodes Nursing Home, the Oakland Cemetery, and the Martin Luther King Center, with unofficial assistance from Georgia Baptist Hospital. This coalition made use of neighborhood associations and the respective NPUs and took its case to the city's Zoning Review Board, which voted five to zero against approval of the special-use permit for the piggyback facility. NIP made the case that truck traffic would damage neighborhoods and add congestion to in-city expressways (Atlanta has a perimeter highway to carry trucks and other through-traffic around the city). The organization also identified another railyard that could be used on the outskirts of the city—hence the name, No *Intown* Piggyback.

On the other side, promising to use joint-venture contracts for minorities and a black lawyer and architect in its plans, CSX obtained the active support of councilmember Morris Finley, author of the city's ordinance on minority contracts. In August 1984, the council voted nine to eight to approve the special-use permit. Opponents turned to the mayor, and Young vetoed the measure, expressing concern over the traffic, its impact on neighborhood-improvement efforts, and its tendency to increase in-town congestion generally.

According to news accounts, the railroad was stunned by its defeat but not deterred.[20] CSX threatened to locate the piggyback facility in another city, and it did extensive advertising to promote its case. The Atlanta *Constitution* provided strong editorial endorsement and gave little attention to neighborhood opposition, even though NIP represented a somewhat unique and broad-based, biracial coalition. Above all, CSX sought and won solid business support from business organizations and from the state Department of Commerce and Industry. Bankers assured the mayor that they were interested in financing further development around the piggyback facility, thus reinforcing CSX's position that its investment would be a catalyst for turning around an economically declining area.[21] The closing of the textile mill a decade earlier provided a useful backdrop for its argument.

NIP tried to counter the economic-development argument by questioning the amount of investment and the number of permanent jobs created: The piggyback facility itself was to be a largely automated operation. Although CSX had activated general business support, NIP enjoyed no comparable response from the neighborhood movement. Inman Park concentrated on the Presidential Parkway, CAUTION never affiliated with NIP, and more distant neighborhoods were not involved.

The railroad employed several strategies to disarm neighborhood opposition, the most obvious of which was to offer concessions. From the beginning, CSX had promised to build a replacement community center, and it now added a proviso that 25 percent of the contracts for construction and related services would go to black firms. The company also offered to establish a fund for neighborhood improvement to be operated through the Metropolitan Community Foundation (which Dan Sweat, then head of CAP, also chaired). Funds were to be donated at the rate of fifty cents per trailer loaded at the facility.

In addition, the company decided to buy the old mill site and explore its renovation as a complex for company offices, an "international trade" fair, and perhaps a restaurant and a "Museum of the South." Combined with the promise of sound barriers and additional landscaping, this offer was enough to garner some neighborhood support, though the core of opposition remained firm. NIP itself would relent only if CSX would work out with the state a plan for a separate truck line from I-20, building it on land occupied by an abandoned rail line. Neither the rail company nor the state were willing to assume the costs of that alternative to city streets as a connector from the interstate to Hulsey Yard.

The rail company sought the mayor's approval in two ways. It called the project a "land-port" complex and offered a special pitch about international trade, making the project sound more glamorous than a mere piggyback railyard. In addition, CSX persuaded the state DOT (that had no money for a dedicated truck route) to work with CSX in developing "a quaint locomotive" to run from the World Congress Center and Underground downtown to Stone Mountain and back. Since international trade was a favorite theme of Mayor Young's and the redevelopment of Underground was a pet project of his, the rail company's appeal was clearly targeted to discourage another mayoral veto.

When the city council voted three months after the veto, the vote was eleven to eight in favor. After considerable hesitation, the mayor decided not to veto. NIP took the matter to court and won at the superior court level, only to see that decision overturned by the Georgia Supreme Court. Subsequent efforts to work out a dedicated truck access line have not succeeded, though they continue. After the facility was completed and operating, the neighborhood complained about the noise, the overall volume of traffic, and congestion on residential side-streets caused by trucks not using the designated route.[22]

Between the two votes, Young visited the mill and the piggyback site and declared it to be "really just a junkyard."[23] He concluded that only businesses connected with the railroad would be interested in developing in the area, and, reversing his earlier position, he dismissed the traffic problem as inconsequential. Although he admitted that the development plans "really could" turn out to be empty promises, he saw no alternative for the site. The mayor termed it "a judgment call" rather than a clear-cut choice.[24] Still, when forced to choose, he lined up with the business-centered alliance over the neighborhood-based coalition.

Some councilmembers were also ambivalent, but the railroad argued that the piggyback facility was part of a larger picture in which Atlanta was a transportation hub for the southeast. In addition, business backers contended that the city needed to have itself viewed as a place receptive to development and that the way to promote that view was to accept the railroad proposal. As one councilmember explained, the council itself had very limited research capacity and could not challenge railroad claims about development and job generation. In fact, the piggyback facility is heavily automated and employs only about eighty people. At this writing, the mill renovation remains an unfulfilled promise and thus provides no jobs.

After the court defeat, NIP turned to the polls, with mixed results. NIP member Mary Bankester challenged an at-large incumbent from the area who had switched from opposition to support for the piggyback facility. Both candidates were white, and the incumbent won narrowly, with strong backing from Mayor Young who supported her and introduced her at a number of black churches during the campaign. NIP also "drafted" Hosea Williams to run against Morris Finley in his district, and Williams won. After his election, Williams held a "summit meeting" of neighborhood representatives, but there was no follow-through. In his days of civil-rights leadership, Williams had specialized in the dramatic gesture, leaving it to others to sustain actions after the initial confrontation. His service on the city council has fallen into somewhat the same pattern; no ongoing effort followed the neighborhood "summit."

The neighborhood movement was unable to recruit a candidate to oppose Young for the mayoralty, and they could not even find a strong challenger for the post of city council president. A neighborhood-based organization formed, called Campaign 85, but it reached no firm consensus on strategy. In the end, it produced only a "report card" and supplied information on candidates. Thus NIP's electoral effort linked with no larger political force, and in the following year (1986), Morris Finley returned to the city council in a special election for an at-large seat.

Unlike CAUTION, NIP was a thoroughly biracial coalition. However, one could imagine that in a city two-thirds black with black control of city hall, black neighborhoods would fare better than white, or better than those with gentrifying whites. The Atlanta experience supports no such conclusion, especially considering two neighborhoods examined earlier — Vine City and Buttermilk Bottom/Bedford-Pine.

Vine City and Buttermilk Bottom Revisited

Situated just west of the expanding business district, Vine City had been brought into the urban-renewal process in the 1960s, when some land was cleared with the understanding that low- and moderate-income housing would be built. None was, partly because federal housing funds diminished but more importantly because city officials, starting with the late years of the Allen administration, worried about too much subsidized housing.

The Atlanta Housing Authority (whose jurisdiction was not confined to the city limits) did build two small projects just beyond the city line. Later, Fulton County created its own housing authority, but it proved ineffective. In the meantime, cleared land in Vine City remained vacant; additional clearance accompanied MARTA, and still no replacement housing was built. A 1980 proposal for housing almost reached fruition, but when it became caught up in a conflict-of-interest issue, Maynard Jackson vetoed the measure. In 1986, with housing still unbuilt, the state Department of Labor proposed buying 8.3 acres of the cleared Vine City land for an office building. Neighborhood opposition forced the department to withdraw its proposal eventually. No office building was constructed, but neither was any housing.

By 1987, Vine City was again the target for nonhousing development. A proposed domed stadium (this would be Atlanta's second stadium in the downtown area — the old one for baseball, the new one for football and supplemental exhibit space) adjoining the Georgia World Congress Center would destroy at least two churches, a school run by one of the churches, and some commercial buildings. Moreover, experience with the stadium built in the 1960s showed that it had had a depressing effect on the surrounding neighborhoods. Parking and traffic generated by stadium crowds make a neighborhood less attractive. At this writing, the domed stadium is in the planning

stage, and Vine City is plàgued by signs of development-related destabiliza-
tion. Landlords are raising rents and looking to sell their properties at enhanced values,[25] and vacant buildings have been hit by an extensive series
of fires that authorities believe are arson.[26] Vine City, of course, still lacks
replacement housing and is faced with extensive nonresidential development.

To the east of the business district is (or, more accurately, was) Buttermilk
Bottom, now sometimes known as Bedford-Pine. Successive fights to preserve
the neighborhood began in Ivan Allen's first term and extended into Maynard Jackson's mayoralty.[27] Perhaps the crucial event in determining the
future of Bedford-Pine was the creation of Park Central Communities as a
nonprofit subsidiary of CAP to control redevelopment. Although federal
rules had strengthened the neighborhood's hand in the early battles, no federal Urban Renewal Administration remained by the 1980s, and guidelines
under the CDBG program were weak.

In short, Park Central was virtually free of federal oversight. Moreover,
city hall under Andrew Young displayed no particular interest in the neighborhood, and its past battles were not part of any public discourse over city
policy. Besides, little was left of the original neighborhood. What had been
Buttermilk Bottom was now the civic center complex, office space, and Ren-
aissance Park (an upscale housing area). Farther east, the public-housing project negotiated by U-Rescue remained in the old Bedford-Pine area, as did a
few owner-occupied homes and some rehabilitated apartments (due also to
U-Rescue). Later battles spearheaded by the Reverend Clark added new subsidized housing in the southern sector of Bedford-Pine.

Park Central had helped to establish and fund a community development
corporation for the area, but by the 1980s, its board had become passive. Most
of the original Bedford-Pine residents were gone; dislocation, delays in housing starts, the failure or displacement of many businesses, and the exodus
of some churches left little basis for neighborhood cohesion. Park Central is thus free of federal or city constraints and of any organized neighborhood voice, and free to shape the remaining land use away from housing and services for the poor. What is taking shape at this writing is more
housing for the affluent on the fringe of downtown; mixed-use office and
luxury housing on some of the vast (and unneeded) parking space behind
the civic center; and an upscale shopping center in the northwest corner
of the renewal area—the site most distant from the nonaffluent blacks remaining in the area.

All of this is quite different from the community's earlier proposals, which
had included a shopping center of neighborhood-oriented stores to be located near the heart of the project area. Yet, when Park Central disregarded
an earlier agreement and changed the shopping-center proposal, no protest
was raised; too little of the neighborhood and its original social infrastructure remained to mount a new battle. Indeed, in the face of neighborhood

passivity, the Downtown Development Authority facilitated the alteration by providing subsidized financing.[28]

Designating Park Central Communities as the redevelopment agent for the area gave CAP an institutional entity for withstanding various waves of neighborhood opposition and enabled the business elite to guide the transformation of Buttermilk Bottom. Occasionally, significant concessions were made—in earlier times, to neighborhood groups, but in the 1980s phase, to black business interests. The latter included joint-venture arrangements with minority firms and, in one case, sole construction by a subsidiary of H. J. Russell and Company, Atlanta's largest black-owned construction company. The neighborhood has thus ceased to play a part in its redevelopment.

In the case of both Vine City and Buttermilk Bottom, black residents were unable to defend against destabilizing development. The Vine City story is not closed yet, but its future as a residential area appears unlikely. The Buttermilk Bottom saga is closing, and neighborhood interests have essentially lost the struggle to CAP. Both areas had the misfortune of lying in the path of CAP's push to renew and expand the central business district.

But what about areas not on the periphery of downtown—areas with affluent residents well-stocked in organizations, fully supplied with professional and organizational skills, and supposedly sophisticated about the processes of urban development?

A North Atlanta Expressway—Georgia 400

Neighborhood opposition had blocked a late-1960s push for a new north Atlanta expressway. Federal funds for the proposed I-485 were withdrawn, and, unlike the case of the right-of-way for the Stone Mountain Tollway, land acquired for the expressway was sold back or sold off. Moreover, in his 1981 mayoral campaign, Andrew Young said he would work to kill the north Atlanta expressway "once and for all."[29] CAP, however, never gave up the idea of an additional expressway connecting Atlanta with its northern suburbs.

Black militants such as Hosea Williams charged that those roads harmed the black community, while helping whites reside outside the city but earn their living in it.[30] When the city council reversed itself and approved a new north Atlanta expressway in 1986, Williams described the action as "anti-poor, anti-black and anti-small business."[31] Off the record, business leaders acknowledged that highways to the suburbs made them less dependent on an increasingly black city-workforce, but the issue received no airing in that form.[32] Instead, the public debate centered on the question of protecting neighborhoods versus linking city and suburb. The Atlanta *Constitution* contended that "we cannot allow separate communities to evolve for lack of access."[33] In opposition, northside civic associations argued two points: The city should not solve the traffic problems for those who had chosen to move out of the city; and mass transit, not highways, should be the favored mode of transportation. Consequently, when Mayor Young shifted his position, he proposed a highway with a MARTA track in the median.[34]

However, the principal proponent of a north Atlanta expressway was not the mayor, but the chairman of the Fulton County Commission, Michael Lomax. A black elected official with aspirations to be mayor, Lomax judged that his position could withstand opposition from northside whites. But Georgia 400 — the state highway number for the reincarnated expressway — is more than a story about career ambition. City endorsement of Georgia 400 illustrates how planning in Atlanta and its environs is done. The process is one in which investors and developers pursue their private aims, sometimes in concert with one another and sometimes not. No public master plan guides or even modifies these development decisions, and public planning and the provision of public facilities are mainly reactions to such decisions. In short, public officials cope with the consequences of private development without being able to guide it.[35]

Just as CSX decided on an in-town piggyback facility and the city accommodated without weighing the broad implications, so on a larger scale business interests have promoted development in north Atlanta and beyond and the city has played only a reactive role. Public planning is largely ad hoc, operating without any explicit conception of what is a socially good form of growth. Signficantly, one of the key technical studies laying the groundwork for advocacy of Georgia 400 was privately financed.[36] To some extent, the absence of a guiding public hand in shaping growth can be attributed to metropolitan fragmentation. But this explanation does not apply to older areas inside the city limits, areas that are also subject to pressures for intensified development. Northside Atlanta has been subject to those pressures at a high level.

Buckhead, the commercial district in the heart of Atlanta's affluent northside, has undergone an investment boom as an office site, with commercial and multifamily residential development also spreading into what was once a vast area of surrounding single-family homes. The development pressure has been intense enough to spawn a phenomenon known as the "neighborhood buy-out": To avoid opposition to rezoning, developers arrange for entire neighborhoods to sell their homes. That "solution" only changes the scale of the pressures at work. When a neighborhood turns commercial, the adjoining one is vulnerable to speculation for development. The process is market-driven, and such transactions are notorious for being guided by "pack psychology," with little attention to long-range consequences. Competition for profits, as the "tragedy of the commons" teaches, does not necessarily serve the social good.[37]

On Atlanta's northside, the state highway department and the city abetted this development by widening streets and secondary roads. As conversion occurs piece by piece, the process gathers momentum and takes on the appearance of inevitability.[38] Eventually, as in Buckhead, area solidarity is broken by the fragmented and staged impact of development.[39] Some sections are bought out; some are heavily affected by development and by the piecemeal expansion of secondary roads; and in others, where intensified development still seems remote, residents may be indifferent. Only when development moves closer do they act to defend their neighborhood—unless they too have come to view the process as inevitable.

City endorsement of Georgia 400 is thus to be understood not merely as the result of a single long-term battle over a proposed expressway. Because this development occurred step by step, it was never a public issue *as a comprehensive process.*

After intensified development had been transforming north Atlanta for some time, the Atlanta Board of Realtors sponsored a public-private symposium on projected growth in Buckhead.[40] The Georgia Power Company contributed a report showing the enormous growth in Buckhead and predicting a continuation of that trend into the future. The report took the position that Georgia 400 was needed to connect Buckhead with the suburbs north of Atlanta. Various business interests, but not the larger public, were thus engaged in analyzing and responding to a process of privately guided development. Yet business interests such as CAP saw the public sector as a major resource for coping with the consequences of a northward shift in private investment preferences.

The pattern was adversely affecting the lower downtown area, making private investment there riskier. Consequently, CAP backed the development of the lower downtown as a sphere of intensified *public investment*, thus counterbalancing its support for the building of roads to accommodate northside growth. Rather than protect its sunk investment in the central business district by constraining the preferences of developers, CAP sought to pass on to the general public the cost of imbalanced growth. By connecting the Buckhead area with the perimeter highway to the north, the proposed Georgia 400 is sure to be an additional stimulus to development in northside Atlanta and its suburbs. It offers no inducement to private investment in the central business district and southward, and it may even make it less likely.

The decision to proceed with Georgia 400 thus has special political significance. Beginning in Jackson's administration, black political leaders favored southside development.[41] "Southside" is ill-defined, but, however defined, it is more proximate to black residents than is northside. How, then, could a prominant black political leader like Michael Lomax openly take the lead in promoting acceptance of Georgia 400? In part, it was a case of northside development making an additional transportation route seem inevitable, even more so since the highway enjoyed the combined backing of the state DOT, the daily newspapers, and CAP. Additionally, black political support gravitated to Georgia 400 because there was no concrete alternative. No coherent coalition existed that could pursue the possibility of using public authority and resources to tilt development toward the southside instead of reinforcing its northward tilt.

The major regional planning body, the Atlanta Regional Commission, was more a creature of suburban jurisdictions than of the city and was in no position to pursue a black policy agenda that pushed hard for southside development. Within the city, the commission has been most closely associated with CAP. For example, Dan Sweat, the head of CAP from 1973 to 1988, came to that position from the post of executive director of the Atlanta Regional Commission.[42]

The primary policy-research organization in the city is Research Atlanta, a nonprofit organization largely dependent on CAP members for funds. As such, it is unlikely to challenge a Georgia Power study or propose restrictions on investor prerogative in the name of balanced growth. In its study of southside development, Research Atlanta called for increased promotion, enhanced governmental incentives, and upgrading the educational level of the workforce.[43] Not even a hint of planning controls was suggested. There is also no black "think tank" to fill the planning vacuum, conduct critical policy studies, or develop alternatives to the policies offered by CAP, its members, and its allies. Although the Atlanta University complex is a fount of black professional talent, the university system is not a likely locus for such an enterprise, given its strong ties to the white business elite.

In this void, CAP and the Chamber of Commerce have argued that Atlanta's major need is a favorable climate for investment. They depicted friction between Mayor Jackson and the business elite as a bad investment climate, and argued that, to erase the effect of that period, the city must accommodate investors and not discourage them with restrictions of any kind. The enormous projects north of Atlanta along the perimeter highway have been cited as evidence that investments *can* be scared away from the city. If development is accommodated, it is further contended, in due time southside will come into its own.

Atlanta and its environs thus provide a political climate of unchecked investor prerogative. That sets the stage on which localized conflicts, such as the struggle over Georgia 400, are worked out. The network of organizations through which Atlanta's business elite carries out policy forecloses the emergence of other coalitions capable of creating alternative policies. Without a different approach to development, Georgia 400 can be defended as a response to a growing need. The general pattern gives particular proposals the appearance of inevitability.

Lomax's decision to support Georgia 400 thus needs to be seen in context. As part of the Jackson administration, Lomax had observed what happens to mayors who try to govern without the cooperation of Atlanta's business elite. Since the building of Georgia 400 seemed unavoidable, why not take the public initiative? The black community might want southside development,[44] and white Atlantans on the northside might prefer that growth be directed away from their neighborhoods. Together, they might even find the general idea of managed growth appealing, but there was no set of arrangements by which they could coalesce around such broad public aims and attempt to guide transportation and development actions.

Preservation Efforts

The linked issues of historic preservation and affordable housing further illuminate the obstacles to building support for an alternative development policy. City-council approval of Georgia 400 came after several setbacks to neighborhood conservation and preservation, not only in Buckhead but in a wide swath of northside neighborhoods, including the close-in Midtown area. In the struggle against intrusive development, one can again see the shaping hand of CAP, as preservationists failed to unify around an alternative to an investor-guided development process. But political fragmentation was greater than what could be attributed to any direct effort by the business elite.

Consider first the case of West Paces Ferry Road, perhaps Atlanta's wealthiest and most prestigious neighborhood. In mid 1983, residents proposed that the area be designated as a Historic and Cultural Conservation District — a zoning change that would increase lot sizes, set height limits, and require that the city's Urban Design Commission review all building and landscaping plans. In the fall, the city council rejected the proposal ten to seven, and its division was instructive. Two neighborhood-oriented members from the eastside were outspoken opponents because the two members from the West Paces Ferry area had disregarded historic preservation on their turf by supporting the Presidential Parkway. Another eastside member, Morris Finley, though generally prodeveloper, also complained that northsiders had not supported efforts to designate the Kirkwood neighborhood in his district as a historic area.[45] Proneighborhood member Mary Davis said, "We will either sink or swim together. The northwest is important, but so is the northeast, the southeast and the southwest."[46]

They sank together. No citywide preservationist coalition formed, but the outcome is not fully explained by friction between councilmembers. Rather, the debate revealed two policy perspectives. Prodeveloper members worried that historic zones would be a prelude to other restrictions, restrictions that might discourage development overall; but preservationists argued that development could be guided without causing stagnation. The prodeveloper argument gave obeisance to the rights of property owners, but *no larger discussion took place of how properties came to have their given values.* Opponents of both the Presidential Parkway and Georgia 400 on occasion made the point that additional expressways provided opportunities for speculative profits, but the matter was never pursued to any great extent nor was the argument expanded to the overall development scene.

Thus, when the West Paces Ferry Road plan was followed by other proposals, particularly those involving sites in Atlanta's Midtown area (on Atlanta's near northside), preservationists had no well-developed rationale for limiting the prerogatives of investors in development projects. CAP argued that property owners should be free to make profits, and it made use of its favorite (but unproved) contention about the need to overcome the bad investment climate of the Jackson era.

The Midtown area was a hotly contested battleground. Preservationists believed that the quality of urban life was at stake and that downtown Atlanta with its concrete-and-steel canyons was precisely what Midtown should avoid. What Midtown *should* do, they said, was keep affordable housing, so that it could hold a large and diverse residential population able to sustain round-the-clock living, rather than the eight-hour life of downtown. However, they lost a series of battles, with the mayor twice vetoing narrow propreservation council votes.

In one of his veto messages, Young displayed a concern for a broad guarantee of property rights;[47] and he also proposed a *private* preservation trust fund that would negotiate with the owners of historic buildings, buy structures, renovate them, resell them to private owners, and use the proceeds to make the trust fund a revolving account. In addition, Young called for a cooperative effort among the city's Urban Design Commission, CAP, and the privately funded and operated Atlanta Preservation Center. Preservationists were confronted with a privatized solution or none at all. Despite a strong showing of popular support for legislation, the council dealt preservation a further blow by tabling a later effort to introduce a comprehensive ordinance on historic areas. The mayor wanted the city to act only in partnership with CAP and without intruding on the market prerogatives of private owners. Preservationists simply could not move ahead on their own and press a reluctant city government into acting.

What was missing from the public debate over preservation was any mention of an "unearned increment,"[48] the notion that public actions contribute to and in some cases determine the value of private property. Indeed, the battle over preservation was lost before it became visible publicly. It was part of a larger struggle over the character of Midtown, which itself was a segment of the still-larger development picture described above.

Midtown

North of the main business district and bisected by Peachtree Street, Midtown has been mainly residential. For a time in the late 1960s, a portion of it was the home of Atlanta's "hippie" colony, and it later became an area for drugs and prostitution.[49] With encouragement from CAP, city and county law enforcement officials cleaned it up in the mid 1970s, and the arts colony then became the ascendant element — giving the area a rich cultural life and providing it with a twenty-four-hour ambience missing from Atlanta's downtown, as it inevitably is from every office-tower downtown.

The opening of three MARTA stations in the Midtown helped make it a target for intensified development. In fact, the Special Public Interest Districts created around each MARTA station allows for such growth *so long as it is mixed use*. The ideal is a combination of commercial space, offices, and housing, but there are no specific residential requirements; in particular, affordable housing is not specified.

As large-scale development began, land prices escalated. This trend tempted developers to replace modest-income housing with luxury housing and nonresidential uses. Realizing that intensified development was decreasing housing along Peachtree and making street life after dark less viable, area residents and businesses sought to stem the change. They formed a committee through a task force of the Midtown Business Association to consider and recommend corrective action.

The task force's housing committee initially called for legislation requiring that all high-density projects be mixed use and include housing affordable to people then living in the area. Various proposals surfaced, and with the committee's urging, the Board of the Midtown Business Association adopted a resolution seeking to maintain the predominantly residential character of Midtown.[50] The committee itself was more specific and proposed legislation requiring new housing where existing housing was demolished, as well as legislation to make the maintenance of existing housing and inclusion of new housing "financially attractive to owners and developers." Its report also advocated special district zoning to give the city more control over development in order to promote preservation, protect the nonluxury housing, provide for such publicly desired uses as theater space, and see that low-scale buildings not disappear completely from the area. The report further suggested the establishment of a trust fund to support facilities for the arts community as well as affordable housing. Developers would be required to either provide replacement housing and structures such as theaters, or contribute to the trust fund. Although the committee report contained concrete recommendations, there was no follow-through. Indeed, the overall task force offered only guidelines to developers, not requirements.

To understand why the follow-through lacked substance, one needs to see how the Midtown Business Association fit into the larger civic network of Atlanta. Perhaps the central consideration is that, although neighborhood residents and businesses are represented, the Midtown Business Association is essentially a subsidiary of CAP; CAP established it and paid its staff in the first year of operation. Major businesses such as Southern Bell, with new office buildings in Midtown, hold membership in and contribute to the organization. Moreover, membership in the Midtown Business Association is not restricted to those who live or operate businesses in the area. The daily newspaper, for example, is a member, and the publisher is on the Board of Directors, as are Dan Sweat (who heads CAP) and a number of public officials. The association's task force report, *Atlanta's Midtown* — a glossy promotional publication, in contrast to the considerably more substantive, mimeographed housing committee report — was prepared jointly with CAP, the city's Bureau of Planning, and the Community Development Department of Georgia Power Company.

Proposed restrictions gave way to guidelines when Dan Sweat of CAP and Mayor Young reacted to the housing committee report by suggesting that it would not be a good idea to make too many demands on developers. No legislation was introduced. CAP's influence had been strong enough to prevent the Midtown Business Association from being a vehicle for mobilizing preservationist forces. Instead, CAP persuaded preservationists to seek to influence the city's planning process by joining with it and the city in working out a mutually agreeable policy.

In 1986, when public controversy over the demolition of an apartment complex occurred, the Midtown Business Association took no stand — despite the declaration of its earlier resolution that the association would "oppose any development which threatens the aforementioned quality of life in Midtown Atlanta." When preservationists sought to enlist the support of the association, top officials dodged taking sides, since its membership (which included realtors and property owners who wanted to sell) was divided on the issue. Besides, Dan Sweat made it clear that development policy was the domain of CAP. The association's task, he argued, was to work to improve the area, not to set policy.

The 1986 battles were followed in 1987 by renewed struggle. At that point, some of the smaller theaters and other arts facilities in the area were faced with expired leases and orders to vacate because properties had been sold to developers. In line with the suggestions made by Mayor Young and Dan Sweat, preservationists (including the arts community) have embarked on a three-way negotiation process with the city and developers.[51] Development interests insist that there be no infringement on the rights of owners; preservationists and arts-community proponents support city requirements to see that affordable housing and arts facilities are provided. Although they have gained no such concessions, the one bright spot for preservationists in the ongoing process is the building of a new Academy Theater as part of a large-scale development. That achievement came about, however, because the Academy Theater had a long-term lease on property owned by the Metropolitan Community Foundation, and a developer wanted to purchase the property.

Since the Metropolitan Community Foundation is headed by Dan Sweat, who also heads CAP, he worked out an exchange. But, as the head of one of the theaters losing its facility observed, most theaters do not have that kind of leverage. He asked the city to amend its zoning law "to define an arts district and make it incumbent on the people who develop there to take the lead in preservation, maintenance and creation of arts facilities."[52] Development interests, however, successfully resisted all requirements, and the protesting manager has now lost his theater and is out of business.

Throughout, the mayor has displayed little concern about historic preservation. Shortly after one of his vetoes, Mayor Young indicated that his concern was about the city's contemporary development. Of its past, he said: "The city has no character. . . . We're building the city's character now."[53] Current development is what Young finds exciting. The past he links with the Jim Crow system, arguing that preservationists should "find a way to make decisions in such a way that if a developer wanted to come in and do something that might be expressive of the new wealth we have in Atlanta right now, that we can create a history of the golden age of integration and development, rather than preserving the old days of segregation and poverty."[54]

Preservationists thus were handicapped in tripartite negotiations because the mayor was largely unsympathetic to their cause and because the developers resisted requirements. Even in the area of theater and other arts facilities, which all sides agreed were desirable for the city, only the preservationists/arts subcommunity supported measures that would impose requirements on developers. The executive director of the Midtown Business Association, for example, took the position that developers were open to such ideas as putting theaters in their large-scale buildings, but that they could only be expected to do what was profitable on expensive Midtown land. She added that, "even with subsidies, this is still prime space. There will be some groups that can't afford Peachtree anymore than all New York groups can afford Broadway. . . . But those that have enough celebrity to fill the seats I feel confident we can find space for."[55]

As an elected official, the mayor might have been expected to contend that developers have social responsibilities. Instead, Young offered this view on preservationism: "No citizen has the right to say to somebody, 'You have an old car, you have to keep an old car, because to destroy the old car is to destroy a classic.' Same thing with a building."[56]

Among other considerations, the mayor's position ignores a fundamental difference between cars and real property. Old cars increase in value only because they age. Property, specifically Midtown property, went up in value in part because of the huge *public* investment in MARTA and other improvements. The market price of a privately owned property appropriates benefit from public expenditure. The mayor refused to acknowledge that fact, as did the private owners themselves.

Thus preservationists — whether their concern was with historic landmarks, affordable housing, or theaters — have lacked the ally that they needed in negotiations. The mayor was out; the council majority they could occasionally muster was too slender to override a mayoral veto; Midtown Business Association officials reflected the position of large property holders; and neighborhood groups, in any case less potent than at their peak, were prone to nurse their resources for their own highly local struggles.

CONCLUSION

In the 1970s, Atlanta's neighborhood movement had made itself a formidable political force. It occupied a strategic balance-of-power position in electoral politics, providing a significant bloc of votes, strong candidates, and all-important volunteers for both citywide and district elections. It proved itself skillful in using litigation and in forcing administrative reviews. Moreover, it displayed influence at the national and state levels, as well as at the local level.

The 1980s were a different story. The neighborhood movement failed to align itself with Andrew Young, the winning mayoral candidate in 1981, and by 1985 it had electoral clout in only a segment of the city. It could not match the business elite and developers in campaign funds, and, in an electorate that had become two-thirds black, its predominantly white composition restricted its appeal. Though there were some successes, the 1980s have been on the whole a period of defeat and frustration for neighborhoods. Apart from wielding an occasional veto, neighborhoods consistently found their interests sacrificed to those of developers and CAP. This chapter has not recounted every single battle by any means, but the pattern is clear. Even when neighborhood organizations were biracial or all-black, they lost. The most important fact about Atlanta neighborhoods is not race in and of itself, but that they are politically fragmented, responding on a highly segmented basis, building alliances issue by issue. The NPU system was designed to overcome this segmentation, but it was not structured for *political* mobilization. The Citywide League of Neighborhoods provided some cross-neighborhood contacts and alliances but lost strength as its electoral position declined.

Atlanta neighborhoods proved eventually to be politically weak because they did not solve the collective-action problem for citywide organization. Since they could build ad hoc alliances and maintain efforts within given areas, theirs was not an inability to sustain any form of collective action.[57] Rather, it was a failure to solve the mega-problem of coordination on a *sustained citywide basis*.[58] CAUTION, for example, fought its battle distinct from NIP. Vine City and Buttermilk Bottom found themselves in not-so-splendid political isolation. Northside fought not even as a unified sector of the city, but as a changing slate of actors — each with a narrow and particular agenda.

It is tempting to account for the failure of the neighborhood movement through the collective-action problem and let the matter rest there. Divisions of race and class are formidable, especially when amplified by geographic fragmentation and particularly if collective action is based on solidary appeals.[59] The NPU system provided a boost for building coalitions across divides of race, class, and geography, but it proved insufficient to the task. Indeed, the task is substantial enough to suggest that a relatively modest effort like the NPU system is incapable on its own of having a durable impact. This system gave neighborhoods a network through which they could communicate and a common stake in preserving the access it provided. But it provided no body of incentives to create or reinforce obligations to a citywide coalition. And it stood alone, *not* as part of an ongoing network among community groups and nonprofit organizations concerned with neighborhood and preservation issues.

However, this explanation stops short. If the neighborhood movement faltered because it failed to solve the collective-action problem at the citywide level, the question is, why was the citywide problem not solved? Or why was there not at least a greater effort to solve it? One response must be that there was weak motivation for mayors in office to attempt it. In Jackson's case, though he was ideologically sympathetic, he had too little time and too many distracting side battles. For Young, there was not only the two-term limit but also the fact that the preservation aspects of a neighborhood program of action had no appeal. Rather than perpetuate a past associated in the black community with poverty and segregation, Young saw his chance to make a mark by a record of building a new Atlanta. He, of course, was not the first politician to display an "edifice complex."

Shortcomings in mayoral leadership are not the whole story. There was also the potency of the rival coalition. The business elite operated with a high level of cohesion and continuity and with a daunting array of resources. Its power added up to more than the sum of its parts. Even potential rivals found it easier to move with than against the business elite, whether the goal was preserving old buildings, housing a local theater, widening minority business opportunities, driving crime out of Midtown, seeking a foundation grant, or constructing nonprofit housing. Alliance with the business elite is the coalition that works — though it is an alliance that comes at the cost of acquiescence to such business interests as no city-imposed requirements on developers, which the Midtown Business Association experience illustrates. There was, then, ample reason for Andrew Young to say that he could not govern without the cooperation of the city's business elite. Perhaps he could have, but not without great difficulty.

The network of contacts and exchanges through which civic cooperation is achieved offers ample evidence of business-elite resources at work. If preservationists want to mobilize support in the Midtown area, they are handicapped without the Midtown Business Association. If the arts colony wants theater space provided, they cannot ignore the Metropolitan Community Foundation. The art museum was built with substantial Woodruff funding. If research, planning, or analysis is needed, the likely sources include Research Atlanta, the Chamber of Commerce, CAP, and the research and community development departments of major corporations such as Georgia Power. The business elite takes the lead in the United Way and other charitable drives, including support of the arts. If the Preservation Center wants to write a grant proposal, the signature of the president of CAP as sponsor or endorser carries weight. Indeed, in Atlanta, the impression develops quickly that all civic roads lead to CAP. It is hard to make a broad-based civic effort without tying into CAP's network.

CAP does not control everything. Neighborhoods enjoy autonomy within their segmented world. Preservationists and various good-government groups are not its puppets, but they are reluctant to alienate themselves totally from CAP or commit themselves to a rival network of civic cooperation. The nature of policymaking itself magnifies the importance of CAP's civic network and the concentration of resources enjoyed by the business elite. Policymaking in Atlanta does not consist of a set of isolated governmental decisions aimed at a changing list of unrelated concerns. Problems are connected over time and across arenas of activity.

Since World War II, under CAP's leadership, the city has been adjusting to the dispersing impact of the automobile on work and life in the metropolitan area. From the Lochner report through the planning and building of MARTA to the approval of Georgia 400, the city's governing coalition has used public authority and funds to connect the business district with a growing and spreading hinterland. These transportation decisions not only cut through neighborhoods but also alter land values and determine the attractiveness of sites for high-density development.

Reacting to a specific incursion into a particular neighborhood does not match the larger dynamics of urban development. That is the lesson of Georgia 400 and of the impact of MARTA on Midtown as well. Driving vice activity and pornography shops out of lower Midtown is not just an isolated instance of neighborhood improvement; instead, it was one step among many (opening up MARTA stations, creating the Midtown Business Association, and building a new art museum, for example) that altered the character and investment potential of the area.

Some of those steps were public (locating MARTA stations), while others were private (the art museum), but in Atlanta, those were not disjointed decisions. CAP plays a guiding role in both public and private spheres. It operates on a large scale, concerned with the consequences of public and private actions citywide and beyond. CAP also operates over the long run, looking not just at immediate impacts and results—though it does not foresee well enough to make *detailed* plans over the long term and it sometimes generates unintended consequences.

An apt illustration was the CAP decision to foster public investment in the lower downtown area by, among other steps, promoting it as a "government center." As part of that effort, CAP supported the construction of the Richard Russell Office Building there, which brought federal regional offices into this new complex. Several of these offices had been located in Midtown, and, ironically, their departure may have contributed to the area's 1970s decline. Yet CAP was still bent on reviving Midtown as an integral part of its center-city strategy. The MARTA system and private money for an arts complex, combined with the law-enforcement antivice drive, provided the needed catalyst.

The downtown elite thus responds to unforeseen and unwanted developments in the context of a policy strategy that, though flexible, is long in term and broad in scope. In general, CAP favors investment in and close to the business district, but without restricting investors. That means imposing social costs on nonbusiness interests, and it also entails the use of public authority and funds to stimulate and complement business efforts and to compensate for their shortcomings. No other element of the community has a comprehensive strategy, and even if some other group did, it would have difficulty mobilizing sufficient resources to act.

Mayor Young understood the situation and made his alliances accordingly. Neighborhood and other community groups continue to behave as if policy is an episodic process of responding to ad hoc challenges. The 1980s show Young's approach to be workable and the neighborhood strategy to be fatally flawed; the mayor enjoys partnership in the governing coalition while the community groups are confined to a reactive and defensive strategy.

7

The Coalition Restabilizes

Changing land use is a political process.

—Atlanta developer

Within every association [and polity] there is the same basic constitutional problem, the same need for an accommodative balance between fragmentary group interests and the aims of the whole.

—Philip Selznick

Andrew Young's mayoralty quickly demonstrated that the neighborhood movement was outside the governing coalition. The movement was not without a political voice on the city council and in the state legislature, but it no longer played a major part in forging the city's policy effort. Instead, as we saw in the previous chapter, neighborhood groups found themselves reacting to, not formulating, policy initiatives. At best they could wield an occasional and partial veto.

The political faltering of the neighborhood movement only indicates what the current governing alignment is not—it is not one in which neighborhood groups are an integral part. But what is it—what motivates it and what holds it together? The short answer is that it is a revised version of the older coalition. Blacks no longer occupy a subordinate position, but neither are they dominant. Nor is black participation in the coalition inclusive; just as before, the black middle class are the political insiders. However, that group has expanded to include not only public officeholders, but blacks in white-owned corporations, such as Coca Cola, Delta, and Rich's Department Store. The main difference between the periods is that blacks control city hall, whereas earlier they only bargained with city hall as one of the city's voting blocs.

As mayor, Andrew Young gave the 1980s coalition a special imprint based on his conviction that he could best govern with the cooperation of the white business elite. That was partly a lesson learned from Maynard Jackson's experience, but in Young's case, the view is even more deeply embedded. His experience as a civil-rights leader taught him that racial changes came in such bedrocks of resistance as Alabama not through electoral or even legal pressure but through economic pressure.[1]

In the Atlanta milieu, with its history of biracial cooperation, Young offered the view that "you never get progress through guilt. You make people change by making them feel more secure."[2] Of Atlanta and his partnership with the business elite, Young observed: "Politics doesn't control the world. Money does. And we ought not to be upset about that. We ought to begin to understand how money works and why money works."[3] As he saw it, the Atlanta partnership was an exchange: power based on electoral control exchanged for a share of the city's economic growth. Young has said that his "job is to see that whites get some of the power and blacks get some of the money."[4] As we have seen, however, not all whites get "some of the power," and there are continuing complaints that too few blacks receive a share of the money.[5]

The central factor in the exchange between electoral power and investment money is the city's Minority Business Enterprise (MBE) program. City legislation calls for 35 percent of city contracts to go to minority businesses either directly through contracts or subcontracts, or in joint ventures that include minority partners. Where that medium of exchange works *to unite* the black political leadership and the white business elite, projects move forward. Where the partnership is not achieved, inaction results.

THE CENTRAL BUSINESS DISTRICT

A city's central business district represents a significant economic configuration. It is not only a major part of the city's tax base but also an employment center. City well-being is therefore heavily entwined with the business district. As an area that is privately owned for the most part, it is subject to the concerns and aspirations of big private investors as well as those in city hall. The central business district is thus a major arena of urban political economy, formed by relationships among investors and between private investors and public officials. Investors can work together politically and economically to pursue a shared vision of how best to protect and promote their common stake in the value of a downtown location, or they can compete with each other, acting alone. Of course, there are gradations between these two extremes. For downtown Atlanta, CAP represents a substantial commitment to pursue a common vision.

In Atlanta, the downtown investment game is complicated by the fact that the city is the state capital, a county seat, and a federal regional headquarters. Additionally, Georgia State University is located in the heart of downtown, and the Georgia Institute of Technology is on the periphery of the business district. All of this amounts to a substantial public presence in downtown land use.

Because the value of any parcel of land is heavily influenced by uses and investment decisions on adjoining parcels, public and private interests are intricately intertwined. How these relationships are worked out should reveal much about how a city is governed. The key element in Atlanta is CAP, the collective voice of Atlanta's biggest property holders in the central business district.

CAP works closely with the Chamber of Commerce, and the two organizations rarely take public stands at odds with one another. But it is CAP that gives downtown business a privately controlled planning capacity and an opportunity to unite around concrete measures so generated. From the Lochner report of the 1940s through urban renewal and MARTA to the present redevelopment of Underground, CAP has succeeded in initiating strategies for the regeneration and growth of downtown—strategies, as these examples indicate, that were embodied in large-scale public projects.

Beyond being a forum for discussion, CAP does not intervene in the private investment decisions of its members. Its efforts are directed at stimulating *public* actions that would enhance the value of downtown property or at least protect it against the centrifugal force of changes such as the automobile. Thus CAP's shrewdest move has been to make itself an integral part of the planning process in Atlanta. While neighborhood and preservationist groups have typically taken a narrow and reactive stance on urban change, CAP has taken a broad and long-range view.

During Ivan Allen's mayoralty, CAP in partnership with the city launched a Central Area Study to consider how to connect downtown with outlying areas (especially with MARTA) and how to knit the business district together in such a way that lower downtown would not continue its gradual decline. The proposal to concentrate governmental facilities in that area addressed the problem of decline. As a section unattractive to private investors, lower downtown could be upgraded by expanding governmental office space.

More than a decade later, as the 1980s opened, the knitting together of the business district remained an unfinished task. As private investment concentrated in the upper business district, the lower portion became increasingly populated with small, marginal businesses. Moreover, as Atlanta lost whites and gained blacks, the patronage for these marginal stores and, in the same vicinity, the old central store of Rich's became heavily black—adding to the investor *image* of a declining area.

For a time, the bright spot in this area was Underground Atlanta. In a city ranked third in the nation in volume of convention business, Underground gave Atlanta a much-needed center of nighttime entertainment. For this stretch of the city, left divided by the 1920s viaducts that elevated traffic above the rail lines, the Underground revival in 1969 as an entertainment district was a timely boost. Small entrepreneurs used the theme of the bygone railroad era, complete with gaslights and player pianos, to make Underground a booming success at the time that the initial Central Area Study (now called Central Area Study I) was completed. But the success was short-lived. Deteriorating quality, incidents of crime and disorder, and MARTA construction combined to bring an end to this entertainment district. After years of decline, the last business closed in February 1982. For CAP, the task of rejuvenating lower downtown and making the business district a vibrant whole was unfinished business for the 1980s. An entertainment district still made sense and not just as a draw for convention-goers. CAP realized that having a business district that closed down at 6:00 P.M. marked Atlanta as still a provincial city.

CAP came up with a three-part strategy: 1) make a new Central Area Study, focused on the quality of life in downtown; 2) redevelop Underground; and 3) promote housing for the affluent on the fringes of the business district. As with the first study, the new planning venture was a cooperative effort between the city and CAP, joined this time by Fulton County.

The plan that emerged from Central Area Study II involves multiple public subsidies for downtown housing—loans drawn from the tax-free bonds of the Urban Residential Finance Authority, tax abatement on the land, and, for housing in Bedford-Pine, written-down land costs. The redevelopment of Underground has taken the form of collaboration between the public and private sectors. The Central Area Study initiatives show the governing coalition at work: CAP formulated a broad strategy, initiated particular actions, and enlisted governmental cooperation and support. Public officials liked the idea of protecting the tax base *and* of becoming identified with a visible set of accomplishments. As we shall see later, partnership with CAP offered Mayor Young projects that moved toward completion, while development pursued outside this partnership produced disappointment. The redevelopment of Underground illustrates the capacity of the governing alliance to overcome what Pressman and Wildavsky call "the complexity of joint action."[6]

UNDERGROUND AND THE GOVERNING COALITION

In the abstract, the revival of Underground appears to be an unimpeachable idea. Besides complementing the city's important convention business, it offers a possible correction, albeit a limited one, in the northward skew of Atlanta's development.[7] In reality, Underground is a controversial and expensive undertaking, estimated originally at $124 million. It is essentially a downtown urban-renewal project, requiring that land be taken from 150 private owners and sold or leased to others. The original owners resisted, and the city council has voiced considerable skepticism.[8]

Underground is also a high-risk project. Its predecessor failed, as did a similar entertainment area in the Omni complex. Underground's viability is intertwined with race. To succeed, the new Underground must appeal not only to convention-goers but also to Atlanta residents — no easy matter in a highly race-conscious metropolitan region, where the Underground vicinity is thought of as a black area. By one estimate, 80 percent of the restaurant industry in Atlanta is "very skeptical about this project."[9] Moreover, while the new Underground was afoot, developer/architect John Portman began talking about an upscale retail and entertainment complex at his Peachtree Center in upper downtown. Here was the prospect of nonsubsidized, private development to meet the convention industry need, but in a locale that would leave a section of the business district unregenerated. The Portman initiative was unappealing to both city hall and CAP. Each wanted new development in lower downtown, but neither had confidence that the Underground project would win in a popular referendum. Thus they set out to build support and detailed an elaborate scheme of financing that enabled them to avoid holding a bond referendum.

Preliminary talks with the Rouse Company of Maryland about making Underground a "festival marketplace" began during Jackson's administration, and Andrew Young carried these forward. In the meantime, a CAP-initiated task force, speaking for CAP, Action Forum, and the Chamber of Commerce, pronounced the project feasible and gave it the business "seal of approval." Skeptics within these organizations voiced no public doubts or criticisms. Newspaper endorsement followed,[10] and Rich's Department Store promised renovation of its downtown store, *if* Underground moved ahead.

Students of implementation regard the game of "piling on" — adding more objectives to a policy initiative — as a major threat to project success.[11] The redevelopment of Underground suggests a different maxim: Adding objectives can broaden support. In the case of Underground, it is informative to consider which objectives were in fact added and which were called for but not included. Four councilmembers wanted to require that 50 percent of all construction and retail jobs be reserved for Atlanta residents. Backers of Underground opposed any such guarantees, and in the end, a compromise resolution "encouraging" that goal was enacted instead. The issue was not raised again by the council, though the grass-roots organization ACORN did later protest against the heavy use of out-of-town construction workers.[12]

The council did insist on strong guarantees of minority business participation. As a consequence, a joint-venture arrangement was worked out through which H. J. Russell Company (the company of construction executive Herman Russell) and Kinley Enterprises (a fast-food company run by Mack Wilbourn) would have a 30 percent share in the limited partnership with the Rouse Company in running the project. In addition, 25 percent of the construction contracts were set aside for minority enterprises. Both private and public money was budgeted to encourage minority retail operations in Underground as well, with the city council setting up a special loan fund and local banks promising to make loans. In short, while job guarantees gave way to a symbolic gesture, business opportunities gave rise to hard bargaining.

There has since been infighting over minority business participation. City policy calls for money to go to *disadvantaged* business enterprises, and several councilmembers have sought to expand the universe of minority businesses included. Some members complained that H. J. Russell Company has obtained a disproportionate share of minority business opportunities. In any event, as a company with 1985 sales of $118 million, it was scarcely "disadvantaged" in any general understanding of that term.[13]

There was no shortage of conflict: between the mayor and the city council, the city and the Rouse Company, within the city council, and within the city administration. Various proposals were made to alter the financing scheme, to cut costs by scaling down the project, to siphon off funds for related projects such as the Grammy Hall of Fame and the Atlanta Science Museum, but none of these gained acceptance.

The complicated legal and financial arrangements posed barriers, but, significantly, they also generated fees. City officials joked that "they would have to rent out the Atlanta Stadium if all the lawyers working on the project were to meet."[14] The army of lawyers and other professionals drawing fees from the project could hardly be expected to voice publicly any doubts about its wisdom.

A $15-million private investment in the project, designed as a tax write-off, was threatened by a change in federal tax law. The original plan to avoid a public referendum by having the Downtown Development Authority issue the bonds had to be revised to circumvent a court ruling. Furthermore, a variety of tax-minded individuals and groups, including the Southeastern Legal Foundation, challenged the new method of financing, while property owners in the project area contested their displacement and exclusion from participation. Finally, because the project claimed major CDBG funds, neighborhood opposition was significant.

None of these complications derailed the project, largely because of the vigorous backing of CAP and the unyielding commitment of Mayor Young. CAP had been strongly behind the project even before Young's election. For example, in 1981, before the official planning began, CAP persuaded the state Building Authority to buy the old railroad depot and an adjacent four acres of land as a possible complement to the city's effort and eventually for a land swap. CAP was pivotal in creating the syndicate that provided $15 million of private "equity" money, and CAP's membership dominated the board of the Downtown Development Authority—making it doubly key to the project's financing. CAP also had clout with several city councilmembers; it helped to persuade Fulton County to contribute to the project and reinforced Rich's renovation plans for its downtown store adjoining Underground. When the project came to an early impasse, Young asked CAP to form an Underground Festival Development Corporation to take charge of the process. The new corporation's board consisted of downtown business executives, and its administrative head was a former CAP staff member, Joe Martin (now slated to succeed Dan Sweat as the chief executive of CAP).

In short, as a unified business voice, CAP could speak authoritatively about the urgency of cooperation. It could also tap skillful and knowledgeable administrative talent and bring to bear a wide array of resources and contacts. Even though there was a profusion of potential barriers to the completion of Underground, CAP in partnership with the mayor could overcome them. Still, the public-private partnership solidified only when a reluctant and cross-pressured city council cooperated after its demands for minority business participation were met. The case of Underground suggests that a unified and powerful business elite, attractive to and allied with an activist mayor, and a program of minority business participation whereby legislative support can be courted are the central elements in a governing coalition that works—one that can move along even enormously complex, costly, and controversial projects.

REDEVELOPMENT PRIORITIES

Other Redevelopment Efforts

In contrast, other simpler projects that lacked CAP support went nowhere. One example is Auburn Avenue, an area that contains a U.S. Park Service-operated historic district commemorating the birthplace of Martin Luther King, Jr., and is known as the faded but traditional center of black business and civic life in Atlanta. Black elected officials feel obligated to continue calling for renovation, and plans from the modest to the elaborate have been drawn; yet the area remains the topic of much discussion but limited action. Neither CAP nor Young has opposed redevelopment of Auburn Avenue; its renovation has simply not been a priority. Auburn Avenue itself is divided: Residents fear gentrification and displacement; small businesses want help so they can renovate and stay; and larger ones, particularly Atlanta Life, want the business end of Auburn redeveloped as an extension of the city's main business district, which it borders. Stalemate prevails.

The specifics of a West End redevelopment effort were different, but the outcome was the same. This close-in neighborhood southwest of the business district was once a white area, which was kept white for a time by the agreements and "understandings" of the Hartsfield era. In the 1960s, blacks began to move in, and later, the city bought and partially cleared fifty acres in the area. Located close to the Atlanta University complex, West End became partly gentrified in the 1970s, meaning that much but not all of its current middle-class population is black. With a MARTA station only two stops from the Five Points station in the heart of downtown, the vacant land in West End has enormous redevelopment potential, even though part of it adjoins a run-down industrial area.

Faced with two proposals for redevelopment in the early 1980s, the mayor and city council chose the one put forward by a subsidiary of the black National Baptist Convention. Critics, including the *Constitution*, raised conflict-of-interest questions: The architect for the development corporation was the mayor's close ally; (his wife was on the mayor's staff as well); and a law partner of the city-council president drew up the incorporation papers for the subsidiary.[15]

Black defenders of the proposal saw it differently. One city councilmember, acknowledging that the Baptist proposal had "the support of a small army of black ministers in Atlanta," described it as "a continuation of the civil rights movement."[16] The commissioner of community development charged its critics with implying "in tone and language that whites can do a better job of developing West End than blacks."[17] The newspaper softened its criticism, but the project nevertheless failed. The black Baptists' development corporation was a new entity, formed by an organization without development experience and with limited contacts inside Atlanta's business community. The mayor tried to revive the project by bringing in Asian financial and development interests as joint-venture partners, but that partnership foundered on misunderstandings. Another attempt to involve the Asian investment group, this time without a joint-venture arrangement, centered around the Garnett Street station of MARTA, but it also came to naught. The missing ingredient in both cases was the Atlanta business elite.

A new redevelopment proposal for some of the West End land is in the offing—this time, a joint venture between a black member of CAP and the white developer who had submitted the earlier rejected proposal.[18] The city appears to have abandoned attempts at redevelopment without the active participation of the Atlanta business community.

Housing

The fate of 1980s housing efforts parallels the redevelopment experience. CAP and the mayor backed an ambitious plan (part of Central Area Study II) to build downtown housing that would attract upper-income residents, making use of tax abatements and subsidized interest rates. Though one plan to use MARTA land near the civic-center station has stalled, other projects, particularly in the Bedford-Pine area, are moving ahead. Significantly, they involve minority business opportunities and thus have the critical elements for success. However, the city council has so far balked at the idea of a direct appropriation to build luxury housing.

Lower-income housing lacks priority. Some of its ablest administrators have left for jobs in economic development or with the Urban Residential Finance Authority—the state agency that gives subsidized interest loans to encourage private housing efforts. Meanwhile, allegations of corruption, conflict of interest, and mismanagement have sprung up around city programs and the Atlanta Housing Authority.[19] Representatives of the mayor's office have met with nonprofit housing groups, but their modest capabilities have little appeal to the mayor and have generated negligible follow-up. For the most part, then, lower-income housing is at a standstill.

Mayor Young is not uninterested in housing for the poor; for example, on one occasion he disguised himself as a panhandler to experience firsthand the treatment of the homeless. Yet there are no city facilities for the homeless. Church groups provide them, with some financial support from the city. But CAP is against a public program, maintaining that a city effort would inevitably be bureaucratic. Considering the management problems rampant in public-sector housing, the argument is persuasive.

Of course, all city officials claim to be interested in better housing for the poor, and, in fact, the Central Area Study II task force on housing adopted a goal of promoting the rehabilitation and preservation of low- and moderate-income housing. However, housing for the nonaffluent, who lack a power base, gives way to competing demands. For example, when one city councilmember sought more money from federal funds for relocating lower-income families from the airport area, the council voted the measure down. The winning contender for that allocation, backed by the mayor, was a $700,000-loan fund for minority businesses going into Underground.[20]

Public Safety

Not all of the policy trade-offs in redevelopment are financial. For example, from the beginning, backers of Underground saw that its success depended on having a low-crime area in downtown. The Central Area Study II task force on public safety initially proposed creating a "safeguard zone" for the hotel and convention district, which would include Underground when it opened. The zone would have strictly enforced laws forbidding panhandling, loitering, and public drunkenness.

Regarding the proposal as an effort to create a vagrant-free zone, Mayor Young's initial reaction was opposition.[21] A CAP staff member suggested that the proposal had been misunderstood: "It is not an attempt to round up the homeless and move them to a concentration camp. . . . But I think everyone agrees that in order to have economic development in the central area, we really have to do something about homeless people walking up and down the streets."[22] CAP explained that more housing was part of the overall plan and that the public-safety task force made a distinction between a "vagrant-free zone" and "a safe area." The mayor then agreed to support stringent enforcement of ordinances against vagrancy and panhandling citywide so long as it was not an effort to displace the homeless.[23]

As the task force proposal evolved, the term "safeguard zone" was dropped, and the final report instead recommended a new police zone for intensified patrolling, to include all of downtown and adjoining residential areas to the east and north.[24] For this newly delineated district, the task force sought 140 more patrol officers (30 just for Underground). Underground would have a police substation *and* a private security force as well. The report again called for tighter ordinances on panhandling and vagrancy and for a limit on the number of street vendors, especially around the main MARTA station.

The outcome of these recommendations is still undetermined, but they have set the agenda of discussion. Increased policing is part of budget deliberations, and the Underground Festival Development Corporation claims that potential Underground merchants must be assured of additional patrols.[25] With Underground now imminent, it seems likely that the request for more policing will be acted on. However, stringent new ordinances affecting street behavior are not being pushed because of a threatened legal challenge from the American Civil Liberties Union.[26]

MINORITY BUSINESS OPPORTUNITIES

Andrew Young is credited with healing the break between Atlanta's black political leadership and the city's white business elite. Part of that healing is attributed to Young's own easygoing style and his strong personal inclination to cooperate with the city's monied interests.[27] Another part, however, dates back to Maynard Jackson's administration and the development of a program to encourage minority business enterprises (MBE). Foreshadowed by an earlier MARTA agreement pushed by black members of Action Forum, Jackson's policy gained a foothold in negotiations over the building and operation of the new Atlanta airport. At first, an MBE program for the airport was strongly resisted, but the city policy that minority firms receive a 25-percent (later 35-percent) share of government-generated contracts proved enormously helpful in holding together the governing coalition.[28]

The white business elite came to realize that fact, and the newspaper shifted its position to become a staunch defender of the policy.[29] When Georgia contractors initially succeeded in a court suit against it, the *Constitution* supported amending the city charter to reestablish the legal footing of the policy.[30] A candid "op-ed" column defended minority set-asides as necessary to prevent black contractors from being frozen out as latecomers to the game. Columnist Tom Teepen described the practice as "sort of the old spoils system — but with a difference. It has clear rules, negotiated publicly through the political process and written into governing law. Its contracts are awarded openly, its results are openly monitored." He added, "The realistic choice, and for that matter the proper choice, may not be between low bids and the spoils system. It may only be between a regulated, publicly scrutinized spoils system and an introverted one."[31]

Bidding on contracts can be extremely complicated. A simple, no-discrimination/low-bid rule leaves many issues unaddressed. Established firms may be able to exclude newcomers by superior knowledge and resources. Also, the bid is only the final stage in a complex process that requires a company to have credit and secured bonding lined up — which is traditionally based on past performance, thus handicapping new businesses and building a subjective factor into the process. Aside from these complications, the bid itself is not airtight on every point, since some terms may be left open for later negotiation. Nor are bids always based on cost; quality considerations sometimes enter in. All in all, judging the merits of proposals inevitably becomes a subjective process. Black business leaders in Atlanta knew that from old experience — when the Atlanta Housing Authority would award bids on the basis of design, not cost alone, and when seventy-eight acres of prime land in the Bedford-Pine urban-renewal project was passed to a CAP subsidiary that had *not* offered the highest sum for the property.

The web of business relations among contractors, lending institutions, and insurance companies, and the leeway that decision makers enjoy are tough screens to break through. In Teepen's words, the process is "introverted." Those on the inside tend to be comfortable with past criteria, such as reputations for proven ability; they are thus reluctant to include new actors and play by new rules. Government policy is therefore crucial. And, as Fulton County Commission Chairman Michael Lomax has stated, local government contracts are the "bread and butter" of minority entrepreneurs.[32]

Perpetuating exclusion does not require intentional discrimination; once established, it is easily sustained by "satisficing,"[33] that is, by continuing to rely on procedures in place that have no overt racial content. Without leverage, little changes. That is why Maynard Jackson's aggressive insistence on minority participation was integral to the reordering of relationships in Atlanta. Airport construction provided especially strong leverage, and Jackson claimed that its contracts created twenty-one black millionaires.[34] All of this said, a minority-participation requirement is by itself no guarantee of an ongoing open process. It may merely enlarge the "club" to include a small, first wave of minority entrepreneurs, especially where there is reliance on joint-venture arrangements.

Under the joint-venture relationship, white contractors are allowed to take on black partners in order to meet minority participation requirements. The original idea was that inexperienced minority entrepreneurs would learn from those well-schooled in the trade. In practice, it turns established businesses into patrons, able to pick and choose those on whom their favor is bestowed. There is also an incentive for white contractors to select joint-venture partners who are well-connected politically. It is precisely this pattern that has become a matter of contention within Atlanta's black community—as is evident, for instance, in the recent plan to buid a City Hall annex.[35] One city councilmember complained that "white contractors call on the same [black] companies."[36]

The minority-business program has also been subject to fraudulent use. When caught, some white contractors complained that they used minority fronts because there was a shortage of legitimate minority subcontractors and joint-venture partners. City hall responded to that excuse by tightening regulations and maintaining a list of eligible minority firms. Although that lessens the likelihood of sham arrangements, it may encourage repeated employment of larger and recognized firms. In any event, the review and selection process continues to generate conflict.[37] One city councilmember reports that "one of the common perceptions is that our MBE [Minority Business Enterprise] program has helped only a few people rather than a lot like it was intended to do."[38]

Some city councilmembers have also been concerned that the MBE program has done little to increase employment opportunities outside the black middle class. Borrowing an idea tried in other cities and touted earlier by ACORN,[39] these critics initially sought a "First Source Jobs Policy" ordinance that would require any developer who receives a city contract to choose some workers from a pool of people identified as poor, handicapped, or unemployed. However, they later settled for toothless legislation calling for developers to make an effort to employ such workers.

Despite conflicts and glitches in the process, the minority-business program has survived and seemingly gained strength. Indeed, the minority-business sector in Atlanta has grown to the point where a variety of business organizations represent it—from the Atlanta Business League and the Atlanta Regional Minority Purchasing Council through the city coalition of black contractors to the tiny but growing Atlanta Hispanic Chamber of Commerce. The minority-business program thus has an organized constituency, whose foundation is partly political. Though it is not free of criticism, it works well for the white business elite, now lacking the direct access to city hall it had enjoyed under Hartsfield and Allen. Joint-venture arrangements consolidate ties with highly useful black allies. The old patron-client relationship could be dressed in the new senior-partner/junior-partner garb of business association. Furthermore, the goodwill of the black middle class is valuable enough for some white businesses to ensure that minority firms are used for purchases and contracts even when city funds are not in use.

For black political leaders, the program is also valuable. After long years of nearly total exclusion, minority-business participation has strong group appeal, with both its symbolic and material value. Money going to black entrepreneurs circulates to black employees and other black businesses more readily than does money going to white entrepreneurs. Public expenditures for black contractors also result in contributions to black candidates — an incentive to maintain the program even though some of its prime beneficiaries hardly qualify as "disadvantaged."

Minority-business participation promotes coalition cohesion, providing exchanges and interactions around concrete opportunities to accomplish personal and group objectives. These are continuing, not one-time, occurrences, that enable norms of cooperation to develop and be sustained. Though the public rhetoric of biracial cooperation is very visible, friction is by no means absent or even denied. But, as one observer noted, black and white leaders describe a "careful detente they have nurtured over the years, drawing on the same anecdotes as if they had rehearsed them together."[40] Indeed, repeated negotiations give them ample opportunity to develop the habit of collaboration and rehearse the anecdotes that justify working together. Black real-estate brokers were central figures in the early years of the coalition, when massive changes in land required rehousing an expanding black population. In the 1980s, black contractors occupy a central place. The network of insiders has enlarged, but it is still small, leaving out most of Atlanta, black and white.

The earlier rehousing task and the later minority-contract requirement each served to provide much of what Russell Hardin has identified as a "network of mutual interaction."[41] Hardin has trenchantly argued that "social states of affairs are often more to be explained by what *can* be tacitly coordinated than by what anyone's preferences or reasoned outcomes might be."[42] Repeated interaction around specific and material goals teaches participants how to cooperate and rewards them for cooperation. That the gains to be made are individual as well as collective confers a form of discipline. Those who fail to cooperate can be excluded.[43] Those outside the network are drawn toward it; those in it are reinforced.

Atlanta is perhaps remarkable in the degree to which complex and controversial projects can be moved along. Whereas studies of policy implementation might lead to the conclusion that such attempts are inevitably stymied, that is not the Atlanta experience. Defenders of the status quo often come out losers. The opposition to the Presidential Parkway, to an in-town piggyback facility, to Georgia 400, to apartment demolition and intensified development along Peachtree Street, to the transformation of Buttermilk Bottom, and to the redevelopment of Underground—each effort failed to stop change. On the other hand, the governing coalition's "network of mutual interaction" could and did produce results.

The decline of the neighborhood movement illustrates the weakness of actors who cannot subordinate what separates them to what unites them. Similarly, opportunists who play to the galleries rather than build insider alliances may be able to defy the norms of cooperation and reciprocity and survive individually, but, as students of legislative behavior have long understood, they pay a price in policy effectiveness. "Go along to get along" works in Atlanta as well as in the halls of Congress. Not everyone need regard such a system as legitimate; all that is required is for enough people to participate in the network to make it the system perceived to be the most workable.[44] As Jane Mansbridge found in her study of the failure of the Equal Rights Amendment, political groupings that cannot make use of selective incentives to encourage discipline are handicapped in their struggle with other groups that do have such inducements.[45]

Atlanta's program of minority-business participation provides selective incentives useful to both the business elite and to black political leaders. For that reason, the program is unlikely to be relinquished without strong resistance from both partners in the coalition, since it augments the strength and flexibility of governing arrangements. The coalition's capacity to achieve cooperation thus rests on a high level of development activity. The divisible and collective benefits draw members toward development even when the considered judgment of some is that a given project is costly, risky, or conducive to unwanted side effects. This almost magnetic attraction of productive cooperation enables the governing coalition to surmount the opposition of defenders of the status quo.

CROSSCURRENTS IN COALITION MOBILIZATION

The governing coalition in Atlanta rests on a narrow popular base. In fact, it seeks to avoid popular referendums—most conspicuously on the redevelopment of Underground, but in other ways as well. The Central Area Study II proposed raising the level of annual general obligation bonds the city can issue without a popular referendum from $8 million to $16 million.[46] In addition, much of the city's development activity is conducted through independent agencies, starting with Park Central Communities during the Massell administration, including the Jackson-era Atlanta Economic Development Corporation, as well as the Underground Festival Development Corporation in Young's mayoralty. These public-private entities are thoroughly insulated from popular control. Two state agencies of significance also issue tax-exempt bonds without a referendum: the Downtown Development Authority, for economic development, and the Urban Residential Finance Authority, for housing. Business interests are heavily represented on both boards, and both have supported the development agenda of the city's governing coalition.

The activities of all five agencies involve programs that are so legally and organizationally complex that their operations are not easily understood by the general public, making oversight difficult. Indeed, their operations are so intricate that they can be depicted in any of a number of ways. Given the importance of interpreting these activities to the public, the inclusion of the major newspaper in the governing coalition is an important feature of the Atlanta political scene. It largely determines whether attention is focused on the amount of job generation, the size and scope of public subsidy, contribution to general economic growth, or some other factor. A missing feature in Atlanta politics, then, is an institutionalized policy-research capacity independent of the governing coalition, ideally one with channels of communication to the larger public.

Indeed, the overall connection between decision makers and the mass citizenry is weak. Significantly, both black and white constituencies represent considerable class diversity (though the white population is more heavily tilted toward the affluent middle class). However, political parties and explicitly political organizations rarely muster the electorate. Churches are especially important in the black community, civic associations among whites, yet each represent diffuse and fragmented forms of political mobilization with weak claims on voter loyalty. Electoral support is thus quite volatile. Race remains the dominant division, but as the John Lewis/Julian Bond congressional primary demonstrated, the white minority can tilt the balance toward one black contender over another.

Against this background, several crosscurrents are at work, which can be illustrated by three interrelated issues: corruption and conflict of interest; insider privilege and perquisites; and police-community relations.

Corruption and Conflicts of Interest

Extensive opportunities for individual reward and a general civic atmosphere of deal making contribute to a persistent problem for the governing coalition. Since the transactions have involved public officeholders in elaborate arrangements with business interests and have deeply infused business practices into government decision making, it should not be surprising that issues of corruption and conflict of interest have emerged. Commercial deals—inevitably a pervasive part of development activity — reward and therefore encourage opportunistic behavior. The profit motive is venerated, and the distinction between public and private interest becomes clouded.

In this atmosphere, the conduct of some local officials has transgressed what is legally permissible. The 1980s have seen both city and county officials convicted, and some have resigned or, in City Council President Arrington's case, withdrawn from a business relationship when it became public. A few publicized incidents have been deemed technically legal but of questionable judgment. Many, but not all, of the public officials involved have been black, leading some to believe that blacks are targeted for probes.[47] But, as one columnist pointed out, a number of white officials in Georgia have also been charged with political corruption.[48]

More to the point may be the volume of development activity and the huge profits it generates, which appear to draw less scrupulous officeholders into questionable behavior or across the line into illegal activity.[49] Full-throttle development creates a distinct civic climate; for example, mostly white Fulton County, during a 1970s building boom, was notorious for a close official association with developers.[50] At the same time, Mayor Jackson was insisting on high standards of public responsibility in Atlanta and had vetoed a housing proposal for Vine City tainted by a conflict of interest that involved a former Housing Authority official and a then-incumbent city councilmember. But Jackson's leadership on the issue was resisted. With development activity on the rise, Jackson proposed a stringent ethics code, with full disclosure of all income from any source for both elected officials and their spouses. The council did not enact it.

Later, John Lewis was the leading advocate of financial disclosure during his five years on the city council, when he accused his fellow councilmembers of cronyism involving business deals and city contracts. He, too, was unable to obtain enactment. Only after he moved on to Congress in 1986 did the council approve even a modest disclosure ordinance. Their complacency on the issue was broken when James Howard, a city councilmember, was convicted of tax fraud for not reporting a "consultant's fee" he received from a developer. Even with the new provision, the city's ethics law remains weak. The Ethics Board reviews conflicts of interest only on request and publishes its reports with names deleted. It has no enforcement power; the law, designed to encourage elected officials to ask for rulings, therefore relies on voluntary compliance.

City-council posts are part time, and some members have, or had, ties to firms conducting business with the city.[51] In addition, developers and contractors are heavy campaign contributors. One developer described the process of "plugging in": "any time you start redeveloping in a mature market, that means every project involves a change in land use. And changing land use is a political process. That involves campaign contributions and close political relationships."[52] On another occasion, he added that "we're a heavily regulated industry. You have to have people think well of you."[53] Unfortunately, his efforts were not restricted to campaign contributions. It was this developer who paid councilmember Howard a consultant fee of $475,000 for help in a particularly lucrative land deal; $50,000 was paid in cash because Howard said he "did not have an active checking account."[54] Howard also received $80,000-worth of house remodeling from the same person, for whose zoning requests he worked.

In Howard's tax-fraud trial, another developer testified that the council-member had solicited $400,000 for a similar "consulting contract," in exchange for which Howard offered to "put a wall around" the developer at city hall. This second developer balked at the fee and spoke with other officials to see whether "what happened to me was common," and he contended that City Council President Arrington then talked with Howard. (Arrington disputes this assertion.) According to testimony, Howard subsequently called the developer and said: "Back off. We could've done it for a lot less. Let's let this thing die."[55] Arrington himself testified that "people didn't really follow" the city ordinance prohibiting conflicts of interest (requiring councilmembers not to *vote* on legislation in which they have a financial stake).[56]

The trial also revealed that Howard sought to have the city's zoning administrator reverse his opinion on another issue involving the developer from whom he was receiving money. According to the zoning administrator's statement, Howard said, "Bill, you're creating a political problem for the mayor. You need to forget about your professional reputation."[57]

City-hall reaction to Howard's conviction was limited. Mainly, there was a studied attempt to focus on the fact that the trial was a tax-fraud case. Mayor Young said, "I think that this was a tax case on his reporting of taxes, and I think that's what the decision ought to be based on. That you ought to pay your taxes."[58] Collegiality may well have discouraged public condemnation by Howard's fellow officials, but newspaper columnists, black and white, were appalled by the council's "cavalier attitude" and its unwillingness to recognize that its institutional integrity was in question.[59] Significantly, Howard has worked as a lobbyist *on city affairs* for the American Federation of State, County, and Municipal Employees even after his conviction.

It is not easy to determine whether James Howard's "consultancy" was a unique arrangement or not. What is clear is that it was the most flagrant in a series of conflict-of-interest episodes. Between 1983 and 1988, the following came to light:

1. As noted earlier, council president Marvin Arrington's hauling company got a Presidential Parkway subcontract in violation of state conflict-of-interest regulations. He gave it up only after the news media broke the story.

To counter his public embarrassment, Jesse Hill and other luminaries in the governing coalition sponsored a dinner in his honor — a move suggesting that insider solidarity matters more than scruples over conflict of interest.[60]

2. President Jimmy Carter supported a commuter highway through east-side Atlanta in exchange for land from the state DOT for his presidential library. Although this occurred after he was out of office and in violation of no statute, it seems to be a case of using the prestige of office to further a personal aim.

3. A $2-million management-consultant contract was awarded without a competitive bid to a firm that Mayor Young had previously worked for.[61]

4. The mayor's brother, a dentist and "international consultant" became a paid lobbyist for a Canadian rail company seeking a MARTA contract.[62]

5. A bid on a $30-million annex to City Hall went to a partnership that included an architect who is a strong political supporter of the mayor and whose wife works on the mayor's staff.[63]

6. Former state senator Leroy Johnson, the executive director of the Atlanta-Fulton County stadium authority, resigned under a cloud of suspicion. The Ethics Board could not corroborate claims that Johnson had solicited payment from a fair promoter seeking use of the stadium grounds, but it did express "serious concern" about Johnson's son being employed in a management role in a 1986 fair and concluded that the arrangement had "the reasonable appearance that [Leroy Johnson] used his influence or allowed his influence to be used to obtain a favored position for his son."[64]

7. The head of the Atlanta Economic Development Corporation refused to make his travel and expense records available to the city council and subsequently resigned.[65]

8. The chief legal counsel for the Atlanta Housing Authority resigned after charges that he had his home remodeled partly at government expense.[66] The authority itself subsequently came under investigation for malfeasance.[67]

9. The chair of the Fulton County Housing Authority was replaced after the news media disclosed that he had not repaid an interest-free loan he received from a major contractor with the authority.[68]

10. The city's housing bureau director was convicted in federal court for demanding illegal "side payments" from tenants in housing he owned.[69]

11. Legal Aid and the NAACP filed suit on behalf of homeowners and began an investigation of "patterns" of favoritism toward certain home-improvement contractors,[70] one in a series of long-standing complaints. For example, an earlier report had shown that at least five of the city's twenty-one housing inspectors held active licenses as real-estate agents and one was a salesperson for a company with a history of code violations.[71]

12. Two Fulton County commissioners were convicted for soliciting bribes, and testimony revealed that vote trading on rezoning issues was common.[72]

13. A state senator at first denied, then admitted, that he was a paid "con-

sultant" for the company seeking approval of a landfill site vocally opposed by his constituents. The matter was to be voted on by the city council right after a National League of Cities convention in Las Vegas. Councilmembers managed to taint their own integrity on the issue by accepting a free dinner from the landfill company at the convention, and the state senator tried to bill the state for his trip to Las Vegas on behalf of the landfill operator.[73]

14. A contract for expansion of the parking decks at the airport was awarded at the mayor's insistence to a company principally owned by Herman J. Russell. When a losing competitor challenged the decision, it was overturned and $900,000 in damages was imposed on the city. The jury foreman said that the consensus was "that the city had acted in a non-businesslike manner in not following its own regulations and by ignoring the strong feelings of its own employees"; i.e., three city purchasing agents who had recommended that bid procedures be followed to the letter.[74]

15. After ordering fire fighters to fill his personal swimming pool (in violation of a city ordinance and during a summer drought), the fire chief was put on administrative leave with the expectation that he would then retire instead of facing dismissal charges.[75] A newspaper columnist linked the chief's behavior to a pattern of mayoral hiring and "dabbling" in administrative matters on nonprofessional grounds.[76]

Since conflict-of-interest issues are not readily measured, it is difficult to compare Atlanta with other cities or even with its own record in earlier years. But the nature and volume of the incidents suggest that there is a serious problem. If the overall trend toward increasingly lax civic integrity does not change, it could become an issue on which an electoral challenge could be built.

Insider Privileges and "Perks"

Conflict-of-interest issues are not isolated phenomena. Any governing coalition — whether in the Soviet Union or capitalist America — is cemented in part by insider privileges and "perks." Regimes may vary in the degree of privilege and in the magnitude of the conflict-of-interest problems they generate, but insider privilege is part of the discipline that governing coalitions use to hold supporters in line and attract new adherents. The aphorism "go along to get along" gives testimony to that principle.

Part-time public officials who put in long hours in hearings and constituent contact may find a "consultant" relationship with a developer not radically different from other insider privileges they observe on a daily basis. Consider some examples of the relationship between Atlanta's business elite and the city government: (1) When Maynard Jackson came into office, he found that banks did not compete for the city's money. Instead, the director of finance had worked out a formula for dividing up city deposits among them. (2) As mentioned earlier, when the Housing Authority awarded seventy-eight acres of land in the Bedford-Pine renewal area for redevelopment, the award did not go to the out-of-town firm that made the highest offer; it went to a subsidiary of CAP. (3) Tax-free bonds issued by the Downtown Development Authority have been offered for such purposes as refurbishing the offices of major accounting and law firms.[77] (4) Developer/architect John Portman has built several "skywalks," a private use of the city's air rights that contributes to the lack of pedestrian activity in Atlanta at night. CAP then asks the city to ameliorate the problem through the use of public funds and public plans. (Portman was not the first to receive this privilege. Rich's Department Store had a pedestrian bridge long before Portman embellished it as a "skywalk.")

Some of the favors are exchanged between private-sector members of the "club." The newspaper's role is instructive: Noted editor Eugene Patterson resigned when publisher Jack Tarver insisted that a columnist not criticize an insider company, Georgia Power; and John Portman has received editorial support to counter criticism of his antipedestrian style of architecture.[78] The pattern is also biracial. When a newspaper series on housing criticized upkeep in a housing complex run by Herman Russell (black contractor, former president of the Chamber of Commerce, and solid insider), the article was criticized editorially and followed by this statement: "We believe the description of West Lake Town Houses that appeared in the Tuesday, November 19 [1985], editions of the Atlanta Constitution and the Atlanta Journal as part of a series on low-income housing does not reflect their actual condition. For another look at the project, see the story on 14A and Editor Jim Mintner's column, 2D."[79]

More recently, the newspaper gave ample evidence of how much Andrew Young is regarded as an insider, in contrast to his predecessor. In a highly publicized incident (detailed in the next section), when Alice Bond (wife of Julian Bond), talked with police about drug dealing and drug use in Atlanta, Young's call to her placed him under investigation for a possible charge of obstruction of justice (the charge, it turned out, was not made). The U.S. attorney, a white Republican from a suburban area north of Atlanta, was accused of "playing politics," and the grapevine buzzed with the opinion he was priming himself for a congressional race by trying to nail Young, as a prominent black Democrat. Atlanta *Constitution* political columnist Frederick Allen came to the attorney's defense, describing him as someone who was restoring public confidence.

Atlanta's political establishment, black and white alike, began a campaign to discredit Barr [the U.S. Attorney] in advance of any action he might take. Democrats have hastened to point out, for instance, that Barr may be planning a run, at some point, against U.S. Representative Buddy Darden in the 7th District. What better campaign tool, they ask, than a reputation as the man who "got" Andy Young? . . . All this was unfair. . . . Barr actually deserves a good deal of credit. It is worth recalling that when he first jumped into the fray, Barr was the only public official — the only authority figure at any level of government — who expressed any interest whatsoever in dealing with what appeared to be a severe breakdown in the integrity of Atlanta's law enforcement system.[80]

Shortly thereafter, the *Constitution* announced Allen's resignation, with Allen offering no elaboration beyond citing a "disagreement" with the editors.[81]

Other insiders enjoy editorial protection as well. When federal indictments put the spotlight on the expense allowances of county commissioners, a *Constitution* editorial defended them:

> More often than not, the officials criticized for treating part-time elective posts like full-time jobs are black. Frankly they are caught in a bind. They are responding to the needs, expectations and demands of the people who elected them. That is not an excuse, just a fact. And those pondering whether the perks given to Fulton officials ought to be cut back or other actions taken to discourage commissioners from treating their jobs as full-time positions need to keep that in mind.[82]

The editorial never explained how using county funds to rent a Mercedes and a Lincoln Town Car helped meet constituent needs.[83]

When the more independent-minded city council came under criticism for a $50,000, "red-carpet" fund used for foreign travel and entertainment of dignitaries,[84] an editorial suggested that the recruitment of international business should be left to Mayor Young (whose travel is often privately funded) and the Chamber of Commerce.[85] In recommending that publicly funded foreign travel be limited, the editorial may have missed an important point: Young's inclination to include both city councilmembers and city administrators in foreign travel may be a "perk" that is useful in maintaining allies for his development policy.

The city council has also shown itself to be keenly aware of the advantages of being able to distribute favors. When one cost-conscious member sought to eliminate their right to distribute free passes to the city-owned golf courses, the council balked. Even though the free passes cost the city $65,000 a year and reap unfavorable publicity, the council voted to retain them by a five to two margin, with nine abstentions.[86] Golf passes were not an isolated practice. Later complaints to the Ethics Board prompted an investigation into a wide array of free tickets given to city officials for activities in city-owned facilities.[87] The issue is not yet resolved, but its specter has further clouded public integrity. The amount of money involved in free tickets and other such privileges is relatively small, but the significance of these practices is that they set a tone of civic conduct. Council behavior affects others. Social agencies — in particular, EOA and the housing authorities — continue to come under criticism for poor-quality service to clients combined with high-level benefits to staff.[88]

Thus far, the system of perquisites and insider privileges has not become a major issue, but the potential is there — especially if the trickle-down approach to development benefits comes into greater question. It is perhaps noteworthy that when James Howard's council seat became vacant, his elected successor was someone who has worked mainly on defending the interests of low-income neighborhoods; for instance, he was one of the sponsors of the first-source ordinance to encourage greater attention to local job needs. Still, the issue of who is served by the current governing regime is largely latent, and it may remain that way. If Atlanta's public sector is visible primarily for self-serving actions, that perception could simply reinforce cynicism and promote indifference.

Police-Community Relations

The question of insider privilege is also related to police conduct in Atlanta. Atlanta has a long history of extensive mayoral and council involvement in police affairs, making the task of departmental management doubly difficult.[89] The Alice Bond matter reveals some of the tensions, although perceptions of that controversy vary widely. Distraught about marital problems, Alice Bond went to the police with allegations concerning drug use. She was interviewed at some length by two white police officers, who were part of an on-going drug investigation. Some of the specifics are in dispute, but it is clear that Alice Bond's initial accusation and main concern was about the woman she believed her husband to be involved with.[90] However, police investigators attempted to draw her into much wider allegations, including hearsay about prominent black Atlantans — among them the mayor and his brother.

The events that followed are sufficiently complex with enough dispute over details to allow observers to interpret the matter in radically different ways. The police chief briefed Young and one of his deputies, telling them that Alice Bond had made damaging allegations. The chief also transferred the initial police officers away from the drug investigation. After the briefing, both the mayor and his deputy spoke with Alice Bond, and she subsequently refused to talk further with the police. Young and his deputy were close friends of the Bond family as well as public officeholders. The mayor said he was only counseling a distraught friend. But a U.S. Attorney began an obstruction-of-justice investigation, which never culminated in a formal charge on the ground of insufficient evidence. Still, conservative critics of city hall contended that the situation had been manipulated by insider influence. A column in a suburban newspaper broadened the accusation.

It is believed by some knowledgeable city watchers that the reason City Council won't appropriate money for a top-quality police department is because of precisely what is happening now. Too good a police department would cramp the lifestyle of some elected officials because qualified officers couldn't be yanked off investigations at the whim of any official, and investigations would be carried to their conclusions.[91]

In contrast with that charge, there are some grounds for believing that the two police investigators overreacted, perhaps out of eagerness to implicate black officials and embarrass the mayor and the police hierarchy. The police memorandum on the questioning of Alice Bond was leaked to the press shortly after being written, and the document and a recording of the interview were turned over to the Federal Bureau of Investigation when the two officers were transferred. Moreover, when reporters eventually heard the tape, it turned out that the summarizing memorandum was selective in the names it mentioned and that it stretched Alice Bond's actual words about hearsay to implicate the mayor.[92]

Thus some black leaders saw the events as part of a concerted effort by white law-enforcement officials at several levels of government to destroy the credibility of blacks in government generally and in policing specifically—in short, "an attempt to get blacks."[93] Alice Bond herself denied that the mayor's telephone call intimidated her and prevented her from talking further. Instead, she accused police officers of lying. In her statement to the internal affairs investigation of the police department (also leaked to the press), she stated that her confidence had been violated, and she now distrusted the police.[94]

If it had been the intention of the police investigators to embarrass the mayor and the police command, they succeeded—and the mayor and police command made their task easy. Rephrasing in the passive voice, as public officials are wont to do, one could say that "mistakes were made." Since they were made all around, a significant question is what was the response to the mistakes. Obviously, such a sensational case rated widespread media coverage, and the mayor even charged that those accused were "being tried in the press through innuendo."[95] The suburban newspapers, outside the city's governing coalition, ignored this criticism. The Atlanta *Constitution*, however, shifted quickly to deflect criticism from the mayor. Frederick Allen's resignation, mentioned above, appears to be part of that pattern. Editorially, the paper was basically supportive of the mayor, though questioning his judgment in telephoning Alice Bond.[96]

In the first days of the controversy, Mayor Young appointed a "blue ribbon" citizens' panel to study the city's handling of the matter. Cochaired by two members of Action Forum, one black and one white, fact finding was thus given to coalition insiders.[97] A subsequent internal police department investigation focused on the officers who questioned Alice Bond, specifically on whether department rules were violated by leaks to the media.[98] The mayor eventually brought the inquiry to a close with a "no-fault" agreement among all the principals.[99]

The Alice Bond controversy highlights only one aspect of the politics of the Atlanta police department. Much more emotion-laden are the questions of law-enforcement procedure involving the use of firearms and of policing techniques generally against blacks suspected of street crime. Given the history of police treatment of blacks in Atlanta, this issue has the potential to mobilize a majority of the city electorate for or against any given office-holder or candidate. The popularity of Reginald Eaves in the black community rested on more than the mere fact that he was the city's first black commissioner of public safety; in office, Eaves had altered police conduct and taken such specific actions as banning hollow-point bullets.

Police behavior has remained an issue even after many years of black control of city hall, and it causes strain within the governing coalition. It has put Mayor Young on the spot — caught between his black constituents, most of whom want strong citizen review of police conduct, and his white business allies and the newspaper, who want social order tightly maintained, especially downtown. Although there have been several controversies, a recent case (involving the shooting death of a black suspect killed by two white police officers at a public-housing project) brought the mayor under especially strong criticism from councilmember Hosea Williams and others in the black community.[100] Beyond the particulars of individual situations, Young's policy stance of favoring more police leeway and stronger methods of maintaining street-level social control invites opposition.[101]

The report of the Central Area Study II task force on public safety suggests how sharp the disagreement may be — and how the mayor and coalition-minded councilmembers like Marvin Arrington could accommodate conflicting pressures.[102] A proposed new downtown police zone, especially if financed by a special tax district, could pave the way for a divided service strategy: a downtown heavily policed with loose reins on enforcement methods; and residential neighborhoods less intensely policed and with more restrictions on police conduct. After all, such a move would be in line with the public-choice literature that treats law enforcement as primarily a problem of market accommodation when there are diverse wants and differing abilities to pay.[103] Providing a segmented form of service would enable Atlanta to meet conflicting expectations by tailoring the city's police service to the type of area served. The potential flaw in this approach is that it might simply fail to provide neighborhoods the level of protection they feel they are entitled to.

CONCLUSION

Atlanta's coalition between black middle-class leaders and white business interests is no simple matter of giving the business elite what they want. Its chief policy thrust — a full-throttle development with almost no restrictions on investors, combined with strong encouragement and opportunities for minority businesses — brings the coalition together and promotes cooperation. Projects that meet these criteria move ahead despite enormous obstacles and numerous pitfalls; those that lack these ingredients make little headway.

The political weakness of this arrangement is that it serves only a small proportion of the black electorate and leaves out a variety of predominantly white groups as well. Within the black community, smaller and less-established businesses both resent and want to join the tiny group of black businesses on the inside. Black employment is also poorly served by these arrangements, but it has proved hard to organize an effective constituency around these job needs. As with white neighborhood and preservationist groups, jobs advocates cannot match the governing coalition's effectiveness.

Police-community relations pose a different set of challenges for black political leaders. City hall comes under criticism for promoting insider interests, but that seems much less politically potent with the city electorate than is the question of street-level police conduct. Here city officials are caught between conflicting concerns from white business allies and black voters. The emotional content of this issue could rupture the governing coalition, creating a split between the white business elite and the predominantly black electorate that gives city hall its popular base.

In the development arena, the governing coalition has thwarted opposition by minimizing popular control. Independent agencies (typically operating under state auspices), public-private entities not accountable to the electorate, and a minimal use of the referendum keep most development policy questions out of electoral politics. Whether policing can be similarly insulated from conflicting community expectations remains to be seen. What is clear is that alliance with the business elite and dependence on a popular base of electoral support subject city hall to severe cross-pressures on this sensitive issue.

Atlanta's public policy since the mid 1940s has been shaped by the composition of its governing coalition *and* by the nature of the interaction and cooperation between coalition partners. External forces and unforeseen developments within Atlanta have presented challenges to the city's governing arrangements, and they have given rise to modifications in the coalition itself. Nevertheless, the governing coalition is not simply a recipient of change; it also causes change. The durability of this coalition, despite changes and challenges, is a striking feature of Atlanta life. The chapters ahead will explore the question of why this coalition has not been split asunder or replaced by alternatives.

8

Policy Innovation and Regime Practice: An Atlanta Overview

Social states of affairs are often much more to be explained by what can *be tacitly coordinated than by what anyone's preferences or reasoned outcomes might be.*

—Russell Hardin

This account of Atlanta has not only focused on how the city's post–World War II governing coalition was formed and modified, but has also given attention to the policy changes that were made along the way. Indeed, one of the distinctive features of postwar Atlanta is the high degree of policy innovation—the degree to which the governing coalition was dedicated to change and brought it about despite considerable opposition.

Public policies are not mere reflections of a community's social composition, nor are they mechanically determined by the economic system. Policy innovations—the critical decisions made in response to social change[1]—emerge from and reflect the character of a city's governing coalition. But they are not simply what the coalition partners want; indeed, regime allies sometimes have conflicting wants. Regime analysis instructs us that *policy innovation is not about individuals and their preferences.* In Atlanta, for example, some business leaders *personally* would have preferred that racial segregation be perpetuated, but the *business community* embraced a policy of moderate change because that policy met their regime-building needs. As members of a biracial governing coalition, business leaders learned to link their desire for economic prosperity with abandonment of die-hard segregation.

What can be learned from the Atlanta experience overall? To begin with, the policies adopted in post–World War II Atlanta are not radically different from those of many other cities over the same time span, and this should not be surprising. All cities in the United States faced the same basic chal-

160

lenges (metropolitan decentralization, changing race relations, and mobile capital), and the ingredients for regime building (private ownership of business and popular control of local government) were the same for all. Yet particulars are important, and neither the character of Atlanta's regime nor the policies it adopted are typical of urban America *in any degree of detail*. By reviewing the specifics of what Atlanta has done and why, we can see how policy actions (and inactions) are tied to the particulars of regime practice.

This chapter zeroes in on the strategies by which each of Atlanta's coalition partners positioned itself for participation in the governing coalition and how the fact of coalition coordination itself favors some policies over others. The political practices that constitute a regime are intertwined with policy initiatives in complex ways, each influencing the other. The character of a regime determines both its capacity to act and the direction that action will take. But policy actions also affect regimes, in some cases profoundly; they may, in fact, help define its character.

THE EARLY POSTWAR PERIOD:
COHESION IN THE FACE OF CONTROVERSY

In the years following World War II, Atlanta more than any other Deep South city was noted for moderation in race relations. The city's mayor avoided race-baiting rhetoric and was often at odds with the state's political leaders on that count. The newspapers added to the city's climate of racial moderation and themselves became objects of derision in state politics for their concern about the treatment of blacks. For a time, Atlanta's stance was mainly symbolic: The city remained heavily segregated, and some of the concrete steps away from Jim Crow practice were taken—as in the case of the integration of public transit—only under the auspices of federal authority.

Even so, the city's racial moderation was of consequence. The mayor, especially, conferred on the city's black middle class a measure of personal respect extraordinary for the Deep South of that time, and this was an important gesture to a group ever restive under the customs of the South. More than that, interracial cooperation enabled Atlanta to achieve peaceful school desegregation in 1961—a time when racial turmoil ran at a high level and massive resistance was still official policy in much of the South. In the politics and race relations of the nation, Atlanta's ability to accomplish smoothly what had been so traumatic in Little Rock and New Orleans was no small matter; it demonstrated that peaceful school desegregation could be realized in a Deep South state.

Significantly, Atlanta's public position of racial moderation and token integration posed no challenge to Atlanta's business elite *as a business group*. Even though the personal predilections of individuals may have been overridden, the group's collective interest in *economic* growth, reinforced by its political alliance with the black middle class, encouraged support for orderly racial change. But student sit-ins at downtown sites were another matter. They were aimed specifically at making deeper and more direct cuts into the prerogatives of business owners and managers. Not surprisingly, under direct challenge, business resistance was strong, and student protests achieved only a partial victory in Atlanta. Full integration of public accommodations came only after new federal laws required it, a step in which coalition-conscious public officials from Atlanta played an important role.

Racial moderation was only one part of an interrelated policy picture in Atlanta. It developed from a form of group reciprocity in which the mayor and white business executives promoted racially responsible behavior by whites, in exchange for which black leaders acquiesced in a policy of massively reordering land use in central Atlanta, giving the downtown elite the buffer zone they wanted around the central business district.

Some years ago, when Robert Whelan and I compared urban renewal in Atlanta and Baltimore, we found some distinctive differences in Atlanta's approach to redevelopment. Although both cities had active programs, Atlanta was more likely to execute total clearance and to shift land from residential to nonresidential use.[2] Atlanta also built more new public housing.[3] Indeed, though Atlanta is not among the nation's largest cities, it has the fifth largest public housing program.[4] And, as we saw in the discussion of the era of negotiated settlements, public housing was only a part of the city's conflict-ridden relocation effort. The FHA 221(d)2 program, nonprofit-sponsored apartments, and negotiated neighborhood transitions were also part of the plan by which land use was changed and new areas opened for black residential use. On all counts, then, Atlanta's program entailed a high level of social conflict.

This extensive program of altering land use, with its enormous potential for conflict, could be managed only by a governing coalition capable of maintaining its unity in the face of intense opposition. For Atlanta, that was not easy, since most displacement fell on the city's black population. Much more was involved, then, than a simple logroll between two groups. It is true that blacks received a community stance of racial moderation in exchange for giving up close-in land and taking "expansion" land farther out. A group bargain was thus involved, but it was only part of the overall process. Particular benefits were also accorded to strategically placed black interests—land for the Atlanta University complex, deposits in black financial institutions, donations to black nonprofit organizations, and profit opportunities for black real-estate brokers and builders.

Extensive bargaining over expansion land and the efforts to gather resources for building new housing are significant in themselves; they created a vast reservoir of skill in biracial negotiation. This habit of biracial bargaining and cooperation could then be applied to new areas of conflict as they arose. Several factors thus converged to maintain the coalition, and individual incentives (or selective incentives, as they are called by students of collective behavior) in particular helped to preserve the overall group bargain. Repeated interactions in dealing with issues that were both concrete and controversial served to cement the coalition and promote cooperation across racial lines.

The activities holding the coalition together were integral to the city's policy effort. They enabled the coalition to maintain cohesion in the face of widespread controversy and community opposition. The richness and depth of biracial cooperation also sustained the governing coalition through the period when student protests generated great tension between the coalition partners and the bases of black leadership began to diversify.

Lest we assume that the outcomes of events in Atlanta were inevitable, it should be remembered that an alternative policy position was quite possible. Small property holders – business and residential, black and white – favored a less active program of restructuring land use. Indeed, some other cities in the South opted for less government action on behalf of redevelopment.[5] And Atlanta's real-estate board was a formidable opponent of public land acquisition, characterizing the city's redevelopment program as a "socialist" violation of private enterprise. However, the various sources of opposition never coalesced into an alliance capable of governing the city. By contrast, throughout the urban-renewal era, mayors Hartsfield and Allen and their downtown business allies worked hard to enlist and keep black allies so that this partnership could retain its capacity to govern.

TRANSITION AND RESTABILIZATION

The 1960s were years of transition. The habit of biracial cooperation was embedded deeply enough to secure the governing coalition for a time, but as the decade wore on, the coalition became unsteady. Federal court decisions and administrative guidelines helped to diversify the city's black leadership further and to give an opening to neighborhood champions. Displacement and residential transition reached proportions that outran the old system of negotiated settlements and eroded the process through which particular benefits and cross-racial interaction bound the coalition.

At this stage, regime change seemed likely. The downtown business elite suffered notable electoral defeats in the first MARTA referendum in 1968 and in a succession of mayoral elections starting in 1969. Business leadership also failed to achieve annexation or some form of metropolitan reorganization to offset the emerging black electoral majority. The feat of the 1951 Plan of Improvement was not repeated, and the failure to enlarge the city boundaries illustrated just how limited the power of the business elite was, standing alone. To achieve metropolitan reorganization required the support of suburban political leaders in an action conspicuous to the mass public. A downtown business elite had little capacity to enlist suburban political allies on a visible issue in which business interests and suburban residential interests were plainly at odds.

The failure to achieve metropolitan reorganization demonstrates yet another point. Social scientists are accustomed to an analytical framework where there is a clear distinction between independent and dependent variables. Drawing on Lowi's policy typology,[6] Paul Peterson constructed an interpretation of city politics in which, within each policy arena, the type of policy (the independent variable) molds the form of political participation and the character of politics (the dependent variables).[7] But policy and politics are, I suggest, related in more complex and less linear ways than this construct allows. The regime analysis I am employing offers a different dynamic. Politics in the form of the governing coalition shapes policy, *and* policy also shapes the regime. The reasoning here is not a simple reversal of the policy-causes-politics argument but rather that policy and politics are circular, each at various points causing and being caused by the other. In this view, causation is in part a matter of enacted change. Some actions are what Selznick calls "character-defining."[8] Sometimes changes in policy come first; sometimes politics (the character of the governing coalition) forges policy. Either can have profound impact—illustrating the argument that the interplay of event and structure is a process of structur*ing*.[9]

In the case at hand, the inability of Atlanta's city hall/business elite alliance to expand the city's boundaries was an event that shaped the regime. Thwarted in its effort to gain (suburban) white voters and restore the earlier electoral coalition, white business executives had to develop a working relationship with black political leaders whose influence lay in having the votes to control city government.

There are other instances as well of policy shaping politics in highly particular ways. Nationally, as federal urban policy shifted from strict to lenient guidelines about citizen participation, community groups have lost an advantage. Likewise, increased emphasis on using public money to leverage private investment serves to weaken the neighborhood position and enhance that of development capital.[10] By facilitating the creation of entities based on a public-private partnership, federal policy encourages the adoption of local policies that, in turn, diminish the political force of popular majorities in city politics. The creation of complex tax districts and arrangements, the use of tax-exempt bonds, and reduced requirements for bond referendums have similar effects on city politics. Atlanta's urban regime, like that in other cities, is constantly subject to the impact of continuing change in federal and state policy.

However, there is more to shaping an urban regime than formal policy enactments. The Atlanta experience illustrates how a unified business elite can deploy its own resources to devise patterns of civic cooperation in which it is a guiding force. In Atlanta, as the old system of negotiated settlements became tattered from the winds of social change, the downtown business elite began a comprehensive program of repair. Its creation of Action Forum, in particular, along with the active involvement of black business leaders in the Chamber of Commerce, CAP, and business trips to promote investment in Atlanta, provided multiple opportunities for biracial interaction centered on the policy agenda of downtown business. Because these arrangements provided networking opportunities, which in turn brought some blacks into the white corporate structure of Atlanta and opened up business opportunities for others, they appealed to black entrepreneurial aspirations. The system of interaction was not one concerned with race relations in general; rather, it was a set of arrangements that linked elements of the black middle class closely with white business interests.

Minority business opportunities, first opened up with MARTA and then broadened and firmly established under Mayor Jackson's program of joint ventures and minority set-asides for city contracts, solidified the business foundation of biracial cooperation. Although white business interests initially resisted some of these programs, black electoral power was too substantial to be disregarded. In this instance, it might be said that politics shaped policy, but that puts the matter too simply. The black-led city government's policy of promoting minority business enterprises meshed smoothly with the networking efforts of downtown business executives, and the two initiatives jelled into a new form of biracial cooperation. Indeed, the agreement to cooperate around business opportunity is now so firm that, as we have seen, other considerations and policy concerns yield to business-guided development — so long as it provides minority business opportunities.

Although the group benefits generated by these arrangements are limited and partly symbolic, the alliance is strengthened by the presence of particular benefits (selective incentives) that reinforce the attachment of black business executives to the coalition. The black business executives, in turn, provide campaign funds and various types of civic leadership that are an integral part of black political mobilization in Atlanta. Hence, the coalition, like its counterpart in the earlier period of negotiated settlements, is self-sustaining enough to withstand considerable community opposition.

The fact that the coalition is held together by interaction and cooperation around business interests gives Atlanta a distinctive policy stance in development. Atlanta, for example, is a nonlinkage city (see pages 170–171). Further, a comparative analysis of UDAGs (Urban Development Action Grants) by Susan Clarke shows that Atlanta stands out as a city that attaches few conditions to government-subsidized development opportunities.[11] The governing coalition's method of operation thus freezes out other considerations and facilitates full-tilt development to the detriment of neighborhood and preservationist interests.

Even where tax abatement and tax-exempt bonds are provided, the city exacts nothing more than paper agreements by businesses "to attempt in good faith" to satisfy the city's goals of wider employment opportunities. No targets are set; no enforcement procedure is employed.[12] The city's Office of Contract Compliance is concerned with assuring that legitimate minority businesses receive a share of city funds through contracts, subcontracts, or joint-venture arrangements—not with promoting more inclusive employment practices. In the few cases where investigative reporting has looked into the employment gains from city subsidies to business, the results show none.[13]

BLACK POLITICAL MOBILIZATION
AND UNCRITICAL MAYORAL SUPPORT

By several indicators, public policy in Atlanta is economically regressive; that is, it favors the interests of upper-strata groups and disregards or harms the interests of lower-strata groups. Consider the following: (1) Unionized city workers have been frustrated in their efforts to pursue higher wages, and strikes have twice been broken; (2) the city's commitment to full-throttle development provides no system of linkage whereby employment needs, job guarantees, affordable housing, historic preservation, or arts facilities are addressed; and (3) a regressive sales tax provides the local funding for MARTA and supplements the property tax as a general source of revenue.

When Andrew Young promoted the latter—a one-cent add-on to the state sales tax for general city revenue—he rebutted critics of the measure by arguing that "a sales tax administered by the state or federal government might be regressive . . . , but not one administered by the city council and me. Not only did we head off a property-tax revolt, but we'll deliver more services to the poor. Only liberal ideologues can call that regressive."[14] The facts offer little support for Young's claim. The state places on Fulton County, not the city of Atlanta, the responsibility for health and welfare services. Two of the major uses to which "windfall" sales-tax revenue has been applied are (1) the redevelopment of Underground as a tourist-oriented shopping and entertainment center and (2) the building of a City Hall annex. Neither project does much for the city's poor; both, however, provide opportunities for minority business enterprises.

Charles King, a sometime critic of Young in the black community and president of the Urban Crisis Center, said that Young is "working under Reagan's 'trickle down' theory, which doesn't work for black people." King added that Young had reassured the white business community but had "sacrificed the poor."[15] A recent study documented that "Atlanta's poor are spending a greater and greater portion of their incomes — often as much as two-thirds — for increasingly dilapidated housing in neighborhoods far removed from the booming employment growth metropolitan Atlanta is famous for."[16] It is not esoteric information, then, that the benefits of development in Atlanta trickle down very little to a large lower class.

Why has there been no revolt against the city's black political leadership? Various events taken together suggest that it is a case of racial solidarity overriding class friction. A black political mobilization against incumbent black political leaders — especially the mayor — is highly unlikely. Blacks in Atlanta were so long excluded from a share of power in running the city that, as a group, they are wary of a public challenge directed at centers of black political control. Black ministers, who are key links between black officeholders and the black public, have indicated that any impairment to an incumbent mayor is perceived as a weakening of black solidarity and a threat to black political power. This perception helps to explain how Maynard Jackson was able to mobilize black clergy against striking municipal employees and how Andrew Young mobilized them for the city sales tax and the Presidential Parkway.

The importance attached to black control of executive power is illustrated in the Atlanta School Compromise of 1973. Black participants in the biracial committee agreed to give up busing as a means to racial balance in exchange for a black school superintendent and other high-level black administrative appointments. One might characterize that trade-off as a move to broaden "patronage" for the black middle class, but that would be a distortion. The new superintendent was not a local person, but someone recruited from California (and his successor was brought in from New York). In other words, the point of the compromise was not to provide jobs for a set body of insiders; it was to gain for blacks as a group the position of power represented by the control of the key post of school superintendent.[17]

Thus far, Atlanta's black mayors and their close allies have been immune to black insurgency. On the other hand, elections involving no incumbent and two black candidates can split the black electorate, as was the case in the 1986 congressional primary between John Lewis and Julian Bond. Although black political power seems secure, this occurrence of a divided electorate in which white voters held the balance of power was enough to give rise to a unity meeting sponsored by Concerned Black Clergy of Metro Atlanta.[18]

One inference from this sequence is that ministers are important gatekeepers for the black electorate in citywide elections. The concerns of the clergy about the tenuousness of black political power and their tendency to be guardians of black solidarity make it unlikely that they would become involved in lower-class insurgency against an incumbent black mayor. They have a strong incentive not to bring attention to class division within the black community. Furthermore, black ministers (somewhat in the manner of precinct bosses of old) ask city officials for favors and considerations for parishioners. This practice adds strength to a tendency to "go along to get along" and makes a critical stance improbable.

Black clergy in Atlanta are not apolitical. They are an integral part of the city's electoral politics, and under the right conditions, they could be part of a mobilization on behalf of the interests of the black lower class. This capacity was demonstrated in the instance of the planned MARTA spur line to Proctor Creek near the Perry Homes public-housing project. The line was promised in the 1971 referendum as evidence that rail service would be extended to poor black areas as well as affluent white ones. At one point in 1986, MARTA appeared to be on the brink of dropping that proposed spur from its plans. A citizens' Committee of 50 was appointed to consider the question of MARTA priorities. When an authority report suggested substituting a busway for the rail system, the planning staff officially recommended against a rail line. However, opposition in the black community, including the clergy, was mustered against the change, and after some hesitation, the Committee of 50 recommended that MARTA honor its 1971 promise and construct the rail line. The Atlanta *Constitution* reversed its position to give strong editorial support to the recommendation, citing the need to maintain trust.[19] Though the rail line is not built at this writing, the episode shows that black political mobilization can be effective in gaining policy concessions for the lower class. The effort was directed, however, not against an incumbent black mayor, but against a biracial MARTA committee containing both city and suburban representation.

What does this interplay of forces imply for the future? Until black mayors can no longer exploit their symbolic position as the embodiment of black political power, they appear to be free to pursue their own alliance-building needs with the white business elite, to the neglect of the black lower class. Innovations in city policy, the sales tax in particular, reflect that latitude. On the other hand, the controversy over the MARTA spur line reveals a mostly latent potential for less regressive policies. Without efforts by the clergy, however, the lower class seems largely unable to enlist support for a broadened set of policy concerns. On its own, the black lower class lacks resources for political organization that are comparable to those available to the black middle class.

BUSINESS UNITY AND INVESTOR PREROGATIVE

The downtown business elite brings many resources to bear in obtaining for itself a central place in the city's governing coalition. Many are plainly revealed in the events that constitute Atlanta's postwar political experience: campaign funds, staff time devoted to civic activity, business contacts extended to black entrepreneurs, and voluntary contributions, to name a few. The Chamber of Commerce uses its membership to promote close business-government association through its "buddy" system, in which chamber members are assigned to keep in contact with members of the city council. The art museum, the new day-care center at the Bowen Homes public-housing project, and land for a downtown park are representative of the business elite's contributions to community facilities.

The business elite is hardly a group indifferent to community well-being; rather, its members are active and involved. What makes this involvement so effective is the high degree of business unity. Although there are certainly tensions within the Atlanta business elite—upper downtown versus lower downtown, Portman versus Cousins as developers, and many more—they do not make their differences public. The banks, the utilities, the major department stores, the daily newspaper, and Coca Cola, in particular, have a long history of acting in concert, and they draw other businesses that may be newer to the Atlanta scene into the same pattern of unified public action. In its relations with the external world, the business elite does not divide into factions; hence, no segment of the business elite can be an ally in a coalition against another segment.

The unity of the business elite rests on several foundations. One is that it is structured to have a single voice. CAP provides the elite with an organization separate from the more inclusive Chamber of Commerce. Within CAP, the elite can discuss issues, formulate plans, and monitor policy performance with the assistance of a staff employed to promote their particular shared interests. There is, of course, the potential for a split between CAP and the Chamber of Commerce, coinciding with a division between large and small business. That has not occurred, though the early days of urban renewal clearly posed that possibility. C. Wright Mills has explored as closely as anyone the tendency of small companies to follow large ones, and his analysis seems on target.[20] In Atlanta as elsewhere, large business has special prestige in the eyes of small business. Moreover, large concerns have the staff and funds to create task forces (formal and informal), to make things happen and sometimes, as in the case of Underground, to overwhelm opposition from smaller businesses. Large corporations are especially useful to formal organizations such as the Chamber of Commerce as a source of both funds and prestige. In Atlanta, Coca Cola epitomizes this phenomenon, and it often serves as the bellwether for the business community.

One of the considerations at work within the business community is that small businesses are reluctant to challenge a position taken by the banks. Credit-worthiness, especially for a small company, is too subjective for businesses to disregard how an action will affect their standing with lending officials. Aside from that, small businesses downtown see their well-being tied closely to that of major enterprises; hence, they have a disincentive to form an opposition. Finally, in Atlanta, major business enterprises utilize their prestige within the business community to have their chief executive officers serve in such capacities as president of the Chamber of Commerce. The chamber is thus not in a position to do battle with CAP on a significant policy question. The same can be said even more forcefully for smaller organizations, such as the Midtown Business Association and various civic clubs.

CAP is small enough to permit plenty of interpersonal interaction, which itself promotes group unity and adherence to norms of cooperation and reciprocity within the group.[21] Within the business community, there are deliberate efforts to inculcate a *group* perspective and surmount the tendency to think parochially about one's own business firm. To rise to a position of general leadership, a businessperson is expected to pass through "rites" of service; that is, to play a number of specific business leadership roles – president of the Chamber of Commerce, board membership in CAP, head of the fund drive for United Way, head of the Arts Alliance, and perhaps serve on the boards of various eleemosynary institutions.[22]

These duties are seen as encouraging a broad business outlook. In addition, the boards of individual companies provide opportunities for interlocking connections through which a business-class perspective can be promoted that is again broader than the interest of a single firm.[23] The Chamber of Commerce also sponsors activities that engender personal bonding among members of the business community. For example, the chamber created Leadership Atlanta with that purpose in mind, especially the need for biracial ties. The chamber also conducts out-of-town and overseas trips for small groups seeking to encourage investment in Atlanta, and these too are seen as a means for building bonds between individuals.

The idea is to have a network of personal relationships that can head off factional splits. Should a divisive issue arise, individuals can resolve it on a personal basis rather than allow differences to harden into a permanent cleavage between opposing sides. These personal networks can also serve to reinforce norms of business unity and civic cooperation. However, fostering such norms is not guaranteed always to succeed; it can be undercut by disputes, especially ones that impinge on business profits. Thus, for the norms to be effective, they require a hospitable environment.

Unity within Atlanta's business community rests in part on its success in maintaining such favorable circumstances for business cooperation, and central to that environment is the ability of business leaders to obtain acceptance of wide investor prerogative. The Chamber of Commerce and CAP diligently promote the idea that a favorable climate of business is essential for investment to occur *and* that the key is an absence of governmentally imposed restrictions on investors. They argue that linkage (that is, requiring developers to contribute in some way to the social good of the community in exchange for the chance to exploit development opportunities) would kill the incentive to invest in Atlanta. Instead, the argument runs, it is necessary to bend over backwards to accommodate those who would invest. And accommodation, not conflict, is the watchword.

CAP especially avoids issues that might deeply divide its members and never asks one segment to sacrifice its particular interests to another. Instead, the organization focuses on getting government support for initiatives that maintain wide investor prerogative and in that way further business unity. For any group, the challenge is how to find norms that promote cooperation and downplay competing interests.[24] Investor prerogative meets that test; it protects business unity by asking no sacrifice while promising gain. Investors thus enjoy the position of a privileged class, subjected to few impinging regulations or requirements. There is no problem of varied responses based on differing legal impacts—there are few enactments to give rise to mixed impacts. Instead, business executives have an incentive to band and hold together in defense of their privileged position.

Investor prerogative at work is illustrated by the example of "skywalks"— pedestrian bridges linking one structure with another. The use of air rights over public streets is not only an extraordinary use of the public domain for private ends but also contributes to a general problem for the community and for downtown business especially. Skywalks lessen street-level pedestrian traffic, making the streets less inviting and less safe for that reason. *Planners and people within the business community recognize the problem.* Yet business opposes a ban on pedestrian bridges as a discouragement to further investment, and the Atlanta *Constitution*, as we saw earlier, has strongly defended the prime advocate of skywalks—developer/architect John Portman. Rather than limiting the construction of bridges as a way of encouraging street-level pedestrian traffic, the city has embarked on various publicly funded efforts to make the street level of the business district more appealing. That is, instead of supporting a restriction on one of their own, business executives back public projects to meet the problem. In this way, the cost is passed on to the general public.

Public policy is thus shaped to protect investor privilege, maintaining unity within the investor class. Since this harmony makes it easier to promote the policy initiatives that accord investors a wide prerogative, the pattern is self-reinforcing. Investor prerogative is both a litmus test for policy proposals and a preserver of business unity in politics. It is also a principle that is protected by insulating development activity from popular electoral control through the extensive use of independent authorities and public-private partnerships.

Although investor prerogative is guarded politically, it also has political consequences. It serves to *enhance* business influence by attracting an array of allies and clients in the following manner. Investor prerogative means that developers and other business enterprises are not obligated to return to the community a share of the profits they garner, even when public authority and public expenditures have played a major part in creating profit opportunities. Whatever is given back to the community is at the discretion of the investor, and business firms do in fact contribute to a variety of community causes, ranging from social services to the fine arts. Aside from direct donations, money is channeled through the United Way, the Atlanta Metropolitan Community Foundation and other foundations, the Arts Alliance, and various special drives. Under a norm of "corporate responsibility," major business leaders head up campaigns for the United Way and the Arts Alliance and serve on the boards of colleges, universities, hospitals, and theaters, as well as in top offices in CAP, the Chamber of Commerce, and various lesser civic organizations. Thus they either give directly to or head up fund drives for a wide array of community activities.

Atlanta's business leaders, then, are not indifferent to community conditions and needs. Robert Woodruff, late Coca Cola magnate, especially was known for his generosity and his willingness to contribute to the social good. Donating as a matter of individual charity, however, is a much different phenomenon from doing so as a matter of legal responsibility. The latter is like paying taxes; it warrants no reciprocal obligation, whereas contributing voluntarily may. Charity can be selective, conferred on a case-by-case basis, and thus provide an opportunity to use contributions as tools for building alliances. Even if the same amounts were involved between legally required and voluntary contributions, their political consequences would be quite different. The one promotes a bond of reciprocity between patron and client; the other simply enhances the resources of the public sector.

The arts-and-entertainment task force of the Central Area Study II illustrates the issue. With mostly business members, the task force turned aside requests that developers, particularly in Midtown, be required to provide funds or replacement facilities for the arts community, a group which is being pushed out of the Peachtree Street corridor and other places. Instead, that group has formed another business-dominated task force charged with the responsibility of finding replacement facilities. The arts colony will thus be dependent on business benevolence. Those theater and arts groups that are provided facilities will be grateful and disinclined to complain about a process that took care of them. Those without facilities will likely fold, and in any event, they will find themselves isolated in their resentment and unable to make common cause with those more fortunate. In this way, investor prerogative not only promotes unity within the investor class but also fosters disunity among those who might become part of an alternative governing coalition.

With all of its strength, investor prerogative is not a principle that is inevitably beyond public scrutiny. The uncritical support given by black clergy to incumbent black mayors perhaps makes it easier for arrangements based on investor prerogative to go uncontested. But a shift in the concerns that the clergy manifest or the emergence of a new link between city officials and the mass public might expose business privilege to greater scrutiny than is now the case. If the politics of the situation is altered, policy change will follow. But politics will not change greatly unless some policy enactment gives expression to new concerns and new political relationships.

DOES ECONOMIC COMPETITION DRIVE POLICY ACTION?

CAP expounds the view that wide investor prerogative is essential for the city's economic well-being, and economic competition between localities does indeed enhance the bargaining position of investors. So it might be argued that the pattern of policy action is mainly a response to Atlanta's position in a competitive market. Yet such an argument oversimplifies an enormously complex situation; economic competition is only one consideration, which must be balanced against others.

Decision makers in the governing coalition interpret the situation and choose the trade-offs, but many considerations are relevant. For example, Atlanta takes risks, such as the redevelopment of Underground. Those expensive projects, especially when amplified by a continuing agenda of publicly funded measures, could cumulatively saddle the city with a large debt. Analysis by Clark and Ferguson indicates that Atlanta has an extraordinarily high long-term debt, second in a sample of sixty-two cities only to New York.[25] At some point, indebtedness itself could become a disincentive to future investment, but there is no formula for this matter. Instead, it depends on a number of factors — from the general economic climate to the revenue-generating success of particular city-backed projects.

Thus, the fact of economic competition does not itself determine what level of risk should be incurred.[26] Opinions differ; several groups in Atlanta have advocated a cautious approach to the altering of land use and the building of publicly funded facilities, but these groups have not been an integral part of the governing coalition. Significantly, the governing alliance did not submit the redevelopment of Underground to public referendum, and there is no reason to believe that the coalition represents a popular consensus.

Aside from risk taking, there is the question of how best to protect and promote the long-range economic appeal of a locality. Full-throttle development is not an answer with which everyone agrees. Developers tend to take a short-term view. Typically they have no long-term investment in the community and hence they have little reason to be concerned about overdevelopment. If high-rise building and intense development in Midtown drive out the arts colony and make the area unattractive over the long run, developers are unlikely to pay the consequences. Many of the companies now developing Midtown are from outside the area and will have moved on to other prospects in ten or fifteen years and thus have little concern about Midtown's livability over the long run. CAP and the downtown businesses it represents do have a long-term stake, and they are the intermediaries between outside investment money and Atlanta's governing coalition. But the local investor class, which also has an interest in investor prerogative, generally opposes constraints on development in Midtown. The arts people who work and live in the area favor restrictions, but they, of course, have no special stake in investor prerogative. CAP, however, is a central element of the governing coalition; the arts community is not. CAP is aware of the problem, as Central Area Study II shows, but it prefers a voluntary response — not necessarily because that is the best guarantee of the city's long-term economic well-being but because wide investor prerogative is one of the underpinnings of that organization's solidarity.

Consider the issue from another angle. CAP and city officials express support for making Atlanta a city that attracts and retains the middle class. During Maynard Jackson's mayoralty, when in-town neighborhoods held an important position electorally, both city hall and CAP actively aided and encouraged the revitalization of older neighborhoods. Under Andrew Young, when the governing coalition reestablished itself on a stable basis without the neighborhood movement, concern for the livability of in-town neighborhoods faded as a policy priority. Mayor Young, however, believes that the future economic well-being of the city requires it to be biracial, which means that a significant white middle-class population must live in Atlanta. Editorially, the Atlanta *Constitution* concurs and has suggested a precise tipping-point of 70 percent black. Beyond that, the newspaper contends, "investors, for whatever reasons, begin to shy away from an area."[27] Yet, instead of embarking on a program of neighborhood conservation to retain the white middle-class population, the city is pursuing a policy of tax abatements and other subsidies to build new close-in housing for the affluent.

In short, the governing coalition has chosen a costlier and riskier approach over a less costly and less risky one. Political antagonism between the governing coalition and the neighborhood movement may have influenced the choice. But it is also the case that the approach selected provides opportunities to include minority enterprises as builders and joint-venture partners in the activity, as well as a variety of other particular benefits to architects, lawyers, and realtors who would gain nothing from simply conserving the status quo. Policy choices are thus best understood as emanating, not from an abstraction called the logic of market competition, but from efforts of the partners in a governing coalition to mobilize a supporting constituency and preserve the cohesion of the coalition itself. What would otherwise seem to be inconsistencies in policy disappear when viewed in light of the maintenance and enhancement needs of the governing coalition.

SELECTIVE INCENTIVES

Harvey Molotch's incisive analysis of urban "growth machines" leads us to consider what holds a governing coalition together.[28] Molotch examines the questions of who has shared interest in growth and who benefits selectively. The Atlanta experience points a step farther. A shared opportunity by itself is not specific and compelling enough to account for the extraordinary effectiveness and durability of the city's governing coalition. Policies that make particular incentives available stand a better chance of being sustained than do policies that simply further a generally desired goal. As students of public choice have long known, arrangements that can solve the collective-action problem are more likely to survive than those that cannot.[29] Development policy in Atlanta is consistent with that principle.

The ample use of particular, material benefits may not be the only way to coordinate the efforts of a governing coalition and reinforce its norms of cooperation, but it is an effective way. Such selective incentives are what game theorists call "side payments"; they help to sustain a coalition when other considerations might lead to defection. Furthermore, because members of the governing coalition understand that particular benefits are useful for collective action, they are drawn toward embracing policies that renew the supply of such benefits and enable the coalition to perpetuate itself.

Selective incentives are linked in an intricate way to investor prerogative, although, on the surface, the two seem unrelated. Investor prerogative is asserted as a general principle, but it is important to see how it operates and exactly what it is. Protection of investor prerogative is not just an aversion to the general use of authority; public subsidies are abundant, eminent domain is used widely, and Central Area Study II proposed the creation of a "safeguard zone" that could impinge substantially on civil liberties. In fact, reliance on eminent domain in land assembly also makes it clear that no simple notion of property rights is at work. Instead, investor prerogative more precisely means eliminating *dis*incentives for a privileged group. Since no sacrifice is asked, solidarity within the investor class is not strained. For the same reason, deliberations within the business elite work toward consensus and the avoidance of divisive positions.

The foundation of collective action is clearly complex. As important as selective incentives are, not everything reduces to them. For example, in Atlanta, the governing coalition chose to retain plans for what it perceived as an uneconomic rail line to a public-housing area in order to preserve trust and cooperation within the coalition. The issue thus did not involve selective incentives, but it did center on the integrity of biracial bargaining. Dropping the rail line would have constituted a repudiation of a past agreement and opened up questions about the reliability of negotiated settlements.

Whether it is investor prerogative, the distribution of selective incentives, norms of corporate responsibility, or a preference for internal consensus building, practices within the governing coalition reflect a sensitivity to the need to promote cooperation. Coalition members are astute enough to see that their cooperation with one another is not automatic — that, instead, it comes about because there are practices that encourage it. Mutual protection and the promotion of cooperation within the governing coalition thus become a measuring rod against which policy proposals are laid. Those that provide selective incentives fare especially well. But other considerations also come into play, and a shared concern for safeguarding cooperation within the coalition affects the acceptability of proposals.

IMPLICATIONS

Because this is not a comparative study, it is not possible to place Atlanta in precise relation to other cities. Yet the pattern of policy initiatives in postwar Atlanta is clear enough to characterize the city generally: The Atlanta regime is activist but not progressive. To illustrate the first quality, the city has aggressively provided infrastructure support to revitalize the central business district and encourage investment. Expressways (initiated before the federal interstate program), mass transit, an in-town stadium, and extensive convention facilities have all been built successfully, despite controversy and costs. Although many other cities have pursued the same agenda, some have not. On each count, Atlanta would fall at the activist end of the spectrum.

Atlanta is perhaps more distinctive, but still far from unique, in the ambitious redevelopment program it has pursued. It also has an extraordinarily large public-housing program, but it is not one based on progressive ideals. Instead, most of the projects were built in outlying areas of the city to move poor residents away from the business district. Compared to Baltimore, for example, Atlanta's redevelopment and rehousing program has been highly disruptive and strongly fixed on relocating people away from the center of the city. Residential isolation has resulted, and except for the still-promised Proctor Creek line of MARTA, the remoteness of its housing remains a problem for much of the lower-class population. Furthermore, road building on the west- and southsides of the city — the areas of greatest black concentration — has never provided easy travel by bus or car. In the 1980s, these sections of the city remain under the influence of earlier attempts to hamper black residential expansion by limiting the number of through-streets.[30] Thus policy initiatives in transportation and redevelopment have a regressive slant. Other regressive features of the regime are clear in the breaking of municipal-employee strikes and in the heavy reliance on a sales tax for MARTA and for general revenue. The city sales tax is piggybacked on the state's, and it is a comprehensive tax with no exemptions for food or other necessities.

The city's most progressive measures have been those that serve the black middle class: first, city support for new private housing developments for blacks in the period starting in the 1940s and running through the 1950s; and recently, strong support for minority-business opportunities. Both of these measures also provide an ample supply of selective incentives. The city departs sharply from a progressive stance on measures that entail restrictions on investor prerogative. For example, the absence of linkage or balanced-growth requirements sets Atlanta apart from many other cities. Employment guarantees, affordable housing, historic preservation, and arts facilities are among the needs raised (but rejected) as potential obligations for developers to meet.

Much that the regime does, as well as declines to do, is justified on the ground of economic enhancement, but that claim does not withstand close scrutiny. First of all, heavy expenditures for socially disruptive transportation links to outlying suburbs are questionable means of furthering the city's economic position.[31] Also, even though Mayor Young professes interest in retaining a large enough white middle class to avoid any tipping-point in the eyes of investors, his efforts concentrate on costly, high-risk new housing in the downtown area, not on less costly, low-risk approaches to neighborhood conservation. Inattention to the arts community and its need for inexpensive facilities seems particularly short-sighted, given the city's desire to promote the convention business and enhance its standing as a cultural center.

Atlanta's overall record in policy innovation suggests several conclusions. One is that Atlanta is not governed by veto groups. The status quo has been broken on several fronts, and activist policies have usually prevailed even in the face of considerable opposition. A second conclusion is that the business elite does not rule in command-and-control fashion. It does not always get its way, not only losing city elections but also failing to achieve a much-desired expansion of city boundaries. In addition, it has made extensive concessions to the black community—first in response to student protests by integrating public accommodations faster and more extensively than it wanted, and second in response to increased black electoral power by accepting requirements for minority participation in city contracts.

Third, increased electoral power has produced significant gains for the black middle class, but little for the black poor and working class. Scarce attention is paid to the employment and housing needs of those who have limited education and income. Class differences in policy gains rule out any simple connection between electoral power and group benefit. The black middle class benefits more than the larger black lower class. Fourth, lack of attention to the white middle class, including the arts community, also rules out economic enhancement of the city as "the" guiding concern. No simple explanation of the pattern of policy innovation works. Straight elite domination, pluralism in the form of numerous veto groups, majoritarian influence through the ballot box, and apolitical economic enhancement — each fails to account for Atlanta's policy pattern. Instead of these alternatives, I have suggested that the internal politics of coalition building best explains why various policy initiatives took the particular form that they did.

The matter is intricate, because policy is not to be understood as a consensus position between coalition partners nor as a simple dividing up of the spoils between winners. The wants of coalition members are drawn toward and constrained by the means through which coalition actions are coordinated. Just as organizational routines shape agency policy, so coordination "routines" shape coalition policy.

The enormous importance of housing efforts in the 1940s and 1950s and minority-business opportunities in the 1970s and 1980s suggests that the distribution of particular benefits is vital. Innovation is never easy. Side payments facilitate cooperation in a way that reasoned argument alone is unable to do. Not surprisingly, policies that provide an ample supply of side payments seem easier to promote — though, as we have seen, the Atlanta regime hardly reduces to that simple formula. Rather, the city's biracial coalition represents two change-oriented elements with broad policy aspirations. Although their efforts could have been stymied and their partnership severed, neither happened. The pursuit of policies that afforded opportunities for selective incentives is an important explanation. But there are other considerations as well, including trust between the partners and forces within both elements of the coalition that promote their internal cohesion.

In conclusion, is Atlanta exceptional? Atlanta's pattern of policy initiatives is not enormously dissimilar from that of several other large cities, but there are differences. Atlanta is decidedly less progressive than some and more uncritically responsive to investors than may be typical. It is also more attentive to the interests of the black middle class than is frequently the case. But what sets Atlanta apart most clearly is the effectiveness of the governing coalition in furthering its agenda despite opposition and an occasional electoral setback. Cumulatively, the governing coalition has compiled an impressive record of massively changing land use, building costly and controversial projects, casting off resistance to desegregation, and incorporating the black middle class into the city's mainstream economic and civic life. If Atlanta is exceptional, its exceptionalism lies primarily in the strength and ability of its governing coalition to carry out an activist agenda in the face of resistance and opposition.

PART THREE
ANALYSIS

With an account of postwar Atlanta now complete, we can turn to the analysis of that experience. Since the focus of the narrative was the development and evolution of the city's regime, it is perhaps in order for me to repeat the general definition of an urban regime and explain some of the implications of that definition for the analysis that follows.

Chapter 1 defined an urban regime as the informal arrangements by which public bodies and private interests function together to make and carry out governing decisions. There are three elements in this definition: (1) a *capacity* to do something; (2) a *set of actors* who do it; and (3) a *relationship* among the actors than enables them to work together.

The first element is *capacity*. A regime is identified by its ability to *make and carry out governing decisions.* I have maintained that the formal authority of government, standing alone, is inadequate for this task. There is thus no command structure that furnishes the capacity to make and carry out governing decisions, and this capacity can vary in strength from time to time and place to place.

The second element is the *set of actors* who, when working together, have the capacity to govern. Since government cannot do it alone (nor can private institutions), the capacity requires both public and private actors. They combine informally the otherwise segmented capacities of governmental bodies and significant nongovernmental community institutions. As a practical matter, given the important resources and activities controlled by business organizations, business interests are almost certain to be one of the elements, which is why regimes are best understood as operating within a political-economy context. Since the set of actors possessing the capacity to make governing decisions represents varied interests, it is appropriate to refer to them as the *governing coalition*. They are diverse actors brought together in the activity of governing.

The third element in the definition is the *relationship* among the actors—how they function together. If they are *not* unified under the formal authority of government to command compliance, then the mechanism of coordination must be *informal*. A crucial question thus becomes how cooperation is achieved. On this point, explanation beyond the bare bones of definition might be helpful.

One possible basis for cooperation is devotion to a common cause, but as a practical matter, such devotion is unlikely to be the only factor. A cause general enough to unite a sufficient body of actors to form a governing coalition is probably too general to guide the behavior of coalition members in a disciplined fashion. And, indeed, a coalition may be largely pragmatic rather than ideological, Atlanta being an apt example.

More specific motivators are likely to play an important part. Reciprocity, for example, is a basic and recurring type of interaction,[1] but it comes in many forms. It might consist of explicit and specified exchanges; however, cooperation in this form lacks flexibility, and transaction costs are high.[2] Tacit and imprecise exchanges are more flexible, but they require a relationship of trust and tend to build up only gradually. Thus, an activity such as expansion of housing for Atlanta blacks in the immediate postwar years can be enormously useful in coalition building; through repeated transactions, trust and confidence in reliability grow. Stable and proven forms of exchange have a potential to be stronger and more flexible than ad hoc ones. Because they represent valued relationships not easily duplicated, established types of exchange and cooperation represent what economists call "sunk costs."[3] Partners in such arrangements are reluctant to give them up and indeed have an incentive to reinforce these relationships.

Reciprocity thus blends into other supports for cooperation—mutual loyalty in particular. No doubt loyalty rests on several foundations, but one of them, in the case of a governing coalition, is that the partners in an alliance need to be able to count on one another to contribute to the *combined* capacity to govern. Indeed, it is helpful if they have a significant degree of loyalty to the governing arrangements themselves, which need not take an abstract form. It need be no more than a set of individuals who are accustomed to cooperating, who are confident that they can rely on one another, and who believe that it is proper to maintain these relationships. The machine politicians of yesteryear, for example, put great stock in loyalty, which they believed was owed to fellow members of an in-group (not always the entire party organization).

Reciprocity and loyalty do not necessarily stand alone. Often they are related to the usefulness of norms in making relationships dependable and reliable.[4] Individuals can be inducted into a system of cooperation quickly by adherence to simple (and often amoral) norms, such as "not making waves." Among coalition members, there may be two levels of norms: (1) those that hold *within* constituent elements of the coalition (e.g., business adherence to the norm of corporate responsibility); and (2) those that hold *between* constituent partners in the alliance (e.g., "go along to get along").

In the relationship among members of a governing coalition, sunk costs in a system of cooperation contribute to stability and adaptability in the partnership. Action Forum in Atlanta, for example, could rapidly become an effective new medium of biracial interaction because it rested on long years of informal exchange, mediated through the mayor's office—first under Hartsfield and later under Allen. Although Action Forum itself marked a change (a step toward more direct dealings between white business leaders and key figures in the black community), it still was an extension of long-established relationships.

In Chapter 1, I used the term "structuring" to emphasize that even relatively durable relationships undergo a continuing process of modification. Biracial cooperation in Atlanta clearly illustrates that pattern. When such relationships display stability, it is because some number of actors are investing time and resources in sustaining and adapting them. Though useful in promoting cooperation, stability is not self-perpetuating; it requires effort and a degree of ingenuity in devising appropriate modifications.

The line between change and continuity in a regime is thus not sharply defined. Adaptations serve stability, but they also modify the original relationship. Does Atlanta in the period between 1946 and 1988, then, represent one regime or a succession of regimes? I regard it as a single regime, because the central membership of the coalition remained constant and the basic mode of promoting cooperation stayed the same. Yet important changes took place. The influence of the black partners in the coalition expanded enormously. And particularly as the racial control of city hall changed, the white partners came to rely more heavily on CAP as an organization, as well as on the head of that organization (Dan Sweat) to personally serve as both advocate of business interests and mediating agent between business executives and black leaders.

Because a regime is a mixture of continuity and change, the characterization imposed—adaptations in a single regime versus a succession of related regimes—is inevitably somewhat arbitrary, a fact I acknowledge. Thus, although postwar Atlanta is treated here as a single regime going through adaptations, the reader should be mindful that the changes that occurred were not inconsequential.

To describe regimes as a mixture of continuity and change implies that they lack sharp boundaries. If so, does the term "urban regime" refer to something real in the actual community experience? In the analysis that follows, I will try to show that regimes are conceptually important. But I also believe that they are concrete, that the idea of regime is not superimposed without regard to actual experience.

The preceding forty-year narrative should provide several illustrations of why I believe that some notion of regime is evident in the conscious behavior of community actors. But one particularly revealing example is that members of Atlanta's governing coalition regard Maynard Jackson's mayoralty as a time of great conflict, while Andrew Young's mayoralty is regarded as a time of accord. That perception arises from the fact that the Jackson administration was a period of high intraregime conflict; Jackson personally, with considerable electoral backing, was inclined toward a progressive stance that placed him at odds with the business elite and put the regime under great stress. By contrast, Young established a close relationship with the business elite. Yet there was high *extraregime* conflict. Struggle with neighborhood groups and preservationists ensued; the Young administration suffered occasional setbacks; many issues involved close votes and intense debate in the city council; and prolonged litigation surrounded the Presidential Parkway in particular. Still, because Young's opposition came from outside the governing coalition, the capacity of the regime to govern was unimpaired and Young is perceived by many insiders as enjoying a harmonious administration. These characterizations of the two mayoralties can rest only on a conception of regime as the governing arrangement for the community.

9

Atlanta's Urban Regime

Nothing makes a prince so much esteemed as to carry on great enterprises.
— Machiavelli

No group is wise enough, good enough, strong enough to assume an omnipotent and omniscient role.
— Dr. Benjamin Mays

The present chapter builds directly on the previous one, but instead of looking at the particulars of policy innovation, it confronts the issue of how Atlanta's governing coalition could prevail over alternative alliances, both of the caretaker[1] and progressive types.[2] In short, it addresses questions at the level of the whole regime — for example, why one governing coalition (with relatively narrow and unsteady popular support) formed and held sway over its challengers for more than forty years. This chapter also considers how the Atlanta regime was able to pursue successfully an activist agenda.

URBAN REGIMES

To understand the durability and effectiveness of Atlanta's regime, we need to examine the ways in which public bodies and private interests function together in governing a community. Because these arrangements form in a political-economy context, regimes need to bridge the principle of popular control of governmental office on the one side and the community's need for an appreciable level of business activity on the other.[3] This political-economy context is a constraint but not a precise determinant. The accord between the electoral and economic sectors of the community can take varied forms. To focus on the character of this bridge, I find it useful to conceive of community life as containing a third, or civic, sector — one that consists of the terms on which cooperation between public bodies and private interests are worked out.

Consider some possible forms that the political-economy accord can take. The business elite itself could dominate elective office, employing professional city management to run the government on a day-to-day basis. For a time, San Antonio[4] and Dallas[5] approximated this pattern. The accommodation was achieved on terms that involved minimal tension because, informally, business and political leadership were the same.

The classic urban machine — a regime in which professional politicians make a career of cultivating constituency electoral support — offers a different scenario. Ward politicians, especially those tied closely to small property holders, may pursue essentially a caretaker role and in the process offer large firms, particularly in manufacturing, what they most want: low taxes.[6] An accommodation may thus be partly tacit, in the sense that politically connected small property holders and large but politically inactive business firms may share policy preferences. Hence, major economic enterprises may enjoy an acceptable policy agenda without having to work actively for it. Manufacturing firms that want minimum taxation and minimum civic responsibilities may be able to achieve their aim by locating outside the city or in a congenial region of the country.[7] Of course, some businesses lack easy mobility,[8] and circumstances change for others. For example, the noninvolvement of an economic elite may itself become an issue, as when the civil-rights movement came to Birmingham.[9]

Numerous variations are possible. Small property holders may be electorally dominant without the intermediary of ward politicians,[10] or professional politicians may form an alliance with the economic elite, not around caretaker policies, but around an activist program of redevelopment — as in Chicago[11] and Pittsburgh.[12] Caretaker regimes solve the problem of civic cooperation — the coordination of efforts across institutional lines — by minimizing the need for it. A few appropriate norms or conventions that serve to keep divisive issues off the agenda and that adhere to a "psychology of scarcity," as in small towns,[13] can maintain public harmony. Since little is being done, no complicated forms of coordination and no broad bases of resource mobilization are called for. But that arrangement is not viable in many circumstances.

The continuing process of change, especially the impact of the automobile on older central cities, provides an incentive for downtown businesses to pursue their collective interest in an activist policy. That was the impetus behind the formation of the predecessor to CAP in Atlanta in 1941 and the formation of similar groups in other cities, such as the Greater Baltimore Committee,[14] the Vault in Boston,[15] and the Bay Area Council in San Francisco.[16] Boosterism and low taxes are the most unifying positions for associations with diverse business membership, but such stances do not fit the activist agenda that major downtown businesses in Atlanta and other cities often have in mind. Hence, an organization separate from the chamber of commerce may be useful for articulating and acting on the collective interests of downtown property holders. These are businesses large and wealthy enough to absorb the shocks of guided change in pursuit of greater long-term stability and prosperity. In short, banks, utilities, and major department stores play a different scale of game from that played by small merchants. For large businesses with local ties, the stakes are bigger and the wherewithal to participate is greater.

Although large downtown businesses possess a collective interest, it is not foreordained that they will cohere into an organization to pursue this shared interest. In Albuquerque, for example, individual, free-wheeling entrepreneurs dominate development in a manner that pays little heed to collective aims.[17] New fast-growing cities, not confined to old boundaries, may provide less incentive to organize for collective action on a redevelopment agenda. Or, businesses in such cities may have limited opportunity to work out norms of cooperation; as Axelrod has suggested, it may be that more open environments with transitory conditions are not very conducive to norms of cooperation.[18] Opportunistic practices may arise, then, in which political brokers arrange ad hoc agreements between particular parties around specific decisions.[19]

As this brief look at urban regimes indicates, the civic sector is interwoven with the electoral and economic sectors of a community's institutional life. The form that civic cooperation takes is influenced by who makes up the electorate, how citizens are associated, and how they are mobilized, as well as by what kinds of businesses make up the local economy and how they are associated. If the electoral, economic, and civic sectors are not discrete spheres of activity, why distinguish them? The answer is that separating the three elements of community political life serves to highlight some important points and perhaps facilitate cross-city comparisons. It may also emphasize that winning elections is not the same as being able to govern.[20] As we have seen in the case of Atlanta, electoral victories and defeats are an unreliable indicator of who participates in the governing coalition. A governing coalition needs to be able to promote economic activity and achieve civic cooperation as well as win elections, and in Atlanta, elected officeholders have been unable to accomplish that without allying with the downtown elite.

Distinguishing the three sectors also helps to stress that the business elite, as in the case of Atlanta, may extend its involvement well beyond the sphere of economic activity.[21] Few statements about urban politics miss the mark wider than Nelson Polsby's rendition of pluralist assumptions about social differentiation: "If a man's major life work is banking, the pluralist presumes he will spend his time at the bank, and not in manipulating community decisions."[22] Polsby saves himself by adding, "This presumption holds until the banker's activities and participations indicate otherwise."[23]

By treating activities as having three different dimensions, we can see how bankers and other members of Atlanta's downtown elite operate in a far wider sphere than simply economic participation. Indeed, when an Atlanta bank sets up a special fund for community development loans or embarks on a specific program of providing loans to minority entrepreneurs, those activities spill over into the civic sphere (and thereby indirectly into the electoral sphere). And, when the business elite constitutes the principal source of campaign funds, it is a direct and significant factor in the electoral sphere, thus encouraging cooperation across institutional lines.

SELECTIVE INCENTIVES AND
CIVIC COOPERATION IN ATLANTA

The electoral and economic spheres are standard enough topics not to require additional discussion here. Instead, I will concentrate on civic cooperation as a dimension of the governance of urban communities. After some preliminary observations about the general nature of civic cooperation, I will consider how that cooperation has occurred in Atlanta and has helped establish the character of the city's regime.

First, let me offer a brief sketch of the problem of collective action, which has been explored at length elsewhere.[24] One aspect of the issue has been described as the free-rider problem.[25] The individual who acts as a utility-maximizer has little incentive to make personal sacrifice (of time, money, inconvenience, etc.) on behalf of the groups to which he or she belongs. Often the effort of a single individual makes no appreciable difference in the outcome of a collective endeavor, and the sacrifice asked of the individual may be out of proportion to the gain *that can be attributed to the action of that individual.* Hence, every individual has an incentive to be a free rider and let the sacrifice of others determine the outcome.

The traditional solution to the collective-action problem has been selective incentives; that is, to supplement group benefits by a system of individual rewards and punishments administered so as to support group aims. Those who go along with the group by paying dues, respecting picket lines, and so on, receive individual rewards and services; those who do not lose valuable benefits or incur sanctions. Voluntary efforts are thus complemented by inducements or coercion, individually applied.

Because not everyone is narrowly opportunistic, selective incentives are not the whole story of collective action.[26] Efforts on behalf of a group purpose may be intrinsically satisfying. Thus political movements and other activities heavily dependent on volunteer efforts rely on emotional commitment to motivate adherents.[27] Volunteer activities may afford opportunities for sociability or identity with a larger group or purpose, which are not dependent on an external system of rewards and punishments.[28] And if adherence to group obligations is widespread enough, norms or conventions of cooperation may prevail over individual opportunism.

At the same time, selective incentives are enormously important. Machine politics, for example, entails an extensive use of selective incentives; providing a form of discipline that reliance on emotional commitment does not offer. One ward politician expressed his disdain for loyalties based on emotional sentiment, suggesting that volunteers dedicated to a cause have little staying power: "What I look for in a prospective captain . . . is a young person—man or woman—who is interested in getting some material return out of his political activity. I much prefer this type to the type that is enthused about the 'party cause' or all 'hot' on a particular issue. Enthusiasm for causes is short-lived, but the necessity of making a living is permanent."[29] The redoubtable George Washington Plunkitt long ago wrote off social reformers as nothing more than "mornin' glories" because they "can't last"; they only "make a show for a while."[30] Emotional commitment has thus long been regarded as inferior to selective material incentives as a way of building a durable political organization.

The reliability of material incentives is presumably what gave the old-style urban organizations their ability to deliver votes with mechanical certainty. To be sure, city machines did not rely on a single motive,[31] but the use of selective incentives did provide discipline and reinforcement for a core of workers that enabled them to prevail over less-disciplined reformers for many years. Furthermore, the machine style of organization proved adaptable enough to accommodate a variety of regimes, from free-spending distributors of patronage to the penurious, from mobilizers of the immigrant masses to defenders of the small property holder, from caretakers to activist remakers of the urban landscape.[32]

Because selective material incentives can be combined with various forms of emotional commitment and group appeal, political organizations that include a substantial reliance on selective incentives have the potential for solving the collective-action problem, which organizations dependent on group incentives alone lack. Moreover, selective incentives can bridge diverse groups by minimizing the issues that divide and building cooperation around those that unite.[33] For example, redevelopment in Atlanta has been an enormously divisive issue from the 1940s to the present, but selective incentives have enabled the biracial governing coalition to cohere while dividing the opposition. Thus selective incentives shape the lines of cooperation and conflict even in difficult situations.

The Atlanta experience brings us from the general problem of collective action to the particular task of civic cooperation at the city level. Here the point is that the task varies; not all urban regimes face the same degree of difficulty in governing the community. A regime devoted to a caretaker style of governance has a much less demanding task than does a regime devoted to an activist style of governance; maintenance of traditional services needs only minimal effort and adherence to a set of conventions or norms that reinforce passivity. The burden of coordinating activity falls mostly on those who would challenge an agenda of routine service provision. Unlike the guardians of a caretaker regime, challengers cannot simply make group appeals to established conventions or norms. They must actively marshal individuals who desire change but who are often unsure that the attempt can succeed or that their own efforts will make a difference. Challengers to a caretaker regime thus face a more profound free-rider problem than do its guardians. Passive support or simple adherence to a convention that is generally accepted costs the individual relatively little and causes minimal strain between individual and group interests; organized opposition is a different matter.

An activist regime confronts a more substantial task. In order to pursue a program such as redevelopment, a governing coalition must be able to sustain efforts by a variety of actors and to ensure that the high level of coordination needed for complicated projects is achieved, sometimes in the face of controversy. These projects typically require a series of immediate efforts and expenditures with delayed returns; risks and short-term inconveniences are often the price of success. As Pressman and Wildavsky have argued, the complexity of joint action stands as a significant barrier to effective program implementation.[34] Policies, such as redevelopment, that require complicated joint action pose potentially major strains between individual interests and group advancement. In these instances, free-rider and related shirking problems are quite profound. It is therefore not surprising that regimes with an ample supply of selective material incentives, such as Chicago under Mayor Daley, have successfully pursued aggressive programs of redevelopment. Much the same could be said of Boston under Kevin White[35] or the Robert Moses empire in New York.[36] Interestingly, both Moses and White started as reformers and embraced machine-style selective incentives in order to conduct active programs of development.

By combining the types of incentive systems and the nature of the civic-cooperation task, a fourfold table of urban regimes and potential regimes for Atlanta emerges (see Table 9.1). The examples illustrate that Atlanta has had experience with a variety of regimes and potential regimes — reminders that postwar efforts to return Atlanta to the caretaker pattern of the early twentieth century were an unsuccessful but not insignificant part of Atlanta's political experience. The protest period of the 1960s again represented a challenge to the governing coalition, but protest groups were unable to constitute themselves into a stable coalition. The lack of selective incentives was accompanied by an absence of discipline; hence, protests never became more

Table 9.1   Incentive System

	selective incentives plus	group appeals only
simple civic cooperation task	early twentieth-century Atlanta	small property holders & neighborhood defenders of status quo in 1940s & 1950s
complex civic cooperation task	business elite/ black middle class	student, Black Power, & neighboorhood protests of the 1960s

than outlets for expressing discontent. Like the good-government reformers of Plunkitt's day, they were "mornin' glories" and failed to become a viable regime.

Axelrod's game-theory research suggests that entities able to cooperate with one another can prevail in competition with those unable to establish cooperative relationships.[37] The Atlanta experience is consistent with that view. Thus protest groups—typically mobilized by accentuating differences or, as the late Saul Alinsky said, "rub[bing] raw the sores of discontent"[38]— have had no success in establishing themselves as central elements in durable coalitions. They have demonstrated little capacity to put together a network for cooperation, relying instead on the intensity of resentment for what inevitably becomes ad hoc mobilization efforts. In contrast to protest groups, the business elite/black middle-class coalition has extensive selective incentives available as they face their complex task of civic cooperation. The table thus suggests that selective incentives are indeed vital to the establishment and maintenance of a regime, especially if it undertakes an activist policy agenda.

The progressive coalition brought together in the election of Maynard Jackson does not fit neatly into any of the four categories, and it is not included in the table. With two-thirds of the city council elected by district, an NPU system enacted and a body of neighborhood civic associations in place, and city hall in a position to decide which minority enterprises were eligible as genuinely minority-controlled, the potential for extensive use of selective incentives by the progressive coalition was considerable. However, the potential was not realized.

To be sure, some selective incentives were available, but any move toward large-scale use of them was stoutly resisted by the business elite. The newspapers and business organizations scrutinized exercises of mayoral discretion for hints of what they regarded as "power grabbing." Any attempt to reward friends and punish enemies was vulnerable to vocal criticism. For their part, neighborhood associations working with the Citywide League of Neighborhoods could and did respond to individual service requests, but the NPU system itself was under close guard to ensure that it did not become involved in electoral politics or in any action that could be linked to voter mobilization. Therefore, the NPU system could not be used to build a wide network of allies. Similarly, the awarding of city contracts was watched critically, unless it came into the orbit of coalition building between the mayor and the downtown business elite, as eventually was the case with the development of the new Atlanta airport.

The business elite also lobbied to create a public-private Atlanta Economic Development Corporation, not under the direct control of city hall. To the extent that it supplanted the mayor's own office of economic development, this entity gave the business community a direct say in how benefits would be distributed. As this example illustrates, much of the business opposition to Maynard Jackson was simply resistance to any move on his part that did not include the business community as a voice in the distribution of benefits. The progressive coalition under Maynard Jackson's leadership thus *found itself restricted in its capacity to become an autonomous source of selective benefits.*

Since selective benefits can come from the private sector as well as from strictly governmental auspices, business resistance to Maynard Jackson's leadership was more than personal sentiment or ideology. It was an effort to preserve a base of business influence. Stated another way, it was an effort to preserve intact a form of civic cooperation centered on the downtown business elite. Selective incentives are more than a means for achieving civic cooperation; they are also an object of struggle. *Control of selective incentives is a significant factor in determining which alignment of groups will be best able to press its case as the community's governing coalition.*

The extent to which the business elite has successfully restricted the range of selective benefits distributed under the auspices of public authority gives the regime in Atlanta a distinctive character. By linking the control of selective benefits to the private sector, the business elite has maintained itself as the centerpiece in the community's network of civic cooperation. Thus, the kind of discipline that enables the regime to execute highly complex tasks of coordination is present but is not directly connected to the electoral sector. It is largely in the hands of the business sector, which concentrates the capacity to promote regime durability and effectiveness in private hands and links it closely to local investors.

Considering how the Atlanta regime is constituted, it is understandable that investors are accorded a wide prerogative and that alternative regimes have difficulty gaining a foothold. Without the membership of the business elite, a governing coalition has little capacity to bring about civic cooperation and govern effectively. Although standpat forces in the immediate postwar years pursued a goal of caretaker government that in itself involved no great task of coordination, they lacked the resources to build the kind of biracial coalition needed to gain control of government in the first place. A mobilized black electorate precluded domination of city politics by whites alone. Since the black constituency was led by a change-oriented and institutionally connected middle class, a caretaker coalition was unlikely. An educated and ambitious black middle class found little common ground with small property holders and status-quo-minded leaders in the white community. After all, in the 1940s and 1950s, the status quo was one of segregation and highly restricted opportunity. In the 1980s, the status quo is less confining, but preservationists and defenders of the quality of residential life do not have much to offer the black middle class as an inducement to an alliance.

Just as major white businesses had the resources to play a game of guided change, so too did the institutionally connected, black middle class. Furthermore, not only did the black middle class and the white business elite share a willingness to pursue change, but they also represented the most highly organized segments of the community. As potential coalition partners, each entered the contest with much of its collective-action problem solved through existing organizations. As a governing coalition, they needed only to bring about a modest degree of federation among existing organizations.[39] Hence, they faced a less arduous mobilization task than did their standpat foes.

Maynard Jackson's progressive alliance gained control of city hall and, with the Citywide League electorally and the NPU system programmatically, had a chance to become the city's governing coalition. However, business control of selective incentives and other key resources weakened Jackson's leadership in the black community and left the mayor with few means for disciplining the neighborhood movement as a partner in the city's governing coalition.

Important as individual rewards and deprivations are, they are not the whole account of promoting successful cooperation. The full extent of the Atlanta business elite's capacity to serve as the guiding hand in the civic sector goes beyond a narrow version of selective incentives. To explore this capacity more fully, we need to consider the several ways in which business is able to promote cooperation across institutional boundaries.

ATLANTA'S BUSINESS ELITE
AND CIVIC COOPERATION

The breadth of community activities in which Atlanta's economic elite takes part perhaps makes it extraordinary. Aside from the usual array of fund drives and luncheon clubs its members head or belong to, the business elite has long provided a framework for promoting biracial contacts and cooperation through such organizations as the Action Forum. It supplies funding and staff for public-private ventures (such as the redevelopment of Underground) and the preparation of programs of action (as in Central Area Study I and II). In the early postwar years, the Metropolitan Planning Commission — the initial proponent of redevelopment — was itself supported partly by private funding from business. CAP has also supported and endorsed grant proposals from such groups as the Atlanta Preservation Center, and it took the initiative in forming the Midtown Business Association.

The downtown elite also underwrites policy analysis through the sponsorship of Research Atlanta, a nonprofit organization engaged in timely studies of issues. The major newspaper is an integral part of the business elite, and it can play up or play down an issue. Similarly, it can give editorial endorsement, or it can ridicule a proposal and berate its backers. Through the Metropolitan Community Foundation, other foundations established by individual business leaders, and various ad hoc efforts (some of which are guided by CAP), the downtown business elite is engaged in an array of projects and programs.

In short, if one is seeking credit, donations, technical expertise, prestigious endorsements, organizational support, business contacts, media backing, or in-depth analyses of problems, then very likely one is thrown into contact with the civic network that emanates from the activities of the downtown business elite. The easiest way to attain an objective is to enlist the support of this far-reaching network. That also means that the objectives most easily attained are the ones the downtown business elite will support. Of course, not every group seeking help obtains it. Not every candidate soliciting campaign funds receives them, nor is every minority businessperson asked to become a joint-venture partner. By preserving wide investor prerogative and drawing on a broad array of business-provided benefits, Atlanta enables the downtown business elite to promote civic cooperation on the basis of "go along to get along." Those terms are well understood.[40]

Starting with the substantial capacity that its own unified membership represents, the economic elite is able to enlist a substantial body of allies, particularly those holding public office. Maynard Jackson's frustrations in trying to work independently of the downtown business establishment provided a vivid lesson. That lesson was not wasted on either his successor, Mayor Andrew Young, or Young's contemporaries — City Council President Marvin Arrington, Fulton County Commission Chairman Michael Lomax, City Council Finance Committee Chair Ira Jackson, and many others. These elected officials also play by the rule "go along to get along." The mayor could, for example, improve the reelection chances of a vulnerable white city councilmember, running at-large, by introducing her at black churches — as Young did in the 1985 election. City Council President Marvin Arrington can reward supporters by naming them to chair council committees, and he can deprive noncooperators of such positions — as he did with neighborhood advocate and champion of financial disclosure, John Lewis. Thus, consistent opposition can be costly, while going along can be beneficial.

As the circle of cooperating allies grows, its effectiveness becomes cumulatively greater. The governing coalition has a kind of gravitational pull; as its own weight increases, its capacity to attract other civic entities increases. As the network of civic cooperation makes its presence felt, others realize that cooperation pays and noncooperation does not. That is what "go along to get along" means, and it constitutes an effective form of discipline based on the selective-incentive principle. So long as the network of cooperators is large enough in its own right and has no rival network to serve as an alternative, there are significant gains to be made by going along and opportunity costs to be paid for opposition.

The situation is broader than rewards and deprivations for individuals, because not just personal opportunities are at issue. It extends to the wider question of how to further projects and promote policy initiatives. Advancing a project or program typically requires many forms of support: money from several sources, endorsements, favorable publicity, and help from those knowledgeable about how to maneuver around a variety of technical and legal pitfalls. Business in Atlanta has no monopoly on any of these, but it is a likely source for all of them. Moreover, business in Atlanta encompasses personal and informal networks that have long and successful experience in bringing together all of the needed forms of support on behalf of civic activity. Thus, they have the record and the reputation of being "the leadership that works."

Coordination of effort on behalf of various projects and programs is only one side of the Atlanta story. The other side is the question of why opposition (especially over huge projects with many ripple effects) never cumulates into an alternative governing coalition. If opposition is widespread and recurring, why does it not lead to a new regime, more in line with popular support? The answer has to do with what I call the "small opportunities" phenomenon,[41] which means that most people most of the time are guided, not by a grand vision of how the world might be reformed, but by the pursuit of particular opportunities. The point is not self-interest over altruism, since altruists also pursue small opportunities — perhaps a nonprofit housing venture, a community theater, a job-training program, saving a black business from financial setback, conservation of park land, a food bank for the hungry, a historic preservation ordinance, or an arts festival.

A group or governing coalition that has a capacity to further small opportunities on go-along-to-get-along terms is in a strong position to attract allies rather than activate opponents. Opposition is costly and gives the term "opportunity costs" special meaning in this context. Therefore, the more concentrated and effective a capacity to further projects is, the harder it is to resist.

If the downtown business elite were less cohesive, its attractiveness as an ally would be diminished. If its resources were less aggressively deployed in building a network of civic cooperation, it would also be less attractive as an ally. It is helpful, then, to realize that the network of civic cooperation is itself a resource for governing the community — a secondary resource, not in its importance (indeed, it is primary on that count), but in the sense that it is built out of other resources. The downtown business elite, *as a unified group*, is able to build that kind of derivative power base, whereas no other group in the community can. The others do not have the range and depth of resources needed for such an effort.

Because the downtown elite is so highly cohesive and because the civic network it has built is both cohesive and wide ranging, alliance with this business elite is a unifying force. It overcomes much of the personal rivalry between officeholders; it knits together what might otherwise be competing agendas of action; and it downplays potentially conflicting ideologies among elective officials. In a nonpartisan setting with no party discipline, politicians typically make their way individually. In appealing to a mass public, they have an incentive to sharpen their ideological images. What counters these otherwise centrifugal tendencies is the cohesive power of the business-centered network of civic cooperation.[42]

For elected officials, alliance with business is not just unifying; it is empowering. Of course, the empowering is contingent. In the hands of a small and cohesive business elite, the concentration of resources useful for civic cooperation benefits political leaders who pursue policies acceptable to business. As Maynard Jackson learned, that concentration of resources can hobble those whose goals are unacceptable to major business interests. Business leaders cannot prevent the formulation of antagonistic policies or veto particular proposals, but a cohesive business elite of the kind that has developed in Atlanta can withhold its capacity to promote civic cooperation from unacceptable policy directions. Without the discipline that accompanies business backing, most policy efforts soon founder.

In the case of Atlanta, the downtown elite not only has a unifying impact on political officeholders, but has also helped shape leadership within the black community. From the 1940s embarkation on a policy of replacement housing for blacks, to the contemporary promotion of joint-venture arrangements, the efforts of the downtown business elite have expanded the number and influence of black businesses and entrepreneurs. Business deals are and have been a major element in the overall network of civic cooperation. Indeed, the network is quite conducive to business activities and fosters their development.

It would be an overstatement to suggest that the white business elite has created a black leadership in its own image, but it is no exaggeration that the network of civic cooperation pulls black leadership strongly in that direction. The result is that the city's elected black officials drive few hard bargains with the white business elite, because an important part of their own constituency is oriented toward concerns shared by the white business elite. The network of civic cooperation is not simply an instrument for promoting coordination in complex projects; the network shapes the very ethos of community participation.

The downtown business elite has thus been attractive as a governing partner and has also used its resources to mold its allies, thereby profoundly influencing the nature of the regime. Reciprocity and its components — the extensive use of selective incentives, deal making, and protection of wide investor prerogatives — have been integral to the expansion of business opportunities for blacks and the emergence of black entrepreneurs. The point is that reciprocity is not just a way of cooperating on specific issues; the constituent elements of reciprocity are also activities that help fashion the character of civic life. To be sure, participation in the governing task and the quest for allies have also had an effect on the business elite, broadening its understanding of what constitutes a favorable economic climate.

UNDERSTANDING BUSINESS POWER IN ATLANTA

The downtown business elite is the key to regime durability and effectiveness in Atlanta. The control that business displays in Atlanta is not command power;[43] it is more indirect. It is the power to occupy a central place in the city's governing coalition in the face of changing national and local conditions. This power is limited in several ways: (1) It is shared with coalition partners; (2) it consists of a capacity to respond to changing conditions, not to determine what will and will not change; and (3) the set of arrangements through which the governing coalition is held together has maintenance needs, which themselves help to shape policy independent of the personal preferences of coalition members. Thus the downtown elite cannot do what it wills; it can only position itself as part of the arrangements through which governance occurs. Elite power in Atlanta is therefore constrained, not so much by the countervailing power of others outside the coalition as by the maintenance needs of the governing coalition itself.

If simple business dominance is not the key to Atlanta's regime, what is? The explanation is best accomplished in several steps, focusing both on the fact of coalition and on the special role of the downtown elite in promoting cooperation. Within a political-economy context, the two coalition partners offer resources that are understood to be complementary: The business elite provides access to investment activity while the black middle class provides electoral leadership. Combined, they form the two major institutional sectors of community life; however, that is only one facet of regime building.

The coalition partners also represent compatible demands. Although they have particular differences, both have embraced policy change: business, in order to adapt the central business district to the impact of the automobile and other dispersing trends; the black middle class, in order to move beyond the days of Jim Crow exclusion. The two elements in the coalition also are amenable to discipline that promotes cooperation. In the case of the business elite, small size, homogeneity of interest and background, and substantial continuity of membership (sometimes across generations, other times provided by traditions within companies to practice "corporate responsibility" to the community) maintain norms of unity and participation. The practice of investor prerogative protects these norms by minimizing the pressure to deviate. Selective benefits and the collective good of a successful alliance with a cohesive business elite provide discipline for the black middle class, more numerous and less homogeneous than its business partner.

Further, transaction-cost economics tells us that an established relationship has an advantage over new relationships.[44] Demonstrated loyalty, tacit knowledge useful in bargaining with familiar partners, and a broad base of mutual understanding encourage the preservation of a working relationship over the search for new partners. In Atlanta, both elements of the governing coalition have developed a durable attachment to their shared alliance.

Any list of explanations is incomplete, however, if it implies a static situation of matching partners. The drama in Atlanta has been and remains dynamic; the partners have shaped each other and contributed to mutual complementarity, compatability, and discipline. Yet the interaction between the two has not been based on equality. Despite black electoral gains, the business elite has had the greater maneuverability and the larger store of resources from which to solve the dual problem of promoting its own internal unity and securing allies who are dependably cooperative.

After all, private ownership of business enterprise confers a resource advantage on the investor class. In Atlanta, this group has used its resources with diligence and skill to cumulate them into still other advantages. In this way, it has assured that the whole of its influence is greater than the sum of its parts. The structural leverage that comes through private ownership can thus be magnified and protected by concrete steps, which, in Atlanta, have consisted of the creation, elaboration, and reinforcement of a still-evolving network of civic cooperation. By putting itself at the center of the community's only wide-scale system of cooperation, the business elite makes itself an indispensable partner in the city's governing coalition. Public officials can govern *with* the grain of business cooperation but cannot govern very effectively against that grain. Incorporation into the business system of civic cooperation is thus empowering, and that fact makes alliance with the downtown elite strongly attractive to public officials and others in the community as well.

The sphere of civic cooperation emphasizes the multifaceted character of business power. The ability to make or withhold investment capital is important, as is being a major source of campaign funds, especially early money. But for us, the sphere of civic cooperation highlights the complex character of business power and *the considerable extent to which that power is contingent on an active and politically effective use of primary resources.* The business elite lacks the supremacy of numbers, but it is able to make itself nearly indispensable to those who can mobilize voters and win mass elections. Its resources and skills enable it to amplify its influence by three steps:

1. It can instill a groupwide view within its own membership; i.e., it is able to heighten its own class consciousness and promote its own class unity.

2. It can use reciprocity in the form of selective incentives and advancement of small opportunities to encourage cooperation from its allies. Cooperation becomes something that community actors cannot disregard or free-ride on, and "going along" offers strong attractions that often override inconveniences, misgivings, and potential indifference.

3. By building a network of civic cooperation, the downtown business elite can offer an empowering relationship to those able to win electoral support. Partnership with the business elite offers the appeal of a coalition able to get things done. Although the casual observer may not see this civic role as overtly political, it does in fact profoundly shape the city's politics.

There is certainly much that Atlanta's business elite cannot do alone, but there is not much of an activist agenda that can be accomplished without its cooperation. The reason is that, even though Atlanta's business elite has no power of command over the community at large and can be defeated on any given issue, it is nevertheless too valuable an ally—especially for those who are oriented to change and accomplishment—to be left out of the picture.

Business control of investment activity is certainly a major component of business influence, but the issue does not end there. Private ownership of major business enterprise entails an enormous store of "slack" resources, and those slack resources are of great *political* value. The economic purpose of business should not obscure the fact that business is also able to play an active political role. Although some businesses do not have a strong incentive to engage actively in local politics, others do. Businesses can, of course, participate in a variety of ways. They may enter individually, as developers with interests in particular sites often do. Atlanta illustrates another possibility; those with collective interests may join together formally and informally and press the case for their shared concerns. CAP is such an organization—of, by, and for the major holders of property in downtown Atlanta.

Politically active businesses can also pursue several strategies for exerting influence. Developers, for instance, often act directly by buying access through campaign contributions or, in some cases, by illicit payments to officeholders.

Such direct forms of influence may predominate, but again Atlanta illustrates a different pattern—Atlanta's downtown elite has invested heavily in shaping the local regime itself.

In most communities, business leaders invest resources in a network of civic organizations and informal contacts through which they create a private capacity to cooperate and promote community projects. With extraordinary skill and vigor, Atlanta's business elite has accomplished that—and more. Having long recognized the value of black allies in the city's politics, they have put substantial resources into *creating a direct business tie with black business interests and other black leaders with important institutional affiliations.* White business leaders have also established working partnerships with local government and have done so throughout the post–World War II period; hence, the pattern of public-private partnership is nothing new to Atlanta.

CONCLUSION

Civic cooperation in Atlanta is a multifaceted process with the business elite at the center, not only tying together a variety of private resources and institutions but maintaining a biracial bridge and an ongoing business/government partnership. As business participation in the governing coalition is examined—and considering that business cannot go it alone—one is drawn to the fact that Atlanta's downtown business elite represents a concentration of resources that cannot be ignored. No other group commands resources that are comparable in quantity, in range, and in crucial importance. In the electoral arena, business supplies campaign funds, and the newspaper is a major source of communitywide communication. In the economic arena, business control of investment money and credit is vital. But the influence of business is more than a long list of particulars. The business elite has parlayed these specifics into the construction of a network of civic cooperation that itself is a major factor in the political life of the community. In understanding the Atlanta regime, it is important to recognize that a business-guided network of civic cooperation has an empowering capacity for those who "go along."

This network imbues the Atlanta regime with a means to achieve publicly significant results that an otherwise divided and fragmented system of authority could not provide. It is this network that makes alliance with the business elite especially attractive and that, through selective incentives and the advancement of small opportunities, draws public officials and different segments of the community into the business orbit of influence. At various points, when the electoral balance was shifting or the governing coalition seemed to be coming apart, the network of civic cooperation was the stabilizing force.

Because the business elite cannot pursue its activist agenda without the cooperation of government, adjustments to change have not been exclusively on business terms. The black middle class itself represents a substantial institutional capacity, especially when in control of city hall, and it has exerted a limited gravitational force of its own. That is why, as adjustment (structuring) has occurred, the business community has sought to constrain the capacity of city hall to provide special incentives and has worked to establish strong *private links* between the downtown elite and the black middle class. The downtown elite has consistently pursued a strategy of building regime effectiveness around privately controlled resources and limiting the potential for public bodies to act on their own.

That a means of coordinating efforts across institutional lines exists is itself important, especially since the direction of this system is lodged in private hands. Not being publicly accountable on criteria of fairness and equity, the network of civic cooperation strengthens the ability of the regime to produce results; those who do not "go along" can be readily disciplined. That situation, of course, raises other questions, including the ancient one about who will guard the guardians and by what criteria.

10

Equity and Effectiveness

A problem of institutional leadership, as of statesmanship generally, is to see that elites do exist and function while inhibiting their tendency to become sealed off and to be more concerned with their own fate than with that of the enterprise as a whole.

— Philip Selznick

The Atlanta regime works in such a way that the downtown elite is a privileged group. The special part that business leaders play is combined with a restricted role for popular participation. Difficulties in managing racial antagonism, especially that expressed by tradition-minded whites, have provided a rationale for limiting popular involvement. One local observer described the situation this way: "Atlanta's not run by public debate but by a sort of equal-opportunity elite. There is almost a fear of democracy: 'Look what democracy gave us. Lester Maddox.' It's the business people who really decide things."[1] The alternative to popular participation is behind-the-scenes negotiations among strategically placed individuals, many of whom have long-term institutional interests in the community. Consequently, politics in Atlanta "is virtually all 'handling'" — handling that grows out of the informal civic network centered in the downtown business elite.[2]

Maynard Jackson's experience as mayor suggests that, without a close partnership between city hall and the business elite, effective governance in Atlanta is difficult; impasse rather than action is likely. Is the community better or worse off because the downtown elite holds a special position in the city's politics? With business-elite involvement, the governing regime appears effective but not necessarily equitable.

Can a regime be both effective and equitable, or is a trade-off inescapable? Some would suggest the latter[3]; they sometimes believe that excessive concern with political equality and democratic participation makes for ungovernability and therefore a loss of effectiveness.[4] Yet there is a counterargument, and this chapter uses the Atlanta experience to illustrate it. Effectiveness is itself a complex phenomenon — too complex to constitute a simple trade-off with equity. Development policy in Atlanta offers an especially instructive case.

THE DEVELOPMENT AGENDA OF BUSINESS

What Atlanta's business elite wants is a vibrant central business district, complete with office towers and, to enhance its appeal as a convention city, an active and culturally rich nightlife. Since Atlanta has long been a regional headquarters town and never primarily a manufacturing place,[5] that economic development strategy makes sense.[6] As a general goal, downtown development serves communitywide interests in a sound tax base, employment opportunities, and provision of desirable amenities. Life, however, is experienced in the particulars. The justness of a regime is not to be judged simply by the general goals it announces or even pursues. By exploring the specifics of Atlanta's development experience and determining how priorities were set, what tradeoffs were made, and why, the interplay between equity and effectiveness becomes concrete.

As we have seen, before World War II, the need to accommodate automobile traffic in a downtown dominated by rail lines made the business elite aware of its collective interest in a transformed center city. It also made the business elite appreciate the importance of public authority and resources. To pursue its economic interest in business-district transformation, two related steps were taken. One was to promote unity of action among the major land holders by forming the Central Atlanta Improvement Association (now CAP). This organization brought the business elite together around their common predicament in the downtown area, without the distracting concerns of small property holders who were less able to cope with and benefit from large-scale transformation. CAP thus gave the business elite a means to unify around its privately defined planning goals and to assert them in the public arena.

The second step was to limit the capacity of public planning agencies to formulate and advance an independent set of development goals. Hence, in the early postwar years, the activist Metropolitan Planning Commission was partly funded by business contributions, and the city itself maintained only a small planning staff. Later, as city planning incurred wide-ranging responsibilities (partly through federal encouragement), the major priority-setting exercises were Central Area Study I and II — both done in partnership between the city and CAP.

Redevelopment in Atlanta has gone through several stages. Although there is no need here to retrace all of the details, some major features bear discussion. First of all, the initial postwar redevelopment strategy was to move the low-income population, especially the black population, away from the central business district and to create a buffer between that population and areas of business investment in the downtown area. Massive displacement to the east and south of the business district were the principal fronts in this change.

Thus, although the goal of a revitalized business district is economically defensible, the way in which it was pursued imposed substantial social costs. The city's redevelopment program obliterated a number of neighborhoods and set in motion a process of rapid residential transition that undermined others. Moreover, the city's efforts to provide new housing, some of it earmarked for displacees, were concentrated in remote areas of Atlanta, convenient neither to downtown nor to suburban jobs. The mass-transit system serves few of these sections, and road building there has also been a low priority. Indeed, for a time, street development was deliberately curtailed as a way of guiding racial transition.[7] Consequently, economic isolation is the lot of many city residents, who are only loosely connected to the world of downtown Atlanta. Not surprisingly, many of these areas are in what the police today call the "combat zone."[8]

A more inclusive form of decision making surely would have resulted in less social disruption. Although it is not clear whether investors would have built the new downtown hotels and office buildings on the scale they did without wide buffer zones, the fact that older cities like Baltimore did less clearance than Atlanta suggests that removal may have been more extensive than was necessary to attract investment.[9] On the other hand, Norman and Susan Fainstein have found evidence that aggressive programs of redevelopment account for some city differences in attracting investment.[10] What is certain is that Atlanta's strategy of promoting downtown investment by displacing a documented sixty-seven thousand residents in a ten-year time span was a major hardship on the city's nonaffluent population, and it widely affected residential patterns. One could even speculate on the ironic possibility that the regime's redevelopment strategy contributed to a result not wanted by the business elite; namely, a city with a black majority. Unquestionably, rapid transition in the racial character of neighborhoods, encouraged by massive relocation, did little to stem white flight. Not surprisingly, then, Atlanta moved from predominantly white to predominantly black very quickly.[11]

Once broad considerations are taken into account, it is not clear that *even in economic terms* the redevelopment scheme of moving quickly and vigorously to create wide buffer zones was the soundest approach over the long run. A more measured policy of displacement might have made future investment less skewed and mass-level racial animosity less strong. At the very least, given that Atlanta continues to have an extremely high poverty rate, the strategy pursued was hardly of universal benefit. Broader representation in the city's redevelopment coalition might have made agreement more difficult and vigorous action less likely, but the consequent reduction in displacement would surely have been more equitable than what was implemented, especially since the most socially vulnerable segment of the population took the brunt of the impact. Vast relocation served Atlanta's neediest population badly, with little evidence of compensating benefits.

Recent development strategy is more complicated in its ramifications. Starting with Central Area Study I in the mid 1960s and continuing through Central Area Study II twenty years later, the city hall/CAP partnership has promoted an intra-business-district development plan. The core of this plan is to make lower downtown into a center of government offices — city, county, state, and federal. Much of that has been achieved or is under way. Local leaders, for example, lobbied federal officials to build what is now the Richard Russell (federal) Office Building in lower downtown, thus gathering into one place offices that had been dispersed, many of which had been in Midtown. Midtown itself has been marked as the area for an arts district and for private investment. In lower downtown, the Underground project serves to remove some of the shabbier small businesses from the section between the government center and the financial district. The pattern here is: (1) government subsidy for, or direct government assumption of, the riskiest forms of investment, located in lower downtown, and (2) unchecked private development in the low-risk Midtown area. The latter is an especially clear example of investor prerogative at work, since government action cleaned up Midtown and enhanced its investment potential by locating three MARTA stops there as well as upgrading the road access. Meanwhile, intensified and unchecked private development in Midtown is producing undesirable side effects; i.e., driving out smaller and more marginal "arts" activities, such as small theaters. Indeed, the pattern of development may undermine the mixed-use character of the area that has helped make it attractive for investment.

The overall development strategy is for private investors to move in concert around a plan that they shaped, but individual actions are based on consent, not coercion; certainly there are no public restrictions or linkages of any kind. Because public subsidy is involved heavily in setting the stage for private investment, the market is not a free and competitive one. It is more nearly an oligopoly, with a small number of large entrepreneurs acting in accord and, in this instance, backed by government. At this stage, the strategy is quite effective in promoting investment. A substantial level of new development and economic revitalization has occurred within the central area, though the trend toward suburbanization continues to dominate. Because of investor prerogative, the return to the city on this investment is mainly an enhanced tax base. And the equity question that has not been debated publicly is whether the tax-base gain alone is a sufficient return, given the extensive public subsidy involved.

There is a further issue, also not fully aired in public debate. Since intensified development is shifting the area chiefly toward office towers, it may constitute a "tragedy of the commons"; that is, a form of development harmful to the community over the long run. The older section of the business district is already suffering from the nine-to-five syndrome of closing down at the end of the office work day, and its vacancy rate is on the rise.[12] The absence of evening pedestrian traffic creates public-safety problems and engenders an increasingly sterile environment — one unlikely to sustain a high level of investment. Just as the unwillingness to halt skywalks results in costly public programs to counteract the consequences (such as the hiring of additional police and efforts to encourage street-level pedestrian traffic), so the unwillingness to impose balanced-development requirements poses the prospect of future public expenditures to compensate for a culturally barren milieu and to overcome the threat of rising vacancies. Even in the short run, intensified development in the Midtown area is shrinking the supply of affordable housing and arts facilities.

Investor prerogative thus seems to promote a high level of private investment, but with mixed consequences. It entails substantial public investment as an immediate inducement; it works hardships on less affluent people and on nonprofit and small enterprises; and it may provide weak protection of the long-term investment potential of the center-city area.[13]

Although there are flaws in the development policy pursued, the question remains whether an alternative regime arrangement could make and carry out a better one. For example, it is not clear that an unplanned, competitive-market approach would be superior. Completely unplanned development based on the individual and uncoordinated actions of developers could generate all of the problems of the present regime, though it probably would not have produced the enormous displacement of the 1950s and 1960s. For the opposite alternative — a policy guided by publicly debated and established plans — the question is whether such an approach would generate a high level of investment.

The present system of planning, led by major private interests, is far from misdirected on all points. The notions of a government center, an arts district, and a focus such as Underground for downtown nightlife are not ill-advised; permitting skywalks downtown and unchecked development in Midtown almost certainly are. Unplanned development might, however, bring about the undesired practices without the defensible ones. After all, developers individually have slack resources with which to unblock resistance to particular projects. In totally open development, the city might still have excessive office-tower building and skywalks.

With a regime committed to public planning and practices such as linkage, the level of investment might be reduced[14] — an uncertain possibility, but still a risk. It is important to remember, then, that, though some segments of Atlanta's population have not benefited from center-city investment and some have even been harmed by it, others have benefited. A substantially lower level of investment would leave some of the citizenry — members of the black middle class, in particular — worse off. Hence it would hardly be an unmixed blessing.

A competitive market with no planning, privately planned development with full investor prerogative, and publicly planned development with a complete array of linkage requirements are three logically distinct alternatives. Actual practice could blend forms. Linkage and mixed-use requirements almost certainly could be imposed on Midtown without discouraging investment. Some proposed developments, such as the in-town piggyback facility, could have been rejected, again without affecting the overall level of investment in the city; and the city undoubtedly would be better off economically and socially without such a major nuisance activity.

However, the most important equity question is not the degree to which investor prerogative could be modified without drying up investment; rather, it concerns alternative strategies of development and a different set of priorities. Given Atlanta's high level of poverty, the current policy of generating jobs by means of the trickle-down effect from privately planned investment is debatable. Some alternatives include: (1) development projects designed, supported, and evaluated in terms of their long-term capacity to generate jobs; (2) education and training for employment in a postindustrial economy, combined with assurances of jobs or higher-education support for students who complete specific requirements; and (3) improved transportation through and from westside and southside Atlanta, as an encouragement to increased investment there and as a boost in mobility for residents in economically isolated areas.[15]

These alternatives highlight the challenge of pursuing equity. As a policy package, the three measures address needs of the lower-income population, in ways that would enhance their economic opportunities and counteract the trend toward "two Atlantas" divided sharply by economic disparities. These are worthy goals, consistent with the idea of fairness to the poor and supportive of conditions that would make for a socially healthier community. There is, however, no reason to believe that the current Atlanta regime would entertain such policy priorities or work diligently to execute them. Such goals as equity for the poor or a socially healthy community are too intangible, too remote from the everyday conditions of regime insiders, to motivate action on their behalf. As Norton Long has observed, "The protagonists of things in particular are well organized and know what they are about; the protagonists of things in general are few, vague, and weak."[16]

Atlanta's regime is strong because it is knit together by narrow concerns. Some issues are group-based and collective but still represent the concerns of particular elements of the community. For example, CAP is well staffed and capable of a long-term view, but its view remains that of only one segment of the community and of only one facet of community life. No less so than other participants in Atlanta's civic life, the downtown business elite is guided by "opportunities" (not always so small) for themselves and not a "grand vision" of what the community could be. Conceivably, coalition insiders could hold an elevated perception of their role, as persons with a responsibility to govern and make decisions based on an idea of community well-being.[17] But the very qualities that give the regime its cohesion — behind-the-scenes deliberations, reciprocity and deal making, and the prevalence of a "go along to get along" outlook — work against an enlarged vision of governing.[18]

THE CASE FOR WIDE REPRESENTATION

Concerted action by a few, negotiated behind the scenes and cemented by selective incentives, can produce a strong capacity to make and carry out policy. But Atlanta's development experience suggests that such a policy will be flawed in important respects, including its failure to address significant social issues. Cohesion, it seems, cannot stand alone as the sole feature of an effective regime. There is a case to be made for wide representation, a case that has two major parts.[19]

One element concerns fairness: Everyone is entitled to a voice in actions that affect them. Since no group is all-wise or free of self-regard, policies *over the long run* are best, or at least fairest, when every group has the opportunity to plead its own case before the other. If we envision public policy, not as a matter of fixed preferences, but as a continuing adaptation based on trial and error, then we can appreciate the case for wide representation as providing a broader base for learning. In forming (and reforming) policy, those who are part of the governing coalition can argue to change practices that adversely affect their interests. Those who are outside of the governing coalition lack that opportunity. Therefore, over time, as policy is adjusted and readjusted, it reflects the interests of those who are represented and disregards the interests of those who are not. That is the essence of the fairness issue.

However, the case for wide representation rests on more than the fairness of broadly based understanding. Democracy also entails the idea of inclusiveness. Beyond mere advocacy, representation affords an opportunity for mutual concern to develop and be nurtured. That notion might itself seem to some hopelessly romantic and idealistic, but consider what often happens within legislative bodies. Camaraderie and shared experience create bonds among representatives who, in other respects, might be adversaries. Legislative norms serve to contain conflict and promote mutual regard. Much the same phenomenon can be seen within Atlanta's governing coalition. Though the picture is complex, partnership with the black middle class in governing the city has broadened the exposure of downtown business executives to community concerns.

Inclusiveness is thus more than aggregating preferences or compromising differences; it is also acting on a responsibility to maintain a bond. For example, in Atlanta, a disposition to preserve biracial communication and cooperation is evident. The existing coalition demonstrates that give-and-take and mutual regard are possible across racial lines, and presumably other divisions could also be bridged. The notion of encompassing governing coalitions is not, then, pure fantasy; the Atlanta experience as well as operating examples in several European countries[20] indicate that, *under favorable conditions*, coalition building can enlarge understanding of community conditions.

Widened representation, however, is not welcomed by Atlanta's business elite. An inclusive governing coalition means more than simply broadening membership; it also means that the investment climate and even specific actions of investors would be subject to the claims of other groups. The business elite thus has a strong incentive to restrict the capacity of other members of the alliance to press such claims. The interplay between coalition partners sheds light on the struggle over wider representation. Although Atlanta's experience in biracial coalition building indicates that expanded concern across racial lines can occur, enlarged understanding can be resisted as well. Again, the experience is worth reviewing.

BIRACIALISM, ATLANTA-STYLE

In 1946, when blacks became an important voting bloc in Atlanta, there were few indications that the city's business elite was more progressive-minded on issues of race than other southern elites. Atlanta's Mayor Hartsfield was himself a conventional segregationist and vocal critic of the NAACP. Yet, under his leadership, the city adopted the practice of according titles of respect and courtesy to black citizens; it hired a small but symbolically significant contingent of black police officers; and it worked informally (and behind the scenes) to use court processes to require the end of Jim Crow seating in public transportation.

Perhaps most notable of all, with the business elite playing an active and visible role in setting the stage at the state level, the city peacefully desegregated its public school system, contributing to an end of massive resistance in the South. Atlanta demonstrated that a Deep South city could comply with the federal mandate to end racially segregated schooling.

When Ivan Allen, Hartsfield's successor as mayor and a central figure among the city's business elite, testified in 1963 in favor of civil-rights legislation, when the city's police chief served on the Kerner Commission (which warned the nation about a racially divided society), when the city and its notables honored Martin Luther King, Jr., on the occasion of his having won the Nobel Peace Prize, and when Allen acted with great personal concern and sensitivity to the tragedy of King's assassination, the nation and good race relations were well served. These are significant accomplishments, unpredictable in 1946, that are not to be discounted because the city's and the business elite's overall record in race relations has shortcomings. The achievements reveal a capacity for cross-racial concern that is noteworthy precisely because American society is so often sundered by racial division.

"Enlightened self-interest," not altruism, is how Atlanta's business elite describes its support for good relations between the races. This attitude led to efforts that allowed blacks to become not only members of the key business organizations in Atlanta but twice president of the Chamber of Commerce. Blacks now serve on the boards of major business corporations in Atlanta, and there is an ongoing effort to promote minority business opportunities. To be sure, each of these endeavors could be faulted for being incomplete, but they are part of a strategy of incorporation, not of racial isolation.[21]

The point of this litany of accomplishments is not to embrace the view of Atlanta as a paragon of racial virtue but to illustrate that white business and political leaders can be motivated to broaden their understanding of community governance. It is also important to recognize that Atlanta's broadened understanding did not occur spontaneously simply from biracial contact. Instead, it resulted from blacks *constituting a growing electoral bloc and pressing for expanded considerations.*

Seen in this light, the history of Atlanta's biracial coalition offers cautions about the role of selective incentives; that is, they form the epicenter from which tensions between regime equity and effectiveness emanate. Consider the Atlanta pattern. In 1946, the black middle class could bargain with the city's white leadership on group terms because the black community had mobilized itself as a substantial voting bloc and had already demonstrated an autonomous economic capacity, including the ability to develop new housing areas. Even though selective incentives strengthened the biracial alliance as a governing coalition, these incentives also weakened the critical perspective of black leaders — hence their acquiescence in massive displacement. And, by 1960, Atlanta's established black leaders had become wary of making demands, even though the regionwide civil-rights movement had entered a new phase of assertiveness. Atlanta's black community embraced the spirit of social change only because student activists and a younger generation of middle-class leadership led the way. These new forces broke through the established lines of biracial accommodation and questioned the insider benefits (selective incentives) available to what these new groups deemed "the old guard."

In the 1970s, representing still another wave of fresh leadership not schooled in the insider game of "go along to get along," Maynard Jackson pushed the city into a new phase of affirmative action, providing a substantial and systematic program of minority business set-asides and joint-venture arrangements and dramatically altering the direction of the police department as well. However, the abundance of selective incentives during Andrew Young's mayoralty has furthered no new policy initiative. Resting on Maynard Jackson's earlier efforts, the Young administration has produced no palpable policy inroads in employment, education, and affordable housing, and investor prerogative continues as the centerpiece of development policy.

In addition to enhancing coalition cohesion, selective incentives also constitute a body of insider privileges. Those who benefit naturally become protective of their position. Insiders are reluctant to unsettle advantageous arrangements, so they do not press other coalition members to widen the agenda of community concerns. Because the business elite has the most slack resources and the greatest capacity to control selective incentives, they are able to devise attractive terms of accommodation, complete with insider privileges that make others less inclined to question the accommodation reached. That is how unity of action is bought at the expense of equity concerns.

The post–World War II period can thus be viewed as a series of adjustments between the downtown elite — not just as investors of capital but also as controllers of selective incentives — and the forces of popular expression. The ballot has been important as a popular means to support leaders who could press upon the downtown elite a set of issues broader than revitalization of the business district. Civil disorder and, typically, the necessity of maintaining the cooperation of elected officials have both enhanced the business elite's understanding of what constitutes a favorable community climate. However, the enormous capacity of business to provide selective incentives, to further small opportunities of particular groups, and, in general, to promote the game of "go along to get along" has drawn enough strategically placed individuals into cooperative arrangements to protect investor prerogative and keep concerns focused mainly on the economic health of the business district.

Whatever the forces of popular expression are able to open up, business control of selective incentives constrains. Hence, during the postwar period, blacks have urged wider racial concerns upon the downtown elite, but the elite has been able to narrow its responses through ample use of selective incentives. Thus the business elite can be drawn into a broader understanding of the community, but it also has a capacity to limit the agenda of concerns. By affording special opportunities to key actors in the black middle class, the business elite keeps the inner circle of the governing coalition small.

COALITIONS AND THE TWO FACES OF EFFECTIVENESS

The evolution of Atlanta's biracial coalition places the tension between equity and effectiveness in a new light. Black participation in the coalition demonstrates that the regime need not confine itself to a narrow development agenda to be effective; effectiveness does not preclude equity considerations. Moreover, the biracial character of the city's governing coalition has in some ways enhanced regime effectiveness, because it broadens the institutional sources that inform and support policy initiatives. An inclusive coalition may be more, rather than less, able to detect changed conditions and formulate supportable responses.[22] In Atlanta, the black voter mobilization of 1946, the student-initiated protests of 1960, expanded black representation through reapportionment, the black revolt in the elections of 1968 and 1969, and Maynard Jackson's election in 1973 each served in retrospect to energize the governing coalition, not debilitate it.

But, as we have seen, unguarded optimism about regime responsiveness is not in order. Aside from business incentives to restrict coalition membership, there are built-in tensions between the range of groups represented and the capacity of a coalition to achieve a coordinated effort. Thus the dynamics of coalition coordination work against wide inclusion; smaller and more homogeneous groups find communication, understanding, and cooperation easier to accomplish.[23] Riker refers to minimal winning coalitions based on the consideration that the benefits of winning are greater when there are fewer claimants.[24] The point here is somewhat different. Riker's formula, after all, is about dividing up a fixed body of benefits; actual governance involves creating and replenishing a body of opportunities. Leiserson seems more on target than Riker in his analysis of internal bargaining costs, which, he argues, are minimized when the number of parties in the coalition is at a minimum.[25] Then there are fewer viewpoints to be reconciled as well as richer opportunities for the insiders to interact closely enough to develop a relationship of trust. As they do, future exchanges occur more easily.

Axelrod has maintained that coalitions with the least internal conflict of interest among members will tend to prevail; hence, he predicts minimal coalitions whose members are adjacent along the ideological spectrum.[26] The Atlanta experience again suggests a somewhat different but not unrelated point. The key factor in Atlanta appeared not to be ideological kinship—both the original postwar coalition of the Hartsfield era and the reconstituted coalition in recent years have had considerable diversity in this regard. The crucial feature seems to be the nature of the interaction, rather than personal ideological predilection. It is an issue not just of congenial objectives but also of modes of operation.[27]

Coalition partners tend to have some objectives that are compatible and others that are not. The question is which set will prevail, and the issue becomes whether or not a mode of operation leads to cooperation. Stable coalitions develop most readily around concrete efforts at problem solving that promise significant material benefits both to individuals and to groups. These are interactions that provide positive reinforcement in the form of tangible and short-term benefits, in which the parties experience an immediate win-win payoff even if there are other (perhaps more distant) dimensions of the issue in which one or both sides have losses. Minority contracting provisions in the building of MARTA, the new airport, and the redevelopment of Underground all had that character, and they laid a foundation for future interaction.

Contrast the dynamics of protest and how they fail to build wide circles of exchange and trust. Protest tactics generally depend on intense emotions, stirred up by the immediacy of a threat. Consequently, protest participants tend to trust only those who share their intensity and are wary of influences originating outside the experiences they know. In this way, protest groups have a built-in limitation on the scope of support they can mobilize. They usually generate backing among those immediately threatened, but only for the apparent duration of the threat. Dissident leaders sometimes believe that a fusing of their efforts with those of other groups blunts the impact of their particular protests. Thus protest groups tend to be segmented and ephemeral.

After all is said about the comparative advantage of some forms of interaction over others as a way to promote coalition cohesion, the matter is not closed. Ease of coordination is double-edged, and facile internal bargaining may come at the expense of openness to the larger environment. Browne and Wildavsky have argued that social organizations gravitate toward internal compatibility, even if the organization itself becomes less adaptable.[28] Their point is that individuals with structured opportunities of inducements to interact learn to cooperate and facilitate interaction, even at the expense of a smooth relationship with others in the external environment of the organization. Atlanta's governing coalition has displayed that trait, with its members working closely together while consistently disregarding the concerns of other elements of the community.

Against this background, the term "effectiveness" assumes at least two dimensions. One involves coordination of effort to carry out a designated project—what Atlanta's downtown elite can contribute so substantially to. But the other dimension concerns breadth of understanding. Policies are formulated in response to problems and friction points, which, in execution, can also give rise to further but unanticipated problems and new friction points. Effectiveness for a regime acting in the name of the whole community thus calls for broad comprehension of social change and awareness of a wide range of situations and potential consequences.

Organization theorists discuss the process of search, or information seeking, as an element of organizational effectiveness; a stronger capacity for search improves selection among possible actions.[29] Thus, as I argued earlier, efficiency in accomplishing specific objectives is not enough; a regime also needs a capacity for search or, as I prefer, social learning.[30] "Search" implies nothing more than a technical process of acquiring facts, whereas "social learning" suggests an extensive understanding accompanied by a disposition to act on that understanding.

Obviously, a coalition that is inclusive, but perhaps not highly cohesive, has a wider capacity to "learn" than does a more narrow coalition that is highly cohesive. Learning, of course, does not eliminate the need for a capacity for coordinated action at some stage. But, a cohesive regime with a weak search capacity is not necessarily better at problem-solving than is a less cohesive regime. Cohesion may narrow understanding of the problem and constrict the effort to solve it. The process of social learning is thus a bridge between equity and effectiveness, opening up considerations that serve equity and increasing the ability to see more dimensions of a problem.

One can as easily talk about tension between the two elements of effectiveness as about the tension between equity and effectiveness. Efficient execution of an agreed-upon project can be achieved by a relatively small body of actors, reinforced in their cohesion by selective incentives. That is what Atlanta's business elite is so successful in promoting. But social learning— for example, understanding the consequences of neighborhood disruption, economic isolation, and growing class disparities—is what the downtown elite resists. As a result, the postwar period has witnessed an ongoing struggle in which the business elite taps the public sector for support for its concerns but tries to prevent that agenda from being brought into question.

The desire to protect investor prerogative curtails social learning; hence, learning comes only when it is pressed on the business elite by those whose position rests on a foundation of popular support. However, the interplay between business and popular expression is complicated, and the regime tends to achieve coordination at the expense of search. As business use of selective incentives draws key actors into the camp of the privileged, cooperation with agreed-upon projects increases, but social learning decreases.

IMPLICATIONS

The Atlanta experience illustrates two general tendencies. One is the usefulness of selective incentives in promoting regime cohesion; the other is the proclivity of selective incentives to hamper social learning by narrowing the terms of coalition cooperation. Once we focus on selective incentives and their impact, the inner workings of the Atlanta regime call into question some of the conventional categories of urban political analysis, particularly the distinction between machine and reform and the related notion of public- and private-regardingness (which is already somewhat discredited).

As a highly cohesive regime, held together primarily by selective incentives, Atlanta more resembles than differs from the Daley machine in Chicago. But by conventional measures, Atlanta is a reform city: nonpartisan elections, no army of patronage workers to turn out the vote, and personality-focused campaigns that rely on the mass media, churches, and civic associations to reach voters. Yet, from a regime perspective, these factors recede in importance. The fact that selective incentives are mainly in the hands of private business instead of a party organization may be less important than the fact that selective incentives are central to regime cohesion. Hence, by focusing on *governmental practice*, the traditional distinction between reform and machine may obscure significant similarities. Moreover, contrary to expectations based in ethos theory, it is the downtown elite and the black middle class who are caught up in reciprocity, "going along," furtherance of small opportunities, and insider deals. These narrow the vision that coalition leaders have of the community and restrict their willingness to see and act on its problems.

The tendency for selective incentives to confine the range of issues dealt with is not peculiar to Atlanta. In an assessment of Chicago, Milton Rakove explained how the Daley machine concentrated on routine services, particular benefits, and small opportunities, but was generally unwilling to promote residential integration, attend to the quality of education, or concern itself with "the broad social issues and programs that are dear to the hearts of the urban reformers."[31] In a similar vein, Independent Alderman Leon Despres said that the effect of the Daley machine was "the muting of protest, incalculable stagnation of the general citizenry, and loss of progress to Chicago."[32]

Thus, another similarity between the two cities is that Atlanta, like Daley's Chicago, has major unaddressed social problems. The city's high poverty rate (especially for its youth), the economically isolated and undertrained workforce, the uninspiring performance of its school system, the social roots of crime, the shortage of affordable housing, and the lack of attention to neighborhood conservation are all serious matters for the city's future. The Atlanta regime may be cohesive and quite effective in executing particular projects, but it does not ably address a wide range of problems. Like Daley's Chicago, it is skilled at building physical structures but not very proficient at launching and carrying out ambitious programs of human development. Yet there is in Atlanta an occasional hint of a regime capable of widening its concerns and enlarging its policy agenda. When black churches play a critical role, as they did in countering MARTA's attempt to eliminate its rail line to a westside public-housing area, the regime responds. The line was saved, and the geographic isolation of a significant population was staved off.

Even though Atlanta's regime has, through informal means, taken on some machine characteristics, it does not signify that reform-style politics — in which political attachments are based on something other than particularistic exchanges – is impossible. Larger concerns do occasionally surface, but the success of vigorous reform politics may depend on the presence of autonomous voluntary associations and a resource-rich middle class, especially one not tied closely to corporate business. It may well be that the lower class especially needs selective incentives for community organization and is therefore politically vulnerable on that count.[33] Of course, reform politics driven by nonparticularistic concerns is not necessarily an inclusive politics. It could be highly ideological and exclusionary.[34] A regime's capacity for wide representation may thus rest on an associational life that is neither narrowly ideological nor dependent on business sponsorship. That issue needs to be placed in structural context.

PROSPECTS FOR CHANGE

Is it possible for Atlanta's governing regime to evolve toward a capacity for greater concern about social equity, or is the system structurally determined to favor investor prerogative and neglect alternative policy priorities? There is no ready answer to that question. The importance of business investment and the substantial store of slack resources in the hands of downtown business are formidable forces for continuity. Yet the political-economy context out of which Atlanta's regime arises is not monolithic. The business elite's privileged position in the city's governing coalition is only partly explained by its control of investment capital; its use of slack resources accounts for much more. It is helpful, then, to return to the concept of structuring introduced earlier.[35] Matters of degree are significant, for seemingly slight changes can ease the way toward more profound ones.

Although most large corporations have extensive slack resources available for political purposes, the Atlanta pattern of a unified downtown elite – experienced in shaping regime arrangements and motivated to do so – is not a universal one. Nor is it certain to endure. As the city ages and business activities continue to decentralize, the importance of downtown investments to key businesses may diminish. Further, many locally run businesses, such as the department stores, are now part of national corporate entities, and they are becoming concerned with operations over a much wider area. Perhaps, as these trends continue, business-elite unity and involvement may decline. If so, the character of the regime would change accordingly. Whether the citizenry of the city would be better or worse off if that happened is a question considered earlier; the answer ultimately depends on the alternative.

The note of caution I would raise relates to regime cohesion and the enormous importance of selective incentives in the governing coalition's capacity to execute complex and nonroutine projects. If a unified business elite were no longer the central supplier of incentives, what would be the nature of the successor regime? Would it be too fragmented to act? Would selective incentives come from other sources, and if so, what might be the consequences? The Daley regime stands as a reminder that a cohesive political organization in control of a substantial body of selective incentives is no guarantee of different policies. Selective incentives could come from individual developers and lone-wolf entrepreneurs, thus continuing to distract attention from wide social concerns and stifling policy alternatives. In other words, a future without a unified business elite is not necessarily a rosier future. Much would indeed depend on how civic cooperation is achieved, who is involved, and how the manner of cooperation constrained the capacity for learning about and acting on a range of community concerns.

Therefore, it is necessary to consider not only the business elite and its future but also other elements of the community. The downtown elite's power, after all, is partially due to the civic vacuum it fills. Contemporary Atlanta is a child of the southern politics analyzed so incisively by V. O. Key.[36] Historically, the South is a region of one- or no-party politics, weak labor unions, and a working class badly divided by racial antagonism. The nonprofit sector in Atlanta has a tradition of dependence on business sponsorship and support, although not all of the business dominance of this sector comes from a Deep South heritage. The Metropolitan Community Foundation is an idea borrowed directly from the business elite in Cleveland, Ohio, and the use of charitable contributions as a source of community influence can be found in a variety of other places, from contemporary Tulsa, Oklahoma,[37] to antebellum New York City.[38]

The central feature of the Atlanta regime is private control of selective incentives and private guidance of civic cooperation generally. In Atlanta, private equals business. Regime openness toward broader community concerns is likely only if the private sector is reconstituted so that nonprofit organizations become a substantial and autonomous force themselves—no easy task. Nonprofits typically are strapped for resources and, if they rely on volunteers, stretched thin. That is why they are so readily attracted to business sponsorship. Still, there are alternative patterns.

The model of how to expand the policy agenda beyond narrow business concerns is the black middle class. Although its autonomy is compromised by the pull of a large set of selective incentives, the black middle class did obtain a foothold in the governing coalition through its independent capacity to mobilize voters and conduct economic transactions. If the black lower class, white neighborhoods, preservationists, and the arts community are going to gain positions in the governing coalition, they have to develop comparable capacities and demonstrate an ability to work together. That is, they have to solve their individual problems of organization and, *in addition*, work out a viable form of cooperation among themselves.

If the needed motivations could be tapped, what could make a difference is the creation on an ongoing set of voluntary and nonprofit groups that are engaged in productive activities: PTAs, day-care, land trusts and land-use compacts, theater and arts groups, neighborhood watch and other crime-deterrence efforts, job-training and business-development corporations, historic- and neighborhood-preservation associations, consumer cooperatives, environmental-protection watchguards and groups interested in promoting green space, antidrug programs, sports leagues, and recreation centers for teenagers—to name a variety of possibilities. These groups are likely to be area-specific as well as functionally specific, thus leaving the public highly fragmented. Forming a federation or making a compact of mutual support is an additional step needed to create a coherent force—one that public officials might embrace as partners in the city's governing coalition.

Numbers alone are not enough. The lesson of Atlanta's black middle class is that electoral strength is significant but unable to stand on its own. Without an independent institutional capacity and a broad federation of groups, business will fill the organizational vacuum. The small-opportunities phenomenon, mixed with the strong attraction of individual incentives, will tie community groups to business patronage. Thus, demanding as the task is, regime reform depends on the reconstitution of the city's civic life, thereby assuring that, in James Madison's words, no single faction would dominate. An array of nonprofit enterprises not dependent on business patronage, neighborhood organizations able to build more than ad hoc alliances, and small-business associations not beholden to the downtown elite would provide a basis for a more inclusive governing coalition—inclusive because it would be coordinated on something other than business-supplied selective incentives. Such a regime might execute fewer mega-projects, but it would also have a greater capacity for social learning.

CONCLUSION

An exploration of the two faces of effectiveness shows that the role of the downtown elite in the governance of Atlanta is quite complex. Business involvement contributes to one facet of effectiveness but limits the other. Given business use of its slack resources to create pockets of privilege for other community actors, it is clear that regime cohesion is gained at the expense of social learning. At the same time, a diversified civic sector might mean less regime cohesion and a decreased capacity to pursue some goals. But business involvement is unlikely to disappear. The downtown elite has too large a stake in the city's future and too many slack resources to be excluded. If a more encompassing governing coalition could be created, it might, then, be able to expand business understanding of what constitutes a sound environment for investment.

Increasing a regime's capacity for social learning is a major challenge. As indicated above, relationships with relatively low transaction costs tend to prevail over those with relatively high costs. The need to economize such costs gives regimes an inclination toward a narrowly composed inner circle. An abundance of selective incentives reinforces that tendency, especially if they are in the hands of a coalition partner interested in reducing its exposure to problem solving demands. That is why, in Atlanta, private control of selective incentives is so important.

Private control of abundant selective incentives also explains why boom times seldom generate successful demands for community problem solving. After all, it is not an absence of problems that accounts for community inaction during those times; social ills do not go away simply because investment in office buildings takes place. Communities presumably could especially afford to act on their problems as economic growth occurs, but boom times provide such abundant opportunities for deals — individual deals — that group demands for community problem solving can be diverted. Although "individual deals" (i.e., selective incentives) are important, once again they are not the whole story. They involve a relatively small number of people.

Despite the importance of selective incentives in promoting coalitional unity, regimes are subject to multiple tendencies. Since city hall is always a key part of any urban regime, the need for electoral support gives rise to a broadening tendency.[39] The difficulty is that the voters are a diffuse public, with few stable means of interaction with elected officials. Their contact is usually shallow and ephemeral, and hence ineffective. That condition enables the business-centered civic network to be extremely effective, coopting or isolating potential opponents and keeping public discontent from amassing into a permanent source of challenge. Thus, electorates as such are not very potent sources of sustained pressure, and, as mass entities, they do little to promote social learning. That is a major reason why the character of a community's associational life is crucial.

The special role of Atlanta's downtown elite in the city's regime is thus not a simple matter of business control of slack resources. The particular political heritage of Atlanta contributes as well — a southern heritage consisting of a working class not independently organized for political mobilization and of a nonprofit sector heavily dependent on business sponsorship. The tension between equity and effectiveness occurs, not because the two are inherently opposed to one another, but because the capacity to promote coordinated coalition action is concentrated in the hands of a privileged group reluctant to expose itself to an array of community concerns. Specifically, the downtown business elite has been able to create a civic network maintained by a set of norms consistent with investor class unity and wide investor prerogative.

Equity considerations are unlikely to carry much weight until Atlanta can expand its capacity for social learning by developing a less one-sided civic sector. However, as I will elaborate in the next chapter, the cohesion of the present regime and its ability to provide small opportunities make it all the more difficult to alter current arrangements and diversify the civic sector. Concentrated resources have a capacity to perpetuate themselves.

11

Rethinking Community Power:
Social Production
versus Social Control

The internal features of one relation are nonetheless a function of the entire network. Any adequate conception of "power structure" must be based upon this fact.
— Richard M. Emerson

Strong centrifugal forces characterize modern societies. Fragmented into myriad special roles, these societies lack an overarching power of command. The formal authority of government is limited, and substantial resources are in private hands. Especially at the local level, the power of public officials may be dwarfed by processes and activities outside governmental control.

Given that communities are divided into various sectors with many independent actors in each, cooperation across institutional lines cannot be achieved simply by formal action. Thus, informally achieved cooperation can greatly enhance the effectiveness of a regime. In other words, if a governing regime is to do more than provide routine services, it must be able to mobilize private as well as public actors. Informally achieved cooperation is therefore vital to the capacity to govern. But these informal arrangements are not neutral; they bias what can and cannot be done with the capacity to govern.[1] That is why the previous chapter explored the tension between equity and effectiveness.

The Atlanta case illustrates the way in which business enterprises are able to shape a city's policy agenda by becoming an integral part of a system of civic cooperation. Atlanta may be atypical in the extent of the civic vacuum which its downtown elite filled, and the city may also be exceptional in the degree of public unity displayed by its business elite. But the Atlanta case also shows that major business enterprises have slack resources, varied in kind, and civic capacities that are useful in the process of governance — attributes that are not easily matched in any community. Hence, business has a somewhat unique ability to make things happen and play a central role in the governing coalition.

Talk of a central role in the governing coalition may conjure up for some readers a familiar story about elite domination. Does a small body of economic notables run Atlanta, and if so, how? Throughout this book, I have attempted to show that, though Atlanta's business elite is extraordinarily influential, it does not exercise command power, nor does it display an ability to control attitudes per se. Indeed, outbreaks of antibusiness sentiment are a recurring feature of the city's politics. Yet antibusiness attitudes that could lead to cumulative restrictions on investor prerogatives are seeds that fall on inhospitable civic ground. They do not find the nutrients they need to grow into sustained actions.

The extraordinary influence of Atlanta's downtown elite stems from its ability to set the terms of civic cooperation, thereby facilitating some courses of action but not others. Is Atlanta exceptional? It may be somewhat unusual in the conjunction of advantages that the city's downtown elite enjoys, but as I argue in this chapter, the Atlanta case illustrates (perhaps more clearly because the business advantage is more pronounced) a way of looking at power that has general applicability. In particular, I suggest that it is inadequate to attribute business influence in Atlanta and other places to a dominant set of beliefs. Beliefs are acted upon in a context, and that context is not the traditional setting of social control. As long as we think about power in a social-control context, we will wind up repeating the pluralist/elitist debate. And that is precisely what we need to move beyond.

In recent years especially, the power debate has centered on arguments about the presence or absence of hegemonic beliefs (i.e., the "third face of power"), which I contend grows out of conflicting ideas about social control. My argument is that social control is not a helpful lens through which to view power and that its unchallenged acceptance has caused *both* the pluralist and elitist schools of thought to misunderstand the character of power *as it operates in modern societies.*

IDEOLOGICAL HEGEMONY

Preliminaries

That Atlanta business is quite influential in city affairs is itself not remarkable. What is noteworthy is that we have difficulty explaining this influence in conventional terms. It is not a form of dominance in which an elite, covert or overt, rules in command-and-control fashion. Business suffers defeats; it finds that it must compromise; and it engages in extensive coalition building. *In some sense*, power in Atlanta is diffuse. No group, business included, appears to be in a position to exercise much in the way of social control.

What, then, does this extraordinary influence consist of? There is little evidence of control by monopolization of the realm of ideas, though here we face some difficult issues. One might argue that there is ideological hegemony in the sense that there is no political challenge to capitalism, and most decision makers embrace the view that the community needs to promote economic growth through the encouragement of business investment. Yet, while there is no significant challenge to the idea of private ownership of capital, there is considerable diversity of opinion about how business investment should be encouraged and what trade-offs should be made on which terms.

Some might argue that this diversity is trivial. As long as the community embraces capitalism, this broad commitment overrides positions on lesser issues. Hence, they would argue, business prevails on policy matters as long as it can maintain the legitimacy of a capitalist political economy. That is a formidable argument; basic commitments would control lesser commitments, and fundamental change would result only from system crisis, loss of legitimacy, and revolution.

Yet it is possible to view the process of change in another way. Change may come about, not through the alteration of basic commitments, but through the piecemeal evolution of new practices and patterns of cooperation and exchange. If, as some students of the human experience claim, life is in the details, then we should be more attentive to details — how they can come to matter and how they can cumulate into new but perhaps unintended patterns.[2] In a sense, power may also lie in the details; that is, in the capacity to guide the piecemeal evolution of new practices and make marginal adjustments in prevailing patterns of cooperation and exchange. Certainly Atlanta's business elite acts as if piecemeal evolution and marginal adjustments are important.

It is at least conceivable that "basic commitments" are little more than crude rationalizations, subject to reinterpretation as practices change. In the view of some observers, we should consider the possibility that the "thought is not father to the deed; in fact, the deed may be father to the thought."[3] Hence, the important developments may not be in broad ideological positions but in the specifics of how people are organized to conduct functionally important activities. Presumably, this is roughly what Marx had in mind when he wrote of turning Hegel on his head.

In this chapter I take particular aim at the notion of ideological hegemony, not because I believe ideas are unimportant or because I wish to lend legitimacy to the status quo, but because the notion of hegemonic beliefs is too easy an explanation of business influence. Without careful refinement, arguments about dominant beliefs can become examples of what Charles Tilly terms one of the "pernicious postulates" of social science; namely, that mental events cause behavior.[4]

Atlanta

Given the centrality of investor prerogative in Atlanta, the city's governing arrangements perhaps sound like just another instance of Warner's "private city."[5] Certainly the ideology of privatism is strong in the governing circles of Atlanta, but that in itself reveals little. Ideas such as privatism may be the result, not the cause, of the dependence of other actors on the business elite.

There is not much in the Atlanta experience to suggest that proper ideological tutoring is the missing ingredient for an effective mobilization against the investor class. The city has, after all, harbored a succession of opposition movements, and citizens are aware that the community could be ordered on some basis other than investor prerogative. Moreover, the events culminating in the election of Maynard Jackson in 1973 brought Atlanta to the brink of regime change.

From the third-face-of-power argument, one would assume that the most difficult barrier for an opposition movement is the initial stage of activity.[6] The progressive coalition that backed Jackson for mayor crossed well over that threshold; it had not only an alternative set of ideas but an electoral majority and an elected mayor as well. Atlanta therefore does not appear to be an example of the third face of power.

The striking feature of the Atlanta experience is the inclination of those in positions of community responsibility to pull back from conflict with the business elite and seek accommodation. That is the recurring tendency particularly of the black middle class, but it is by no means unique to that group.

On analysis, it seems that the underlying structure of the situation works against the massing of opposition, and it is this structure that needs to be explored. But in order to do so, we need first to consider why the social-control paradigm generates unwanted assumptions and makes it easy for third-face-of-power/ideological-hegemony explanations to be devised.

Social-Control Paradigm

As Thomas Kuhn has shown, we view the world in terms of implicit models of how it works.[7] The questions we ask grow out of these paradigms, not out of unmediated reactions to "the facts." Indeed, we may even ignore certain facts or discount them as anomalies rather than take them as disconfirming evidence for implicit but cherished models.

The conventional power debate is based in such a paradigm, one that defines power in Weberian terms as a matter of dominance and assumes that politics is about the legitimacy of forms of social control. In this model of society, the central issue is the cost of compliance—the difficulty of maintaining a comprehensive scheme of control. Pluralists see the cost of compliance as *the* factor that engenders pluralism, especially in systems with constitutional and other restrictions on the use of coercion. Antipluralists believe that consent and legitimacy are engineered to reduce the cost of control and that system transformation can therefore be brought about by withdrawing consent and abrogating legitimacy. The conventional power debate thus centers on how the cost of compliance is handled.[8]

In lieu of an extensive review of the literature, let me offer the following quotations to illustrate how widely the cost-of-compliance issue pervades our understanding of power.

Subjects can gain a degree of independence from their rulers on matters of importance to themselves if they can make the costs of domination so high that domination no longer looks worthwhile to the rulers. Resources are not infinite after all, and exercising control nearly always requires an outlay of resources. Domination, it is fair to say, always does. Thus, control is almost always to some extent costly to the ruler; and domination is sure to be — though it may be cheap, it does not come free.[9]

— Robert A. Dahl

As any elite group (or historical bloc) attempts to achieve domination over society, it will attempt to lower the costs of compliance by developing an ideology of its own legitimacy.[10]

— David D. Laitin

There are three main reasons why the greater extensiveness of a power relation sets limits to its comprehensiveness and intensity. First, the greater the number of power subjects, the greater the difficulty of supervising all of their activities. Second, the greater the number of power subjects, the more extended and differentiated the chain of command necessary to control them, creating new subordinate centers of power that can be played off against each other and that may themselves become foci of opposition to the integral power holder. Third, the greater the number of subjects, the greater the likelihood of wide variation in their attitudes toward the power-holder.[11]

— Dennis H. Wrong

To maintain control of a structure, repeated investments of power are required.[12]

— Edward C. Banfield

In a system in which the political head must continually 'pay' to overcome formal decentralization and to acquire the authority he needs, the stock of influence in his possession cannot all be 'spent' as he might wish.[13]

— *Edward C. Banfield*

If there is an aspiring ruling class, it may *try* to rule; but the complexity of social action will defeat it.[14]

— *Stephen L. Elkin*

Rule in the ruling-class thesis depends heavily on a form of comprehensive planning that cannot be done. . . . The class, directly or through its agents, must be able to identify decisions that are crucial to its interest and to analyze them in sufficient detail to devise a course of action — all in a rapidly changing environment. The difficulties are patent.[15]

— *Stephen L. Elkin*

The hegemon's being recognized as legitimate is one way to reduce the cost of extracting contributions from the allies. This highlights the important role of the cost of coercion in the theory of hegemony.[16]

— *James E. Alt, Randal L. Calvert, and Brian D. Humes*

As certain of the structural factors within the system of control weaken, more resources are required for the enforcement of control and more attention needs to be devoted to problems of policy design.[17]

— *Ian Lustick*

A placid poor get nothing, but a turbulent poor sometimes get something.[18]

— *Frances Fox Piven and Richard A. Cloward*

Sources of power are protected and enlarged by the use of that power not only to control the actions of men and women, but also to control their beliefs. What some call superstructure, and what others call culture, includes an elaborate system of beliefs and ritual behaviors which defines for people what is right and what is wrong and why; what is possible and what is impossible; and the behavioral imperatives that follow from these beliefs.[19]

— *Frances Fox Piven and Richard A. Cloward*

As several of the quotes above make clear, pluralism is regarded as a direct outgrowth of the cost of compliance. And Dahl, in one of the passages, emphasizes the point by arguing that subordinates can drive up the cost of exercising control, thereby reducing dominance. From the opposite side of the political spectrum, Gramsci and other writers in his tradition make much the same argument in positing a relationship between consent and force.[20]

The two sides agree that a few rule; they disagree over the nature of mass compliance. What pluralists see as genuine, their critics see as manipulated. The general paradigm about dominance and the cost of compliance is refined into competing scenarios. For pluralists, assent must be authentic; if it can be engineered, then the threat of mass noncompliance is unavailable to drive power in a pluralist direction. For critical scholars, unless assent is artificial and occasional outbreaks of opposition are manifestations of deeper antagonisms, then there is little ground on which elites can be said to dominate.

The differing scenarios about mass compliance extend to other issues. For pluralists, political stability is solid because popular consent is genuine. For their critics, political stability is tenuous; raised political consciousness can bring the underlying antagonism to the surface and expose elite manipulation. Thus, mass political consciousness becomes vital in achieving regime transformation. This second scenario requires closer examination. It seems to assume that mass resentment of elite rule is a reflection of the underlying structure of the situation. From this assumption flows another: that the political task is to give expression to what is artificially pent up.

Ralf Dahrendorf explains it this way: "The dialectic of power and resistance is the motive force of history."[21] He argues that, "in every imperatively coordinated association," there is not only a group in power, but there also is always "one aggregate of positions and their incumbents which represent the institutionalized doubt in the legitimacy of the *status quo* of the distribution of authority."[22] Dahrendorf sees resistance to domination as fuel for change. The ruling group is the defender of the status quo in authority relations; subordinate groups are the source of change—but only if they can develop leadership and a mobilizing ideology.[23] Students of urban politics who write from a class-struggle perspective make much the same argument.[24]

Starting with an assumption that the underlying structure of the situation is one of domination by the few and resistance by the many, one expects overt conflict to reflect that antinomy. If there is no conflict, it is natural to believe that something has interfered with it, probably mediating forces (e.g., elite control of the means of communication and of socialization) that bring about false or fragmented consciousness.

I contend that this line of argument arises from the social-control paradigm itself: If the many have reason to resent domination by the few, then the many should join together in opposition to the established regime and transform it into one more responsive to themselves. Pluralists discount the possibility that there is a basis for resentment; otherwise they would find mass noncompliance with the regime. Critical scholars believe that there are genuine grounds for resentment, but they credit elites with the ability to manipulate mass consciousness and its expression.

The empirical picture is sufficiently complex for each side to find supporting evidence for its position and dismiss the case for the opposing school of thought. That evidence, I maintain, is weak because the line of inquiry is the product of an inadequate paradigm. For both sides in the debate, the cost-of-compliance factor is what March calls "force depleting."[25] When an elite seeks compliance and legitimacy, it makes concessions to the mass citizenry, *unless* it has gained compliance by manipulation and deception.[26] It would thus seem that withdrawing consent and resisting a regime would constitute an effective way of extracting concessions and perhaps bringing a system to the crisis point.[27] Within this model, challenge is costly to a ruling group and, if intense enough, could deplete its store of resources. What the social-control model does not explain is why a significant challenge might be inconsequential, perhaps resulting only in the challenging group's being left out of what is still a productive enterprise.

A SOCIAL-PRODUCTION MODEL OF POWER

A Tillian View of Society

Consider the Atlanta case again. Investor prerogative is resented sufficiently to occasion substantial opposition, but when that develops, it is the opposition, not the power of the governing coalition, that weakens. Can this pattern be explained without positing elite control of popular consciousness? I believe so. First of all, there is Ira Katznelson's argument that "city trenches" emanating from the separation of home from workplace help divide society and prevent the emergence of a solidified opposition to the capitalist order.[28] The appeal of this argument is that it points to the underlying structure of the situation and the inherent difficulties it poses for bringing opposition together.

Although Katznelson offers helpful insights, I propose to take the argument further and suggest how, in communities like Atlanta, the underlying structure of the capitalist order affords the investor class a strong opportunity to protect itself politically. By its very nature, capitalism divides authority and furnishes investors with the means to maintain an autonomous sphere of economic activity. Indeed, capitalist society provides for a relatively loose form of social control. Hence, Norton Long has aptly described the local community as an "ecology of games,"[29] and Charles Perrow speaks of society as having "low coherence."[30]

Going a step further, Charles Tilly makes a persuasive case against regarding modern society as a cohesive whole.[31] In his view, society's institutions do not constitute a smoothly functioning machine. Further, society is not bound by an integrating body of thought, a shared conception of the world, or even a set of norms and values that most people subscribe to. Instead, Tilly says, what holds the world together is a somewhat loose network of institutional arrangements. Though fraught with tension and conflict, these arrangements promote action on behalf of various social goods. Tilly's thesis is akin to Long's ecology of games, though with a greater emphasis on conflict. The maintenance of the network (or "ecology") is a matter of struggle, with contenders variously accommodating and resisting one another.

In Tilly's understanding of society, instead of a single fulcrum of control, there are strategically advantageous points from which to wage struggle and promote some forms of collective action at the expense of others. There is no consensus. Conceptions of the world and other big beliefs are vague and compatible with a variety of applications. Cognition is limited, and people hold contradictory views, with beliefs often yielding to situational pressures anyway. What counts is how ideas are implemented, the decision rules people develop, and the working alliances they form. Many activities are autonomous, and many middle-range accommodations are worked out. In some ways, the Tillian world is chaotic; certainly it is loosely coupled, and most processes continue without active intervention by a leadership group.

Social Production

In this kind of incohesive, loosely joined society, the paradigmatic issue is not the cost of compliance, since comprehensive control is out of the question. In a fragmented world, the issue is how to bring about enough cooperation among disparate community elements to get things done—and to do so in the absence of an overarching command structure or a unifying system of thought.

Governance requires the power to combine necessary elements for a publicly significant result—whether it is building a downtown expressway system, developing new housing for blacks in the outer area of the westside, hiring black police officers in a Jim Crow city, redeveloping substandard areas next to the business district, peacefully desegregating the school system in an era of massive resistance, launching a mass-transit system, putting on a National Black Arts Festival, or rebuilding Underground Atlanta as a major entertainment district.[32] Atlanta's postwar governing coalition has accomplished all of this and more.

The capacity to assemble and use needed resources for a policy initiative is what I call the social-production model. The implications of defining governance in this way—not as a task of comprehensive control, but as bringing together essential elements in an otherwise fragmented world—are far-reaching. For instance, if society is incohesive to begin with, then opposition may amount to little. Governance is not the same as heading up an enterprise in which everyone's role is significant, so everyone must participate. Instead, in the overall scheme of things, scattered noncompliance means little.

In a social-control model, resistance can escalate the cost of control, and subordinates can tax the workability of a system by withholding compliance.

That is not the case in a social-production model, where opposition is inconsequential unless it can be organized on a mass basis and transformed into an alternative capacity to govern. Thus a challenge group has to do much more than withhold compliance if it is to be effective at a regime level. It must also be able to bring together and use a body of support that is suitable and durable enough to govern.

In the social-control model, the cost burden is on the governing body.[33] In the social-production model, *the cost burden is on the challenge group.* The implications for regime change are enormous. We can see why, within the workings of such a model, a unified business elite is virtually irreplaceable. And we can appreciate, for example, why Richard Daley made peace with Chicago's business elite on first coming into office, even though they had opposed his election. Operating from a social-control model, pluralists grasp only part of the situation. Because they know that control is costly, they understand the difficulty of assembling an effective capacity to accomplish things governmentally. But, because they fail to think in regime terms, they do not understand the gravitational pull of an effective governing capacity once it is created, nor do they perceive the attraction between potential partners for a regime capable of governing. Elitists acknowledge the attraction, but they link it to ideological kinship — because they also operate from a social-control model.

The potential for a governing partnership does not guarantee that it will be realized. But trial and error moves public officials in the direction of finding suitable allies for the task of governance. Those who try, as Atlanta's Maynard Jackson did at first, to carry out an activist agenda without extensive business involvement frequently end up frustrated. In Atlanta as elsewhere, whenever a mayor attempts to carry out a progressive program, stalemate often results.[34] In the United States especially, progressive regimes are almost always found, not in communities with a large but resource-poor lower class, but in a few communities with a resource-rich but noncorporate middle class.[35] For most areas, as in Atlanta, policy effectiveness seems to depend on being able to garner business support. These comments do not signify that voting power is unimportant, only that it is inadequate by itself to sustain a governing coalition. In nonpartisan Atlanta, with its well-organized black middle class, this group is able to use electoral leverage to gain and hold a place in the governing coalition. But it needs complementary resources, and the white downtown elite fits as a "natural ally."

Participants thus do not behave as if the underlying structure of the situation is one of polarity between the few who dominate and the many who are dominated within an integrated system of control. Instead, they act as if the capacity to govern is in question. Where are the needed resources? How can cooperation be induced? Who can provide a reliable foundation of support? With a view of the situation defined by questions such as these, the most attractive allies are those who are organized, who control essential resources, and who have a capacity to engage in a dependable system of cooperation. It is the diffuseness and incoherence of capitalist society that makes the investor class attractive as a political ally. That attraction is magnified at the local level, where the formal authority of government is especially weak, and it is magnified even more in cities like Atlanta, where the business elite fills a vacuum of civic organization.

Comparing the Two Models

Once we make the transition from a paradigm of social control to one of social production, we can see how and why challenging a regime is not simply a question of mobilizing opposition. It means restructuring the way in which people and groups are related to one another and providing new avenues of cooperation between them. That is unlikely to happen in a simple mobilization of dissent. Opposition can gain concessions, but only if it can threaten the foundation of support for the governing coalition; that is why elections matter. Opposition can replace one governing coalition with another, but only if the new coalition has a capacity to govern; that is why electoral victory is not enough.

In a world of diffuse authority, a concentration of resources is attractive. What is at issue is not so much domination and subordination as a capacity to act and accomplish goals. The power struggle concerns, not control and resistance, but gaining and fusing a capacity to act — *power to*, not *power over*. There is, of course, a point at which the two kinds of power merge, and a superior power to form a regime spills over into a kind of domination. But that is not a consideration that actors usually regard as foremost — especially given limited cognition and an inclination to act on the small opportunities that are at hand.

Realistically, we can expect that most people most of the time will not see the "big picture." They pursue immediate opportunities and respond to immediate threats — which, again, is not the same as seeking narrow, self-serving interests. The aims can be altruistic or community-serving; they may entail the advancement of a worthy institution or cause. But faced with a situation in which significant results are not easily attained, most actors will embrace the chances that are readily available. Confronted by a concentration of resources and a prevailing network of cooperating agents in an otherwise chaotic world, those who are results-oriented generally adjust their agendas to pursue the opportunities compatible with that situation; they "go along" rather than sign up for a long-term struggle to reconstitute the regime.

For most people, linking goals to an eventual reordering of the community is not a reasonable strategy.[36] After all, what any one group can do depends on what others will also do. Popular support for regime restructuring would thus require the following: (a) A substantial body of people would have to believe that a new order of things is superior *and* workable; (b) they would also have to believe that a sufficient alliance could be composed to constitute the new order—and the more far-reaching the change the new order represents, the more substantial the alliance needed to bring it off; and (c) they would have to be willing to risk immediate interests in established arrangements for the sake of long-term gains from a by-no-means-assured new order. That is a very large cognitive and motivational order, and one likely to be met only under extraordinary circumstances.[37]

My point is not that Atlanta is the best of all possible worlds but rather that the business elite does not have to control "the processes of mental production" in order to occupy a central place in the city's regime. The situation itself, characterized by weak and diffuse authority, greatly favors any group that can act cohesively and control a substantial body of resources over time. To appreciate that fact and its implications, it is necessary to put aside any notion that mass compliance and legitimacy in a system of comprehensive control are the central issues in the analysis of power. Much more to the point is the question of who can achieve coordination of effort among a select few who are strategically placed. Defining power in this way leads to the realization that the investor class, at least in Atlanta, has a considerable advantage in protecting its position politically. An expansive use of that position is likely to continue unless other elements of the community are able to lessen their dependence on business patronage and establish independent forms of civic organization.

Investor prerogative engenders resentment, but it does not seem to contain the seeds of its own destruction. In a system of divided authority and social incohesion, those who are change-oriented are attracted to, not repelled by, a group that controls enough resources to have leverage in an otherwise gridlocked world.[38] Who, then, will forego the benefits of "going along" in order to bring about regime transformation—especially if the choices are organizing for total realignment or pursuing particular and realizable aims? To reduce the costs of mustering an effective regime challenge, outside support is likely to be essential.

In summary, once we discard the notion that there is a comprehensive scheme of social control, then we can also abandon both pluralist and elitist understandings of power. Governance occurs, not as an act of will or domination, but as a coordination of efforts by those who have complementary aims. Community power accrues to those with a capacity to act in what is an otherwise diffuse system of authority. That, the Atlanta experience suggests, is neither elite rule nor pluralism, as conventionally understood.

Just as physics teaches that it is sometimes useful to treat light as a particle and other times as a wave, so political analysis may find it useful to treat power sometimes in terms of the social-control model and other times in terms of the social-production model. On questions of community governance, the social-production model seems especially appropriate.

CONCLUSION

In this chapter, I have presented a set of assumptions about how society operates. These form what I call a social-production model, a model intended to illuminate the workings of regime politics. By contrasting social production with social control, I have emphasized that urban regimes do not involve comprehensive efforts to control local communities or even the belief systems of local publics; influence yes, control no.

Urban regimes are arrangements for acting, for accomplishing policy goals, for managing friction points between groups, for adapting to an exogenous process of social change. These arrangements are informal; they enable public bodies and private interests to function together in making and implementing governing decisions. Because they are informal, these arrangements involve no overarching form of command. They facilitate the mobilization of resources and the coordination of efforts through an ability to promote cooperation. The inadequacies of formal governmental authority are the foundation for urban regimes and account for the necessity of developing informal arrangements to bring about civic cooperation.

If society lacks high coherence and formal authority is weak, then a capacity to govern cannot be taken as a given. The very fragmentation of modern society enhances the value of a capacity to promote cooperation that can link institutional sectors. That is the ability Atlanta's business elite has demonstrated, and it is what makes this group attractive as a potential ally.

In order to understand conflict and coalition formation in urban regimes, we need to recognize that these regimes are empowering to their members. Conflicts — between races, over particular interests, between haves and have-nots, over ideology, between development and residential interests, and many more — are constrained by the fact that governance requires informal collaboration between the major institutional sectors of the community. Groups can refuse to collaborate, but, if they do, nongovernance may occur on the issues they care about, and nongovernance is a form of powerlessness. Hence, there is an attraction toward arrangements that allow governance to occur, an attraction to the situation of empowerment.

It is this attraction that is at the heart of business influence. A city's major business enterprises control too many vital resources, organizational as well as economic, to be excluded. Regime form is contingent on the ability and willingness of business groups to unify and establish patterns of civic cooperation, and on the ability and willingness of nonbusiness groups to organize separately and autonomously. Thus, the ways in which nongovernmental sectors of the community are associated provide the context for empowerment. The capacity to produce governing decisions rests on the existence and use of an informal arrangement of civic cooperation, a fact that works against simple polarization. In Atlanta, it works against any tendency for nonbusiness interests to come together and challenge the governing role of business elites.

Urban regimes and civic cooperation are shaped less by ideology than by the ability to allocate small opportunities. These opportunities include selective material benefits that are important in solving the free-rider problem in collective action and in providing a means to apply discipline. But small opportunities also encompass the opportunity to be purposeful (even when the purpose is a small one) and the opportunity to accomplish a task (even when the task is a narrow one). In a given community, the politics of regime structuring is influenced by such issues as who allocates small opportunities and on what basis *and* who is able institutionally to discern and act on important policy questions. In the case of Atlanta, it is the business elite that has a major voice in allocating small opportunities as well as an institutional capacity to plan and act on key long-range questions.

Civic cooperation is not a uniform need of urban regimes. As suggested earlier, a caretaker regime, concerned mainly with the provision of routine services, requires simple coordination compared to an activist regime, such as the one in postwar Atlanta. An activist policy agenda is associated nationally with the term "positive state," meaning a state that is extensively committed to problem solving and service provision. Sometimes business and government have been regarded as antagonists, under the assumption that the positive state is engaged primarily in the regulation of business enterprise, the meeting of popular needs, and the promotion of a progressive income distribution. In this scenario, government and business are, in John Kenneth Galbraith's words, "countervailing powers." Such a scenario fails to capture much of the policy activity at the national level, and at the local level is quite misses the point. As the Atlanta experience illustrates, government and business are mutually attracting. Business resources are essential in policymaking; that is, essential in "positive" governance. Partnership with business can therefore be empowering, which is what the social-production model highlights.

Some of my earlier work dealt with the structural reasons why local officials are drawn to partnership with business.[39] I now believe that argument did not go far enough. Business is neither a reluctant nor a passive partner in governance, simply resting on its structural laurels. Atlanta's postwar political experience is a story of active business-elite efforts to make the most of their economic and organizational resources in setting the terms on which civic cooperation occurs. Thus downtown business has not been content to sit back and be courted as a source of investment capital. Instead, the business elite has engaged actively in formulating a policy agenda and in structuring a set of arrangements through which that agenda could be advanced. In doing so, the business elite has relied extensively on public authority and public revenue. The regime is thus empowering for the business elite; in partnership with local government, it can accomplish much more than it can alone.

The dependence of downtown business on governmental action is an underappreciated point. The city's black middle class has perhaps grasped the point more fully than any other group in the community, and it has exacted significant concessions. But black efforts to pursue a broadly progressive agenda have come mainly from individuals who were not regime insiders — student protest leaders in the early 1960s and Maynard Jackson, who came into office without an apprenticeship in insider negotiation. Neither student leaders nor Jackson as mayor were able to sustain their efforts.

Business-elite say in the affording of small opportunities has been integral to the incorporation of the black middle class on terms that advance rather than "countervail" business policy interests. The black working class is not yet organized around its economic interest and is relegated to the position of recipient class in a system of trickle-down benefits.

Preservationists, the arts subcommunity, and the largely white neighborhood movement have found themselves hampered by business-elite control of small opportunities. Their dependence on business patronage emerges from their own inability to coalesce and create a cohesive network of civic cooperation. Generally, the resources of such voluntary associations and other nonprofit groups are meager and their inclination to federate is weak. By contrast, the business corporation concentrates organizational and economic resources in the hands of a few; where there are strong mutual interests, as among the downtown business elite, these few are able to act with considerable unity and promote an extensive system of civic cooperation. Given the weakness of governmental authority and fragmentation in the nonprofit sector, the business elite is uniquely able to enhance the capacity of a local regime to govern.

An imbalance in abilities to contribute to the capacity to govern is thus at the core of the Atlanta regime. Until that imbalance is corrected, biased governance and weak governance appear to be the only real alternatives. That is the lesson to be learned from a social-production model.

12

Conclusion

An economist is one who observes something that works in practice and wonders if it will work in theory.
                                                                    —Victor Fuchs

Logic is a wonderful weapon, but it won't work unless you consider all of the facts.
                                                           —Alfred Sheinwold

In earlier work, I argued that the attributes of business elites and other upper-strata groups made them appealing to public officials as allies. The social-production model elaborates that position, indicating why, for example, Atlanta's downtown elite is attractive as a partner not only with city hall but also with various community groups. This elite controls resources of the kind and in the amount able to enhance the regime's capacity to govern. Minus these business-supplied resources, governing in Atlanta—with its substantial civic vacuum—would consist of little more than the provision of routine services. In Atlanta, then, the very capacity for strong governance is dependent on active business collaboration.

The position of Atlanta's business elite in the affairs of the community is *not* that of a passive partner in a courtship conducted by public officials. The elite has collective aims that it is organized to pursue. Hence, business influence in Atlanta is no mere matter of holding mobile capital; the business elite is an active part of the governing coalition and uses that position to further the claims that it makes on public authority and public resources.

The process through which this happens involves a complex interplay between majority rule and the unequal distribution of resources. The social-production model makes us appreciate that democracy is not simply the aggregation of individual preferences. An integral part of politics, no less in

234

democracies than in other forms of government, is the coordination of institutional capacities in the task of governance.

SELECTED REGIME PATTERNS

Students of international regimes maintain that less costly forms of cooperation prevail over more costly ones.[1] In employing a social-production model, I reach a related but somewhat different conclusion. Cost is only one side of the equation. Even though caretaker regimes are less costly to operate, they have given way to more activist regimes in Atlanta and many other places. The reason is that groups vary in their capacity to pay the cost of coordination, and some groups — Atlanta's business elite, as a case in point — are determined to be central partners in activist regimes and have the resources to do it. In Atlanta, the business elite has been able not only to achieve partnership in the governing coalition but also to help create a regime capable of executing complex and controversial projects.

Obviously Atlanta represents conditions that do not exist everywhere. Although detailed information on the civic life of many cities is not at hand, enough is known about other cases to allow some very general comparisons. Regimes involve arrangements through which elements of the community are engaged in producing publicly significant results *and providing a variety of small opportunities.* The latter task often overshadows broader questions and makes it possible for governing coalitions to gain cooperation even though their larger goals enjoy only weak or uneven popular support.

The small-opportunities phenomenon is especially important because it accounts for the tendency of a capacity for coordination to accumulate strength. That is why the metaphor of gravitation describes the workings of a regime. The greater the ability of a regime arrangement to contribute to and coordinate project efforts, the more other elements of the community are attracted to "going along." The gravitational pull of one body also depends on how much mass is concentrated in other bodies; two equal units counterbalance one another, whereas one large unit holds several small ones in its orbit. So it is with a coordinating capacity. Small capacities for coordination have weak pull in the presence of a large capacity. Politically, that enables the large coordinating capacity to divide and rule over small capacities — for example, accommodating one theater group willing to "go along" while forcing an "opposition" theater group out of an area of intensifying development. Thus, not going along means surrendering opportunities, particularly if one coordinating capacity dominates the civic scene.

The analogy of gravitational force is limited in what it explains. Civic actors are not fixed bodies exerting a mechanistic influence on one another. They may unite and form a larger group; that is what Atlanta's downtown elite accomplished in order to avoid operating in fragmented style as single business enterprises or as competing factions. Civic actors may also ally with others to create a "federation" that joins different centers of institutional strength; that is what the black middle class did to enhance its appeal as a coalition ally in 1946. Furthermore, the governing regime itself is a form of federation, though not necessarily among equals.

The creation of a regime from scratch is imaginable but not likely. The cost of coordination would be enormous — hence the strong relevance of the problem of collective action to regime formation. Federation among existing organizations is one way the problem can be solved,[2] but this means that existing collectivities (or better yet, alliances of collectivities) are especially attractive — more so if they, in turn, can contribute resources to the overall task of coordination and governance.

The special features of Atlanta's downtown elite are highlighted in this context of regime formation as a problem in collective action. Being a highly cohesive entity makes the elite attractive. The unity of the business elite also provides it with ample resources *of the kind* that enable it to enforce discipline on behalf of civic cooperation. Because the ability of Atlanta's public sector to offer selective incentives is limited, the business elite has a unique capacity to make side payments, afford small opportunities, and deliver on them as a way of promoting coordination. It is thus able to play a key regime-building role, largely on its own terms.

Regime building is a form of collective action; it is like one association being able to use selective incentives to overcome a free-rider problem whereas other associations lack a comparable store of incentives. The one association can pursue its collective good, others cannot. There is an added complication to this situation, because the selective incentives that attach to an ongoing association make its members reluctant to give up that association for other possible attachments.

Atlanta is not totally unique in having a unified business elite engaged in regime building. Dallas and San Antonio offer parallel situations, where the business elite replaced relatively weak forms of patronage politics and filled the resulting civic vacuum.[3] Kindred patterns of regime building may be found in other communities. In Flint, Michigan, the enormous resources of the Mott Foundation have been a major force in promoting coordination, bringing business and government together, and concerting civic action around a number of complex projects.[4] Pittsburgh is a case where a business elite took the initiative in allying with a strong form of patronage politics (the Democratic machine under David Lawrence) to create a cohesive regime, similar in many respects to Atlanta's nonpartisan regime.[5] In other cities, public-sector entrepreneurs have played the key role in regime building. Richard Daley in Chicago,[6] Richard Lee in New Haven,[7] and Kevin White in Boston[8] are among the well-documented cases of entrepreneurial mayors. In the New

York area, Robert Moses[9] and Austin Tobin[10] are two noted administrators who built regimes within limited functional boundaries.

Entrepreneurs do not start with nothing; they build mainly with institutional blocks already available. When Daley became mayor, for example, he held onto the position of county party chairman to retain command of the Democratic machine, and he allied with downtown business and other established centers of power. Thus, entrepreneurship is largely a federation strategy, and its success depends partly on existing centers of institutional strength and the ties among them. A dominant entrepreneur is not essential. Atlanta's regime, for example, is not tied to the organizational skill of any single person, though many individuals have played major roles—including mayors Hartsfield and Allen, A. T. Walden and Jesse Hill from the black community, Robert Woodruff within the business elite, and Dan Sweat as head of CAP. Even though some of the key individuals have held elected office, the cohesion of the Atlanta regime is not highly dependent on public leadership. By contrast, regime cohesion in some other cities does seem to depend greatly on the skill of important officeholders—Chicago is an obvious example—though, of course, cohesion never rests on a single factor.

Successful federation depends partly on the nature of the policies pursued. For many years, Mayor Erastus Corning of Albany maintained a machine-centered regime, but on the basis of a caretaker policy with largely passive business participation.[11] Progressive policies, however, present a much different problem. They involve a regime in a difficult coordination task but do not attract business allies with substantial slack resources. Business is likely to represent a strong gravitational counterforce, particularly if it is itself highly organized. For progressive administrations, regime cohesion and durability is often a problem, as Maynard Jackson's initial experience and the case of the Lindsay administration in New York City illustrate.[12] As suggested earlier, the few places where progressive regimes have taken hold seem to be smaller cities with a resource-endowed middle class relatively unattached to corporate business.[13] In Atlanta, by contrast, the black middle class that was such a vital constituency to Maynard Jackson was also tied to the downtown elite.

Progressive policies often meet resistance, but as the Atlanta case shows, business-backed redevelopment policies also encounter substantial opposition. Yet the latter often prove viable while the former do not. The reason seems to lie in the nature of the policy itself, which has much to do with the kinds of incentives that may be available to overcome resistance. Redevelopment projects generate abundant selective incentives and lend themselves to coalition building.[14] Also, business leaders will concur with the wide use of selective incentives to divide and decrease opposition to displacement for economic development projects.[15] On the other hand, the Atlanta experience suggests that business leaders may regard allocations of assistance, especially those not tied to business-backed projects, as a "power grab" by elected officials. The one use of selective incentives they will actively support, the other they tend to oppose. Regime cohesion thus comes to be linked closely with policy stance.

Regime patterns, then, differ along a number of dimensions: the array of organizations and collectivities available for federation, personal leadership skill, and particular policy stance.[16] In short, regimes can be constructed in alternative ways and around different policy orientations. Although patterns are not predetermined mechanistically, it is clear that some regimes are easier to assemble and maintain than others. It is also clear that groups vary in their capacity to meet the costs of coordination entailed in regime building.

The politics of regime formation enables us to see how complicated actual urban democracies are. As will be explored in the section below, the egalitarian principle of "one person, one vote" has limited play within a setting of unequal social and economic resources, especially when those resources are useful in coordinating the diverse activities found in urban communities.

THE POLITICAL RAMIFICATIONS OF UNEQUAL RESOURCES

From Aristotle to Tocqueville to the present, keen political observers have understood that politics evolves from and reflects the associational life of a community. How people are grouped is important — so much so that, as the authors of the *Federalist* essays understood, the formation and reformation of coalitions is at the heart of political activity. Democracy should be viewed within that context; i.e., realizing that people do not act together simply because they share preferences on some particular issue.

Overlooking that long-standing lesson, many public-choice economists regard democracy with suspicion. They fear that popular majorities will insist on an egalitarian redistribution of benefits and thereby interfere with economic productivity. As worded by one economist, "The majority (the poor) will always vote for taxing the minority (the rich), at least until the opportunities for benefiting from redistribution run out."[17] In other words, majority rule will overturn an unequal distribution of goods and resources. This reasoning, however, involves the simple-minded premise that formal governmental authority confers a capacity to redistribute at the will of those who hold office by virtue of popular election. The social-production model of politics employed here offers a contrasting view. Starting from an assumption about the costliness of civic cooperation, the social-production model suggests that an unequal distribution of goods and resources substantially modifies majority rule.

In operation, democracy is a great deal more complicated than counting votes and sorting through the wants of rational egoists. In response to those who regard democracy as a process of aggregating preferences within a system characterized by formal equality, a good antidote is Stein Rokkan's aphorism, "Votes count but resources decide."[18] Voting power is certainly not insignificant, but policies are decided mainly by those who control important concentrations of resources. Hence, governing is never simply a matter of aggregating numbers, whether for redistribution or other purposes.

How governing coalitions are put together is the focus of this book. An underlying question throughout has been why one alignment has prevailed over others. The Atlanta case suggests that a key factor is control of resources in a quantity and of a kind that can lead groups to ally with one set of arrangements instead of another. Thus any element of the community that has a unique capacity to promote action—whether by making side payments, affording small opportunities, or some other means—has a claim on membership in the governing coalition.

Of course, the election of key public officials provides a channel of popular expression. Since democracy rests on the principle of equal voting power, it would seem that all groups do share in the capacity to become part of the governing regime. Certainly the vote played a major role in the turnaround of the position of blacks in Atlanta. Popular control, however, is not a simple and straightforward process. Much depends on how the populace is organized to participate in a community's civic life. Machine politics, for example, promotes a search for personal favors. With electoral mobilization dependent upon an organizational network oriented toward patronage and related considerations, other kinds of popular concerns may have difficulty gaining expression.[19] The political machine thus enjoys a type of preemptive power, though the party organization is only one aspect of the overall governing regime.

On the surface, Atlanta represents a situation quite different from machine politics. Nonpartisan elections and an absence of mass patronage have characterized the city throughout the post–World War II era. Yet it would hardly be accurate to describe civic life in Atlanta as open and fluid. Nonpartisanship has heightened the role of organizations connected to business, and the newspapers have held an important position in policy debate. At the same time, working-class organizations and nonprofit groups unsupported by business are not major players in city politics.

Within Atlanta's civic sector, activities serve to piece together concerns across the institutional lines of the community, connecting government with business and each with a variety of nonprofit entities. The downtown elite has been especially adept at building alliances in that sector and, in doing so, has extended its resource advantage well beyond the control of strictly economic functions. Responding to its own weakness in numbers, the business elite has crafted a network through which cooperation can be advanced and potential cleavages between haves and have-nots redirected.

Consider what Atlanta's postwar regime represents. In 1946, the central element in the governing coalition was a downtown business elite organized for and committed to an active program of redevelopment that would transform the character of the business district and, in the process, displace a largely black population to the south and east of the district. At the same time, with the end of the white primary that same year, a middle-class black population, long excluded from power, mobilized its electoral strength to begin an assault on a firmly entrenched Jim Crow system. Knowing only those facts, one might well have predicted in 1946 that these two groups would be political antagonists. They were not. Both committed to an agenda of change, they worked out an accommodation and became the city's governing coalition. The alliance has had its tensions and even temporary ruptures, but it has held and demonstrated remarkable strength in making and carrying out policy decisions.

To understand the process, the Atlanta experience indicates that one must appreciate institutional capacities and the resources that various groups control. That is why simple preference aggregation is no guide to how coalitions are built. The downtown elite and the black middle class had complementary needs that could be met by forming an alliance, and the business elite in particular had the kind and amount of resources to knit the alliance together.

Politics in Atlanta, then, is not organized around an overriding division between haves and have-nots. Instead, unequally distributed resources serve to destabilize opposition and encourage alliances around small opportunities. Without command of a capacity to govern, elected leaders have difficulty building support around popular discontent. That is why Rokkan's phrase, "Votes count but resources decide," is so apt.

UNEQUAL RESOURCES AND URBAN REGIMES

Regimes, I have suggested, are to be understood in terms of (1) who makes up the governing coalition and (2) how the coalition achieves cooperation. Both points illustrate how the unequal distribution of resources affects politics and what differences the formation of a regime makes. That the downtown elite is a central partner in the Atlanta regime shapes the priorities set and the trade-offs made. Hence, investor prerogative is protected practice in Atlanta, under the substantial influence of the business elite *within* the governing coalition. At the same time, the fact that the downtown elite is part of a governing coalition prevents business isolation from community affairs. Yet, although "corporate responsibility" promotes business involvement, it does so in a way that enhances business as patron and promoter of small opportunities.

Similarly, the incorporation of the black middle class into the mainstream civic and economic life of Atlanta is testimony to its ability to use electoral leverage to help set community priorities. The importance of the mode of cooperation is also evident. Although much of what the regime has done has generated popular resistance, the black middle class has been persuaded to go along by a combination of selective incentives and small opportunities. Alliance with the business elite enabled the black middle class to achieve particular objectives not readily available by other means. This kind of enabling capacity is what gives concentrated resources its gravitational force.

The pattern thus represents something more than individual cooptation. The black middle class as a group benefited from new housing areas in the early postwar years and from employment and business opportunities in recent years. Some of the beneficiaries have been institutional—colleges in the Atlanta University system and a financially troubled bank, for example. Because the term "selective incentives" implies individual benefits (and these have been important), the more inclusive term "small opportunities" provides a useful complement. In both cases, the business elite is a primary source; they can make things happen, provide needed assistance, and open up opportunities. At the same time, since the downtown elite needs the cooperation of local government and various community groups, the elite itself is drawn toward a broad community-leadership role. Although its bottom-line economic interests are narrow, its community role can involve it in wider concerns. Selective incentives, however, enable the elite to muffle some of the pressure that might otherwise come from the larger community.

Once we focus on the regime and the importance of informally achieved cooperation, we can appreciate better the complex way in which local politics actually functions. Public-choice economists, fearful that democracy will lead to redistribution, misunderstand the process and treat politics as a causal force operating in isolation from resources other than the vote. That clearly is unwarranted. Atlanta's business elite possesses substantial slack resources that can be and are devoted to politics. Some devotion of resources to political purposes is direct, in the form of campaign funds, but much is indirect; it takes on the character of facilitating civic cooperation for those efforts deemed worthy.

The business elite is small and homogeneous enough to use the norms of class unity and corporate responsibility to maintain its cohesion internally. In interacting with allies, the prevailing mode of operation is reciprocity, reinforced in many cases by years of trust built from past exchanges. The biracial insiders have also been at their tasks long enough to experience a sense of pride in the community role they play. Even so, the coalition is centered around a combination of explicit and tacit deals. Reciprocity is thus the hallmark of Atlanta's regime, and reciprocity hinges on what one actor can do for another. Instead of promoting redistribution toward equality, such a system perpetuates inequality.

Reciprocity, of course, occurs in a context, and in Atlanta, it is interwoven with a complex set of conditions. The slack resources controlled by business corporations give them an extraordinary opportunity to promote civic cooperation. Where there is a compelling mutual interest, as within Atlanta's downtown elite, businesses have the means to solve their own collective-action problem and unite behind a program of action. Their resources also enable them to create a network of cooperation that extends across lines of institutional division, which makes them attractive to public officials and other results-oriented community groups. In becoming an integral part of a system of civic cooperation, Atlanta's business elite has used its resource advantage to shape community policy and protect a privileged position. Because the elite is useful to others, it attracts and holds a variety of allies in its web of reciprocity. The concentration of resources it has gathered thus enables the elite to counter demands for greater equality.

SOCIAL LEARNING VERSUS PRIVILEGE

Instead of understanding democratic politics as an instance of the equality (redistribution)/efficiency (productivity) trade-off, I suggest an alternative. Policy actions (and inactions) have extensive repercussions and involve significant issues that do not fit neatly into an equality-versus-efficiency mold. There is a need, then, for members of the governing coalition to be widely informed about a community's problems, and not to be indifferent about the information. That is what representative democracy is about.

For their part, in order to be productive, business enterprises need a degree of autonomy and a supply of slack resources. It is also appropriate that they participate in politics. However, there are dangers involved in the ability of high-resource groups, like Atlanta's business elite, to secure for themselves a place in the governing coalition and then use that inside position along with their own ample resources to shape the regime on their terms. Elsewhere I have called this "preemptive power,"[20] and have suggested that it enables a group to protect a privileged position. The ability to parcel out selective incentives and other small opportunities permits Atlanta's business elite to enforce discipline on behalf of civic cooperation by vesting others with lesser privileges — privileges perhaps contingently held in return for "going along."

The flip side of discipline through selective incentives is a set of contingent privileges that restrict the questions asked and curtail social learning. Thus one of the trade-offs in local politics can be phrased as social learning versus privilege. Some degree of privilege for business may be necessary to encourage investment, but the greater the privilege being protected, the less the incentive to understand and act on behalf of the community in its entirety.

The political challenge illustrated by the Atlanta case is how to reconstitute the regime so that both social learning and civic cooperation occur. The risk in the present situation is that those who govern have only a limited comprehension of the consequences of their actions. Steps taken to correct one problem may create or aggravate another while leaving still others unaddressed. Those who govern can discover that only, it seems, through wide representation of the affected groups. Otherwise, choices are limited by an inability to understand the city's full situation.

No governing coalition has an inclination to expand the difficulties of making and carrying out decisions. Still, coalitions can be induced to attempt the difficult. For example, Atlanta's regime has been centrally involved in race relations, perhaps the community's most difficult and volatile issue. Relationships within the governing coalition have been fraught with tension; friction was unavoidable. Yet the coalition achieved a cooperative working relationship between the black middle class and the white business elite. In a rare but telling incident, black leaders insisted successfully that a 1971 pledge to build a MARTA spur to a black public-housing area not be repudiated. The newspaper opined that trust within the coalition was too important to be sacrificed on the altar of economizing. Thus the task of the governing regime was expanded beyond the narrow issue of serving downtown in the least expensive manner possible; concerns *can* be broadened.

Although no regime is likely to be totally inclusive, most regimes can be made more inclusive. Just as Atlanta's regime was drawn into dealing with race relations, others can become sensitive to the situations of a larger set of groups. Greater inclusiveness will not come automatically nor from the vote alone. Pressures to narrow the governing coalition are strong and recurring. Yet, if civic cooperation is the key to the terms on which economic and electoral power are accommodated, then more inclusive urban regimes can be encouraged through an associational life at the community level that reflects a broad range of perspectives. The problem is not an absence of associational life at that level but how to lessen its dependence on business sponsorship, how to free participation in civic activity from an overriding concern with protecting insider privileges, and how to enrich associational life so that nonprofit and other groups can function together as they express encompassing community concerns.

This step is one in which federal policy could make a fundamental difference. In the past, starting with the urban-redevelopment provision in the 1949 housing act and continuing through the Carter administration's UDAG program, cities have been strongly encouraged to devise partnerships with private, for-profit developers, thus intensifying already strong leanings in that direction. Since these were matters of legislative choice, it seems fully possible for the federal government to move in another direction and encourage nonprofit organizations. The federal government could, for example, establish a program of large-scale assistance to community development corporations and other nonprofit groups. Some foundations now support such programs, but their modest efforts could be augmented. Programs of community service required by high schools and colleges or spawned by a national-level service requirement could increase voluntary participation and alter the character of civic life in local communities. It is noteworthy that neighborhood mobilization in Atlanta was partly initiated by VISTA (Volunteers in Service to America) workers in the 1960s and continued by those who stayed in the city after completing service with VISTA. This, however, is not the place to prescribe a full set of remedies; my aim is only to indicate that change is possible but will probably require a stimulus external to the local community.

SUMMING UP

If the slack resources of business help to set the terms on which urban governance occurs, then we need to be aware of what this imbalance means. The Atlanta case suggests that the more uneven the distribution of resources, the greater the tendency of the regime to become concerned with protecting privilege. Concurrently, there is a narrowing of the regime's willingness to engage in "information seeking" (or social learning). Imbalances in the civic sector thus lead to biases in policy, biases that electoral politics alone is unable to correct.

A genuinely effective regime is not only adept at promoting cooperation in the execution of complex and nonroutine projects, but is also able to comprehend the consequences of its actions and inactions for a diverse citizenry. The promotion of this broad comprehension is, after all, a major aim of democracy. Even if democratic politics were removed from the complexities of coordination for social production, it still could not be reduced to a set of decision rules. Arrow's theorem shows that majority choices cannot be neutrally aggregated when preference structures are complex,[21] as indeed they are bound to be in modern societies.

Democracy, then, is not simply a decision rule for registering choices; it has to operate with a commitment to inclusiveness. Permanent or excluded minorities are inconsistent with the basic idea of equality that underpins democracy. That is why some notion of social learning is an essential part of the democratic process; all are entitled to have their situations understood. Thus, to the extent that urban regimes safeguard special privileges at the expense of social learning, democracy is weakened.

Those fearful that too much community participation will lead to unproductive policies should widen their own understanding and consider other dangers on the political landscape. Particularly under conditions of an imbalance in civically useful resources, the political challenge is one of preventing government from being harnessed to the protection of special privilege. The social-production model reminds us that only a segment of society's institutions are under the sway of majority rule; hence, actual governance is never simply a matter of registering the preferences of citizens as individuals.

The character of local politics depends greatly on the nature of a community's associational life, which in turn depends greatly on the distribution of resources other than the vote. Of course, the vote is significant, but equality in the right to vote is an inadequate guarantee against the diversion of politics into the protection of privilege. If broad social learning is to occur, then other considerations must enter the picture. "One person, one vote" is not enough.

Appendix A.

A Socioeconomic Profile of Atlanta and Other Black-Majority Cities

In a world geared exclusively to reciprocity, the rich use their freedom to get richer and the poor, alas, use theirs to become poorer.
— William K. Muir

One of the gravest dangers facing the Movement is the alienation, the drawing away of the black middle class from the black impoverished masses.
— John Oliver Killens

The figures in Table A.1 compare Atlanta with the seven other cities over two hundred thousand in population which have a black majority. Among these cities, all have lost population between 1970 and 1980, and again between 1980 and 1986. Atlanta stands out in this group as the fastest growing metropolitan area. Atlanta is second only to Washington, D.C., in proportion of population that is black and also second to Washington in proportion of the population who have completed college.

Using the ratio of the population employed in professional managerial *occupations* as a measure of postindustrialism, and the ratio in the goods-producing *sector* as a measure of industrialism, Atlanta falls decidedly on the postindustrial side. Washington has by far the largest proportion of its population in professional and managerial positions and the smallest proportion of its workforce in the goods-producing sector. Falling second and third behind Washington, New Orleans and Atlanta are virtual twins on these two measures. Richmond, Atlanta's fellow state capital, also has a similar profile. Newark and Detroit fall at the opposite end of the spectrum, as the most heavily industrial and blue-collar of the eight cities.

Although Atlanta is predominantly a services and white-collar city in this set, it is also a city of economic extremes.[1] It is second only to Newark in

Table A.1 Atlanta Compared with Other Black-Majority Cities over 200,000 in Population

	Atlanta	Baltimore	Birmingham	Detroit	New Orleans	Newark	Richmond	Washington, D.C.
City Population[2] (000s)								
1986	422	753	278	1,086	554	316	218	626
1980	425	787	284	1,203	558	329	219	638
Population Change (%)								
1980–86	−0.7	−4.3	−2.1	−9.7	−0.7	−4.0	−0.5	−1.9
1970–80	−14.1	−13.0	−5.6	−20.5	−5.9	−13.9	−12.0	−15.7
SMSA Population (000s)								
1986	2,561	2,280	911	4,335*	1,334	1,889*	810	3,563
1980	2,138	2,200	884	4,488*	1,256	1,879*	761	3,251
Change 1980–86 (%)	+19.8	+3.6	+3.1	−3.4	+6.2	+0.5	+6.4	+9.6
City 1980								
Black	66.6	54.8	55.6	63.0	55.3	58.3	51.3	70.3
Hispanic	1.4	1.0	0.7	2.4	3.5	18.6	1.0	2.8
Housing								
owner occupied	41.3	47.2	53.3	57.9	39.7	21.1	47.1	35.5
built 1960 or later	37.7	15.8	31.6	8.6	27.2	17.6	33.3	22.2
Median Family Income	$13,591	$15,721	$15,210	$17,033	$15,003	$11,989	$16,820	$19,099

Table A.1 Atlanta Compared with Other Black-Majority Cities over 200,000 in Population (*Continued*)

	Atlanta	Baltimore	Birmingham	Detroit	New Orleans	Newark	Richmond	Washington, D.C.
Poverty level								
All	27.5	22.9	22.0	21.9	26.4	32.8	19.3	18.6
Under 18	39.2	32.5	31.3	31.5	38.7	46.3	30.3	27.0
Household income								
< $10,000	45.3	40.2	43.1	38.7	43.7	49.6	36.3	30.5
> $50,000	4.6	2.5	2.1	2.7	4.4	1.3	3.4	7.7
Education								
High School or more	60.2	48.4	60.4	54.2	59.2	44.6	57.1	67.1
4 years college or more	20.5	11.3	13.0	8.3	17.7	6.3	19.8	27.5
Persons over 16 employed in								
Professional & Managerial occupations	24.2	19.5	19.9	16.6	24.3	12.3	24.1	32.6
Goods-Producing Sector	18.4	24.0	22.4	31.2	18.3	35.4	22.6	8.1

Figures are in percentages except where otherwise specified.

*PSMA

Table A.2   Atlanta Profile over Time

	1950	1960	1970	1980	1985–86
City area (square miles)	37	136	132	131	131
City population (000s)	331	488	495	425	422
SMSA population (000s)	727	1017	1390	2138	2561
City statistics (%)					
Black	36.6	38.3	51.4	66.6	67.6
High school graduate	33.0	40.5	46.5	60.2	n.a.
Owner occupied housing	39.9	45.6	41.1	41.3	n.a.
Goods producing	23.5	23.6	22.6	18.4	n.a.
Professional &					
managerial	16.7	18.2	21.0	24.2	n.a.
Poverty rate*	n.a.	24.2	15.9	23.7	n.a.

*Poverty-rate figures are for families in 1959, 1969, 1979.

the proportion of poverty-level population and in households below $10,000 in income, and it has the second lowest median income of the cities compared here. Although it is also second to Washington, D.C., in percentage of households with over $50,000 in annual income, some subtraction shows that Atlanta is also tied with Newark for the smallest percentage of households between $10,000 and $50,000. Finally, Atlanta is the newest city physically, with the highest percentage of housing built since 1960; however, the city falls toward the middle in proportion of homeowners.

Table A.2 traces Atlanta's growth in the period since World War II, showing a huge jump in area and population following the 1952 annexation under the Plan of Improvement. Rising black population, though slowed by the annexation, is rapid thereafter. Increasing educational levels and proportion of the population employed in professional and managerial occupations are also evident, but perhaps contrary to expectations, these changes are not accompanied by improvements in economic position. Homeownership rates rose with annexation, but then declined and held steady. Poverty rates have fluctuated, as have the national figures (which were over 22 percent in 1959, then dropped to 11 percent in the mid 1970s before rising to 14 percent in the mid 1980s). The Atlanta figures are higher and have shown little improvement over time. The trend toward a postindustrial or services-oriented economy is also evident in the table.

Appendix B.
A Chronology of Major Events, 1946–1988

Events are defined not by any measure of detail, specificity or concreteness within the chronology of happenings but by their significance as markers of transition.
— Philip Abrams

The knowledge of things in particular removes from people's minds that delusion into which they . . . fall . . . by looking at things in general.
— Machiavelli

1937	W. Hartsfield elected mayor on reform platform, backed by and closely allied with downtown elite.
1941	Formation of downtown business association, predecessor to CAP.
1946	Lochner plan begins massive displacement for expressways.
1946	Blacks protest police conduct and ask for hiring of black police.
1946	End of white primary followed by black voter mobilization.
1946	Beginning negotiations over "Negro expansion" areas for housing.
1948	First black police officers hired.
1949	Hartsfield reelected mayor with black support.
1950–1957	Political and legal moves and countermoves over redevelopment, overcoming small business and neighborhood opposition and culminating in a biracial coalition around five projects providing expansion land for the Atlanta University system, new areas for black housing development, and removal of low-income residences near the central business district.
1952	Plan of Improvement goes into effect, quadrupling land size of city and bringing affluent white northsiders into city.
1953	Dr. R. Clement elected as first black member of Atlanta school board.

251

1957	Mayor Hartsfield reelected despite strong challenge by die-hard segregationist L. Maddox.
1958	Negotiations lead to a court case through which public transportation in Atlanta is desegregated.
1960	Sit-ins signal generational change in black community.
1961	Peaceful school desegregation and negotiated desegregation of most downtown public accommodations.
1961	Chamber of Commerce president I. Allen elected mayor over L. Maddox.
1963	Mayor Allen testifies in favor of national civil-rights bill.
1965	Protests begin over C. W. Hill school in Buttermilk Bottom.
1965	Mayor Allen easily reelected; first black city councilmember elected.
1966	Neighborhood protests widen, civil disorder occurs, and mayor establishes Housing Resources Committee.
1968	Black opposition contributes to MARTA referendum defeat.
1969	Creation of Action Forum and Leadership Atlanta.
1969	In-town neighborhood movement originates with opposition to expressways.
1969	S. Massell elected mayor with black support over business-elite-backed candidate; M. Jackson elected as vice-mayor.
1970–1973	Census shows black majority for first time; efforts to enlarge city limits fail.
1971	MARTA referendum passes in city of Atlanta and counties of Fulton and DeKalb with substantial black support after minority business and employment agreements and assurances that rail lines will serve westside Atlanta.
1973	Biracial school compromise reached, with limited busing and the naming of a black superintendent.
1973	New city charter, with two-thirds council and two-thirds school board elected by district; mandates citizen participation in planning.
1973	First black mayor, M. Jackson, elected, with overwhelming support in black community and with backing from the Citywide League of Neighborhoods.
1974	Council adopts NPU system, and mayor provides advocacy planning staff, to implement citizen-participation mandate.
1974	Mayor pushes affirmative action in city contracts and city hiring and calls for businesses to employ blacks in high positions.
1974–1975	Brockey letter from CAP to mayor, followed by newspapers' "City in Crisis" series, signaling conflict between Mayor Jackson and the business elite; followed by Pound Cake Summit meetings; eventually business accepts minority contracting, and bank loans to black entrepreneurs are facilitated.
1975	Drolet letter, breaking "diplomatic relations" between Citywide League of Neighborhoods and CAP.

1978   First black president of Chamber of Commerce, J. Hill, elected.

1981   Second black president of Chamber of Commerce, H. Russell, elected.

1981   A. Young elected mayor without business support but negotiates new understanding of cooperation with downtown elite.

1982   Mayor Young comes into conflict with in-town neighborhoods and preservationists over Presidential Parkway and subsequent issues.

1985   Mayor Young reelected without serious neighborhood challenge.

Appendix C.
A Note on Method and Sources

> *Historical sociology is more a matter of how one interprets the world than of what bit of it one chooses to study.*
>
> —Philip Abrams

Reflections on the Historical Approach

Early in my teaching career, one of my students, wise in his naiveté, gave me an insight into the ways of social science when he concluded his essay with: "And these are the conclusions on which I base my facts." V. O. Key and Frank Munger phrased the matter more delicately: "The answers one gets depend in part on the kinds of questions one asks."[1] Thomas Kuhn has a more elaborate argument, suggesting that the scientific paradigms from which testable hypotheses are drawn have built into them criteria of evidence and expectations of normality that narrow and limit understanding.[2] Much of any theory, he maintains, is tacit and assumed rather than directly investigated.

However the issue is expressed, what we see rests partly on the mental preparation we bring to the act of seeing, and expanded understanding requires that we break through set preconceptions. Scientific progress, Kuhn goes so far as to argue, comes more from the posing of new questions, the formulation of new paradigms, and the emergence of new forms of evidence than it does from the normal-science method of hypothesis testing.

One need not embrace Kuhn's argument fully to appreciate that scientific analysis is more than a technical process, more than using agreed-upon criteria of evidence to test clearly demarked propositions. Judgment and subjectivity cannot be abolished. In the cold light of experience, both theory and evidence are human constructs, inevitably imperfect and limited in their capacity to explain the world around us. No research technique can ignore that unyielding fact: Even though judgment itself is sure to have shortcomings, no technique obviates its necessity.

As one moves from the realm of physical phenomena to that of social phenomena, limitations in the scientific method multiply. The nature of the research enterprise itself is open to debate. For example, unlike many social scientists, historians are disinclined to search for universal conclusions or identify "iron laws" of human behavior. Instead, they offer the detailed texture of a phenomenon — whether it be a movement, an institution, a person, an era, or some combination of these. But here a Kuhnian caution is again in order. Pure description is as illusory as pure science. As a practical matter, comprehensible description, even if highly detailed (perhaps *especially* if highly detailed), involves selecting some features and neglecting others.[3] It entails, not just judgment, but prejudgment as well.

Moreover, as historians examine the past, they cannot escape these limitations. The past cannot simply be resurrected; its totality is beyond recapture. Nor is it just a matter of information lost with the passage of time. The present is also incomprehensible in its totality. We understand by selective perception. As Herbert Simon argues, limited cognition is part of the human condition.[4]

If neither untainted theory nor pure description is possible, what is the alternative? Even logical deduction has limitations, especially in the consideration of human behavior. Although deduction is an important tool of scientific analysis generally, historians often have a special appreciation of something beyond its reach, namely, paradox. Many historical phenomena display opposing tendencies; hence, characterization often takes the form, not of elaborating the implications of pure types, but of explaining how divergent needs or clashing propensities are reconciled. Appreciation of paradox pushes us toward complexity, not simplification: toward bridging differences, not defining them out of existence.

Arthur Stinchcombe talks about concepts in depth, an interplay between theory and observation.[5] As he sees it, any abstract concept or, for that matter, any first stab at conceptualization is likely to be oversimplified and shallow. Assuming that our powers of studied observation are more robust than our capacities for ready generalization, then analysis — actual analysis — takes the form of an interaction between concept and observation of detail. And it genuinely is *inter*action. Good concepts illuminate significant details, and telling details point to illuminating concepts.

Isolated details can, of course, point in quite different directions. That is why historians emphasize context. Evidence consists, not of interesting facts standing alone, but of *patterns* of detail. The soundness of a political characterization (of a person, movement, institution, etc.) depends on the explanatory power of the conceptualization and on the consistency of detail. Here we confront fully the interaction of concept and observation. If a concept does not illuminate concrete historical events, it is not useful. If it is contradicted by a *pattern* of detail, then it is inadequate at best.

Reliance on the pattern of detail makes the matter of historical research "softer" (that is, more obviously caught up in matters of judgment) than hypothesis testing. But it also offers flexibility in identifying relevant evidence. Of course, even advocates of normal science acknowledge that multiple forms of evidence are better than a single form. However, implicit in that position is the admission that judgment ultimately plays a crucial role. Moreover, the research task, at least at the level of competing paradigms, is adversarial, and historical research is always potentially at that paradigm level. An adversarial process, especially one involving interpretation of historical findings, is not necessarily a win-or-lose-all proposition. The process of challenge and response which surrounds historical research does not mean that a given concept or interpretation must be *either* accepted *or* rejected. Refinement, modification, and qualification are possible alternatives.

The larger process of challenge and response among scholars is only an extension of the individual researcher's movement back and forth between concept and observation. Because historical research is subjective to a significant degree, the check on the soundness of characterization comes from the challenges of others, and such challenges of necessity involve both conceptualization and consistency of detail. Many heads are better than one as a check on subjectivity.

In this study, I have argued that governance in Atlanta can usefully be understood by the concept of an urban regime. By implication, I also suggest that this same concept would be a fruitful starting point in the study of governance in other communities. In short, I contend that "urban regime" is an illuminating concept, casting light on Atlanta's political experience and, potentially, on the experience of other communities as well.

Just as I do not claim that the concept of urban regime developed from start to finish in my imagination (I owe special and direct debts to Floyd Hunter and to Stephen Elkin[6]), I do not expect the concept to be frozen at the version presented by me. The interaction of concept and observation is ongoing, and none of us does more than offer a guidepost in the journey.

Sequential Causation and the General and the Particular

Is this study to be regarded as a guide to future research on Atlanta or as a pointer for research in other communities? My hope is that it will be both. I have tried to conceptualize the study in a way that would open up comparative analyses, while remaining sensitive to the particulars of Atlanta. Pressing the question further, is the primary aim to capture the specifics of the Atlanta case or to generate a body of explanatory statements with wide application? There is no simple answer. Pure description, I have suggested, is as illusory as pure theory. The special virtue of historical research is that it forces us to see that the distinction between theory and description is artificial and imposed.

Historical analysis makes assumptions about causation, the main one being that social phenomena are to be understood as having multiple causes.[7] Research proceeds by analyzing the *conjunction* of factors, not by isolating single variables.[8] History is unable to replicate endless observations under laboratory conditions. Instead, it proceeds from the notion of sequence. Events have manifold causes, many of which we may never identify or even be conscious of. But by following events sequentially, we gain some understanding of what remains constant, what changes, and what is associated with each. Given a significant degree of social inertia, a historical sequence holds some set of factors constant, but it also allows for others (including the intentions of purposive actors) to change. The examination of a sequential process is a rough counterpart to laboratory control. History does not purport to be an exact science, but it does allow for systematic study.

At various stages in historical processes, alternative courses of action are visible. Some are followed, others are not. Because there is often struggle surrounding the selection process, Barrington Moore calls the courses not selected "suppressed alternatives."[9] The question of what conjoins to enable one alternative to prevail over another is central.

In this study of Atlanta, alternative regime forms not selected are a focal point of observation. What was associated with the prevailing regime that was missing from the "suppressed alternatives"? Within assumptions of manifold and sequential causation, my research task was to report on the Atlanta experience, but to do so in a way that could be applied to other communities. That meant trying to state observations in general terms or relating particular components of the Atlanta experience to a general condition.

Over time, it should be possible to cumulate observations about sets of conditions (again, including the intentions of purposive actors) that are associated with various regime forms and how they change. That is the kind of enterprise historical political sociology is concerned with. Given assumptions of manifold and sequential causation, however, one finds no clear line between description and theory *as an account of the emergence, modification, and decline* in regime forms.

There is a drive toward parsimony, toward identifying key variables and formulating general propositions. But, if the focus of the study is the *conjunction* of factors — and the mix of factors are always changing over time — then the analysis can never produce a neat formula of explanation to apply universally. Universality assumes a degree of constancy that history does not provide. I do not deny that there are regularities in human behavior; I only assert that something as complex as the shaping of an urban regime must be understood as a confluence that itself is not permanent. By observing the flow of events over time, we can see what combination of factors have recurring weight and what changing factors alter the course of events. But complex causation and few cases make analysis difficult. Moreover, the historical process is not mechanical because the flow of events is much affected by human intentions, understandings, and misunderstandings. As they change, the conjunction of factors change, complicating explanation.

The more complex the explanation, the more it resembles description; that is, a unique account of the flow of events from one point to another.[10] Having said earlier that there is no such thing as pure description, I need to clarify that a unique account cannot be atheoretical. The theory may be almost wholly implicit and it may be both implicit and inconsistent, but any intelligible account embodies theory. That is why the authors of case narratives should strive, within reasonable limits, to make their theoretical arguments explicit. Explicit theorizing makes it easier to determine if an argument is internally consistent and also compatible with the observable events purportedly explained. And explicit theorizing is what I have attempted in this account of Atlanta.

By being explicit, we are pushed to examine our own claims about what factors conjoin and with what consequences. Since the character of conjunctions is itself undergoing change, this search is always a catch-up game, but that is all the more reason for diligence.

Evidence on Events in Atlanta

The events that I attempt to explain are those related to the governance of the city of Atlanta for a period beginning in 1946 and ending in 1988. Thus the "what" is governance, not the whole gamut of community life. The "where" is the central-city community of Atlanta, not the whole metropolitan area — though the latter has a substantial impact on the former. The "when" starts with the black voter mobilization in 1946, which clearly meant a new conjunction of elements in the political life of Atlanta. There is no notable divide in the community's political life that coincides with 1988 (though it is near the end of Andrew Young's second term as mayor and it marks the close of Dan Sweat's fifteen-year tenure as head of CAP).

I have used the completion of Central Area Study II as the curtain-falling policy event in order to conclude research and finish the manuscript. Several matters were pending or emerged shortly after that point: the domed stadium; defeat of a bond referendum; negotiations over a comprehensive historic preservation ordinance; preliminary moves in preparation for the 1989 mayoral race, with Maynard Jackson as the precampaign favorite; deteriorating conditions at the Bankhead Court public housing project; the selection of Joe Martin to take over the reins at CAP; a red-lining and bank-practices controversy; and the replacement of the editor of the *Constitution*. None of these issues were followed to closure, but as 1988 came to an end, none pointed to a likely change in basic regime character. But that story awaits future scholars.

What sources did I use to identify events in the governance of Atlanta from 1946 to 1988? Exhaustive primary investigation was not practical, since this book spans a very substantial length of time. For the period preceding Maynard Jackson's election in 1973, I relied heavily on my own earlier research on redevelopment in Atlanta as well as a large body of secondary literature. Atlanta is a city widely studied and reported on. That is an enormous advantage, and the secondary literature is quite abundant, not only for the early years but also for the Jackson era and into the 1980s.

Second, I made extensive use of the Atlanta *Constitution*, especially for the period from 1971 through 1988. (My earlier study had extended from 1950 to 1970 and also had involved substantial use of newspaper coverage, including the morgue of the *Journal* and *Constitution*.) A brief explanation is in order about the relationship between the Atlanta *Constitution* (the morning newspaper) and the Atlanta *Journal* (the afternoon newspaper). In 1946, these were separately owned dailies, though their earlier rivalry had diminished. After they came under the same ownership in 1950, Sunday and holiday editions were jointly published. Although they still retain separate editorial pages except when jointly published, for most news coverage they are now essentially two editions of the same newspaper. I have used the *Constitution* as the "edition" more widely available outside Atlanta. Other newspapers with occasional coverage of Atlanta have also been used, as have a variety of documents, reports, and newsletters from both public agencies and private associations in Atlanta. However, for the 1970s and especially the 1980s, the main source of documentary evidence is the *Constitution*. Its coverage is the most comprehensive, and it has the added advantage of being a source that was available to the various actors on the community stage. What is cited in the *Constitution* is fully public information. I say this in order to emphasize that my account of Atlanta's regime is not an account of a hidden conspiracy or a secret protocol. The facts were widely known in their particulars, though perhaps few people reflected much on the *pattern* of events.

Finally, I interviewed ninety-seven individuals, a few more than once, from the autumn of 1982 to the summer of 1988. These participants in the civic and political life of Atlanta fall into the following categories by race and sex: black, 35; white, 62; female, 36; and male, 61. And by category of community participant, as follows:[11] business, 22; public official, 52; and community-based, 27.

Keeping to the V. O. Key tradition, I did my interviews in person, without a tape recorder and on a not-for-attribution basis;[12] I do not quote from them. This is a disappointment for those who hope to preserve an oral-history record, and while I respect and encourage that objective, my aim was different. I use newspapers and other published sources for on-the-record quotations.

In talking with participants in Atlanta's political and civic life, I was not concerned with what they were willing to say for the record. Instead, I aimed for a conversation in which respondents would reflect on their involvement and how it fit into the larger picture. I was less concerned with their recall of events (which would have been fragmentary and subjective, in any case) than with their insight into the flow of events in the community. Consequently I do not use interviews primarily as a record of events; they serve as an aid to me in interpretation. My approach put a premium on talking to a variety of individuals, giving respondents full encouragement to reflect openly on their own sense of the situation. Interviews, then, were not so much evidence about events as they were a source of background and context.

The events recounted from 1946 to 1988 can thus be examined through published records. Even the backstage negotiations for which Atlanta is noted find their way into the record; although some details are never reported, the events themselves and their outcomes can be observed by the diligent and systematic observer. And it is the flow of events and outcomes that is at the heart of my account of the Atlanta experience.

It is certainly possible that another researcher might report some details other than the ones I have recounted, but the soundness of my version rests on the pattern of events I have identified. Different details in themselves would not be damaging, but a contradicting *pattern* of events would call into question the adequacy of my characterization of Atlanta's governing arrangements. Because the record is accessible and the research process ongoing, challenge is within the realm of possibility—as it should be with any set of findings.

"Urban regime" is the concept I offer, and a public record of events is the source of details I draw from. Because I can claim that neither my conceptualization nor my use of evidence is unflawed, it is now my responsibility to say: Let the process of challenge and response begin.

Notes

PREFACE

1. V. O. Key, Jr., *Southern Politics in State and Nation* (New York: Alfred A. Knopf, 1949), 106.

2. Clarence N. Stone, "Preemptive Power: Floyd Hunter's 'Community Power Structure' Reconsidered," *American Journal of Political Science* 32 (February 1988): 82–104.

3. Clarence N. Stone, *Economic Growth and Neighborhood Discontent: System Bias in the Urban Renewal Program of Atlanta* (Chapel Hill: University of North Carolina Press, 1976).

4. Clarence N. Stone, "Systemic Power in Community Decision Making," *American Political Science Review* 74 (December 1980): 978–990.

5. See Barbara Ferman, *Governing the Ungovernable City* (Philadelphia: Temple University Press, 1985); cf. Norton E. Long, "The Local Community as an Ecology of Games," *American Journal of Sociology* 64 (November 1958): 251–261.

6. Douglas Yates, *The Ungovernable City* (Cambridge, Mass.: MIT Press, 1977); Charles R. Morris, *The Cost of Good Intentions* (New York: W. W. Norton & Co., 1980); Martin Shefter, *Political Crisis/Fiscal Crisis: The Collapse and Revival of New York City* (New York: Basic Books, 1985).

7. Robert L. Crain, *The Politics of School Desegregation* (Chicago: Aldine, 1968); David L. Kirp, *Just Schools* (Berkeley and Los Angeles: University of California Press, 1982); Alan Lupo, *Liberty's Chosen Home* (Boston: Beacon Press, 1988).

8. Stephen L. Elkin, *City and Regime in the American Republic* (Chicago: University of Chicago Press, 1987).

9. Edward C. Banfield, *The Unheavenly City Revisited* (Boston: Little, Brown, 1974); but see the telling historical argument by Amy Bridges, *A City in the Republic* (Cambridge: Cambridge University Press, 1984).

10. Paul E. Peterson, *City Limits* (Chicago: University of Chicago Press, 1981).

11. Paul Kantor, with Stephen David, *The Dependent City* (Glenview, Ill.: Scott, Foresman, 1988).

12. John H. Mollenkopf, *The Contested City* (Princeton, N.J.: Princeton University Press, 1983); and Todd Swanstrom, *The Crisis of Growth Politics* (Philadelphia: Temple University Press, 1985).

13. Quoted in Carl Grafton, Review of *The New Class War, American Political Science Review* 77 (December 1983): 1050.

14. Stephen L. Elkin, "Capitalism in Constitutive Perspective: The Commercial Republic in America" (Paper prepared for delivery at the Annual Meeting of the American Political Science Association, September 1988, Washington, D.C.).

15. Robert Michels, *Political Parties* (New York: Dover Publications, 1959); see also James G. March and Herbert A. Simon, *Organizations* (New York: John Wiley & Sons, 1965), especially 136–171.

16. Mancur Olson, Jr., *The Logic of Collective Action* (Cambridge, Mass.: Harvard University Press, 1965); see also Dennis H. Wrong, *Power: Its Forms, Bases and Uses* (New York: Harper & Row, 1980).

17. Russell Hardin, *Collective Action* (Baltimore: Johns Hopkins University Press, 1982).

18. Michael Taylor, *The Possibility of Cooperation* (Cambridge: Cambridge University Press, 1987), 20.

19. Key, *Southern Politics,* 3.

CHAPTER 1. URBAN REGIMES:
A RESEARCH PERSPECTIVE

1. James G. March, "The Business Firm as a Political Coalition," *Journal of Politics* 24 (November 1962): 662–678.

2. Chester I. Barnard, *The Functions of the Executive* (Cambridge, Mass.: Harvard University Press, 1968).

3. Oliver E. Williamson, *The Economic Institutions of Capitalism* (New York: Free Press, 1985).

4. Ibid., 10.

5. See Norton E. Long, "The Local Community as an Ecology of Games," *American Journal of Sociology* 64 (November 1958): 251–261.

6. Cf. Graham T. Allison, *Essence of Decision* (Boston: Little, Brown, 1971).

7. See Philip Selznick, *Leadership in Administration* (New York: Harper & Row, 1957).

8. Cf. Bryan D. Jones and Lynn W. Bachelor, *The Sustaining Hand* (Lawrence: University Press of Kansas, 1986).

9. See especially Martin Shefter, "The Emergence of the Political Machine: An Alternative View," in *Theoretical Perspectives on Urban Politics,* by Willis D. Hawley and others (Englewood Cliffs, N.J.: Prentice-Hall, 1976).

10. Clarence N. Stone, Robert K. Whelan, and William J. Murin, *Urban Policy and Politics in a Bureaucratic Age,* 2d ed. (Englewood Cliffs, N.J.: Prentice-Hall, 1986), 104.

11. Stephen L. Elkin, *City and Regime in the American Republic* (Chicago: University of Chicago Press, 1987).

12. See ibid.

13. Cf. Jones and Bachelor, *Sustaining Hand,* 214–215.

14. But see Elkin, *City and Regime;* Martin Shefter, *Political Crisis/Fiscal Crisis: The Collapse and Revival of New York City* (New York: Basic Books, 1985); and Todd Swanstrom, *The Crisis of Growth Politics* (Philadelphia: Temple University Press, 1985).

15. Robert H. Wiebe, *The Search for Order, 1877–1920* (New York: Hill and Wang, 1967), 10.

16. Russell Hardin, *Collective Action* (Baltimore: Johns Hopkins University Press, 1982); and Michael Taylor, *The Possibility of Cooperation* (Cambridge: Cambridge University Press, 1987).

17. Mancur Olson, Jr., *The Logic of Collective Action* (Cambridge, Mass.: Harvard University Press, 1965).

18. Hardin, *Collective Action.*

19. Robert Axelrod, *The Evolution of Cooperation* (New York: Basic Books, 1984).

20. Hardin, *Collective Action;* and David D. Laitin, *Hegemony and Culture* (Chicago: University of Chicago Press, 1986).

21. Taylor, *Possibility of Cooperation.*

22. Charles Tilly, *Big Structures, Large Processes, Huge Comparisons* (New York: Russell Sage Foundation, 1984), 27.

23. Philip Abrams, *Historical Sociology* (Ithaca, N.Y.: Cornell University Press, 1982). For a similar understanding applied to urban politics, see John R. Logan and Harvey L. Molotch, *Urban Fortunes* (Berkeley and Los Angeles: University of California Press, 1987).

24. Cf. Anthony Giddens, *Central Problems in Social Theory* (Berkeley and Los Angeles: University of California Press, 1979).

25. Cf. James G. March and Johan P. Olsen, "The New Institutionalism," *American Political Science Review* 78 (September 1984): 734-749.

26. Abrams, *Historical Sociology,* 331.

27. Ibid.

28. Michael L. Porter, "Black Atlanta: An Interdisciplinary Study of Blacks on the East Side of Atlanta, 1890-1930" (Ph.D. diss., Emory University, 1974); Walter White, *A Man Called White* (New York: Arno Press and the New York Times, 1969); and Dana F. White, "The Black Sides of Atlanta," *Atlanta Historical Journal* 26 (Summer/Fall 1982): 199-225.

29. Kenneth T. Jackson, *The Ku Klux Klan in the City, 1915-1930* (New York: Oxford University Press, 1967); and Herbert T. Jenkins, *Forty Years on the Force: 1932-1972* (Atlanta: Center for Research in Social Change, Emory University, 1973).

30. Charles H. Martin, *The Angelo Herndon Case and Southern Justice* (Baton Rouge: Louisiana State University Press, 1976); Kenneth Coleman, ed., *A History of Georgia* (Athens: University of Georgia Press, 1977), 294; and Writer's Program of the Works Progress Administration, *Atlanta: A City of the Modern South* (St. Clairshores, Mich.: Somerset Publishers, 1973), 69.

31. Lorraine N. Spritzer, *The Belle of Ashby Street: Helen Douglas Mankin and Georgia Politics* (Athens: University of Georgia Press, 1982).

CHAPTER 2. PREWAR BACKGROUND

1. Dana F. White and Timothy J. Crimmins, "How Atlanta Grew: Cool Heads, Hot Air, and Hard Work," in *Urban Atlanta: Redefining the Role of the City,* ed. Andrew Hamer, Research Monograph no. 84 (Atlanta: College of Business Administration, Georgia State University, 1980).

2. Paul E. Peterson, *The Politics of School Reform, 1870-1940* (Chicago: University of Chicago Press, 1985).

3. Howard L. Preston, "Parkways, Parks, and 'New South' Progressivism: Planning Practice in Atlanta, 1880-1917," in *Olmstead South: Old South Critic/New South Planner,* ed. Dana F. White and Victor A. Kramer (Westport, Conn.: Greenwood Press), 223-238; White and Crimmins, "How Atlanta Grew."

4. Cf. Robert H. Wiebe, *The Search for Order, 1877–1920* (New York: Hill and Wang, 1967).

5. Eugene J. Watts, *The Social Bases of City Politics: Atlanta, 1865–1903* (Westport, Conn.: Greenwood Press, 1978); Peterson, *Politics of School Reform.*

6. Peterson, *Politics of School Reform,* 126–127.

7. Howard L. Preston, *Automobile Age Atlanta: The Making of a Southern Metropolis, 1900–1935* (Athens: University of Georgia Press, 1979), 54–61.

8. Quoted in Franklin M. Garrett, *Atlanta and Environs: A Chronicle of Its People and Events,* 2 vols. (Athens: University of Georgia Press, 1954), 2:822.

9. On business civic positions, see Charles P. Garofalo, "Business Ideas in Atlanta, 1916–1935" (Ph.D. diss., Emory University, 1972); and Blaine A. Brownell, "The Commercial-Civic Elite and City Planning in Atlanta, Memphis and New Orleans in the 1920s," *Journal of Southern History* 41 (1971): 339–368.

10. Preston, *Automobile Age Atlanta,* 149.

11. Cf. Mancur Olson, Jr., *The Logic of Collective Action* (Cambridge, Mass.: Harvard University Press, 1965); and Russell Hardin, *Collective Action* (Baltimore: Johns Hopkins University Press, 1982).

12. Cf. C. Wright Mills, "The Middle Class in Middle Sized Cities," *American Sociological Review* 11 (October 1946): 520–529.

13. Floyd Hunter, *Community Power Structure* (Chapel Hill: University of North Carolina Press, 1953).

14. Clarence N. Stone, "Partnership New South Style: Central Atlanta Progress," *Proceedings, The Academy of Political Science* 36, no. 2 (1986): 100–110.

15. Garrett, *Atlanta and Environs,* 2:867–868.

16. Harold H. Martin, *William Berry Hartsfield: Mayor of Atlanta* (Athens: University of Georgia Press, 1978).

17. Hunter, *Community Power Structure,* 78; See also 70 and 81.

18. William F. Holmes, "Part Five: 1890–1940," in *A History of Georgia,* ed. Kenneth Coleman (Athens: University of Georgia Press, 1977), 313–314; Charles F. Palmer, *Adventures of a Slum Fighter* (Atlanta: Tupper and Love, 1955); cf. Steven P. Erie, *Rainbow's End* (Berkeley and Los Angeles: University of California Press, 1988), 107–139.

19. Martin, *William Berry Hartsfield.*

20. Ibid., 23.

21. Ibid., 23–24; and Herbert T. Jenkins, *Forty Years on the Force: 1932–1972* (Atlanta: Center for Research in Social Change, Emory University, 1973).

22. See Writer's Program of the Works Progress Administration, *Atlanta: A City of the Modern South* (St. Clair Shores, Mich.: Somerset Publishers, 1973), 94–106.

23. In the early years of the twentieth century, rivalry between the *Journal* and the *Constitution* was central in the city's bifactional politics (Dewey W. Grantham, Jr., *Hoke Smith and the Politics of the New South* [Baton Rouge: Louisiana State University Press, 1958]). That rivalry ended well before World War II, and in 1950, any remaining competition came to an end when Cox Enterprises added ownership of the *Constitution* to its ownership of the *Journal.*

24. Peterson, *Politics of School Reform,* especially 188–195.

25. Ibid., 195.

26. Ibid., 193.

27. C. Vann Woodward, *The Strange Career of Jim Crow* (New York: Oxford University Press, 1957); V. O. Key, Jr., *Southern Politics in State and Nation* (New York: Alfred A. Knopf, 1949).

28. Grantham, *Hoke Smith.*

29. Ann Wells Ellis, "The Commission on Interracial Cooperation, 1919-1944" (Ph.D. diss., Georgia State University, 1975); Ridgeley Torrence, *The Story of John Hope* (New York: Macmillan, 1948), especially 230-234; John M. Matthews, "Studies in Race Relations in Georgia, 1890-1930" (Ph.D. diss., Duke University, 1970).

30. Ellis, "Commission on Interracial Cooperation," 57.

31. Walter White, *A Man Called White* (New York: Arno Press and the New York Times, 1969), 29-38; and Dana F. White, "The Black Sides of Atlanta," *Atlanta Historical Journal* 26 (Summer/Fall 1982): 215-216.

32. Torrence, *Story of John Hope,* 229-230; and C. A. Bacote, "The Negro in Atlanta Politics," *Phylon* 16 (1955): 342.

33. Michael L. Porter, "Black Atlanta: An Interdisciplinary Study of Blacks on the East Side of Atlanta, 1890-1930" (Ph.D. diss., Emory University, 1974); and White, "Black Sides of Atlanta," 216-218.

34. White, "Black Sides of Atlanta," 218.

35. John Dittmer, *Black Georgia in the Progressive Era, 1900-1920* (Urbana: University of Illinois Press, 1977), 13; White, "Black Sides of Atlanta," 215.

36. Blaine A. Brownell, *The Urban Ethos in the South, 1920-1930* (Baton Rouge: Louisiana State University Press, 1975), 183-184; and Preston, *Automobile Age Atlanta,* 96-102.

37. Preston, *Automobile Age Atlanta,* 97-98.

38. Dittmer, *Black Georgia,* 46-48; Robert J. Alexander, "Negro Business in Atlanta," *Southern Economic Journal* 17 (1951): 454-455.

39. Dittmer, *Black Georgia,* 48.

40. Porter, "Black Atlanta."

41. Cf. Philip Abrams, *Historical Sociology* (Ithaca, N.Y.: Cornell University Press, 1982).

CHAPTER 3. THE ERA OF NEGOTIATED SETTLEMENTS

1. See Appendix A.

2. For a sense of this tradition, see Norman Shavin and Bruce Galphin, *Atlanta: Triumph of a People* (Atlanta: Capricorn Corp., 1982), 343-447.

3. Roy LeCraw defeated Hartsfield by the narrow margin of eighty-three votes in the fall of 1940, then gave up the office of mayor in March 1942 to enter the armed forces. Hartsfield was elected mayor in the special election that followed, then defeated LeCraw in a 1945 rematch. On Hartsfield, see Franklin M. Garrett, *Atlanta and Environs: A Chronicle of Its People and Events,* 2 vols. (Athens: University of Georgia Press, 1954), vol. 2; Herbert T. Jenkins, *Forty Years on the Force: 1932-1972* (Atlanta: Center for Research in Social Change, Emory University, 1973); Harold H. Martin, *William Berry Hartsfield: Mayor of Atlanta* (Athens: University of Georgia Press, 1978); and Bradley R. Rice, "If Dixie Were Atlanta," in *Sunbelt Cities: Politics and Growth since World War II,* ed. Richard M. Bernard and Bradley R. Rice (Austin: University of Texas Press, 1983).

4. Garrett, *Atlanta and Environs,* 2:956-959; Charles H. Martin, *The Angelo Herndon Case and Southern Justice* (Baton Rouge: Louisiana State University Press, 1976), 172-173.

5. See Ivan Allen, Jr., with Paul Hemphill, *Mayor: Notes on the Sixties* (New York: Simon and Schuster, 1971), 48-50.

6. Virginia H. Hein, "The Image of 'A City Too Busy to Hate': Atlanta in the 1960's," *Phylon* 33 (Fall 1972): 205-221.

7. Floyd Hunter, *Community Power Structure* (Chapel Hill: University of North Carolina Press, 1953).

8. Jenkins, *Forty Years,* 45; Pat Watters, *The South and the Nation* (New York: Pantheon Books, 1969), 214-215.

9. Bradley R. Rice, "The Battle of Buckhead: The Plan of Improvement and Atlanta's Last Big Annexation," *Atlanta Historical Journal* 25 (1981): 5-22.

10. Clarence N. Stone, *Economic Growth and Neighborhood Discontent: System Bias in the Urban Renewal Program of Atlanta* (Chapel Hill: University of North Carolina Press, 1976).

11. Numan V. Bartley, *From Thurmond to Wallace: Political Tendencies in Georgia, 1948-1968* (Baltimore: Johns Hopkins University Press, 1970), 35-56; M. Kent Jennings and Harmon Zeigler, "Class, Party, and Race in Four Types of Elections: The Case of Atlanta," *Journal of Politics* 28 (1966): 391-407; and Martin, *William Berry Hartsfield,* 25.

12. Lorraine N. Spritzer, *The Belle of Ashby Street: Helen Douglas Mankin and Georgia Politics* (Athens: University of Georgia Press, 1982), 68-74.

13. Martin, *William Berry Hartsfield,* 49; Numan V. Bartley, *The Creation of Modern Georgia* (Athens: University of Georgia Press, 1983), 194; Bradley R. Rice, "Lester Maddox and the 'Liberal' Mayors," in *Proceedings and Papers of the Georgia Association of Historians* (Marietta, Ga.: Kennesaw College), 78-87.

14. Martin, *William Berry Hartsfield,* 53.

15. Ibid., 46.

16. Quoted in ibid., 47.

17. Numan V. Bartley, "Part Six: 1940 to the Present," in *A History of Georgia,* ed. Kenneth Coleman (Athens: University of Georgia Press, 1977), 363.

18. Douglass Cater, "Atlanta: Smart Politics and Good Race Relations," *Reporter,* 11 July 1957, 18-21; see also Martin Luther King, Sr., with Clayton Riley, *Daddy King: An Autobiography* (New York: William Morrow & Co., 1980); and Hunter, *Community Power Structure,* 114-148.

19. Martin, *William Berry Hartsfield,* 50.

20. Details may be found in C. A. Bacote, "The Negro in Atlanta Politics," *Phylon* 16 (1955): 333-350; and Jack L. Walker, "Negro Voting in Atlanta: 1953-1961," *Phylon* 24 (Winter 1963): 379-387.

21. Martin, *William Berry Hartsfield,* 50-52; Jenkins, *Forty Years,* 44-53, 148-149.

22. Martin, *William Berry Hartsfield,* 51-52.

23. Ibid., 51.

24. Ibid., 72; Jenkins, *Forty Years,* 48-49.

25. Edward C. Banfield, *Big City Politics* (New York: Random House, 1965), 28-29.

26. Quoted in Martin, *William Berry Hartsfield,* 42; see also Rice, "Lester Maddox."

27. Rice, "Battle of Buckhead"; and Garrett, *Atlanta and Environs,* 2:1005-1006; Jenkins, *Forty Years,* 61-65; Dana F. White and Timothy J. Crimmins, "How Atlanta Grew: Cool Heads, Hot Air, and Hard Work," in *Urban Atlanta: Redefining the Role of the City,* ed. Andrew M. Hamer, Research Monograph no. 84 (Atlanta: College of Business Administration, Georgia State University, 1980), 36; and Hunter, *Community Power Structure,* 94-100, 214-220.

28. Bacote, "The Negro in Atlanta Politics"; Banfield, *Big City Politics,* 25.

29. Rice, "Battle of Buckhead."

30. The quoted phrases are from Martin Luther King, Sr., in King with Riley, *Daddy King,* 122; see also Cater, "Atlanta."

31. Martin, *William Berry Hartsfield,* 49.

32. On an earlier case, one to sue for equal pay for teachers, and an explanation

of why black ministers were especially well placed to challenge Jim Crow practices, see King with Riley, *Daddy King*, 125.

33. Jenkins, *Forty Years*, 108-109; King with Riley, *Daddy King*, 154-157.

34. Shavin and Galphin, *Atlanta*, 254.

35. Atlanta *Journal*, 21 March 1946; see also Rice, "If Dixie Were Atlanta."

36. Robert A. Thompson, Hylan Lewis, and Davis McEntire, "Atlanta and Birmingham: A Comparative Study in Negro Housing," in *Studies in Housing and Minority Groups*, ed. Nathan Glazer and Davis McEntire (Berkeley and Los Angeles: University of California Press, 1960), 20.

37. Ibid., 39.

38. This account relies on Thompson, Lewis, and McEntire, "Atlanta and Birmingham."

39. Ibid., 22.

40. Jesse O. Thomas, *My Story in Black and White* (New York: Exposition Press, 1967), 97-98.

41. See M. Kent Jennings, *Community Influentials: The Elites of Atlanta* (New York: Free Press of Glencoe, 1964), 111-114; and Allen with Hemphill, *Mayor*, 12.

42. Martin, *William Berry Hartsfield*, 100-101.

43. On the importance of the respect and courtesy that Hartsfield showed blacks, see King with Riley, *Daddy King*, 121; and Pat Watters, *Down to Now: Reflections on the Southern Civil Rights Movement* (New York: Pantheon Books, 1971), 41-42.

44. Thompson, Lewis, and McEntire, "Atlanta and Birmingham," 38.

45. Jenkins, *Forty Years*, 107-108.

46. Thompson, Lewis, and McEntire, "Atlanta and Birmingham."

47. Ibid., 35.

48. Ibid., 46-51.

49. For details, see Thompson, Lewis, and McEntire, "Atlanta and Birmingham."

50. Ibid., 33.

51. Ronald H. Bayor, "Planning the City for Racial Segregation: The Highway-Street Pattern in Atlanta," *Journal of Urban History* 15 (November 1988): 3-21. On the continuing pattern of isolation, see *New York Times*, 1 January 1989.

52. Quoted in Ann Wells Ellis, "'Uncle Sam Is My Shepherd': The Commission on Interracial Cooperation and the New Deal in Georgia," *Atlanta Historical Journal* 30 (Spring 1986): 47.

53. Cf. Harvey Molotch, "The City as a Growth Machine," *American Journal of Sociology* 82 (September 1976): 309-331.

54. For details, see Stone, *Economic Growth*.

55. Jewel Bellush and Murray Hausknecht, eds., *Urban Renewal* (Garden City, N.Y.: Anchor Books, 1967); and Harold Kaplan, *Urban Renewal Politics* (New York: Columbia University Press, 1963).

56. Atlanta *Daily World*, 23 March 1950.

57. V. O. Key, Jr., *Southern Politics in State and Nation* (New York: Alfred A. Knopf, 1949), 106.

58. For details, see Jennings, *Community Influentials*, 114-128, 140-141.

59. Jennings, *Community Influentials*, 142, 154.

60. Thompson, Lewis, and McEntire, "Atlanta and Birmingham," 39-40.

61. The phrase is from Jeffrey L. Pressman and Aaron Wildavsky, *Implementation*, 3d ed. (Berkeley and Los Angeles: University of California Press, 1984).

62. See, for example, the Atlanta *Constitution* (hereafter referred to as *AC*), 12 April 1958.

63. Mayor Hartsfield to Alderman Douglas, 11 June 1958 (City Hall memo).

64. For details, see Stone, *Economic Growth*, 231.

65. Charles P. Garofalo, "Business Ideas in Atlanta, 1916-1935" (Ph.D. diss., Emory University, 1972), 5.

66. Details in the controversy are found in Jennings, *Community Influentials,* 143-152; and Stone, *Economic Growth,* 69-71.

67. Quoted in Jennings, *Community Influentials,* 151.

68. Quoted in ibid.

69. Atlanta *Journal,* 18 December 1959.

70. Atlanta *Journal,* 9 March 1960.

71. On Allen's election, see Allen with Hemphill, *Mayor;* Jennings and Zeigler, "Class, Party"; Bartley, *From Thurmond to Wallace;* and Rice, "Lester Maddox."

72. See Banfield, *Big City Politics,* 29; Seymour Freedgood, "Life in Buckhead," *Fortune,* September 1961, 184.

73. For details on this phase of the relocation problem, see Stone, *Economic Growth,* 71-76.

74. *Hearings before the U.S. Commission on Civil Rights: Housing, Atlanta, Georgia, April 10, 1959* (Washington, D.C.: GPO, 1959).

75. Citizens Advisory Committee for Urban Renewal, Minutes, meeting of 13 July 1961.

76. Committee Minutes, 4 June 1959.

77. *AC,* 17 October 1958. On the role of newspapers, see John R. Logan and Harvey L. Molotch, *Urban Fortunes* (Berkeley and Los Angeles: University of California Press, 1987), 71.

78. Watters, *South and the Nation,* 227.

79. Ibid., 215.

80. Richard Hebert, *Highways to Nowhere: The Politics of City Transportation* (Indianapolis: Bobbs-Merrill, 1972), 97.

81. Allen with Hemphill, *Mayor,* 22.

82. Harry Holloway, *The Politics of the Southern Negro* (New York: Random House, 1969), 199-201.

83. Bartley, *Creation of Modern Georgia,* 195.

84. Hein, "Image," 205.

85. Numan V. Bartley, *The Rise of Massive Resistance* (Baton Rouge: Louisiana State University Press, 1969), 333; idem, "Part Six: 1940 to the Present," in *A History of Georgia,* ed. Kenneth Coleman (Athens: University of Georgia Press, 1977), 369-370; idem, *Creation of Modern Georgia,* 195; Hein, "Image"; and Alton Hornsby, Jr., "A City That Was Too Busy to Hate," in *Southern Businessmen and Desegregation,* ed. Elizabeth Jacoway and David R. Coleburn (Baton Rouge: Louisiana State University Press, 1982), 120-136.

86. Martin, *William Berry Hartsfield,* 135-136; Bartley, *Rise of Massive Resistance,* 295-296.

87. Bartley, "1940 to the Present," 369.

88. Hornsby, "City That Was Too Busy to Hate"; Bartley, *Rise of Massive Resistance,* 333-334.

89. Allen with Hemphill, *Mayor,* 32-33.

90. Bartley, *Creation of Modern Georgia,* 195.

91. Hein, "Image," 205-206.

92. Hornsby, "City That Was Too Busy to Hate," 131-132.

93. Bartley, *Rise of Massive Resistance,* 195.

94. Martin, *William Berry Hartsfield,* 152.

95. Watters, *South and the Nation,* 54, 213-214; Hein, "Image," 208.

96. Hein, "Image," 206; Jenkins, *Forty Years,* 111.

97. Hein, "Image," 206.
98. Pat Watters and Reese Cleghorn, *Climbing Jacob's Ladder: The Arrival of Negroes in Southern Politics* (New York: Harcourt, Brace & World, 1967), 240; Hein, "Image," 206.
99. Quoted in Hornsby, "City That Was Too Busy to Hate," 135.
100. Martin, *William Berry Hartsfield,* 152; Watters, *South and the Nation;* 218; Jenkins, *Forty Years,* 112.
101. Watters and Cleghorn, *Climbing Jacob's Ladder,* 240.
102. Jenkins, *Forty Years,* 112.
103. Martin, *William Berry Hartsfield,* 154; Rice, "If Dixie Were Atlanta," 47.
104. Rice, "If Dixie Were Atlanta," 48.
105. Watters, *South and the Nation,* 144.
106. George J. Lankevich, *Atlanta: A Chronological and Documentary History* (Dobbs Ferry, N.Y.: Oceana Publications, 1978), 128.
107. The quoted phrase is from Cater, "Atlanta," 18.

CHAPTER 4. PROTESTS AND COALITIONAL STRESS

1. V. O. Key, Jr., "A Theory of Critical Elections," *Journal of Politics* 17 (February 1955): 3-18; Walter Dean Burnham, *Critical Elections and the Mainsprings of American Politics* (New York: W. W. Norton & Co., 1970); cf. Martin Shefter, *Political Crisis/Fiscal Crisis: The Collapse and Revival of New York City* (New York: Basic Books, 1985).
2. William J. Grimshaw, "The Daley Legacy: A Declining Politics of Party, Race, and Public Unions," in *After Daley: Chicago Politics in Transition,* ed. Samuel K. Gove and Louis H. Masotti (Urbana: University of Illinois Press, 1982); idem, "The Political Economy of Machine Politics" (paper presented at the Annual Meeting of the American Political Science Association, September 1987, Chicago).
3. Martin Luther King, Sr., with Clayton Riley, *Daddy King: An Autobiography* (New York: William Morrow & Co., 1980), 133; see also 152.
4. Ibid., 134.
5. Ivan Allen, Jr., with Paul Hemphill, *Mayor: Notes on the Sixties* (New York: Simon and Schuster, 1971), 35.
6. Ibid., 35-36.
7. Benjamin E. Mays, *Born to Rebel: An Autobiography* (Athens: the University of Georgia Press, 1971), 291.
8. Jack L. Walker, "Protest and Negotiation: A Case Study of Negro Leadership in Atlanta, Georgia," *Midwest Journal of Political Science* 7 (May 1963): 99-124.
9. Atlanta *Journal,* 16 February 1960.
10. Howard Zinn, *SNCC: The New Abolitionists* (Boston: Beacon Press, 1965), 17.
11. Mays, *Born to Rebel,* 292-294.
12. Edward C. Banfield, *Big City Politics* (New York: Random House, 1965), 34.
13. Stephen B. Oates, *Let the Trumpet Sound: The Life of Martin Luther King, Jr.* (New York: A Plume Book, New American Library, 1982), 160.
14. King with Riley, *Daddy King,* 152.
15. Ann Wells Ellis, "The Commission on Interracial Cooperation, 1919-1944" (Ph.D. diss., Georgia State University, 1975).
16. King with Riley, *Daddy King,* 135.
17. Ibid.

18. Howell Raines, *My Soul Is Rested: Movement Days in the Deep South Remembered,* reprint (New York: Penguin Books, 1977), 92.

19. King with Riley, *Daddy King,* 169.

20. Cf. V. O. Key, Jr., *Southern Politics in State and Nation* (New York: Alfred A. Knopf, 1949); Jasper B. Shannon, *Toward a New Politics in the South* (Knoxville: University of Tennessee Press, 1949); Numan V. Bartley, *The Creation of Modern Georgia* (Athens: University of Georgia Press, 1983); and Earl Black and Merle Black, *Politics and Society in the South* (Cambridge, Mass.: Harvard University Press, 1987).

21. King with Riley, *Daddy King,* 146; Mays, *Born to Rebel,* 282-285, 296.

22. Oates, *Let the Trumpet Sound,* 160.

23. King with Riley, *Daddy King,* 156.

24. Ibid.

25. King with Riley, *Daddy King,* 155-156, 160.

26. Mays, *Born to Rebel,* 288-291; Raines, *My Soul Is Rested,* 85.

27. Allen with Hemphill, *Mayor,* 39-42.

28. Mays, *Born to Rebel,* 294.

29. Ibid., 65-66.

30. Allen with Hemphill, *Mayor,* 50.

31. Ibid., 29.

32. Ibid.

33. Ibid.

34. Ibid., 30.

35. Allen with Hemphill, *Mayor,* 49-50.

36. Ibid., 54-55; Alton Hornsby, Jr., "The Negro in Atlanta Politics, 1961-1973," *Atlanta Historical Bulletin* 21 (Spring 1977): 10-11; Bradley R. Rice, "Lester Maddox and the 'Liberal' Mayors," in *Proceedings and Papers of the Georgia Association of Historians* (Marietta, Ga.: Kennesaw College), 82-84.

37. Atlanta *Constitution* (hereafter referred to as *AC*), 6 September 1961.

38. Rice, "Lester Maddox," 83.

39. Hornsby, "Negro in Atlanta Politics," 11-12; Bradley R. Rice, "If Dixie Were Atlanta," in *Sunbelt Cities: Politics and Growth since World War II,* ed. Richard M. Bernard and Bradley R. Rice (Austin: University of Texas Press, 1983), 49; M. Kent Jennings and Harmon Zeigler, "Class, Party, and Race in Four Types of Elections: The Case of Atlanta," *Journal of Politics* 28 (1966): 391-407.

40. Allen with Hemphill, *Mayor,* 69-70.

41. Hornsby, "Negro in Atlanta Politics," 14-16; Charles E. Silberman, *Crisis in Black and White* (New York: Random House, 1964), 202-204; Allen with Hemphill, *Mayor,* 70-72.

42. Silberman, *Crisis in Black and White,* 203.

43. Allen with Hemphill, *Mayor,* 71.

44. Hornsby, "Negro in Atlanta Politics," 15; Silberman, *Crisis in Black and White,* 203.

45. Allen with Hemphill, *Mayor,* 72.

46. Hornsby, "Negro in Atlanta Politics," 12-13.

47. Arthur I. Waskow, *From Race Riot to Sit-In, 1919 and the 1960s* (Garden City, N.Y.: Doubleday & Co., 1966), 240.

48. Hornsby, "Negro in Atlanta Politics," 16-17.

49. Ibid., 15-18; David L. Lewis, *King: A Biography,* 2d ed. (Urbana: University of Illinois Press, 1978), 233-235.

50. Louis E. Lomax, *The Negro Revolt* (New York: Harper & Row, 1962), 84;

Lewis, *King,* 243; David J. Garrow, *Bearing the Cross: Martin Luther King, Jr., and the Southern Christian Leadership Conference* (New York: William Morrow & Co., 1986), 369, 530.

51. Quoted in Lewis, *King,* 234.

52. Quoted in ibid.

53. Hornsby, "Negro in Atlanta Politics," 19; and Peter Ross Range, "Making It in Atlanta: Capital of Black-Is-Bountiful," *New York Times Magazine,* 7 April 1974.

54. Hornsby, "Negro in Atlanta Politics," 17.

55. Allen with Hemphill, *Mayor,* 100-115.

56. Ibid., 109.

57. For various accounts, see ibid., 97-99; Mays, *Born to Rebel,* 271-273; Jim Bishop, *The Days of Martin Luther King, Jr.* (New York: G. P. Putnam's Sons, 1971), 367-368; and Raines, *My Soul Is Rested,* 410-415.

58. Quoted in Allen with Hemphill, *Mayor,* 205.

59. Clarence N. Stone, *Economic Growth and Neighborhood Discontent: System Bias in the Urban Renewal Program of Atlanta* (Chapel Hill: University of North Carolina Press, 1976), 94-95.

60. Allen with Hemphill, *Mayor,* 152-164.

61. See Furman Bisher, *Miracle in Atlanta* (Cleveland, Ohio: World Publishing Co., 1966); and Norman Shavin and Bruce Galphin, *Atlanta: Triumph of a People* (Atlanta: Capricorn Corp., 1982), 282-283.

62. Allen with Hemphill, *Mayor,* 157.

63. For details of this project, see Stone, *Economic Growth,* 92-106.

64. Ibid., 97-98.

65. See, for example, the *AC,* 26 July 1965.

66. Stone, *Economic Growth,* 92-114.

67. Quoted in ibid., 100-101.

68. Statement of 8 March 1965, quoted in ibid., 102.

69. Stone, *Economic Growth,* 105.

70. For an account of the pioneering sponsorship by Wheat Street Baptist Church, see James W. English, *Handyman of the Lord: The Life and Ministry of the Reverend William Holmes Borders* (New York: Meredith Press, 1967), 110-151.

71. For details, see Fred R. Crawford, *A Comprehensive and Systematic Evaluation of the Community Action Program and Related Programs Operating in Atlanta, Georgia* (Atlanta: Center for Research in Social Change, Emory University, 1969).

72. James A. Bayton, *Tension in the Cities* (Philadelphia: Chilton Book Co., 1969), 39; Crawford, *Evaluation,* 22.

73. Stone, *Economic Growth,* 127, 237.

74. Details of the ensuing events are contained in ibid., 107-112.

75. See ibid., 107-112, 153-164.

76. For details, see J. Shepherd, "White Power in Black Atlanta," *Look,* 13 December 1966, 137-140.

77. Clayborne Carson, *In Struggle: SNCC and the Black Awakening of the 1960s* (Cambridge, Mass.: Harvard University Press, 1981), 193.

78. Carson, *In Struggle,* 189-201; Cleveland Sellers, *The River of No Return: The Autobiography of a Black Militant and the Life and Death of SNCC* (New York: William Morrow & Co., 1973), 185-187.

79. Quoted in Carson, *In Struggle,* 194.

80. Stone, *Economic Growth,* 119-121.

81. For somewhat varying accounts of the incident, see Reese Cleghorn, "Allen of Atlanta Collides with Black Power and Racism," *New York Times Magazine,* 16

October 1966; Sellers, *River of No Return,* 174-178; Allen with Hemphill, *Mayor,* 179-192; and Lester A. Sobel, ed., *Civil Rights, 1960-66* (New York: Facts on File, 1967), 445-447.

82. See Lester A. Sobel, ed., *Civil Rights: Volume 2, 1967-68* (New York: Facts on File, 1973), 44-46; *Report of the National Advisory Commission on Civil Disorders* (New York: Bantam Books, 1968), 52-56, 154.

83. Stone, *Economic Growth,* 124-127.

84. *AC,* 26 July 1965.

85. Atlanta *Journal,* 18 March 1966.

86. Allen with Hemphill, *Mayor,* 177-180.

87. Marshall Kaplan, Gans, and Kahn, *The Model Cities Program: The Planning Process in Atlanta, Seattle, and Dayton* (New York: Praeger Publishers, 1970).

88. Bayton, *Tension in the Cities,* 35-41.

89. Stone, *Economic Growth,* 127-128.

90. For details, see ibid., 132-138.

91. For details, see ibid., 142-151; see also Martha Derthick, *New Towns In-Town* (Washington, D.C.: Urban Institute, 1972), 47-54.

92. Stone, *Economic Growth,* 151.

93. Ibid., 142-143.

94. Quoted in ibid., 143.

95. Mays, *Born to Rebel,* 297-298.

96. For details, see Richard Hebert, *Highways to Nowhere: The Politics of City Transportation* (Indianapolis: Bobbs-Merrill, 1972), 109-113; Timothy L. Almy, William B. Hildreth, and Robert T. Golembiewski, "Case Study I— Assessing Electoral Defeat: New Directions and Values for MARTA" (Mass Transit Management: Case Studies of the Metropolitan Atlanta Rapid Transit Authority; A Report Prepared by the University of Georgia Department of Political Science for the U.S. Department of Transportation, Urban Mass Transportation Administration, University Research and Training Program); and Andrew M. Hamer, *The Selling of Rail Rapid Transit* (Lexington, Mass.: Lexington Books, 1976), 145-177.

97. Almy, Hildreth, and Golembiewski, "Case Study I," I-4.

98. Ibid., I-6.

99. Ibid., I-10.

100. Hornsby, "Negro in Atlanta Politics," 23-26.

CHAPTER 5. CHALLENGE AND RESPONSE

1. Alton Hornsby, Jr., "The Negro in Atlanta Politics, 1961-1973," *Atlanta Historical Bulletin* 21 (Spring 1977): 22-23.

2. Ibid., 23.

3. Peter Ross Range, "Making It in Atlanta: Capital of Black-Is-Bountiful," *New York Times Magazine,* 7 April 1974, 76.

4. Neal R. Peirce, *The Deep South States of America: People, Politics, and Power in the Seven Deep South States* (New York: W. W. Norton & Co., 1974), 356.

5. Hornsby, "Negro in Atlanta Politics," 27-28; Mack H. Jones, "Black Political Empowerment in Atlanta: Myth and Reality," *Annals of the American Academy of Political and Social Science* 439 (September 1978): 102.

6. Stephen Burman, "The Illusion of Progress: Race and Politics in Atlanta, Georgia," *Ethnic and Racial Studies* 2 (October 1979): 446.

7. Atlanta *Constitution* (hereafter referred to as *AC*), 5 January 1971.

8. Hornsby, "Negro in Atlanta Politics," 27.

9. Robert K. Whelan and Michael W. McKinney, "Black-White Coalition Politics and the Atlanta Mayoralty Race of 1973" (paper presented at the Annual Meeting of the Georgia Political Science Association, February 1974, Athens, GA.).

10. Jones, "Black Political Empowerment," 102; and Peirce, *Deep South States,* 360–361.

11. *Washington Post,* 10 October 1971; see also Hornsby, "Negro in Atlanta Politics," 29; and Jones, "Black Political Empowerment," 102.

12. Whelan and McKinney, "Black-White Coalition Politics"; and Duncan R. Jamieson, "Maynard Jackson's 1973 Election as Mayor of Atlanta," *Midwest Quarterly* 18 (October 1976): 18.

13. Jones, "Black Political Empowerment," 107.

14. Whelan and McKinney, "Black-White Coalition Politics."

15. Peter K. Eisinger, *The Politics of Displacement: Racial and Ethnic Transition in Three American Cities* (New York: Academic Press, 1980), 68–69.

16. Quoted in ibid., 103.

17. Jones, "Black Political Empowerment," 105–106.

18. *AC,* 9 October 1973; see also Whelan and McKinney, "Black-White Coalition Politics"; Jamieson, "Maynard Jackson's 1973 Election"; and F. Glenn Abney and John D. Hutcheson, Jr., "Race, Representation, and Trust," *Public Opinion Quarterly* 45 (1981): 91–101.

19. Quoted in Fred Powledge, "A New Politics in Atlanta," *New Yorker,* 31 December 1973, 39.

20. Ibid., 39–40.

21. For details, see Marilyn F. Grist, "Neighborhood Interest Groups and Atlanta Public Policy" (Master's thesis, Georgia State University, 1984), especially 70–84; Richard Hebert, *Highways to Nowhere: The Politics of City Transportation* (Indianapolis: Bobbs-Merrill, 1972), 113–119; and *AC,* 12 August 1987.

22. Hebert, *Highways to Nowhere,* 113–114.

23. Grist, "Neighborhood Interest Groups," 75.

24. Hebert, *Highways to Nowhere,* 115–116.

25. *AC,* 12 August 1987.

26. Ibid.

27. Quoted in ibid.

28. Ibid.

29. *AC,* 10 February 1980.

30. Hebert, *Highways to Nowhere,* 119; see also *AC,* 22 January 1977.

31. Charles E. Little, "Atlanta Renewal Gives Power to the Communities," *Smithsonian* 7 (July 1976): 100–107.

32. Grist, "Neighborhood Interest Groups," 48.

33. Hebert, *Highways to Nowhere,* 116.

34. Grist, "Neighborhood Interest Groups," 50–51.

35. *AC,* 12 August 1987.

36. Grist, "Neighborhood Interest Groups," 49.

37. Southern Center for Studies in Public Policy, *Consensus Politics in Atlanta: School Board Decision-Making 1974–1978* (Atlanta: Clark College, 1979), 17, 28.

38. For details on the NPU system, see Little, "Atlanta Renewal"; Grist, "Neighborhood Interest Groups," 51–69; and John O. Hutcheson, Jr., "Citizen Representation in Neighborhood Planning," *American Planning Association Journal* 50 (Spring 1984): 183–193.

39. Quoted in Little, "Atlanta Renewal," 101.

40. Dale Henson and James King, "The Atlanta Public-Private Romance: An Abrupt Transformation," in *Public-Private Partnership in American Cities,* ed. R. Scott Fosler and Renee A. Berger (Lexington, Mass.: Lexington Books, 1982), 334.

41. Eisinger, *Politics of Displacement,* 80–83; Adolph Reed, Jr., "A Critique of Neo-Progressivism in Theorizing about Local Development Policy: A Case from Atlanta," in *The Politics of Urban Development,* ed. Clarence N. Stone and Heywood T. Sanders (Lawrence: University Press of Kansas, 1987), 205–206.

42. Henson and King, "Atlanta Public-Private Romance," 335.

43. Quoted in ibid., 332–333.

44. Eisinger, *Politics of Displacement,* 165–166.

45. Ibid., 162.

46. Ibid.

47. Ibid., 163–165; Reed, "Critique of Neo-Progressivism," 210.

48. For details, see Jones, "Black Political Empowerment"; and Reed, "Critique of Neo-Progressivism."

49. Reed, "Critique of Neo-Progressivism," 210.

50. Jones, "Black Political Empowerment," 108–109; and Austin Scott, "Police Hassle Dims Atlanta Mayor's First Six Months," *Washington Post,* 7 July 1974, A2.

51. *AC,* 19 September 1974.

52. *AC,* 22 November 1974.

53. *AC,* 14 February 1975.

54. *AC,* 10 April 1975.

55. *AC,* 23 December 1974; 17 April 1975.

56. *AC,* 12 January 1975; see also 4 October 1974; 25 January 1975.

57. *AC,* 17 January 1975.

58. Jones, "Black Political Empowerment," 111–112.

59. *AC,* 24 November 1974; see also Henson and King, "Atlanta Public-Private Romance," 331–332.

60. Henson and King, "Atlanta Public-Private Romance," 331.

61. Jones, "Black Political Empowerment," 112; *AC,* 24 March 1975.

62. *AC,* 21 November 1974.

63. *AC,* 20 February 1975; and 3 April 1975.

64. *AC,* 24 March 1975.

65. On Tarver's role, see Peirce, *Deep South States,* 358–359; Jack Bass and Walter DeVries, *The Transformation of Southern Politics* (New York: Basic Books, 1976), 142, 146, 151; Hebert, *Highways to Nowhere,* 123–124; and Pat Watters, *The South and the Nation* (New York: Pantheon Books, 1969), 186–189. On the newspaper more generally, especially in its relation with the community, see *New York Times,* 24 April 1988; *Christian Science Monitor,* 28 November 1988; *Washington Post,* 15 July 1988, 5 November 1988, and 13 November 1988.

66. Quoted in Eisinger, *Politics of Displacement,* 98.

67. Quoted in *AC,* 22 September 1975.

68. Steve Ball and Diane Ball, "Atlanta: The Evolution of Changing Heritage," *Real Estate Atlanta* 5 (January/February 1976): 128.

69. *AC,* 22 September 1975.

70. *AC,* 7 April 1975.

71. Austin Scott, "Mayor Shifts Atlanta Power," *Washington Post,* 6 July 1975, A4.

72. David A. Crane, "The Evolving Strategy," *Real Estate Atlanta* 5 (January/February 1976): 104.

73. Ibid., 108.

74. For details, see Ball and Ball, "Atlanta," 127-128.

75. Quoted in ibid., 127.

76. Cf. Jane J. Mansbridge, *Why We Lost the ERA* (Chicago: University of Chicago Press, 1986).

77. Grist, "Neighborhood Interest Groups," 48.

78. Jones, "Black Political Empowerment," 114-115; Austin Scott, "Sanitation Workers' Strike in Atlanta Loaded with Ironies," *Washington Post,* 17 April 1977, A3.

79. See Eisinger, *Politics of Displacement.*

80. Scott, "Police Hassle."

81. Note the business reactions reported in *AC,* 23 March 1975; and 2 April 1975.

82. See Paul E. Peterson, *City Limits* (Chicago: University of Chicago Press, 1981); but see also Roger Friedland and Donald Palmer, "Park Place and Main Street: Business and the Urban Power Structure," *Annual Review of Sociology* 10 (1984): 393-416.

83. *AC,* 11 August 1987.

84. Ibid.

85. Lewis Grizzard, "Committee of One," *AC,* 1975 (CAP clipping file); and *AC,* 1 November 1987.

86. Henson and King, "Atlanta Public-Private Romance," 317.

87. Margaret Shannon, "Blacks in the Board Room," Atlanta *Constitution Magazine,* 21 April 1974.

88. Timothy L. Almy, William B. Hildreth, and Robert T. Golembiewski, "Case Study I — Assessing Electoral Defeat: New Directions and Values for MARTA" (Mass Transit Management: Case Studies of the Metropolitan Atlanta Rapid Transit Authority; A Report Prepared by the University of Georgia Department of Political Science for the U.S. Department of Transportation, Urban Mass Transportation Administration, University Research and Training Program), I-6.

89. For details, see Almy, Hildreth, and Golembiewski, *Case Study I.*

90. Ibid., I-7.

91. Quoted in ibid., I-3.

92. Quoted in ibid.

93. Ibid., I-6.

94. *Newsweek,* 6 December 1971, 78-79.

95. Almy, Hildreth, and Golembiewski, *Case Study I,* I-12, 16.

96. Scott L. Walker, "Rail Rapid Transit: Its Rebirth, Capabilities and Role in Promoting Urban Economic Development, an Atlanta Case Study" (B.A. thesis, Princeton University, 1986), 95-96.

97. For details, see Carl W. Proehl, Jr., and Robert T. Golembiewski, "Marta and the 15¢ Fare" (Mass Transit Management: Case Studies of the Metropolitan Atlanta Rapid Transit Authority; A Report Prepared by the University of Georgia Department of Political Science for the U.S. Department of Transportation, Urban Mass Transportation Administration, University Research and Training Program).

98. On Atlanta specifically, see Andrew M. Hamer, *The Selling of Rail Rapid Transit* (Lexington, Mass.: Lexington Books, 1976); Walker, "Rail Rapid Transit," 85-101.

99. Hebert, *Highways to Nowhere,* 119-120, 131-132.

100. Walker, "Rail Rapid Transit," 18-19.

101. Proehl and Golembiewski, "Marta," II-3.

102. Shannon, "Blacks in the Board Room"; and Norman Shavin and Bruce Galphin, *Atlanta: Triumph of a People* (Atlanta: Capricorn Corp., 1982), 288.

103. For details, see Barbara L. Jackson, "Desegregation: Atlanta Style," *Theory Into Practice* 17, no. 1 (1978): 43-53; Joel L. Fleishman, "The Real against the Ideal —

Making the Solution Fit the Problem: The Atlanta School Agreement of 1973," in *Roundtable Justice: Case Studies in Conflict Resolution,* ed. Robert B. Goldmann (Boulder, Colo.: Westview Press, 1980), 129–180; Research Atlanta, *School Desegregation in Metro Atlanta, 1954–1973* (Atlanta: Research Atlanta, 1973); and the Southern Center for Studies in Public Policy, *Consensus Politics.*

104. Jesse Burkhead, *Input and Output in Large-City High Schools* (Syracuse, N.Y.: Syracuse University Press, 1967), 72–74.

105. Quoted in Research Atlanta, *School Desegregation,* 4.

106. Southern Center for Studies in Public Policy, *Consensus Politics,* 18.

107. Fleishman, "Real against the Ideal."

108. For details about these negotiations, see ibid.

109. Jackson, "Desegregation," 48.

110. *AC,* 1 October 1987.

111. Ibid.

112. Hebert, *Highways to Nowhere,* 130–131.

113. Quoted in *AC,* 1 October 1987.

114. Southern Center for Studies in Public Policy, *Consensus Politics,* 50, 57–75.

115. Barbara L. Jackson, "Urban School Desegregation from a Black Perspective," in *Race and Schooling in the City,* ed. Adam Yarmolinsky, Lance Liebman, and Corinne S. Schelling (Cambridge, Mass.: Harvard University Press, 1981), 211.

116. Quoted in *AC,* 1 October 1987; contrast Fleishman, "Real Against the Ideal."

117. Detailed figures are contained in Research Atlanta, *School Desegregation.*

118. Fleishman, "Real Against the Ideal."

CHAPTER 6. THE NEIGHBORHOOD MOVEMENT FALTERS

1. Jack Bass and Walter DeVries, *The Transformation of Southern Politics* (New York: Basic Books, 1976), 154.

2. Ibid., 148–149.

3. Charles S. Bullock III, and Bruce A. Campbell, "Racist or Racial Voting in the 1981 Atlanta Municipal Election," *Urban Affairs Quarterly* 20 (December 1984): 149–164; Atlanta *Constitution* (hereafter referred to as *AC*), 1 November 1981.

4. *AC,* 5 October 1981.

5. *AC,* 6 October 1981.

6. *AC,* 5 October 1981.

7. Both quotes are from *AC,* 11 August 1987.

8. *AC,* 1 November 1981.

9. *AC,* 25 December 1983; 18 January 1985; and 18 December 1985.

10. For an account of the controversy, see Suzanne M. Hall, "Progress or Preservation: The Presidential Parkway Controversy, 1946–1986," *Atlanta History* 36 (Spring/Summer 1987): 22–38.

11. *AC,* 23 October 1984.

12. The quoted phrase is from a letter by President James T. Laney of Emory University in Donham, *Campus Report* (Emory), 1 February 1982, 12.

13. *AC,* 29 April 1983; 12 June 1983.

14. *AC,* 12 February 1984; 16 September 1984.

15. *AC,* 29 April 1983; 1 July 1984.

16. Since neighborhood resistance has persisted, with substantial council backing, state officials now make no such statements.

17. *AC,* 19 December 1984.
18. *AC,* 22 December 1984.
19. *AC,* 15 April 1988.
20. *AC,* 27 November 1984.
21. *AC,* 12 November 1984.
22. *AC,* 10 March 1987; 7 April 1987.
23. *AC,* 27 November 1984.
24. Ibid.
25. *AC,* 4 August 1988.
26. *AC,* 12 December 1988.
27. For details, see Clarence N. Stone, *Economic Growth and Neighborhood Discontent: System Bias in the Urban Renewal Program of Atlanta* (Chapel Hill: University of North Carolina Press, 1976), 99–114, 153–164; and Dale Henson and James King, "The Atlanta Public-Private Romance: An Abrupt Transformation," in *Public-Private Partnership in American Cities,* ed. R. Scott Fosler and Renee A. Berger (Lexington, Mass.: Lexington Books, 1982), 319–330.
28. *AC,* 2 April 1986.
29. *AC,* 23 April 1983; 5 June 1983.
30. Urban economists concur; see Kenneth A. Small, "Transportation and Urban Change," in *The New Urban Reality,* ed. Paul E. Peterson (Washington, D.C.: Brookings Institution, 1985), 213–223.
31. *AC,* 31 May 1986.
32. But see *AC,* 28 April 1983; and 15 May 1983.
33. *AC,* 18 June 1983.
34. *AC,* 1 June 1983.
35. Dana Blankenhorn and Russell Shaw, "Atlanta Grew and Grew," *Atlanta* (April 1985): 57–58, 126–128; Beth Dunlop, "An Accidental City with a Laissez-faire Approach to Planning," *AIA Journal* (April 1975): 52–55.
36. *AC,* 3 June 1984.
37. Garrett Hardin, "The Tragedy of the Commons," *Science,* 13 December 1968, 1243–1248.
38. See the comments by Mayor Young, *AC,* 28 March 1985.
39. *AC,* 16 May 1983; 13 January 1985; 20 December 1985.
40. *AC,* 7 May 1985.
41. Adolph Reed, Jr., "A Critique of Neo-Progressivism in Theorizing about Local Development Policy: A Case from Atlanta," in *The Politics of Urban Development,* ed. Clarence N. Stone and Heywood T. Sanders (Lawrence: University Press of Kansas, 1987), 199–215.
42. Clarence N. Stone, "Partnership New South Style: Central Atlanta Progress," *Proceedings, The Academy of Political Science* 36, no. 2 (1986): 100–110.
43. Research Atlanta, *Economic Development in Metropolitan Atlanta, Part II: Southside Development Strategies* (Atlanta, July 1984).
44. See, for example, AC, 18 December 1984.
45. *AC,* 3 November 1983.
46. *AC,* 2 November 1983.
47. May 22, 1986.
48. Henry George, *Progress and Poverty* (New York: Modern Library, 1932).
49. James T. Wooten, "Atlanta's Hip Strip," *New York Times Magazine,* 14 March 1971.
50. Resolution adopted by the Midtown Business Association Board, 1 May 1984.
51. *AC,* 7 October 1987.

52. *AC,* 29 September 1987.

53. *AC,* 5 June 1986. See the contrasting assessment by Arthur Frommer — *AC,* 5 November 1988.

54. *AC,* 8 October 1987.

55. Ibid.

56. *AC,* 5 June 1986.

57. Cf. Russell Hardin, *Collective Action* (Baltimore: Johns Hopkins University Press, 1982); Jeffrey R. Henig, *Neighborhood Mobilization* (New Brunswick, N.J.: Rutgers University Press, 1982); and David J. O'Brien, *Neighborhood Organization and Interest-Group Processes* (Princeton, N.J.: Princeton University Press, 1975).

58. Cf. Claus Offe, *Disorganized Capitalism* (Cambridge, Mass.: MIT Press, 1985), 170–220.

59. James Q. Wilson, *Political Organizations* (New York: Basic Books, 1973).

CHAPTER 7. THE COALITION RESTABILIZES

1. Andrew Young, "A Sanction That Would Affect the 'Passive Majority,'" *Washington Post,* 10 August 1986; Atlanta *Constitution* (thereafter referred to as *AC*), 24 July 1983.

2. *AC,* 22 September 1985.

3. Ibid.

4. Ibid.

5. See, for example, *AC,* 14 August 1987; 6 September 1987; *Wall Street Journal,* 19 February 1988; *New York Times,* 14 July 1988; and *Washington Post,* 18 July 1988.

6. Jeffrey L. Pressman and Aaron Wildavsky, *Implementation,* 3d ed. (Berkeley and Los Angeles: University of California Press, 1984), 87 and passim.

7. *AC,* 1 January 1984.

8. *AC,* 3 March 1984.

9. *AC,* 28 June 1987.

10. *AC,* 28 July 1983; 16 August 1983; and 5 May 1984. See also Harvey Newman, Barbara Ray, and Joseph Hacker, "A Content Analysis of Consensus Building in Local Policy Making: The Underground Atlanta Project" (paper presented at the Annual Meeting of the Urban Affairs Association, March 1988, St. Louis, Mo.).

11. Eugene Bardach, *The Implementation Game* (Cambridge, Mass.: MIT Press, 1977), 85–90.

12. *AC,* 14 December 1987.

13. *AC,* 8 May 1986.

14. *AC,* 21 July 1985.

15. *AC,* 27 February 1984; 28 March 1984; 3 May 1984; 6 May 1984.

16. *AC,* 27 February 1984.

17. Turpeau to *AC,* 13 May 1984.

18. *AC,* 25 January 1988.

19. *AC,* 19 November 1985; 11 January 1986; 12 December 1986; 16 August 1987.

20. *AC,* 13 November 1987; 17 November 1987; 23 November 1987.

21. *AC,* 6 December 1986.

22. *AC,* 3 December 1986.

23. *AC,* 11 December 1986.

24. "Central Area Study II: Executive Summary of the Public Safety Task Force Final Report," July 1987, 5–7, Appendix III.

25. *AC,* 12 May 1987.

26. *AC,* 13 December 1986.

27. *AC,* 1 January 1984.

28. For the flavor of that period, see Bruce Galphin, "Politics Are Black and White and Spread All Over," *Atlanta* 15 (October 1975): 10ff., esp. 20.

29. *AC,* 29 May 1987; 30 May 1987; 21 September 1987.

30. *AC,* 13 October 1984. Since then, the U.S. Supreme Court in *Richmond v. Croson* has narrowed the grounds on which minority contracting can be promoted, and the Georgia Supreme Court (in *American Subcontractors Association, Georgia Chapter v. City of Atlanta*) declared that the Atlanta program did not pass the new strict-scrutiny standard. A new plan is under consideration at this writing, and one option is a program that would target small and disadvantaged companies without regard to race— *Wall Street Journal,* 6 March 1989.

31. *AC,* 20 October 1984.

32. *Christian Science Monitor,* 29 May 1987.

33. On this term, see Herbert A. Simon, *Administrative Behavior,* 3d ed. (New York: Free Press, 1976).

34. *Christian Science Monitor,* 29 May 1987.

35. *AC,* 27 May 1987; 15 June 1987; 6 September 1987.

36. *AC,* 6 September 1987.

37. *AC,* 3 May 1987.

38. *AC,* 6 September 1987.

39. See also William J. Wilson, *The Truly Disadvantaged* (Chicago: University of Chicago Press, 1987).

40. *AC,* 11 August 1987.

41. Russell Hardin, *Collective Action* (Baltimore: Johns Hopkins University Press, 1982), 228.

42. Hardin, *Collective Action,* 221.

43. Cf. Jane J. Mansbridge, *Why We Lost the ERA* (Chicago: University of Chicago Press, 1986), 118-122.

44. Cf. Kim Lane Scheppele and Karol E. Soltan, "The Authority of Alternatives," in *Authority Revisited,* ed. J. Roland Pennock and John W. Chapman, Nomos 24 (New York: NYU Press, 1987), 169-200.

45. Mansbridge, *Why We Lost.*

46. The proposal to increase the city's capacity to issue bonds without a referendum itself requires referendum approval under state law, and the proposal was defeated when put before the voters in November 1988—*AC,* 10 November 1988. It is almost certain to be resubmitted.

47. *AC,* 31 October 1987; and 1 November 1987.

48. *AC,* 3 November 1987.

49. Note for example the reports on the Reginald Eaves trial—15 April 1988; 20 April 1988; 8 May 1988.

50. *AC,* 28 October 1984.

51. *AC,* 9 October 1983.

52. *AC,* 30 November 1986.

53. *AC,* 9 October 1983.

54. *AC,* 2 December 1986.

55. *AC,* 1 December 1986.

56. *AC,* 6 December 1986.

57. *AC,* 9 December 1986.

58. *AC,* 20 December 1986.

59. *AC,* 26 July 1986.
60. *AC,* 31 May 1985.
61. *AC,* 19 September 1985.
62. Ibid.
63. *AC,* 13 July 1986.
64. *AC,* 5 January 1987.
65. *AC,* 16 January 1986.
66. *AC,* 19 May 1985.
67. *AC,* 7 July 1988.
68. *AC,* 17 March 1983.
69. *AC,* 2 August 1987; 6 October 1987; 3 November 1988.
70. *AC,* 13 December 1986.
71. *AC,* 18 November 1985.
72. *AC,* 8 May 1988; see also 14 April 1988.
73. *AC,* 29 December 1987; 11 January 1988.
74. *AC,* 20 January 1988.
75. *AC,* 3 August 1988; 5 August 1988.
76. *AC,* 30 July 1988. For similar charges regarding the airport, see *AC,* 11 May 1983.
77. *AC,* 16 September 1983.
78. *AC,* 21 January 1987; Atlanta *Journal,* 24 June 1986. The news media are, however, fully aware that tall buildings and sparse street life harm the attractiveness of Atlanta as a city. See the business section coverage of a speech by travel writer Arthur Frommer—*AC,* 5 November 1988.
79. *AC,* 24 November 1985.
80. *AC,* 20 May 1987.
81. *AC,* 10 June 1987.
82. *AC,* 18 November 1987.
83. *AC,* 10 November 1987.
84. *AC,* 18 July 1987; 14 August 1987.
85. *AC,* 17 July 1987.
86. *AC,* 8 March 1988.
87. *AC,* 2 November 1988; 22 November 1988; 29 November 1988.
88. *AC,* 25 May 1988; 16 June 1988; 7 July 1988; 16 December 1988; 17 December 1988.
89. Herbert T. Jenkins, *Forty Years on the Force: 1932–1972* (Atlanta: Center for Research in Social Change, Emory University, 1973); and *AC,* 19 June 1987.
90. *AC,* 2 December 1987.
91. Quoted in *AC,* 19 June 1987.
92. *AC,* 11 June 1987.
93. *AC,* 19 June 1987.
94. *AC,* 2 December 1987.
95. *AC,* 12 June 1987.
96. *AC,* 12 June 1987; 18 June 1987.
97. More than a year later, the quietly issued report addressed no one's conduct specifically and recommended only that "standard operating procedures in the Police Bureau be redefined"—*AC,* 2 August 1988.
98. *AC,* 2 December 1987.
99. *AC,* 23 December 1987.
100. *AC,* 20 September 1987; 30 September 1987.
101. Miami *Herald,* 27 February 1983; *AC,* 23 July 1987; 30 July 1987.
102. On Arrington, see *AC,* 25 February 1987; 30 July 1987.

103. Robert L. Bish and Vincent Ostrom, *Understanding Urban Government* (Washington, D.C.: American Enterprise Institute, 1973).

CHAPTER 8. POLICY INNOVATION
AND REGIME PRACTICE: AN ATLANTA OVERVIEW

1. On the distinction between routine and critical (or "character-defining") decisions, see Philip Selznick, *Leadership in Administration* (New York: Harper & Row, 1957), 29-64.

2. Clarence N. Stone and Robert K. Whelan, "Urban Renewal Policy and City Politics: Urban Renewal in Atlanta and Baltimore," in *Proceedings of the Georgia Political Science Association* (Athens: Institute of Government, University of Georgia, 1972), 196-197.

3. Ibid., 201.

4. Howard Openshaw, "Atlanta's Housing Imbalance," *Atlanta Economic Review* 23 (May-June 1973): 52 ff.

5. Stephen L. Elkin, *City and Regime in the American Republic* (Chicago: University of Chicago Press, 1987); Robert K. Whelan, "New Orleans: Mayoral Politics and Economic-Development Policies in the Postwar Years, 1945-86," in *The Politics of Urban Development*, ed. Clarence N. Stone and Heywood T. Sanders (Lawrence: University Press of Kansas, 1987).

6. Theodore J. Lowi, "American Business, Public Policy, Case Studies, and Political Theory," *World Politics* 16 (1964): 677-715.

7. Paul E. Peterson, *City Limits* (Chicago: University of Chicago Press, 1981).

8. Selznick, *Leadership in Administration,* 35.

9. Philip Abrams, *Historical Sociology* (Ithaca, N.Y.: Cornell University Press, 1982).

10. On the general importance of federal policy for local coalitions, see John H. Mollenkopf, *The Contested City* (Princeton, N.J.: Princeton University Press, 1983).

11. Susan E. Clarke, "The Effects of Interest Representation Modes on Local Economic Development Policies" (paper presented at the Annual Meeting of the American Political Science Association, August/September 1985, New Orleans, La.); idem, "More Autonomous Policy Orientations," in *The Politics of Urban Development*, ed. Clarence N. Stone and Heywood T. Sanders (Lawrence: University Press of Kansas, 1987).

12. See, for example, the "Declaration of Protective Covenants for Southwide Industrial Park," 1986, 17. Although a modest effort toward widening employment opportunities has recently been enacted, its enforcement potential is uncertain—see Atlanta *Constitution* (hereafter referred to as *AC*), 29 July 1988.

13. *AC*, 2 March 1986.

14. Quoted in the *Washington Post,* 3 January 1983.

15. Ibid. See also David L. Sjoquist, "The Economic Status of Black Atlantans" (paper prepared for the Atlanta Urban League, April 1988).

16. *AC*, 16 October 1987, citing James W. Fossett, "The Downside of Housing Booms: Low Income Housing in Atlanta, 1970-1985" (Metropolitan Opportunity Project of the University of Chicago, September 1987).

17. See the comments by Lonnie King in *AC*, 1 October 1987.

18. *AC*, 5 September 1986; 6 September 1986.

19. *AC*, 18 August 1986.

20. C. Wright Mills, "The Middle Class in Middle Sized Cities," *American Sociological Review* 11 (October 1946): 520–529.

21. Cf. Russell Hardin, *Collective Action* (Baltimore: Johns Hopkins University Press, 1982), 195–197.

22. A similar process is employed in other cities; on Dallas, see Elkin, *City and Regime*, 72–73.

23. Cf. J. Allen Whitt, *Urban Elites and Mass Transportation* (Princeton, N.J.: Princeton University Press, 1982); Beth Mintz and Michael Schwartz, *The Power Structure of American Business* (Chicago: University of Chicago Press, 1985); Michael Useem, "Which Business Leaders Help Govern?" in *Power Structure Research,* ed. G. William Domhoff (Beverly Hills, Calif.: Sage, 1980), 199–225; and idem, "The Inner Circle and the Political Voice of Business," in *The Structure of Power in America,* ed. Michael Schwartz (New York: Holmes & Meier, 1987), 143–153.

24. Cf. Mary Douglas, *How Institutions Think* (Syracuse, N.Y.: Syracuse University Press, 1986), 46.

25. Terry N. Clark and Lorna C. Ferguson, *City Money* (New York: Columbia University Press, 1983), 51. Atlanta officials have disputed the interpretation of this figure, emphasizing that much of it is covered by revenue bonds and not general obligation bonds.

26. Cf. Clarence N. Stone, "Elite Distemper versus the Promise of Democracy," in *Power Elites and Organizations,* ed. G. William Domhoff and Thomas R. Dye (Newbury Park, Calif.: Sage, 1987), 277.

27. *AC,* 12 February 1987.

28. Harvey Molotch, "The City as a Growth Machine," *American Journal of Sociology* 82 (September 1976): 309–331. See also John R. Logan and Harvey L. Molotch, *Urban Fortunes* (Berkeley and Los Angeles: University of California Press, 1987), 50–98.

29. Mancur Olson, Jr., *The Logic of Collective Action* (Cambridge, Mass.: Harvard University Press, 1965).

30. Ronald H. Bayor, "Planning the City for Racial Segregation: The Highway-Street Pattern in Atlanta," *Journal of Urban History* 15 (November 1988): 3–21. Earlier decisions that led to the hurried construction and isolated location of public housing, in particular Bankhead Courts, have also continued to plague the city. See *New York Times,* 1 March 1989; *AC,* 24 and 30 January 1989, 2 February 1989.

31. Cf. Katherine L. Bradbury, Anthony Downs, and Kenneth A. Small, *Urban Decline and the Future of American Cities* (Washington, D.C.: Brookings Institution, 1982), 243.

PART 3. ANALYSIS

1. Alvin W. Gouldner, "The Norm of Reciprocity: A Preliminary Statement," in *Friends, Followers, and Factions,* ed. Steffen W. Schmidt and others (Berkeley and Los Angeles: University of California Press, 1977).

2. See Oliver E. Williamson, *The Economic Institutions of Capitalism* (New York: Free Press, 1985).

3. Ibid.

4. Cf. Russell Hardin, *Collective Action* (Baltimore: Johns Hopkins University Press, 1982).

CHAPTER 9. ATLANTA'S URBAN REGIME

1. See especially Oliver P. Williams, "A Typology for Comparative Local Government," *Midwest Journal of Political Science* 5 (May 1961): 150–164.

2. See especially Pierre Clavel, *The Progressive City* (New Brunswick, N.J.: Rutgers University Press, 1986).

3. Stephen L. Elkin, *City and Regime in the American Republic* (Chicago: University of Chicago Press, 1987).

4. David R. Johnson, "San Antonio: The Vicissitudes of Boosterism," in *Sunbelt Cities: Politics and Growth since World War II,* ed. Richard M. Bernard and Bradley R. Rice (Austin: University of Texas Press, 1983).

5. Elkin, *City and Regime;* and Carol E. Thometz, *The Decision-Makers: The Power Structure of Dallas* (Dallas: Southern Methodist University Press, 1963).

6. Todd Swanstrom, *The Crisis of Growth Politics* (Philadelphia: Temple University Press, 1985); Clavel, *Progressive City,* especially 57–61; Robert K. Whelan, "New Orleans: Mayoral Politics and Economic-Development Policies in the Postwar Years, 1945–86," in *The Politics of Urban Development,* ed. Clarence N. Stone and Heywood T. Sanders (Lawrence: University Press of Kansas, 1987); and Todd Swanstrom and Sharon Ward, "Albany's O'Connell Organization" (paper presented at the Annual Meeting of the American Political Science Association, September 1987, Chicago).

7. See especially John H. Mollenkopf, *The Contested City* (Princeton, N.J.: Princeton University Press, 1983).

8. Roger Friedland and Donald Palmer, "Park Place and Main Street: Business and the Urban Power Structure," *Annual Review of Sociology* 10 (1984): 393–416.

9. Aldon D. Morris, *The Origins of the Civil Rights Movement* (New York: Free Press, 1984).

10. Heywood T. Sanders, "The Politics of Development in Middle-sized Cities: From New Haven to Kalamazoo," in *The Politics of Urban Development,* ed. Clarence N. Stone and Heywood T. Sanders (Lawrence: University Press of Kansas, 1987).

11. Edward C. Banfield, *Political Influence* (New York: Free Press, 1961); Larry Bennett, "In the Wake of Richard Daley: Chicago's Declining Politics of Party and Shifting Politics of Development" (paper presented at the Annual Meeting of the American Political Science Association, September 1987, Chicago).

12. Jeanne R. Lowe, *Cities in a Race with Time* (New York: Random House, 1967), 110–163; Roy Lubove, *Twentieth-Century Pittsburgh* (New York: John Wiley & Sons, 1969); and Barbara Ferman, "Democracy Under Fire: The Politics of Economic Restructuring in Pittsburgh and Chicago" (paper prepared for delivery at the Annual Meeting of the American Political Science Association, September 1989, Atlanta).

13. See especially Arthur J. Vidich and Joseph Bensman, *Small Town in Mass Society,* rev. ed. (Princeton, N.J.: Princeton University Press, 1968).

14. Katherine Lyall, "A Bicycle Built-for-Two: Public-Private Partnership in Baltimore," in *Public-Private Partnership in American Cities,* ed. R. Scott Fosler and Renee A. Berger (Lexington, Mass.: Lexington Books, 1982), 17–57.

15. Mollenkopf, *Contested City.*

16. Ibid.; and Chester Hartman, *The Transformation of San Francisco* (Totowa, N.J.: Rowman & Allanheld, 1984).

17. Peter A. Lupsha, "Structural Change and Innovation: Elites and Albuquerque Politics in the 1980s," in *The Politics of Urban Development,* ed. Clarence N. Stone and Heywood T. Sanders (Lawrence: University Press of Kansas, 1987).

18. Robert Axelrod, *The Evolution of Cooperation* (New York: Basic Books, 1984), 100–101.

19. Lupsha, "Structural Change and Innovation."

20. Barbara Ferman, *Governing the Ungovernable City* (Philadelphia: Temple University Press, 1985).

21. See also Swanstrom, *Crisis of Growth Politics.*

22. Nelson W. Polsby, *Community Power and Political Theory: A Further Look at Problems of Evidence and Inference* (New Haven, Conn.: Yale University Press, 1980), 117.

23. Ibid.

24. See especially Mancur Olson, Jr., *The Logic of Collective Action* (Cambridge, Mass.: Harvard University Press, 1965); Russell Hardin, *Collective Action* (Baltimore: Johns Hopkins University Press, 1982).

25. For a more complex view of shirking, see Michael Taylor, *The Possibility of Cooperation* (Cambridge: Cambridge University Press, 1987).

26. See especially Hardin, *Collective Action;* cf. Chester I. Barnard, *The Functions of the Executive* (Cambridge, Mass.: Harvard University Press, 1968).

27. Jane J. Mansbridge, *Why We Lost the ERA* (Chicago: University of Chicago Press, 1986).

28. Cf. James Q. Wilson, *Political Organizations* (New York: Basic Books, 1973).

29. Quoted in James Q. Wilson, *The Amateur Democrat* (Chicago: University of Chicago Press, 1962), 70–71.

30. William L. Riordon, *Plunkitt of Tammany Hall* (New York: E. P. Dutton, 1963), 17–20.

31. Steven P. Erie, *Rainbow's End* (Berkeley and Los Angeles: University of California Press, 1988); and Ester R. Fuchs and Robert Y. Shapiro, "Government Performance as a Basis for Machine Support," *Urban Affairs Quarterly* 18 (June 1983): 537–550.

32. See, for example, Swanstrom and Ward, "Albany's O'Connell Organization"; Erie, *Rainbow's End.*

33. Cf. Milton Rakove, *Don't Make No Waves, Don't Back No Losers* (Bloomington: Indiana University Press, 1975), 60–89.

34. Jeffrey L. Pressman and Aaron Wildavsky, *Implementation,* 3d ed. (Berkeley and Los Angeles: University of California Press, 1984).

35. Ferman, *Governing the Ungovernable City;* Martha W. Weinberg, "Boston's Kevin White," *Political Science Quarterly* 96 (Spring 1981): 87–106.

36. Robert A. Caro, *The Power Broker* (New York: Alfred A. Knopf, 1974).

37. Axelrod, *Evolution of Cooperation.*

38. Quoted in Charles E. Silberman, *Crisis in Black and White* (New York: Random House, 1964), 220.

39. David O'Brien, *Neighborhood Organization and Interest-Group Processes* (Princeton, N.J.: Princeton University Press, 1975).

40. See, for example, Atlanta *Constitution,* 3 November 1985.

41. The phrase is borrowed from a review of Kurt Waldheim's *In the Eye of the Storm* by Charles William Manes ("The United Nations in a Divided World," *Washington Post* Book World, 2 March 1986, 5). Manes observes that, "like his countrymen, Waldheim was moved not by great visions but by small opportunities." The notion of small opportunities is akin to "satisficing"; Herbert A. Simon, *Administrative Behavior,* 3d ed. (New York: Free Press, 1976).

42. Cf. the discussion of party cohesion as a collective good by Gary W. Cox, *The Efficient Secret* (Cambridge: Cambridge University Press, 1987), especially 144.

43. Clarence N. Stone, "Preemptive Power: Floyd Hunter's 'Community Power Structure' Reconsidered," *American Journal of Political Science* 32 (February 1988): 82-104.

44. Oliver E. Williamson, "Organizational Innovation: The Transaction-Cost Approach," in *Entrepreneurship,* ed. Joshua Ronen (Lexington, Mass.: Lexington Books, 1983), 101.

CHAPTER 10. EQUITY AND EFFECTIVENESS

1. Otis White, editor of *Georgia Trend,* quoted in Erla Zwingle, "Atlanta: Energy and Optimism in the New South," *National Geographic* 174 (July 1988): 24.

2. Ibid.

3. Arthur M. Okun, *Equality and Efficiency: The Big Tradeoff* (Washington, D.C.: Brookings Institution, 1975); cf. Paul E. Peterson, *City Limits* (Chicago: University of Chicago Press, 1981).

4. Samuel P. Huntington, "The Democratic Distemper," *Public Interest* 41 (Fall 1975): 9-38; Michael Crozier, Samuel P. Huntington, and J. Watanuki, *The Crisis of Democracy* (New York: New York University Press, 1975); and Edward Shils, "The Political Class in the Age of Mass Society: Collectivistic Liberalism and Social Democracy," in *Does Who Governs Matter?* ed. Moshe M. Czudnowski (DeKalb: Northern Illinois University Press, 1982).

5. See Appendix A.

6. See also John D. Kasarda, "Urban Change and Minority Opportunities," in *The New Urban Reality,* ed. Paul E. Peterson (Washington, D.C.: Brookings Institution, 1985); but note the caution in Katherine L. Bradbury, Anthony Downs, and Kenneth A. Small, *Urban Decline and the Future of American Cities* (Washington, D.C.: Brookings Institution, 1982).

7. Ronald H. Bayor, "Planning the City for Racial Segregation: The Highway-Street Pattern in Atlanta," *Journal of Urban History* 15 (November 1988): 3-21.

8. Zwingle, "Atlanta," 17.

9. Clarence N. Stone and Robert K. Whelan, "Urban Renewal Policy and City Politics: Urban Renewal in Atlanta and Baltimore," in *Proceedings of the Georgia Political Science Association* (Athens: Institute of Government, University of Georgia, 1972).

10. Susan S. Fainstein and others, *Restructuring the City* (New York: Longman, 1986), 270.

11. The effects of racial composition are complex. Black control of a key jurisdiction is empowering, but state authority over localities can negate expansive use of city government. Moreover, to the extent that a metropolitan area is divided between a predominantly black central city and overwhelmingly white suburbs, planning and policymaking are handicapped by racial antagonisms. Even economic development is greatly affected — statistically, the proportion of population that is black shows up as a disincentive to investment (Bradbury, Downs, and Small, *Urban Decline;* also Clarence N. Stone, Robert K. Whelan, and William J. Murin, *Urban Policy and Politics in a Bureaucratic Age,* 2d ed. (Englewood Cliffs, N.J.: Prentice-Hall, 1986), 283.

12. Atlanta *Constitution,* 8 October 1988.

13. See especially the comments by Arthur Frommer, reported in *AC,* 5 November 1988.

14. Business claims on this point should, however, be viewed with a degree of skepticism. There is a long history of investors in Georgia claiming that demands on

business are unacceptable. One historian, for example, recounts that, during the 1908 gubernatorial campaign, the reform candidate, Hoke Smith, was attacked for driving out capital. A knitting mill in Barnesville, Georgia, suspended operation and posted a sign saying: "Closed for want of orders, owing to too much reform legislation" (Dewey W. Grantham, Jr., *Hoke Smith and the Politics of the New South* [Baton Rouge: Louisiana State University Press, 1958], 188). Having survived child-labor legislation and other reforms of that era, business in Georgia, one suspects, is able to survive other demands as well.

15. For similar general recommendations, see Norton E. Long, "Can the Contemporary City Be a Significant Polity?" (paper given at the Annual Meeting of the Urban Affairs Association, March 1983, Flint, Mich.). For similar recommendations based on an analysis of Atlanta conditions, see David L. Sjoquist, "The Economic Status of Black Atlantans" (paper prepared for the Atlanta Urban League, April 1988).

16. Norton E. Long, "The Local Community as an Ecology of Games," *American Journal of Sociology* 64 (November 1958): 255.

17. Cf. Shils, "Political Class."

18. Cf. E. E. Schattschneider, *The Semi-Sovereign People* (New York: Holt, Rinehart & Winston, 1960), 39.

19. Cf. Jane J. Mansbridge, *Beyond Adversary Democracy* (New York: Basic Books, 1980).

20. Mancur Olson, *The Rise and Decline of Nations* (New Haven, Conn.: Yale University Press, 1982); and Peter J. Katzenstein, *Small States in World Markets* (Ithaca, N.Y.: Cornell University Press, 1985).

21. For examples of a strategy of isolation rather than incorporation, see Robert J. Norrell, *Reaping the Whirlwind* (New York: Vintage, 1986), especially 129; and Ian Lustick, *Arabs in the Jewish State* (Austin: University of Texas Press, 1980), 77, 263-264.

22. Cf. Katzenstein, *Small States*.

23. Russell Hardin, *Collective Action* (Baltimore: Johns Hopkins University Press, 1982); Michael Taylor, *The Possibility of Cooperation* (Cambridge: Cambridge University Press, 1987).

24. William H. Riker, *The Theory of Political Coalitions* (New Haven, Conn.: Yale University Press, 1962).

25. Michael Leiserson, "Factions and Coalitions in One-Party Japan: An Interpretation Based on the Theory of Games," *American Political Science Review* 62 (September 1968): 770-787.

26. Robert Axelrod, *Conflict of Interest* (Chicago: Markham Publishing Co., 1970); see also Michael Leiserson, "Power and Ideology in Coalition Behavior," in *The Study of Coalition Behavior,* ed. Sven Groennings, E. W. Kelly, and Michael Leiserson (New York: Holt, Rinehart & Winston, 1970).

27. Cf. Matthew A. Crenson, *The Un-Politics of Air Pollution* (Baltimore: Johns Hopkins University Press, 1971), 149-154.

28. Angela Browne and Aaron Wildavsky, "Implementation as Exploration," in *Implementation,* 3d ed., by Jeffrey L. Pressman and Aaron Wildavsky (Berkeley and Los Angeles: University of California Press, 1984), 236.

29. James G. March and Herbert A. Simon, *Organizations* (New York: John Wiley & Sons, 1965), 105-106; Anthony Downs, *Inside Bureaucracy* (Boston: Little, Brown, 1967), 167-190.

30. Clarence N. Stone, "Efficiency versus Social Learning: A Reconsideration of the Implementation Process," *Policy Studies Review* 4 (February 1985): 484-496.

31. Milton Rakove, *Don't Make No Waves, Don't Back No Losers* (Bloomington: Indiana University Press, 1975), 16.

32. Quoted in ibid., 79.

33. Though this pattern is consistent with ethos theory, the issue is more complicated than that; see Jeffrey R. Henig, *Neighborhood Mobilization* (New Brunswick, N.J.: Rutgers University Press, 1982); and David J. O'Brien, *Neighborhood Organization and Interest-Group Processes* (Princeton, N.J.: Princeton University Press, 1975).

34. See, for example, Lillian B. Rubin, *Busing and Backlash* (Berkeley and Los Angeles: University of California Press, 1972).

35. Philip Abrams, *Historical Sociology* (Ithaca, N.Y.: Cornell University Press, 1982).

36. V. O. Key, Jr., *Southern Politics in State and Nation* (New York: Alfred A. Knopf, 1949).

37. Bertil Hanson, "Tulsa: Oil Folks at Home," in *Urban Politics in the Southwest,* ed. Leonard E. Goodall (Tempe: Institute of Public Administration, Arizona State University, 1967).

38. Amy Bridges, *A City in the Republic* (Cambridge: Cambridge University Press, 1984), 154–155.

39. Cf. Rufus P. Browning, Dale Rogers Marshall, and David H. Tabb, *Protest Is Not Enough* (Berkeley and Los Angeles: University of California Press, 1984).

CHAPTER 11. RETHINKING COMMUNITY POWER:
SOCIAL PRODUCTION VERSUS SOCIAL CONTROL

1. At the national level, though the formal authority of government is much greater in relation to society (but society is infinitely more complex), informal arrangements often take the form of "subgovernments." The literature is too vast to be cited, but among the more thoughtful discussions are Grant McConnell, *Private Power and American Democracy* (New York: Alfred A. Knopf, 1966); and Theodore J. Lowi, *The End of Liberalism* (New York: W. W. Norton & Co., 1979). The debate at the national level is not over whether or not informal arrangements are important, but over whether or not, beyond subgovernments, there is a cross-sector elite capable of uniting government, business, and the military around a small number of top-level decisions. That there is such a group was argued in C. Wright Mills, *The Power Elite* (New York: Oxford University Press, 1956). Subsequent writers concerned with mechanisms of informal coordination include G. William Domhoff, *Who Rules America Now* (Englewood Cliffs, N.J.: Prentice-Hall, 1983); Beth Mintz and Michael Schwartz, *The Power Structure of American Business* (Chicago: University of Chicago Press, 1985); and Michael Useem, *The Inner Circle* (New York: Oxford University Press, 1984).

2. For an illustration, see Gary W. Cox, *The Efficient Secret* (Cambridge: Cambridge University Press, 1987).

3. Charles Perrow, *Complex Organizations,* 3d ed. (New York: Random House, 1986), 116.

4. Charles Tilly, *Big Structures, Large Processes, Huge Comparisons* (New York: Russell Sage Foundation, 1984), 26–33.

5. Sam Bass Warner, Jr., *The Private City* (Philadelphia: University of Pennsylvania Press, 1968).

6. Steven Lukes, *Power: A Radical View* (London: Macmillan, 1974).

7. Thomas S. Kuhn, *The Structure of Scientific Revolutions,* 2d ed. (Chicago: University of Chicago Press, 1970). See also Jeffrey C. Isaac, *Power and Marxist Theory* (Ithaca, N.Y.: Cornell University Press, 1987).

8. Gerhard E. Lenski, *Power and Privilege* (Chapel Hill: University of North Carolina Press, 1984), 50–66.

9. Robert A. Dahl, *Dilemmas of Pluralist Democracy* (New Haven, Conn.: Yale University Press, 1982), 33.

10. David D. Laitin, *Hegemony and Culture* (Chicago: University of Chicago Press, 1986), 107.

11. Dennis H. Wrong, *Power: Its Forms, Bases and Uses* (New York: Harper & Row, 1980), 20.

12. Edward C. Banfield, *Political Influence* (New York: Free Press, 1961), 313.

13. Ibid., 241.

14. Elkin uses the cost-of-compliance factor to argue that power is not a very useful concept in political analysis. See Stephen L. Elkin, "Pluralism in Its Place," in *The Democratic State,* ed. Roger Benjamin and Stephen L. Elkin (Lawrence: University Press of Kansas, 1985).

15. Ibid., 184.

16. James E. Alt, Randall L. Calvert, and Brian D. Humes, "Reputation and Hegemonic Stability," *American Political Science Review* 82 (June 1988): 448.

17. Ian Lustick, *Arabs in the Jewish State* (Austin: University of Texas Press, 1980), 237, 252.

18. Frances Fox Piven and Richard A. Cloward, *Regulating the Poor* (New York: Pantheon Books, 1971), 338.

19. Frances Fox Piven and Richard A. Cloward, *Poor People's Movements* (New York: Pantheon Books, 1977), 1.

20. Carl Boggs, *The Two Revolutions: Gramsci and the Dilemmas of Western Marxism* (Boston: South End Press, 1984); but cf. Adam Przeworski, *Capitalism and Social Democracy* (Cambridge: Cambridge University Press, 1985).

21. Ralf Dahrendorf, *Essays in the Theory of Society* (Stanford, Calif.: Stanford University Press, 1968), 227.

22. Ralf Dahrendorf, *Class and Class Conflict in Industrial Society* (Stanford, Calif.: Stanford University Press, 1959), 176.

23. Ibid.; see also Wrong, *Power,* 117.

24. See, for example, Manuel Castells, *The City and the Grassroots* (Berkeley and Los Angeles: University of California Press, 1983); Ira Katznelson, "The Crisis of the Capitalist City: Urban Politics and Social Control," in *Theoretical Perspectives on Urban Politics,* by Willis D. Hawley and others (Englewood Cliffs, N.J.: Prentice-Hall, 1976); and Michael P. Smith, *City, State, and Market* (New York: Basil Blackwell, 1988).

25. James G. March, "The Power of Power," in *Varieties of Political Theory,* ed. David Easton (Englewood Cliffs, N.J.: Prentice-Hall, 1966), 39–70.

26. Cf. Lenski, *Power and Privilege,* 50–56; and Arthur Stein, "Hegemon's Dilemma," *International Organization* 38 (1984): 355–386.

27. See, for example, Piven and Cloward, *Poor People's Movements.*

28. Ira Katznelson, *City Trenches* (Chicago: University of Chicago Press, 1981).

29. Norton E. Long, "The Local Community as an Ecology of Games," *American Journal of Sociology* 64 (November 1958): 251–261.

30. Perrow, *Complex Organizations,* 117.

31. Tilly, *Big Structures.*

32. A social theorist especially concerned with power as an enabling capacity is Talcott Parsons (*Politics and Social Structure* [New York: Free Press, 1969]). Parsons, however, seems to fall into the trap of seeing society as an entity apart, that can itself be empowered separate from the conflicts among and within the various elements

composing it; contrast Tilly (*Big Structures,* 20-26). A recent work sensitive to the enabling dimension of power, but in a context of social conflict, is that of Isaac (*Power*). Though not directly concerned with power, Barbara Ferman's recent work (*Governing the Ungovernable City* [Philadelphia: Temple University Press, 1985]) on coalition building and governability is also highly relevant to the question of enabling capacity.

33. Cf. the earlier quote by Dahl.

34. Cf. Ferman, *Governing the Ungovernable City;* Todd Swanstrom, *The Crisis of Growth Politics* (Philadelphia: Temple University Press, 1985); and Douglas Yates, *The Ungovernable City* (Cambridge, Mass.: MIT Press, 1977).

35. Pierre Clavel, *The Progressive City* (New Brunswick, N.J.: Rutgers University Press, 1986); see also Sophie N. Body-Gendrot, "Grass-roots Mobilization in the Thirteenth Arrondissement of Paris," in *The Politics of Urban Development,* ed. Clarence N. Stone and Heywood T. Sanders (Lawrence: University Press of Kansas, 1987).

36. See Laitin, *Hegemony and Culture,* 107.

37. Cf. Claus Offe, *Disorganized Capitalism* (Cambridge, Mass.: MIT Press, 1985), 170-220.

38. Cf. Jennifer L. Hochschild, *The New American Dilemma* (New Haven, Conn.: Yale University Press, 1984).

39. Clarence N. Stone, "Systemic Power in Community Decision Making," *American Political Science Review* 74 (December 1980): 978-990.

CHAPTER 12. CONCLUSION

1. Robert Keohane, *After Hegemony* (Princeton, N.J.: Princeton University Press, 1984).

2. David J. O'Brien, *Neighborhood Organization and Interest-Group Processes* (Princeton, N.J.: Princeton University Press, 1975).

3. Stephen L. Elkin, *City and Regime in the American Republic* (Chicago: University of Chicago Press, 1987); David R. Johnson, "San Antonio: The Vicissitudes of Boosterism," in *Sunbelt Cities: Politics and Growth since World War II,* ed. Richard M. Bernard and Bradley R. Rice (Austin: University of Texas Press, 1983).

4. Bryan D. Jones and Lynn W. Bachelor, *The Sustaining Hand: Community Leadership and Corporate Power* (Lawrence: University Press of Kansas, 1986), 183-184.

5. See especially Barbara Ferman, "Democracy under Fire: The Politics of Economic Restructuring in Pittsburgh and Chicago" (paper prepared for delivery at the Annual Meeting of the American Political Science Association, September 1989, Atlanta).

6. Larry Bennett, "In the Wake of Richard Daley: Chicago's Declining Politics of Party and Shifting Politics of Development" (paper presented at the Annual Meeting of the American Political Science Association, September 1987, Chicago); Barbara Ferman, *Governing the Ungovernable City* (Philadelphia: Temple University Press, 1985); and William J. Grimshaw, "The Political Economy of Machine Politics" (paper presented at the Annual Meeting of the American Political Science Association, September 1987, Chicago).

7. Robert A. Dahl, *Who Governs?* (New Haven, Conn.: Yale University Press, 1961); and Raymond E. Wolfinger, *The Politics of Progress* (Englewood Cliffs, N.J.: Prentice-Hall, 1974).

8. Ferman, *Governing the Ungovernable City;* John H. Mollenkopf, *The Contested City* (Princeton, N.J.: Princeton University Press, 1983); and Martha W. Weinberg, "Boston's Kevin White," *Political Science Quarterly* 96 (Spring 1981): 87–106.

9. Robert A. Caro, *The Power Broker* (New York: Alfred A. Knopf, 1974).

10. Jameson W. Doig, "Coalition-Building by a Regional Agency," in *The Politics of Urban Development,* ed. Clarence N. Stone and Heywood T. Sanders (Lawrence: University Press of Kansas, 1987).

11. Steven P. Erie, *Rainbow's End* (Berkeley and Los Angeles: University of California Press, 1988); and Todd Swanstrom and Sharon Ward, "Albany's O'Connell Organization" (paper presented at the Annual Meeting of the American Political Science Association, September 1987, Chicago).

12. See especially Charles R. Morris, *The Cost of Good Intentions* (New York: W. W. Norton & Co., 1980).

13. See Pierre Clavel, *The Progressive City* (New Brunswick, N.J.: Rutgers University Press, 1986).

14. Harvey Molotch, "The City as a Growth Machine," *American Journal of Sociology* 82 (September 1976): 309–331.

15. See, for example, Jones and Bachelor, *Sustaining Hand,* 97–101.

16. Cf. Jeffrey R. Henig, *Neighborhood Mobilization* (New Brunswick, N.J.: Rutgers University Press, 1982).

17. John Bonner, *Introduction to the Theory of Social Choice* (Baltimore: Johns Hopkins University Press, 1986), 34.

18. Stein Rokkan, "Norway: Numerical Democracy and Corporate Pluralism," in *Political Oppositions in Western Democracies,* ed. Robert A. Dahl (New Haven, Conn.: Yale University Press, 1966), 105; see also Erie, *Rainbow's End.*

19. Matthew A. Crenson, *The Un-Politics of Air Pollution* (Baltimore: Johns Hopkins University Press, 1971); see also Edwin H. Rhyne, "Political Parties and Decision Making in Three Southern Counties," *American Political Science Review* 52 (December 1958): 1091–1107.

20. Clarence N. Stone, "Preemptive Power: Floyd Hunter's 'Community Power Structure' Reconsidered," *American Journal of Political Science* 32 (February 1988): 82–104.

21. Norman Frohlich and Joe A. Oppenheimer, *Modern Political Economy* (Englewood Cliffs, N.J.: Prentice-Hall, 1978), 19–31.

APPENDIX A

1. See also Clarence N. Stone, *Economic Growth and Neighborhood Discontent: System Bias in the Urban Renewal Program of Atlanta* (Chapel Hill: University of North Carolina Press, 1976), 27.

2. All data in Table 1 are taken from census reports.

APPENDIX C

1. V. O. Key and Frank Munger, "Social Determinism and Electoral Decision," in *American Voting Behavior,* ed. Eugene Burdick and Arthur J. Brodbeck (Glencoe, Ill.: Free Press, 1959), 299.

2. Thomas S. Kuhn, *The Structure of Scientific Revolutions,* 2d ed. (Chicago: University of Chicago Press, 1970).

3. See Patrick Gardiner, *The Nature of Historical Explanation* (Oxford: Oxford University Press, 1961).

4. Herbert A. Simon, *Administrative Behavior,* 3d ed. (New York: Free Press, 1976).

5. Arthur L. Stinchcombe, *Theoretical Methods in Social History* (New York: Academic Press, 1978); see also Philip Abrams, *Historical Sociology* (Ithaca, N.Y.: Cornell University Press, 1982), especially 190–226.

6. Floyd Hunter, *Community Power Structure* (Chapel Hill: University of North Carolina Press, 1953); and Stephen L. Elkin, *City and Regime in the American Republic* (Chicago: University of Chicago Press, 1987).

7. Abrams, *Historical Sociology;* Gardiner, *Historical Explanation.*

8. Theda Skocpol, *States and Social Revolutions* (Cambridge: Cambridge University Press, 1979).

9. For an overview of Moore's historical method, see Dennis Smith, *Barrington Moore, Jr.: A Critical Appraisal* (Armonk, N.Y.: M. E. Sharpe, 1983).

10. Mark A. Stone, "Chaos, Prediction and LaPlacean Determinism," *American Philosophical Quarterly* 26 (April 1989): 123–131.

11. The categories refer to the major role of the interviewee in the civic and political life of Atlanta, not necessarily the position that they held at the time of the interview. Numbers do not total ninety-seven because a few respondents played more than one major role. Public officials included both elected and administrative; community-based refers to neighborhood activists, preservationists, and the arts community.

12. See Alexander Heard's Introduction to *Southern Politics in State and Nation,* by V. O. Key, Jr. (Knoxville: University of Tennessee Press, 1984), xxi.

References

Abney, F. Glenn, and John D. Hutcheson, Jr. 1981. "Race, Representation, and Trust." *Public Opinion Quarterly* 45: 91–101.

Abrams, Philip. 1982. *Historical Sociology.* Ithaca, N.Y.: Cornell University Press.

Alexander, Robert J. 1951. "Negro Business in Atlanta." *Southern Economic Journal* 17: 451–464.

Allen, Ivan, Jr., with Paul Hemphill. 1971. *Mayor: Notes on the Sixties.* New York: Simon and Schuster.

Allison, Graham T. 1971. *Essence of Decision.* Boston: Little, Brown.

Almy, Timothy L., William B. Hildreth, and Robert T. Golembiewski. 1981. "Case Study I—Assessing Electoral Defeat: New Directions and Values for MARTA." Mass Transit Management: Case Studies of the Metropolitan Atlanta Rapid Transit Authority. A Report Prepared by the University of Georgia Department of Political Science for the U.S. Department of Transportation, Urban Mass Transportation Administration, University Research and Training Program.

Alt, James E., Randall L. Calvert, and Brian D. Humes. 1988. "Reputation and Hegemonic Stability." *American Political Science Review* 82 (June): 445–466.

Axelrod, Robert. 1970. *Conflict of Interest.* Chicago: Markham Publishing Co.

———. 1984. *The Evolution of Cooperation.* New York: Basic Books.

Bacote, C. A. 1955. "The Negro in Atlanta Politics." *Phylon* 16: 333–350.

Ball, Steve, and Diane Ball. 1976. "Atlanta: The Evolution of a Changing Heritage." *Real Estate Atlanta* 5 (January/February): 122–128.

Banfield, Edward C. 1961. *Political Influence.* New York: Free Press.

———. 1965. *Big City Politics.* New York: Random House.

———. 1974. *The Unheavenly City Revisited.* Boston: Little, Brown.

Banfield, Edward C., and James Q. Wilson. 1963. *City Politics.* Cambridge, Mass.: Harvard University Press.

Bardach, Eugene. 1977. *The Implementation Game.* Cambridge, Mass.: MIT Press.

Barnard, Chester I. 1968. *The Functions of the Executive.* Cambridge, Mass.: Harvard University Press.

Bartley, Numan V. 1969. *The Rise of Massive Resistance.* Baton Rouge: Louisiana State University Press.

———. 1970. *From Thurmond to Wallace: Political Tendencies in Georgia, 1948–1968.* Baltimore: Johns Hopkins University Press.

————. 1977. "Part Six: 1940 to the Present." In *A History of Georgia,* ed. Kenneth Coleman. Athens: University of Georgia Press.

————. 1983. *The Creation of Modern Georgia.* Athens: University of Georgia Press.

Bass, Jack, and Walter DeVries. 1976. *The Transformation of Southern Politics.* New York: Basic Books.

Bayor, Ronald H. 1988. "Planning the City for Racial Segregation: The Highway-Street Pattern in Atlanta," *Journal of Urban History* 15 (November 1988): 3–21.

Bayton, James A. 1969. *Tension in the Cities.* Philadelphia: Chilton Book Co.

Bellush, Jewel, and Murray Hausknecht, eds. 1967. *Urban Renewal.* Garden City, N.Y.: Anchor Books.

Bennett, Larry. 1987. "In the Wake of Richard Daley: Chicago's Declining Politics of Party and Shifting Politics of Development." Paper presented at the Annual Meeting of the American Political Science Association, September, Chicago.

Bish, Robert L., and Vincent Ostrom. 1973. *Understanding Urban Government.* Washington, D.C.: American Enterprise Institute.

Bisher, Furman. 1966. *Miracle in Atlanta.* Cleveland, Ohio: World Publishing Co.

Bishop, Jim. 1971. *The Days of Martin Luther King, Jr.* New York: G. P. Putnam's Sons.

Black, Earl, and Merle Black. 1987. *Politics and Society in the South.* Cambridge, Mass.: Harvard University Press.

Blau, Peter M. 1964. *Exchange and Power in Social Life.* New York: John Wiley & Sons.

Body-Gendrot, Sophie N. 1987. "Grass-roots Mobilization in the Thirteenth Arrondissement of Paris." In *The Politics of Urban Development,* ed. Clarence N. Stone and Heywood T. Sanders. Lawrence: University Press of Kansas.

Boggs, Carl. 1984. *The Two Revolutions: Gramsci and the Dilemmas of Western Marxism.* Boston: South End Press.

Bond, Julian. 1968. *Black Candidates: Southern Campaign Experiences.* Atlanta: Voter Education Project, Southern Regional Council.

Bonner, John. 1986. *Introduction to the Theory of Social Choice.* Baltimore: Johns Hopkins University Press.

Borders, William Holmes. 1975. "Crisis/Another View: Economic and Political Power Must Mesh." Atlanta *Constitution,* 7 April.

Bowman, Ann O. 1988. "City Government Promotion of Economic Development." Paper prepared for presentation at the Annual Meeting of the Urban Affairs Association, March, St. Louis, Mo.

Bradbury, Katherine L., Anthony Downs, and Kenneth A. Small. 1982. *Urban Decline and the Future of American Cities.* Washington, D.C.: Brookings Institution.

Bridges, Amy. 1984. *A City in the Republic.* Cambridge: Cambridge University Press.

Browne, Angela, and Aaron Wildavsky. 1984. "Implementation as Exploration," In *Implementation,* 3d ed., by Jeffrey L. Pressman and Aaron Wildavsky. Berkeley and Los Angeles: University of California Press.

Brownell, Blaine A. 1971. "The Commercial-Civic Elite and City Planning in Atlanta, Memphis and New Orleans in the 1920s." *Journal of Southern History* 41: 339–368.

————. 1975. *The Urban Ethos in the South, 1920–1930.* Baton Rouge: Louisiana State University Press.

Browning, Rufus P., Dale Rogers Marshall, and David H. Tabb. 1984. *Protest Is Not Enough.* Berkeley and Los Angeles: University of California Press.

Bullock, Charles S., III, and Bruce A. Campbell. 1984. "Racist or Racial Voting in the 1981 Atlanta Municipal Election." *Urban Affairs Quarterly* 20 (December): 149–164.

Burkhead, Jesse. 1967. *Input and Output in Large-City High Schools.* Syracuse, N.Y.: Syracuse University Press.

Burman, Stephen. 1979. "The Illusion of Progress: Race and Politics in Atlanta, Georgia." *Ethnic and Racial Studies* 2 (October): 441–454.

Burnham, Walter Dean. 1970. *Critical Elections and the Mainsprings of American Politics.* New York: W. W. Norton & Co.

Caro, Robert A. 1974. *The Power Broker.* New York: Alfred A. Knopf.

Carson, Clayborne. 1981. *In Struggle: SNCC and the Black Awakening of the 1960s.* Cambridge, Mass.: Harvard University Press.

Castells, Manuel. 1983. *The City and the Grassroots.* Berkeley and Los Angeles: University of California Press.

Cater, Douglass. 1957. "Atlanta: Smart Politics and Good Race Relations." *Reporter* 11 July, 18–21.

Chafe, William H. 1980. *Civilities and Civil Rights.* New York: Oxford University Press.

Clark, Terry N., and Lorna C. Ferguson. 1983. *City Money.* New York: Columbia University Press.

Clarke, Susan E. 1985. "The Effects of Interest Representation Modes on Local Economic Development Policies." Paper presented at the Annual Meeting of the American Political Science Association, August/September, New Orleans, La.

———. 1987. "More Autonomous Policy Orientations." In *The Politics of Urban Development,* ed. Clarence N. Stone and Heywood T. Sanders. Lawrence: University Press of Kansas.

Clavel, Pierre. 1986. *The Progressive City.* New Brunswick, N.J.: Rutgers University Press.

Cleghorn, Reese. 1966. "Allen of Atlanta Collides with Black Power and Racism." *New York Times Magazine,* 16 October, 32ff.

Coleman, Kenneth, ed. 1977. *A History of Georgia.* Athens: University of Georgia Press.

Cox, Gary W. 1987. *The Efficient Secret.* Cambridge: Cambridge University Press.

Crain, Robert L. 1968. *The Politics of School Desegregation.* Chicago: Aldine.

Crane, David A. 1976. "The Evolving Strategy." *Real Estate Atlanta* 5 (January/February): 104ff.

Crawford, Fred R. 1969. *A Comprehensive and Systematic Evaluation of the Community Action Program and Related Programs Operating in Atlanta, Georgia.* Atlanta: Center for Research in Social Change, Emory University.

Crenson, Matthew A. 1971. *The Un-Politics of Air Pollution.* Baltimore: Johns Hopkins University Press.

Crozier, Michael, Samuel P. Huntington, and J. Watanuki. 1975. *The Crisis of Democracy.* New York: New York University Press.

Dahl, Robert A. 1961. *Who Governs?* New Haven, Conn.: Yale University Press.

———. 1982. *Dilemmas of Pluralist Democracy.* New Haven, Conn.: Yale University Press.

Dahrendorf, Ralf. 1959. *Class and Class Conflict in Industrial Society.* Stanford, Calif.: Stanford University Press.

———. 1968. *Essays in the Theory of Society.* Stanford, Calif.: Stanford University Press.

Derthick, Martha. 1972. *New Towns In-Town.* Washington, D.C.: Urban Institute.

Dittmer, John. 1977. *Black Georgia in the Progressive Era, 1900–1920.* Urbana: University of Illinois Press.

Doig, Jameson W. 1987. "Coalition-Building by a Regional Agency." In *The Politics of Urban Development,* ed. Clarence N. Stone and Heywood T. Sanders. Lawrence: University Press of Kansas.

Domhoff, G. William. 1978. *Who Really Rules? New Haven and Community Power Reexamined.* New Brunswick, N.J.: Transaction.

———. 1983. *Who Rules America Now.* Englewood Cliffs, N.J.: Prentice-Hall.

———. 1986. "State Autonomy and the Privileged Position of Business." *Journal of Political and Military Sociology* 14: 149–162.

Douglas, Mary. 1986. *How Institutions Think.* Syracuse, N.Y.: Syracuse University Press.

Downs, Anthony. (1967). *Inside Bureaucracy.* Boston: Little, Brown.

Dunlop, Beth. 1975. "An Accidental City with a Laissez-faire Approach to Planning." *AIA Journal* (April): 52–55.

Edds, Margaret. 1987. *Free at Last.* Bethesda, Md.: Adler & Adler.

Eisinger, Peter K. 1980. *The Politics of Displacement: Racial and Ethnic Transition in Three American Cities.* New York: Academic Press.

Elkin, Stephen L. 1985. "Pluralism in Its Place." In *The Democratic State,* ed. Roger Benjamin and Stephen L. Elkin. Lawrence: University Press of Kansas.

———. 1987. *City and Regime in the American Republic.* Chicago: University of Chicago Press.

———. 1988. "Capitalism in Constitutive Perspective: The Commercial Republic in America." Paper prepared for delivery at the Annual Meeting of the American Political Science Association, September, Washington, D.C.

Ellis, Ann Wells. 1975. "The Commission on Interracial Cooperation, 1919–1944." Ph.D. diss., Georgia State University.

———. 1986. "'Uncle Sam Is My Shepherd': The Commission on Interracial Cooperation and the New Deal in Georgia." *Atlanta Historical Journal* 30 (Spring): 47–63.

Emerson, Richard M. 1962. "Power-Dependence Relations." *American Sociological Review* 27: 31–41.

English, James W. 1967. *Handyman of the Lord: The Life and Ministry of the Reverend William Holmes Borders.* New York: Meredith Press.

Erie, Steven P. 1988. *Rainbow's End.* Berkeley and Los Angeles: University of California Press.

Fainstein, Susan S., and others. 1986. *Restructuring the City.* New York: Longman.

Ferman, Barbara. 1985. *Governing the Ungovernable City.* Philadelphia: Temple University Press.

———. 1989. "Democracy Under Fire: the Politics of Economic Restructuring in Pittsburgh and Chicago." Paper prepared for delivery at the Annual Meeting of the American Political Science Association, September, Atlanta.

Fleishman, Joel L. 1980. "The Real Against the Ideal—Making the Solution Fit the Problem: The Atlanta School Agreement of 1973." In *Roundtable Justice: Case Studies in Conflict Resolution,* ed. Robert B. Goldmann, 129–180. Boulder, Colo.: Westview Press.

Fleming, Douglas L. 1986. "The New Deal in Atlanta: A Review of the Major Programs." *Atlanta Historical Journal* 30: 23–45.

Fossett, James W. 1987. "The Downside of Housing Booms: Low Income Housing in Atlanta, 1970–1985." Metropolitan Opportunity Project of the University of Chicago, September.

Freedgood, Seymour. 1961. "Life in Buckhead." *Fortune,* September, 109ff.

Friedland, Roger, and Donald Palmer. 1984. "Park Place and Main Street: Business and the Urban Power Structure." *Annual Review of Sociology* 10: 393–416.

Fuchs, Ester R., and Robert Y. Shapiro. 1983. "Government Performance as a Basis for Machine Support." *Urban Affairs Quarterly* 18 (June): 537–550.

Gardiner, Patrick. 1961. *The Nature of Historical Explanation.* Oxford: Oxford University Press.

Garofalo, Charles P. 1972. "Business Ideas in Atlanta, 1916–1935." Ph.D. diss., Emory University.

Garrett, Franklin M. 1954. *Atlanta and Environs: A Chronicle of Its People and Events,* 2 vols. Athens: University of Georgia Press.

Garrow, David J. 1986. *Bearing the Cross: Martin Luther King, Jr., and the Southern Christian Leadership Conference.* New York: William Morrow & Co.

Gaventa, John. 1980. *Power and Powerlessness.* Urbana: University of Illinois Press.

George, Henry. 1932. *Progress and Poverty.* New York: Modern Library.

Giddens, Anthony. 1979. *Central Problems in Social Theory.* Berkeley and Los Angeles: University of California Press.

Gouldner, Alvin W. 1977. "The Norm of Reciprocity: A Preliminary Statement." In *Friends, Followers, and Factions,* ed. Steffen W. Schmidt and others. Berkeley and Los Angeles: University of California Press.

Grafton, Carl. 1983. Review of *The New Class War* by Francis Fox Piven and Richard A. Cloward. *American Political Science Review* 77 (December): 1050.

Grantham, Dewey W., Jr. 1958. *Hoke Smith and the Politics of the New South.* Baton Rouge: Louisiana State University Press.

Grimshaw, William J. 1982. "The Daley Legacy: A Declining Politics of Party, Race, and Public Unions." In *After Daley: Chicago Politics in Transition,* ed. Samuel K. Gove and Louis H. Masotti. Urbana: University of Illinois Press.

———. 1986. "Unraveling the Enigma: Mayor Harold Washington and the Black Political Tradition." Paper presented at the Annual Meeting of the American Political Science Association, August, Washington, D.C.

———. 1987. "The Political Economy of Machine Politics." Paper presented at the Annual Meeting of the American Political Science Association, September, Chicago.

Grist, Marilyn F. 1984. "Neighborhood Interest Groups and Atlanta Public Policy." Master's thesis, Georgia State University.

Grizzard, Lewis. 1975. "Man with the Money: Mills Lane Got It Done." Atlanta *Constitution.* (CAP clipping file.)

Hall, Suzanne M. 1987. "Progress or Preservation: The Presidential Parkway Controversy, 1946–1986." *Atlanta History* 36 (Spring/Summer): 22–38.

Hamall, Thomas K. 1975. "Crisis/Another View: City Hall Can Help Unite Us." Atlanta *Journal/Constitution,* 13 April.

Hamer, Andrew M. 1976. *The Selling of Rail Rapid Transit.* Lexington, Mass.: Lexington Books.

———, ed. 1980. *Urban Atlanta: Redefining the Role of the City.* Research Monograph no. 84. Atlanta: College of Business Administration, Georgia State University.

Hanson, Bertil. 1967. "Tulsa: Oil Folks at Home." In *Urban Politics in the Southwest,* ed. Leonard E. Goodall. Tempe: Institute of Public Administration, Arizona State University.

Hardin, Garrett. 1968. "The Tragedy of the Commons." *Science,* 13 December, 1243–1248.

Hardin, Russell. 1982. *Collective Action.* Baltimore: Johns Hopkins University Press.

Hartman, Chester. 1984. *The Transformation of San Francisco.* Totowa, N.J.: Rowman & Allanheld.

Heard, Alexander. 1949, 1984. Introduction to *Southern Politics in State and Nation,* by V. O. Key, Jr. Knoxville: University of Tennessee Press.

Hebert, Richard. 1972. *Highways to Nowhere: The Politics of City Transportation.* Indianapolis: Bobbs-Merrill.

Hein, Virginia H. 1972. "The Image of 'A City Too Busy to Hate': Atlanta in the 1960's." *Phylon* 33 (Fall): 205–221.

Henig, Jeffrey R. 1982. *Neighborhood Mobilization*. New Brunswick, N.J.: Rutgers University Press.

Henson, Dale, and James King. 1982. "The Atlanta Public-Private Romance: An Abrupt Transformation." In *Public-Private Partnership in American Cities,* ed. R. Scott Fosler and Renee A. Berger, 293–337. Lexington, Mass.: Lexington Books.

Hochschild, Jennifer L. 1984. *The New American Dilemma*. New Haven, Conn.: Yale University Press.

Holloway, Harry. 1969. *The Politics of the Southern Negro*. New York: Random House.

Holmes, William F. 1977. "Part Five: 1890–1940." In *A History of Georgia,* ed. Kenneth Coleman. Athens: University of Georgia Press.

Hornsby, Alton, Jr. 1977. "The Negro in Atlanta Politics, 1961–1973." *Atlanta Historical Bulletin* 21 (Spring): 7–33.

———. 1982. "A City That Was Too Busy to Hate." In *Southern Businessmen and Desegregation,* ed. Elizabeth Jacoway and David R. Colburn, 120–136. Baton Rouge: Louisiana State University Press.

Hunter, Floyd. 1953. *Community Power Structure*. Chapel Hill: University of North Carolina Press.

Huntington, Samuel P. 1968. *Political Order in Changing Societies*. New Haven, Conn.: Yale University Press.

———. 1975. "The Democratic Distemper." *Public Interest* 41 (Fall): 9–38.

Hutcheson, John D., Jr. 1981. "The Neighborhood Planning Ordinance in Atlanta." Paper presented at the Annual Meeting of the American Political Science Association, September, New York.

———. 1984. "Citizen Representation in Neighborhood Planning." *American Planning Association Journal* 50 (Spring): 183–193.

Isaac, Jeffrey C. 1987. *Power and Marxist Theory*. Ithaca, N.Y.: Cornell University Press.

Jackson, Barbara L. 1978. "Desegregation: Atlanta Style." *Theory Into Practice* 17, no. 1: 43–53.

———. 1981. "Urban School Desegregation from a Black Perspective." In *Race and Schooling in the City,* ed. Adam Yarmolinsky, Lance Liebman, and Corinne S. Schelling. Cambridge, Mass.: Harvard University Press.

Jackson, Kenneth T. 1967. *The Ku Klux Klan in the City, 1915–1930*. New York: Oxford University Press.

Jamieson, Duncan R. 1976. "Maynard Jackson's 1973 Election as Mayor of Atlanta." *Midwest Quarterly* 18 (October): 7–26.

Jenkins, Herbert T. 1973. *Forty Years on the Force: 1932–1972*. Atlanta: Center for Research in Social Change, Emory University.

Jennings, M. Kent. 1964. *Community Influentials: The Elites of Atlanta*. New York: Free Press of Glencoe.

Jennings, M. Kent, and Harmon Zeigler. 1966. "Class, Party, and Race in Four Types of Elections: The Case of Atlanta." *Journal of Politics* 28: 391–407.

Johnson, David R. 1983. "San Antonio: The Vicissitudes of Boosterism." In *Sunbelt Cities: Politics and Growth since World War II,* ed. Richard M. Bernard and Bradley R. Rice. Austin: University of Texas Press.

Jones, Bryan D., and Lynn W. Bachelor. 1986. *The Sustaining Hand: Community Leadership and Corporate Power*. Lawrence: University Press of Kansas.

Jones, Mack H. 1978. "Black Political Empowerment in Atlanta: Myth and Reality." *Annals of the American Academy of Political and Social Science* 439 (September): 90–117.

Kantor, Paul, with Stephen David. 1988. *The Dependent City*. Glenview, Ill.: Scott, Foresman.

Kaplan, Harold. 1963. *Urban Renewal Politics.* New York: Columbia University Press.

Kasarda, John D. 1985. "Urban Change and Minority Opportunities." In *The New Urban Reality,* ed. Paul E. Peterson. Washington, D.C.: Brookings Institution.

Katzenstein, Peter J. 1985. *Small States in World Markets.* Ithaca, N.Y.: Cornell University Press.

Katznelson, Ira. 1976. "The Crisis of the Capitalist City: Urban Politics and Social Control." In *Theoretical Perspectives on Urban Politics,* by Willis D. Hawley and others. Englewood Cliffs, N.J.: Prentice-Hall.

————. 1981. *City Trenches.* Chicago: University of Chicago Press.

Key, V. O., Jr. 1949. *Southern Politics in State and Nation.* New York: Alfred A. Knopf.

————. 1955. "A Theory of Critical Elections." *Journal of Politics* 17 (February): 3–18.

Key, V. O., Jr., and Frank Munger. 1959. "Social Determinism and Electoral Decision." In *American Voting Behavior,* ed. Eugene Burdick and Arthur J. Brodbeck. Glencoe, Ill.: Free Press.

King, Martin Luther, Sr., with Clayton Riley. 1980. *Daddy King: An Autobiography.* New York: William Morrow & Co.

Kirp, David L. 1982. *Just Schools.* Berkeley and Los Angeles: University of California Press.

Kuhn, Thomas S. 1970. *The Structure of Scientific Revolutions.* 2d ed. Chicago: University of Chicago Press.

Ladd, Everett Carll, Jr. 1972. *Ideology in America.* New York: W. W. Norton & Co.

Laitin, David D. 1986. *Hegemony and Culture.* Chicago: University of Chicago Press.

Lankevich, George J. 1978. *Atlanta: A Chronological and Documentary History.* Dobbs Ferry, N.Y.: Oceana Publications.

Leiserson, Michael. 1968. "Factions and Coalitions in One-Party Japan: An Interpretation Based on the Theory of Games." *American Political Science Review* 62 (September): 770–787.

————. 1970. "Power and Ideology in Coalition Behavior." In *The Study of Coalition Behavior,* ed. Sven Groennings, E. W. Kelly, and Michael Leiserson. New York: Holt, Rinehart & Winston.

Lenski, Gerhard E. 1984. *Power and Privilege.* Chapel Hill: University of North Carolina Press.

Lewis, David L. 1978. *King: A Biography.* 2d ed. Urbana: University of Illinois Press.

Lindblom, Charles E. 1977. *Politics and Markets.* New York: Basic Books.

Little, Charles E. 1976. "Atlanta Renewal Gives Power to the Communities." *Smithsonian* 7 (July): 100–107.

Logan, John R., and Harvey L. Molotch. 1987. *Urban Fortunes.* Berkeley and Los Angeles: University of California Press.

Lomax, Louis E. 1962. *The Negro Revolt.* New York: Harper & Row.

Long, Norton E. 1958. "The Local Community as an Ecology of Games." *American Journal of Sociology* 64 (November): 251–261.

————. 1983. "Can the Contemporary City Be a Significant Polity?" Paper given at the Annual Meeting of the Urban Affairs Association, March, Flint, Mich.

————. 1986. "The City as a Political Community." *Journal of Community Psychology* 14 (January): 72–80.

Lowe, Jeanne R. 1967. *Cities in a Race with Time.* New York: Random House.

Lowi, Theodore J. 1964. "American Business, Public Policy, Case Studies, and Political Theory." *World Politics* 16: 677–715.

————. 1979. *The End of Liberalism.* New York: W. W. Norton & Co.

Lubell, Samuel. 1952. *The Future of American Politics.* New York: Harper.

Lubove, Roy. 1969. *Twentieth-Century Pittsburgh.* New York: John Wiley & Sons.

Lukes, Steven. 1974. *Power: A Radical View.* London: Macmillan.

Lupo, Alan. 1988. *Liberty's Chosen Home.* Boston: Beacon Press.

Lupsha, Peter A. 1987. "Structural Change and Innovation: Elites and Albuquerque Politics in the 1980s." In *The Politics of Urban Development,* ed. Clarence N. Stone and Heywood T. Sanders. Lawrence: University Press of Kansas.

Lustick, Ian. 1980. *Arabs in the Jewish State.* Austin: University of Texas Press.

Lyall, Katherine. 1982. "A Bicycle Built-for-Two: Public-Private Partnership in Baltimore." In *Public-Private Partnership in American Cities,* ed. R. Scott Fosler and Renee A. Berger, 17–57. Lexington Books.

McConnell, Grant. 1966. *Private Power and American Democracy.* New York: Alfred A. Knopf.

Manes, Charles W. 1986. "The United Nations in a Divided World." *Washington Post Book World,* 2 March, 5.

Mannheim, Karl. 1936. *Ideology and Utopia.* New York: Harcourt, Brace.

Mansbridge, Jane J. 1980. *Beyond Adversary Democracy.* New York: Basic Books.

———. 1986. *Why We Lost the ERA.* Chicago: University of Chicago Press.

March, James G. 1962. "The Business Firm as a Political Coalition." *Journal of Politics* 24 (November): 662–678.

———. 1966. "The Power of Power." In *Varieties of Political Theory,* ed. David Easton, 39–70. (Englewood Cliffs, N.J.: Prentice-Hall.

March, James G., and Johan P. Olsen. 1984. "The New Institutionalism." *American Political Science Review* 78 (September): 734–749.

March, James G., and Herbert A. Simon. 1965. *Organizations.* New York: John Wiley & Sons.

Marshall Kaplan, Gans, and Kahn. 1970. *The Model Cities Program: The Planning Process in Atlanta, Seattle, and Dayton.* New York: Praeger Publishers.

Martin, Charles H. 1976. *The Angelo Herndon Case and Southern Justice.* Baton Rouge: Louisiana State University Press.

Martin, Harold H. 1978. *William Berry Hartsfield: Mayor of Atlanta.* Athens: University of Georgia Press.

Matthews, John M. 1970. "Studies in Race Relations in Georgia, 1890–1930." Ph.D. diss., Duke University.

Mays, Benjamin E. 1971. *Born to Rebel: An Autobiography.* Athens: University of Georgia Press.

Michels, Robert. 1959. *Political Parties.* New York: Dover Publications.

Miller, Clem. 1962. *Member of the House: Letters of a Congressman,* ed. John W. Baker. New York: Charles Scribner's Sons.

Mills, C. Wright. 1946. "The Middle Class in Middle Sized Cities." *American Sociological Review* 11 (October): 520–529.

———. 1956. *The Power Elite.* New York: Oxford University Press.

Mintz, Beth, and Michael Schwartz. 1985. *The Power Structure of American Business.* Chicago: University of Chicago Press.

Mollenkopf, John H. 1983. *The Contested City.* Princeton, N.J.: Princeton University Press.

Molotch, Harvey. 1976. "The City as a Growth Machine." *American Journal of Sociology* 82 (September): 309–331.

Morris, Aldon D. 1984. *The Origins of the Civil Rights Movement.* New York: Free Press.

Morris, Charles R. 1980. *The Cost of Good Intentions.* New York: W. W. Norton & Co.

Muir, William K. 1977. *Police: Streetcorner Politicians.* Chicago: University of Chicago Press.

Newman, Harvey, Barbara Ray, and Joseph Hacker. 1988. "A Content Analysis of Consensus Building in Local Policy Making: The Underground Atlanta Project." Paper presented at the Annual Meeting of the Urban Affairs Association, March, St. Louis, Mo.

Norrell, Robert J. 1986. *Reaping the Whirlwind.* New York: Vintage.

Oates, Stephen B. 1982. *Let the Trumpet Sound: The Life of Martin Luther King, Jr.* New York: New American Library.

O'Brien, David J. 1975. *Neighborhood Organization and Interest-Group Processes.* Princeton, N.J.: Princeton University Press.

Offe, Claus. 1985. *Disorganized Capitalism.* Cambridge, Mass.: MIT Press.

Okun, Arthur M. 1975. *Equality and Efficiency: The Big Tradeoff.* Washington, D.C.: Brookings Institution.

Olson, Mancur, Jr. 1965. *The Logic of Collective Action.* Cambridge, Mass.: Harvard University Press.

———. 1982. *The Rise and Decline of Nations.* New Haven, Conn.: Yale University Press.

Openshaw, Howard. 1973. "Atlanta's Housing Imbalance." *Atlanta Economic Review* 23 (May–June): 52ff.

Oppenheimer, Joe. 1975. "Some Political Implications of 'Vote Trading and the Voting Paradox: A Proof of Logical Equivalence.'" *American Political Science Review* 69 (September): 963–966.

Palmer, Charles F. 1955. *Adventures of a Slum Fighter.* Atlanta: Tupper and Love.

Parsons, Talcott. 1969. *Politics and Social Structure.* New York: Free Press.

Peirce, Neal R. 1974. *The Deep South States of America: People, Politics, and Power in the Seven Deep South States.* New York: W. W. Norton & Co.

Perrow, Charles. 1986. *Complex Organizations.* 3d ed. New York: Random House.

Peterson, Paul E. 1981. *City Limits.* Chicago: University of Chicago Press.

———. 1985. *The Politics of School Reform, 1870–1940.* Chicago: University of Chicago Press.

Piven, Frances Fox, and Richard A. Cloward. 1971. *Regulating the Poor.* New York: Pantheon Books.

———. 1977. *Poor People's Movements.* New York: Pantheon Books.

Polsby, Nelson W. 1980. *Community Power and Political Theory: A Further Look at Problems of Evidence and Inference.* New Haven, Conn.: Yale University Press.

Porter, Michael L. 1974. "Black Atlanta: An Interdisciplinary Study of Blacks on the East Side of Atlanta, 1890–1930." Ph.D. diss., Emory University.

Powledge, Fred. 1973. "A New Politics in Atlanta." *New Yorker,* 31 December, 28–40.

Pressman, Jeffrey L., and Aaron Wildavsky. 1984. *Implementation.* 3d ed. Berkeley and Los Angeles: University of California Press.

Preston, Howard L. 1979. *Automobile Age Atlanta: The Making of a Southern Metropolis, 1900–1935.* Athens: University of Georgia Press.

———. 1979. "Parkways, Parks, and 'New South' Progressivism: Planning Practice in Atlanta, 1880–1917." In *Olmstead South: Old South Critic/New South Planner,* ed. Dana F. White and Victor A. Kramer, 223–238. Westport, Conn.: Greenwood Press.

Proehl, Carl W., Jr., and Robert T. Golembiewski. 1981. "Marta and the 15¢ Fare." Mass Transit Management: Case Studies of the Metropolitan Atlanta Rapid Transit Authority. A Report Prepared by the University of Georgia Department of Political Science for the U.S. Department of Transportation, Urban Mass Transportation Administration, University Research and Training Program.

Przeworski, Adam. 1985. *Capitalism and Social Democracy.* Cambridge: Cambridge University Press.

Raines, Howell. 1977. *My Soul Is Rested: Movement Days in the Deep South Remembered.* Reprint. New York: Penguin Books.

Rakove, Milton. 1975. *Don't Make No Waves, Don't Back No Losers.* Bloomington: Indiana University Press.

Range, Peter Ross. 1974. "Making It in Atlanta: Capital of Black-Is-Bountiful." *New York Times Magazine,* 7 April, 28ff.

Reed, Adolph, Jr. 1987. "A Critique of Neo-Progressivism in Theorizing about Local Development Policy: A Case from Atlanta." In *The Politics of Urban Development,* ed. Clarence N. Stone and Heywood T. Sanders. Lawrence: University Press of Kansas.

Research Atlanta. 1973. *School Desegregation in Metro Atlanta, 1954–1973.* Atlanta: Research Atlanta.

Rhyne, Edwin H. 1958. "Political Parties and Decision Making in Three Southern Counties." *American Political Science Review* 52 (December): 1091–1107.

Rice, Bradley R. 1981. "The Battle of Buckhead: The Plan of Improvement and Atlanta's Last Big Annexation." *Atlanta Historical Journal* 25: 5–22.

―――. 1983. "If Dixie Were Atlanta." In *Sunbelt Cities: Politics and Growth since World War II,* ed. Richard M. Bernard and Bradley R. Rice. Austin: University of Texas Press.

―――. 1983. "Lester Maddox and the 'Liberal' Mayors." In *Proceedings and Papers of the Georgia Association of Historians,* 78–87. Marietta, Ga.: Kennesaw College.

Riker, William H. 1962. *The Theory of Political Coalitions.* New Haven, Conn.: Yale University Press.

Riordon, William L. 1963. *Plunkitt of Tammany Hall.* New York: E. P. Dutton.

Rokkan, Stein. 1966. "Norway: Numerical Democracy and Corporate Pluralism." In *Political Oppositions in Western Democracies,* ed. Robert A. Dahl, 70–115. New Haven, Conn.: Yale University Press.

Rubin, Lillian B. 1972. *Busing and Backlash.* Berkeley and Los Angeles: University of California Press.

Sanders, Heywood T. 1987. "The Politics of Development in Middle-sized Cities: From New Haven to Kalamazoo." In *The Politics of Urban Development,* ed. Clarence N. Stone and Heywood T. Sanders. Lawrence: University Press of Kansas.

Schattschneider, E. E. 1960. *The Semi-Sovereign People.* New York: Holt, Rinehart & Winston.

Scheppele, Kim Lane, and Karol E. Soltan. 1987. "The Authority of Alternatives." In *Authority Revisited,* ed. J. Roland Pennock and John W. Chapman, Nomos 24, 169–200. New York: New York University Press.

Scott, Austin. 1974. "The New Mayor, Atlanta Style." *Washington Post,* 27 January 1974, C2.

―――. 1974. "Police Hassle Dims Atlanta Mayor's First Six Months." *Washington Post,* 7 July 1974, A2.

―――. 1975. "Mayor Shifts Atlanta Power." *Washington Post,* 6 July 1975, A1.

―――. 1977. "Sanitation Workers' Strike in Atlanta Loaded with Ironies." *Washington Post,* 17 April 1977, A3.

Sellers, Cleveland. 1973. *The River of No Return: The Autobiography of a Black Militant and the Life and Death of SNCC.* New York: William Morrow & Co.

Selznick, Philip. 1957. *Leadership in Administration.* New York: Harper & Row.

Shannon, Margaret. 1974. "Blacks in the Board Room." Atlanta *Constitution Magazine,* 21 April, 8ff.

Shannon, Jasper B. 1949. *Toward a New Politics in the South.* Knoxville: University of Tennessee Press.

Shavin, Norman, and Bruce Galphin. 1982. *Atlanta: Triumph of a People.* Atlanta: Capricorn Corp.

Shefter, Martin. 1976. "The Emergence of the Political Machine: An Alternative View." In *Theoretical Perspectives on Urban Politics,* by Willis D. Hawley and others. Englewood Cliffs, N.J.: Prentice-Hall.

————. 1985. *Political Crisis/Fiscal Crisis: The Collapse and Revival of New York City.* New York: Basic Books.

Shils, Edward. 1982. "The Political Class in the Age of Mass Society: Collectivistic Liberalism and Social Democracy." In *Does Who Governs Matter?,* ed. Moshe M. Czudnowski. DeKalb: Northern Illinois Press.

Silberman, Charles E. 1964. *Crisis in Black and White.* New York: Random House.

Simon, Herbert A. 1976. *Administrative Behavior.* 3d ed. New York: Free Press.

Sitton, Claude. 1961. "Atlanta Example: Good Sense and Dignity." *New York Times Magazine,* 6 May, 22ff.

Sjoquist, David L. 1988. "The Economic Status of Black Atlantans." Paper prepared for the Atlanta Urban League, April.

Skocpol, Theda. 1979. *States and Social Revolutions.* Cambridge: Cambridge University Press.

Small, Kenneth A. 1985. "Transportation and Urban Change." In *The New Urban Reality,* ed. Paul E. Peterson. Washington, D.C.: Brookings Institution.

Smith, Dennis. 1983. *Barrington Moore, Jr.: A Critical Appraisal.* Armonk, N.Y.: M. E. Sharpe.

Smith, Michael P. 1988. *City, State, and Market.* New York: Basil Blackwell.

Sobel, Lester A., ed. 1967. *Civil Rights, 1960–66.* New York: Facts on File.

————. 1973. *Civil Rights: Volume 2, 1967–68.* New York: Facts on File.

Southern Center for Studies in Public Policy. 1979. *Consensus Politics in Atlanta: School Board Decision-Making 1974–1978.* Atlanta: Clark College.

Spritzer, Lorraine N. 1982. *The Belle of Ashby Street: Helen Douglas Mankin and Georgia Politics.* Athens: University of Georgia Press.

Stein, Arthur. 1984. "Hegemon's Dilemma." *International Organization* 38: 355–386.

Stinchcombe, Arthur L. 1978. *Theoretical Methods in Social History.* New York: Academic Press.

Stone, Clarence N. 1976. *Economic Growth and Neighborhood Discontent: System Bias in the Urban Renewal Program of Atlanta.* Chapel Hill: University of North Carolina Press.

————. 1980. "Systemic Power in Community Decision Making." *American Political Science Review* 74 (December): 978–990.

————. 1985. "Efficiency versus Social Learning: A Reconsideration of the Implementation Process." *Policy Studies Review* 4 (February): 484–496.

————. 1986. "Power and Social Complexity." In *Community Power: Directions for Future Research,* ed. Robert J. Waste, 77–113. Beverly Hills, Calif.: Sage.

————. 1986. "Partnership New South Style: Central Atlanta Progress." *Proceedings, The Academy of Political Science* 36, no. 2: 100–110.

————. 1987. "Elite Distemper versus the Promise of Democracy." In *Power Elites and Organizations,* ed. G. William Domhoff and Thomas R. Dye. Newbury Park, Calif.: Sage.

————. 1988. "Preemptive Power: Floyd Hunter's 'Community Power Structure' Reconsidered." *American Journal of Political Science* 32 (February): 82–104.

Stone, Clarence N., and Robert K. Whelan. 1972. "Urban Renewal Policy and City Politics: Urban Renewal in Atlanta and Baltimore." In *Proceedings of the Georgia Political Science Association,* 173–213 (Athens: Institute of Government, University of Georgia).

Stone, Clarence N., Robert K. Whelan, and William J. Murin. 1986. *Urban Policy and Politics in a Bureaucratic Age.* 2d ed. Englewood Cliffs, N.J.: Prentice-Hall.

Stone, Mark A. 1989. "Chaos, Prediction and LaPlacean Determinism." *American Philosophical Quarterly* 26 (April): 123–131.

Swanstrom, Todd. 1985. *The Crisis of Growth Politics.* Philadelphia: Temple University Press.

Swanstrom, Todd, and Sharon Ward. 1987. "Albany's O'Connell Organization." Paper presented at the Annual Meeting of the American Political Science Association, September, Chicago.

Taylor, Michael. 1987. *The Possibility of Cooperation.* Cambridge: Cambridge University Press.

Thomas, Jesse O. 1967. *My Story in Black and White.* New York: Exposition Press.

Thometz, Carol E. 1963. *The Decision-Makers: The Power Structure of Dallas.* Dallas: Southern Methodist University Press.

Thompson, Robert A., Hylan Lewis, and Davis McEntire. 1960. "Atlanta and Birmingham: A Comparative Study in Negro Housing." In *Studies in Housing and Minority Groups,* ed. Nathan Glazer and Davis McEntire. Berkeley and Los Angeles: University of California Press.

Tilly, Charles. 1981. Introduction to *Class Conflict and Collective Action,* ed. Louise A. Tilly and Charles Tilly. Beverly Hills, Calif.: Sage.

———. 1984. *Big Structures, Large Processes, Huge Comparisons.* New York: Russell Sage Foundation.

Tindall, George B. 1967. *The Emergence of the New South, 1913–1945.* Baton Rouge: Louisiana State University Press.

Toppin, Edgar A. 1967. "Walter White and the Atlanta NAACP's Fight for Equal Schools." *History of Education Quarterly* 7 (Spring): 3–21.

Torrence, Ridgeley. 1948. *The Story of John Hope.* New York: Macmillan.

Townsend, James L. 1975. "Crisis/Another View: The Cinderella of the '60s Needs To Be More Mature." Atlanta *Constitution,* 2 April.

Useem, Michael. 1980. "Which Business Leaders Help Govern?" In *Power Structure Research,* ed. G. William Domhoff. Beverly Hills, Calif.: Sage.

———. 1984. *The Inner Circle.* New York: Oxford University Press.

———. 1987. "The Inner Circle and the Political Voice of Business." In *The Structure of Power in America,* ed. Michael Schwartz. New York: Holmes & Meier.

Vidich, Arthur J., and Joseph Bensman. 1968. *Small Town in Mass Society,* rev. ed. Princeton, N.J.: Princeton University Press.

Waligorski, Conrad P. 1984. "Conservative Economist Critics of Democracy." *Social Science Journal* 21 (April): 99–116.

Walker, Jack L. 1963. "Negro Voting in Atlanta, 1953–1961." *Phylon* 24 (Winter): 379–387.

———. 1963. "Protest and Negotiation: A Case Study of Negro Leadership in Atlanta, Georgia." *Midwest Journal of Political Science* 7 (May): 99–124.

Walker, Scott L. 1986. "Rail Rapid Transit: Its Rebirth, Capabilities and Role in Promoting Urban Economic Development, an Atlanta Case Study." B.A. thesis, Princeton University.

Warner, Sam Bass. Jr. 1968. *The Private City.* Philadelphia: University of Pennsylvania Press.

Waskow, Arthur I. 1966. *From Race Riot to Sit-In, 1919 and the 1960s.* Garden City, N.Y.: Doubleday & Co.

Watters, Pat. 1969. *The South and the Nation.* New York: Pantheon Books.

————. 1971. *Down to Now: Reflections on the Southern Civil Rights Movement.* New York: Pantheon Books.

Watters, Pat, and Reese Cleghorn. 1967. *Climbing Jacob's Ladder: The Arrival of Negroes in Southern Politics.* New York: Harcourt, Brace & World.

Watts, Eugene J. 1978. *The Social Bases of City Politics: Atlanta, 1865–1903.* Westport, Conn.: Greenwood Press.

Weinberg, Martha W. 1981. "Boston's Kevin White." *Political Science Quarterly* 96 (Spring): 87–106.

Whelan, Robert K. 1987. "New Orleans: Mayoral Politics and Economic-Development Policies in the Postwar Years, 1945–86." In *The Politics of Urban Development,* ed. Clarence N. Stone and Heywood T. Sanders. Lawrence: University Press of Kansas.

Whelan, Robert K., and Michael W. McKinney. 1974. "Black-White Coalition Politics and the Atlanta Mayoralty Race of 1973." Paper presented at the Annual Meeting of the Georgia Political Science Association, February, Athens, Ga.

White, Dana F. 1982. "The Black Sides of Atlanta." *Atlanta Historical Journal* 26 (Summer/Fall): 199–225.

White, Dana F., and Timothy J. Crimmins. 1980. "How Atlanta Grew: Cool Heads, Hot Air, and Hard Work." In *Urban Atlanta: Redefining the Role of the City,* ed. Andrew M. Hamer, Research Monograph no. 84. Atlanta: College of Business Administration, Georgia State University.

White, Walter. 1969. *A Man Called White.* New York: Arno Press and the New York Times.

Whitt, J. Allen. 1982. *Urban Elites and Mass Transportation.* Princeton, N.J.: Princeton University Press.

Wiebe, Robert H. 1967. *The Search for Order, 1877–1920.* New York: Hill and Wang.

Williams, Oliver P. 1961. "A Typology for Comparative Local Government." *Midwest Journal of Political Science* 5 (May): 150–164.

Williamson, Oliver E. 1983. "Organizational Innovation: The Transaction-Cost Approach." In *Entrepreneurship,* ed. Joshua Ronen. Lexington, Mass.: Lexington Books.

————. 1985. *The Economic Institutions of Capitalism.* New York: Free Press.

Wilson, James Q. 1962. *The Amateur Democrat.* Chicago: University of Chicago Press.

————. 1973. *Political Organizations.* New York: Basic Books.

Wilson, William J. 1987. *The Truly Disadvantaged.* Chicago: University of Chicago Press.

Wolfinger, Raymond E. 1974. *The Politics of Progress.* Englewood Cliffs, N.J.: Prentice-Hall.

Woodward, C. Vann. 1957. *The Strange Career of Jim Crow.* New York: Oxford University Press.

Writer's Program of the Works Progress Administration. 1973. *Atlanta: A City of the Modern South.* St. Clair Shores, Mich.: Somerset Publishers.

Wrong, Dennis H. 1980. *Power: Its Forms, Bases and Uses.* New York: Harper & Row.

Yates, Douglas. 1977. *The Ungovernable City.* Cambridge, Mass.: MIT Press.

Young, Andrew. 1986. "A Sanction That Would Affect the 'Passive Majority.'" *Washington Post,* 10 August 1986.

Zinn, Howard. 1965. *SNCC: The New Abolitionists.* Boston: Beacon Press.

Zwingle, Erla. 1988. "Atlanta: Energy and Optimism in the New South." *National Geographic* 174 (July): 5–28.

Index

306